Kanban in Action

MARCUS HAMMARBERG
JOAKIM SUNDÉN

MANNING
SHELTER ISLAND

For online information and ordering of this and other Manning books, please visit www.manning.com. The publisher offers discounts on this book when ordered in quantity. For more information, please contact

Special Sales Department
Manning Publications Co.
20 Baldwin Road
PO Box 261
Shelter Island, NY 11964
Email: orders@manning.com

Manning Publications Co.
20 Baldwin Road
PO Box 261
Shelter Island, NY 11964

Development editors: Beth Lexleigh, Cynthia Kane
Copyeditor: Melinda Rankin
Proofreader: Tiffany Taylor
Typesetter: Marija Tudor
Cover designer: Marija Tudor

ISBN: 9781617291050
Printed in the United States of America

brief contents

contents

foreword

A great deal of your brain's capacity is devoted to absorbing, processing, acting on, and storing visual information. What we see inspires us to act now and instills patterns for future action. If we have nothing to look at, we have little to act on.

See and understand

Visual systems like kanban draw their power from our preference for visual information. Take a look, for example, at the following simple map. You see the water, the buildings, the roads, and a host of other information. You recognize this immediately. Within the blink of an eye, you understand context, form, and substance.

Here is a list of everything I cared to write down from that map. This is a partial list. And it's in a font size necessary not to fill pages with text:

- Salmon Bay Marine Center
- Lake Washington Ship Canal
- W. Commodore Way
- 20th Ave W
- Gilman Place W
- W Elmore Street
- 21st Ave W
- Gilman Ave W
- Shilshole Ave NW
- W Fort Street
- 26th Ave W
- 24th Ave W

You can quickly see that long lists of things provide less context and take more time to process than a map.

Our goal with visual systems like kanban is to build a map of our work. We want the form and substance of our work. We want to understand the system, immediately and intuitively. We want our kanban board to be explicit about roles, responsibilities, work in progress, rate of completion, the structure of our processes, impediments, and more.

That's a lot of information.

What we've found since launching kanban as a software design tool nearly a decade ago is this:

Seeing the work and the process creates understanding.

Once we see our work, we build a shared understanding of it. Then we can do away with messy process conventions that have plagued software development for years. The kanban board can become a simple single point that lets anyone come and understand the current state of the project.

This means software teams can finally speak the same language as the business! The division between IT and the rest of the company can dissolve. A translator has arrived.

Seeing is half the battle

In this book, Marcus and Joakim list three elements of a project using kanban:

- Visualize
- Limit work in process
- Manage flow

I like this list.

For *Personal Kanban*, we use the first two (visualize your work and limit work in process) and see the third as following naturally. But I like the list of three because it drives this point home:

Work does not fit—it flows.

Smashing work into arbitrary amounts of time has profound negative impacts on rate of completion, escaped defects, and morale. The stress of unnecessary deadlines or overenthusiastic feature sets deprecates both people and product. The focus becomes making work fit into the deadline period, rather than completion with quality.

Completion of work with quality is possible only if work is flowing at a truly sustainable pace. Finding and maintaining that pace is possible only if active work in process (WIP) is less than the capacity of those doing the work. Cramming things in before deadlines will almost always result in breaking your WIP limit.

Too much WIP destroys flow

With a reasonable WIP limit, we encourage the flow of work. Tasks are completed in a measured fashion with an eye on quality. Overhead from managing too much WIP disappears. And, not surprisingly, productivity skyrockets.

This is the short form of what Marcus and Joakim have given you in this book. They provide fantastic and patient detail. If this is your entrée into kanban, welcome. You couldn't have asked for better guides.

JIM BENSON
AUTHOR OF THE 2013 SHINGO AWARD-WINNING
PERSONAL KANBAN

preface

Marcus's journey

I was introduced to agile via Scrum and started to use it, guerilla-style, at a large insurance company in Sweden. Before long, it spread; and within a few years the company had more than 50 Scrum teams. But it still didn't feel right, because the work processes for many teams weren't a good fit with the start-stop nature of Scrum. Also, most teams didn't span the entire process; the teams mostly consisted of developers who were handed requirements and who then delivered to a separate testing phase. I felt the itch to try to incorporate more of the complete process that the work went through.

This itch led me to start investigating other practices in the agile community. Before long, and through some helpful pointers from Joakim, I found and started to read up on kanban. In 2010 and 2011, I attended trainings on kanban and kanban coaching given by David J. Anderson. These further confirmed my feeling that kanban and Lean were what I had been looking for.

Joakim's journey

In 2008, I was consulting as a Scrum Master in a three-team software development project in a large Swedish company's IT department. To deepen my understanding of agile software development, I was reading up on Lean software development—which led me to the amazing story of Toyota and a lot of literature about Lean thinking and the Toyota Way. The studying reached a climax of sorts when I went on a study tour to Toyota HQ in Japan together with Mary and Tom Poppendieck, authors of Lean software development books, in the spring of 2009.

In late 2008, my client came to the conclusion that most, if not all, clients paying for software development eventually draw—that things are moving too slowly. They wanted more development done more quickly, but without cutting scope or quality. Inspired by the Lean thinking around one-piece contiguous flow, I suggested that we should stop planning batches of work in Scrum sprint-planning meetings every two or three weeks (a cadence that felt more and more arbitrary to us) and instead try to focus on one or a few work items and collaboratively get them done as quickly as possible, in a continuous flow of value. The dozen or so team members agreed to not have more than two work items in development and two in testing at any time, and that only when something was finished would we pull new work items from the backlog to plan them just-in-time.

I soon learned about something called kanban that seemed similar to what we were doing, first through Corey Ladas's blog and then through the work of David J. Anderson. In 2009, I connected with the community through the first Lean Kanban conference in the UK. I was immediately attracted by the pragmatic approach of looking at what had actually worked for different teams and companies in their respective contexts, at a time when I felt that a lot of the agile community focus was on faith-based approaches like "How is Scrum telling us how to solve this?"

The next year, I participated in David J. Anderson's first kanban coaching workshop ever (now called Advanced Master Class) in London, together with, among others, experienced practitioners like Rachel Davies, David P. Joyce, and Martine Devos. I cofounded Stockholm Lean Coffee in 2010, where kanban enthusiasts have kept meeting every week since. In 2011, I was invited to attend the first Kanban Leadership Retreat hosted by David J. Anderson, during which I became one of the first "David J. Anderson approved" kanban trainers.

The common journey

Together with our colleague at Avega Group at the time, Christophe Achouiantz, we started developing a practical introduction to kanban in 2010. It was an immediate success and the starting point for a long series of conference talks in both Europe and the US, including in-client trainings, tutorials, and workshops, sometimes conducted individually, sometimes by the two of us together. The practical approach of our work resonated well with many people who attended our talks and tutorials, and we received a lot of positive feedback.

It was after a conference tutorial at JFokus (a great conference organized by Mattias Karlsson, another Avega Group colleague) that Marcus got a call from Manning Publications, asking him if he was interested in writing a book. He immediately felt that he should do it together with Joakim. We decided to write the book in the same manner as the presentation we had created, using a practical approach and a lighthearted style.

about this book

Do you want to better understand how your work works and what is happening on your team or in your workplace? Would you benefit from being able to focus on a few small things instead of constantly having to switch between multiple projects? Do your users and stakeholders want new features delivered now rather than some other day? Do you think that you and your coworkers need to keep improving and learning?

Then *kanban* is for you.

Do you want to get started with kanban as soon as possible, without spending too much time on abstract theory and history and splitting hairs about different methods? Do you want to know how people in the kanban community have used kanban in practice to face different challenges?

Then *this book* is for you.

This book is a down-to-earth, no-frills, get-to-know-the-ropes introduction to kanban. It's based on lots of practice, many observations, and some hearsay (!) from two guys who have worked with and coached dozens of kanban teams. We've also talked and taught at conferences and actively participated in user groups and the kanban community over the last few years.

In this book, you'll read about simple but powerful techniques to *visualize work*: how to design a kanban board, how to track work and its progress, how to visualize queues and buffers, and even such nitty-gritty details as how colors and other enhancements can help you to organize and track your work items.

You'll also pick up a lot of practical advice about how to *limit your work in process* throughout the workflow, such as how to set the limit in different ways depending on context, and how to understand when and how to change it.

With these two tools in hand—kanban and this book—you're ready to get down to business and *help your work flow* through the system as you learn and improve your process further and further. You'll learn about things like classes of service, how planning and estimation are done in kanbanland, about queues and buffers and how to handle them, and—well, you'll learn a lot of things that you'll need to help your team become a little better every day.

But wait, there's more. You'll learn about metrics and how to use them to improve, and we'll present several games and exercises you can use to understand the principles of kanban and get new people to join you on the kanban bus. Hey, we even throw in a small section on kanban pitfalls and common criticisms, just for good measure.

This is a practical book, and we won't spend a lot of time on the underlying theory or the history behind kanban. There are already great books on these topics (hint: pick up some books about Lean, agile, and Toyota), and they do a much better job at that than we could ever dream of doing. But we won't leave you high and dry; some theory will be needed to make good use of the practical advice we're giving, and we'll supply it to you.

But this book is not only for beginners. Judging from all the questions we receive about kanban, and from all the light bulbs that get turned on during our practically oriented talks and training courses for people who have been working with kanban for some time, as well as for novices, you'll get a lot out of this book even if you're far from new to kanban.

Let's get started and see some *kanban in action*!

The structure of this book

This book is divided into three parts, each with a different purpose, aimed at being your companion as you learn kanban:

- *Part 1, "Learning kanban"*—This is an introduction to kanban in the form of a short story. The idea is that you can quickly skim through this part to get a feeling for what kanban is and learn enough about it to get you up and running, just like the fictional team you'll meet in chapter 1. After this introduction, you'll have all the tools and knowledge you need to start using kanban in real life—you'll be able to start learning by doing kanban. If stories aren't your thing, or if you don't like our storytelling style, you can skip this chapter and jump straight into the next part.
- *Part 2, "Understanding kanban"*—This part gives you deeper knowledge about the *why* (the principles and ideas behind kanban) and the *how* (lots of practical tips on applying the principles in your context). We'll take a closer look at the core principles of kanban. There will be many commonly used solutions and variations on these, which people in the community have applied in different contexts. Our descriptions will be practical and will give you more tools and tips

to continue to build your knowledge. The team from chapter 1 will pop in from time to time to ask questions.

- *Part 3, "Advanced kanban"*—OK, you're up and running with your board, you're familiar with how WIP limits work, and you're focused on helping the work to flow. Now what? In chapters 8–12, you'll learn how to use kanban principles to manage risk, facilitate self-organization, plan, and improve. We've also included a chapter on common pitfalls and how to avoid them. Don't let the "advanced" scare you: it's not that complicated, it's just that these practices aren't what you start with typically when you're new to kanban.

We make no claim that you'll come out a kanban master at the end of this book, but it will make a good companion on your learning journey. Matched with the practical experience you'll gain from trying stuff out, this will be a great learning combination.

How to read this book

You can choose several ways to read this book:

- *If you want to get started as fast as possible,* spend an hour reading part 1 ("Learning kanban"), and implement some of the things you learn right away.
- *When you need inspiration or get stuck,* browse through part 2 ("Understanding kanban") and steal ideas or be inspired by how others have approached similar challenges.
- *If you want to know why things are how they are in kanban-land,* read part 2 and learn where kanban comes from and the principles and ideas on which it's based. You'll get a hefty dose of practical tips along the way.
- *If you're already using kanban and are curious about the next step,* take a closer look at the topics in part 3 ("Advanced kanban"). You'll be sure to pick up something new that applies to your situation.
- *When people ask you to teach them kanban,* find fun and educational games in part 4 ("Teaching kanban") to play with them, and tell them about your findings and experiences. And then get them a copy of this book!

You can also read the entire book from cover to cover. This will give you a gradually deeper and wider understanding of kanban. We believe that the best learning experience will come from combining the topics in this book with practical experience.

Author Online

Purchase of *Kanban in Action* includes free access to a private web forum run by Manning Publications where you can make comments about the book, ask technical questions, and receive help from the authors and from other users. To access the forum and subscribe to it, go to www.manning.com/KanbaninAction. This page provides information on how to get on the forum once you're registered, what kind of help is available, and the rules of conduct on the forum.

Manning's commitment to our readers is to provide a venue where a meaningful dialog between individual readers and between readers and the authors can take place. It's not a commitment to any specific amount of participation on the part of the authors, whose contribution to the forum remains voluntary (and unpaid). We suggest you try asking the authors some challenging questions lest their interest stray!

The Author Online forum and the archives of previous discussions will be accessible from the publisher's website as long as the book is in print.

about the authors

Before we set out on this journey together, it might be interesting for you to get to know us a bit. Here we are—plain and simple:

JOAKIM is a thinker, the brains in our dynamic duo. He often lets a person talk for quite a while before he makes up his mind what to say, and then he responds with something profound meant to make them think. This annoys some people, because they usually just want to know what "to do." He has solid theoretical knowledge in all things Lean, agile, and about the Toyota Production System. And he has a lot of practical experience to go along with it, too.

In his spare time, Joakim is a foodie and a movie buff, and quotes from obscure Danish dogma movies sneak into his conversations from time to time (much to the confusion of those around him).

Joakim has four kids (ages zero to nine) and a wife (Anna) and still manages to be engaged in the progress of the company he works for (Spotify) and the Lean and agile communities in Sweden and around the world. He's a regular speaker at international conferences.

MARCUS is a doer and thus the muscle of the pair, to continue with the "dynamic duo" metaphor. He prefers to try something out and fail rather than think about doing it right the first time. This leads to him having do stuff over and over again—much to his irritation and the amusement of others.

Marcus has approached the Lean and kanban communities from a developer's perspective and has a strong interest in the practices that make these ideas work in the wild: test-driven development, pair programming, specification by example, and impact mapping, among others.

When he has time, he can be found blogging or at the Salvation Army or reading up on the latest brass-band news. Trying to incorporate much of that into work-related situations is both hard and pretty much useless, as you can probably imagine.

Marcus is married to Elin, and they have three boys (5, 3, and 3 years old[1]). By the time you read this, they will all have moved to Indonesia, where Marcus will work for the Salvation Army. He will lead the work at a foundation, for the Salvation Army's 6 hospitals and 13 clinics in Indonesia. This will, of course, be done in an agile, Lean fashion, drawing inspiration from and using the techniques found in this book. Marcus will also teach brass instruments to the youngsters at the Salvation Army orphanages.

1 Yes, the last two are twins.

about the cover illustration

The figure on the cover of *Kanban in Action* is Tokugawa Ieyasu (1543 – 1616), the founder and first shogun of the Tokugawa Shogunate of Japan, which ruled from the Battle of Sekighara in 1600 until the Meji Restoration in 1868. A shogun was the military leader in feudal Japan, and because of the power concentrated in his hands, he was the de facto leader of Japan, in place of the nominal head of state, the mikado or emperor. Ieyasu seized power in 1600, received appointment as shogun in 1603, abdicated from office in 1605, but remained in power until his death in 1616. He claimed to have taken part in over 90 battles during his lifetime, as either a warrior or a general. He had a number of qualities that enabled him to stay in power and wield authority—he was both careful and bold—at the right times and in the right places. Calculating and subtle, he switched alliances when he thought he would benefit from the change.

We would like to share one of Ieyasu's recorded quotes with our readers, a quote that is applicable to both our personal and professional lives: "Life is like unto a long journey with a heavy burden. Let thy step be slow and steady, that thou stumble not. … Find fault with thyself rather than with others."

acknowledgments

If you've read an acknowledgements section before, you know that it always starts with thanking the families of the writers. We now know why. They are the people from whom we have taken time: writing while they fall asleep, writing instead of spending time with them, giving them cryptic answers when we were somewhere on page 267 instead of at the playground where we should have been. And *still* they supported us throughout this project. Without them and without their support, this book would not have been possible.

We owe the community around us a big thank you for this opportunity—all the people we have learned from, and continue to learn from, every day and who in many cases know this stuff better than we do. We're standing on the shoulders of giants. Thanks for your shoulders and your encouragement during this process.

There are other people we want to mention who have been particularly helpful, inspiring, and supportive: Christophe Achouiantz, Torbjörn Gyllebring, David J. Anderson, Jim Benson, Corey Ladas, David P. Joyce, Benjamin Mitchell, Karl Scotland, Mattias Skarin, Don Reinertsen, Alan Shalloway, Mary and Tom Poppendieck, Håkan Forss, Måns Sandström, Eric Willeke, Jabe Bloom, Mike Burrows, Dennis Stevens, and all the folks at the Kanban Leadership Retreat. We've learned a lot and had a great time with the Stockholm Lean Coffee bunch, including Håkan Forss and all the other wonderful people there.

An array of people also helped us with reviews and feedback, for which we are very grateful. A special thank you to Rasmus Rasmussen and Viktor Cessan for your insights, and to the following reviewers: Adam Read, Barry Warren Polley, Burk Hufnagel, Chris

Gaschler, Craig Smith, Daniel Bretoi, Dror Helper, Ernesto Cardenas Cangahuala, Jorge Bo, Karl Metivier, Marius Butuc, Richard Bogle, and Sune Lomholt.

Special thanks to Jim Benson for providing the foreword to our book, to Danny Vinson for his careful technical proofread of the manuscript shortly before it went to production, and to Robert Vallmark for producing the great-looking[2] avatars—you really helped us improve the book's visuals!

We have been fortunate to work together with the great crew at Manning, and we are convinced that Manning set aside their best people just for us.

Thank you to Bert Bates for helping us push the envelope on how a Manning book could look and feel. We're fortunate to have had access to your head at the beginning of this process. And of course, thank you to publisher Marjan Bace for letting us write the book this way.

A big thank you to Beth Lexleigh and Cynthia Kane, our development editors, for your effortless reviewing and pushing when things were slow. You took our ramblings and turned them into a real book.

Thanks to all the other people at Manning who helped us in ways big and small, in no particular order: Michael Stephens, Maureen Spencer, Tiffany Taylor, Kevin Sullivan, Mary Piergies, Janet Vail, and Candace Gillhoolley.

MARCUS

I first want and need to thank God—the foundation of everything I am and do.

My personal thank you goes to Elin and the boys (Albert, Arvid, and Gustav), who have supported me during this process. I even got some design help from Albert from time to time.

To my father and mother who raised me to be what I am today (for better or for worse): "Tack mamma och pappa, för allt ni gjort för mig."

To all the people in my close community whom I've turned to with questions and worries from time to time—a mega thank you. I got nothing but cheering and support from you guys: Torbjörn Gyllebring, Håkan Forss, Måns Sandström, Anders Löwenborg, Hugo Häggmark, Tomas Näslund, Per Jansson, Kalle Ljungholm—love you guys.

To Avega Group and Aptitud (my employers during the time of writing): thank you for letting me take on this project. Avega even paid me for it! It blew me away, when you offered that! You're great, both of you!

And finally, to Joakim—this book would have been rubbish without you. It might have been finished earlier, but no one would have read it. I've learned more than a lot from you and continue to do so. Thanks, man!

---

[2] Great looking and funny caricatures, although not very flattering to us. Joakim's avatar received the comment "It looks like an Italian version of you after you've had too much pizza," and Jim Benson asked why Marcus looked like Jeff Goldblum.

JOAKIM

My participation in this book would not have been possible without the support from my family. To the family that gave me life and amazing opportunities (in chronological order): my grandparents Albin, Ingeborg, and Molly; my parents Ove and Elisabet and their siblings and their families; my sister Anna and my brother Henrik—thank you for making me who I am. I'm extremely grateful to the love of my life, Anna, and our children Alva, Saga, Albin, and Iko—your support has been phenomenal, as always.

Thank you Marcus for involving me in this book; for your endless patience with my slow and sparse contributions; for constantly soldiering on and writing; for coping with my not always very polite criticisms, recommendations, and ideas for big rewrites to be mainly carried out by you; for the huge effort you've put into the drudgery of formatting, pixel-pushing, and so on; for pushing me yet never rushing me or making me feel bad for not contributing enough (I did that myself); for your cheerful and supporting personality; in short, for being Marcus!

Part 1

Learning kanban

Part 1 is a practical introduction to kanban. The goal of this part is to enable you to get up and running using kanban while also giving you a basic understanding of the principles behind it and peeking into some advanced topics to whet your appetite for more.

We start off with a short story that follows a typical software development team as they are introduced to, and get started using, kanban. If you don't like the story-telling approach, you can skip straight to the next chapter; we'll cover most of the things from chapter 1 in more detail in subsequent chapters.

1 Team Kanbaneros gets started

Marcus and Joakim are at a conference presenting a practical introduction to kanban. They're finishing the presentation; let's join them in action.

"To sum up: kanban is an approach to software development based on the principles of Lean. It has quickly been picked up by many organizations around the world. You can pick it up too! Starting tomorrow, you should stop starting and start finishing. And with that," Joakim concluded, "our quick, practical introduction to kanban ends. But remember what we said earlier—you could get started tomorrow. Getting up and running with this isn't hard—the effects can have a dramatic impact on your productivity."

"Thank you all for coming! We'll be hanging around here for a couple of minutes if you have any questions," Marcus added, trying to close the discussion in order to end the presentation on time—for once.

Daphne

As Joakim started to clean the whiteboard and remove all the stickies from the wall, Marcus answered a couple of quick questions, pointing some people to the slides available for download as he headed toward the exit. He didn't get far, though. Halfway to the exit a woman abruptly stopped him.

"What's this? Why are you leaving? Don't tell me we missed it all?!" The woman looked disappointed and almost as though she'd been cheated.

"Missed what? The presentation? Yes, it just finished, but you can catch the video online," Marcus replied.

"Oh no!" she cried out. "We only came here for this presentation! It looks like *someone* missed the starting time of the presentation." She nodded toward a man leading a group into the room.

"Well, we'll probably do something in the autumn as well if you want to see the live presentation," Marcus said, trying to smooth things over.

"That won't cut it—we want to get started right away! Our whole team is here; even the business guys were joining us for this tutorial, on my recommendation." She looked genuinely sad. "Hi, I'm Daphne, by the way."

"OK; why don't you book Marcus or me for a day of consultation, then?" Joakim suggested as he joined them, introducing himself to Daphne.

Cesar

"Well, we could, but there have been quite a lot of complaints from both the team and people working with it already. We wanted to do something about this and hoped that we would pick up something to help today." The words came from an imposing man who had caught up with Daphne.

"What kind of problems are you talking about?" Joakim asked the man.

"The team feels swamped with work, and people who are waiting for them to deliver stuff thinks it takes forever," he said plainly. Daphne cut in: "Despite us having a lot of work to do, we have long discussions about which project is more important to start first. Yet we still fail to pick the right one."

"And … well, there's more, but we don't want to take up your time. You were leaving, right?" the man said, leaving the question hanging.

"Unless you have a better suggestion?" Marcus replied quickly. This sounded like the beginning of a fun challenge.

"This is what we're going to do. I'll buy some consultation from the two of you right here and now," the imposing boss-man said. "Your slide there on the screen says 'start tomorrow.' I'm giving you a chance to put your money where your mouth is. How much time can you spare?" He paused and locked his eyes on Marcus and Joakim.

"We have two hours until we need to get going," Joakim said, looking at his watch.

"Well in that case: get us up and running with kanban in two hours," the boss-man said, extending his hand.

"We won't be able to help you solve all your problems, only put you on the right path," Joakim said, looking at Marcus. They nodded to each other. "Right—we have two hours to spare. Challenge accepted!"

Welcome to kanban in action!

You've embarked on a learning journey about kanban, and this introductory chapter will teach you the basics of kanban by means of a story. No previous knowledge of kanban is needed. You'll follow coaches Marcus and Joakim (yes, that's us) as they teach kanban to a software development team and help the team apply what they learn to their way of working.

This made-up story is meant to be an introduction that easily and gently takes you through the basics of kanban. In this chapter, you'll learn how to use visualization techniques such as the kanban board and its work items to better understand how your work *works*. You'll learn how to limit the amount of work in process, and you'll come to understand how doing so makes your work flow faster and helps you identify improvement opportunities. You'll also learn a bit about using metrics for improvement.

In the reviews we've gotten on this chapter, there have been two camps. Many people love this storytelling approach; others seem to ... not like it as much. If you don't want to start with a story, you can skip to the subsequent chapters directly. Everything we mention in this chapter will be treated in much more depth in later chapters. But we hope you'll read this chapter, too, and get a lot out of it. After reading this chapter, you should be able to get up and running with kanban yourself, by applying the principles we're teaching the team in the story.

In the rest of the book, we'll go into the details: the principles behind kanban and a lot of variants and practices that kanban teams around the world have evolved. If you feel that we've left you with questions in the first part, you'll certainly find the answers in the latter parts of the book.

But first things first; let's get back to the story!

1.1 Introductions

The entire team was gathered in the next room. They introduced themselves to Marcus and Joakim by describing each other, a technique they seemed to be pretty experienced with, judging from the bold statements made.

Adam

"Adam is a tester. He's been around for quite some time and is almost always skeptical: of new stuff, of the others' capabilities, but mostly of the quality of the work the others do. He tries to deliver his criticism in a nice way; sometimes he succeeds."

"Adam likes to work his way. He doesn't like change—change means regression testing."

Beth

"Beth is a new employee. She's responsible for requirements analysis on the team. That includes everything from asking the business what it wants and writing it down to making sure the developers understand what they should do."

"Beth is always looking for new ways to work."

Cesar

"Cesar *is* the business. He practically built the first version of the application the team is working on, an internet bank, all by himself way back when."

"Now he has left the IT part of things and is in charge of the business part of the operation. He still likes to think of himself as a developer and is often found 'on the floor.'"

Daphne

"Daphne is a kick-ass developer. She has been known to sling more code in an hour than most developers do in a week."

"But she likes to work alone; other people slow her down. Sitting down with Cesar and deciding how stuff should work—that's the best way to work, if you ask Daphne. Things fly out then. All these other ceremonies and hierarchies are in her way."

Eric

"Eric is a developer by day … because he has to be. But at night he's a guitar hero, playing in local pubs and other venues. Soon the big break will come. Soon."

"Writing code is all right, but it's often hard to see why we do it."

"Eric likes to get things done so that he can continue to answer questions on http://guitar.stackexchange.com."

Frank

"Frank is the manager of the IT side of the operation. He has 36 people under him, and he tries to meet with everyone at least once every other month, but there are lots of other meetings to attend."

"He cares about the product, but he has a hard time keeping up with all the new features. Frank tries to develop his people whenever he has extra time."

"Great," Marcus said. "I've found a room over here with a whiteboard in it. Do you have your stickies, Jocke?"

"Yes, of course," Joakim replied, with his please-no-stupid-questions face. He's an agile coach; naturally he has stickies with him at all times.

"Great—let's go, then," Marcus said, leading the way.

"Who can tell us what your team does?" Joakim asked when they stood around the board.

"That's probably me," Cesar said, pulling out his laptop.

"No, please! No slides!" Eric cried out in pain. "Tell him—we don't have time for that."

"Yes, you're probably right," Cesar responded, a bit stumped. "Here's the short version."

The team is a small development team consisting of the group gathered here. They work for a big insurance company with responsibility for the newly released mobile bank application. Because their team is pretty small, they can govern themselves for the most part. There's reporting to be done to other parts of the business, but they can make their own decisions about the work they do, with Cesar having final say in every important decision. The team is in charge of creating new features in the mobile bank, as well as supporting and maintaining the software that's in production.

"Why do you need our help?" Marcus asked. While waiting for an answer, he wrote the heading *Challenges* on a flipchart.

"I can probably answer a bit of that." Frank, the project leader, stepped forward. "We've been experiencing difficulties in keeping up the pace of expected deliveries. There has been a lot of complaining from different stakeholders in the organization about not getting their features in time."

"And that gets worse by the minute," Cesar added. "People no longer trust the quality of our work, and they definitely don't trust our estimates and delivery dates."

"We, on the team, for our part," Daphne added, "feel totally swamped and don't know what to do first. When we're trying to please everybody, it leads to sudden changes in priorities, and everything is 'PRIO 1.'"

The team then told Marcus and Joakim that it was common for stakeholders to hand tasks directly to the team members. These requests often came from senior people in the organization, making it difficult for the developers to say no. Furthermore, those items were sometimes tasks someone else was already working on. Marcus patiently wrote down the challenges as bullet points on the flipchart.

* We often deliver late
* Estimates are often inaccurate
* Team is swamped with work
* Priorities are unclear
* Work is coming to the team from everywhere
* Unclear who's working on what

"Thank you, but that's probably enough," Daphne interrupted. "The clock is ticking, you know; you only had two hours to spare, right? Let's get practical."

"Yeah, let's get back to the task at hand." Frank grew impatient now. "Where do we start?"

"We understand that you're eager to get started," Joakim answered. "But you should also understand that kanban is a bit different from other methods. Take Scrum or Rational Unified Process (RUP), for example; they prescribe what roles you should have, what meetings you should run, even how you should run them, and so on. Kanban, on the other hand, starts where you are, helps you understand your current situation, and helps you identify the next step to improve it."

"Yes, it's important for us, and for you, to understand where you are right now in order to help you," Marcus cut in, afraid that Joakim would come across as too theoretical, "but we can definitely get started now, and you'll understand more about this as we go. We'll keep this list of challenges here as a sort of agenda for our short time together."

"What is your team called, by the way?" Joakim asked.

"From now on it should be: the Kanbaneros!" Frank said, in his best Mexican accent. The rest of the group laughed, and Marcus wrote it down on the flipchart.

"Let's start with some show-and-tell to make our work a little more visual, shall we?" Joakim began.

1.2 The board

"How do you know what you're working on as a team and how work enters your workflow? If you're not even sure yourselves, how could the stakeholders know, right?" Joakim went up to the whiteboard and grabbed a marker.

"Where do you keep your backlogs today?" Joakim asked. "I guess you have some kind of list of what you need to work on?"

Beth

"Of course we do," Beth quickly replied. Joakim and Marcus could sense that she felt a bit insulted by the question. "I make sure to enter and categorize all the requirements in JIRA,[1] our project-issue tracking system."

"Yes, and I go in there as often as I get a chance and try to keep the ordering, with respect to priorities, up to date." Frank added that he felt the project-tracking system was in good shape.

"This makes it easy to see who is working on what and the progress for each item," Cesar added.

"Can we access your JIRA system right now?" Marcus asked, pointing to Daphne's laptop.

"Yeah—of course," Daphne answered, and she flipped the laptop open.

"Good. Let's write down what you're working on right now," Joakim suggested. "Write each item on a separate sticky note, and keep it brief; it's enough if all of you understand roughly what it refers to." He opened the pack of sticky notes with his patented one-hand grip in less than a second, much to the amused admiration of the group (or so he imagined). He handed out yellow notes to the team.

"Please write legibly, using the thicker sharpies and not the ballpoint pens." Even though Marcus had given the exact same instructions hundreds of times, he always felt a bit patronizing when doing so, but he had learned the hard way that tiny scribbling makes it much more difficult for people to understand and feel involved in exercises like these. "When you're done, post the items on the whiteboard."

Joakim asked the team to post the work in priority order from top to bottom. There were a couple of minutes spent running back and forth to the screen, but pretty soon six items had been posted in a nice column on the board. When the running had settled down, Joakim faced the team and asked, "Do you agree, team? Is this what you're working on right now?"

"Yes," came the answer, almost instantly and simultaneously from Cesar, Frank, and Beth. Adam and the developers, Daphne and Frank, looked down at the floor and said nothing.

"There's no right or wrong here," Marcus said. "What's important is that we get the true picture of your current situation. Anything else?"

After a couple of seconds, Adam came clean. "Well, it's not entirely true … we have a lot of stuff that we do that doesn't get entered in JIRA."

Adam

"What are those items?" Joakim asked. "Can you give us examples?"

It turned out that those items could vary a lot both in size and in what they were: additional requirements, small support tasks, favors repaid to other departments, and maintenance of

[1] JIRA is an electronic issue- and ticket-tracking application from Atlassian: www.atlassian.com/software/jira/overview/.

systems were some examples. Often, someone senior who wanted something done handed it to a team member in the corridor.

"Those tasks are hard to turn down," Adam said. "We don't know how to prioritize or what we're allowed to say no to. But I guess we could do a better job telling you about them."

"Well, to me it seems that we're missing JIRA tickets," Beth said. "If people are working on stuff that isn't registered in there, then we can't trust JIRA."

"Is there anything you could do about that?" Joakim continued.

"Well, I guess it will sort itself out if we make sure to add everything to JIRA, right?" Beth said. "Then all the work will be in one place, and it's easy to share with people who don't sit next to us."

"That's right," Joakim said. "Any drawbacks to an electronic tool?"

"Not where I stand, no," Eric was quick to say.

"Hmmm—things often get lost in JIRA," Beth commented. "We have, on more than one occasion, had doubles of work, for example. There's a fair amount of searching to find anything in there."

"How could we make work easier to find and see?" Joakim asked.

"Well," Beth began, "we would have to see it all the time, I presume. Like writing on the wall or something."

"Bingo!" Marcus could not hold back anymore. "Put the work on the wall! For every work item you're working on, create a little note and put it up on the wall. You'd be surprised how big a difference such a small thing will make for your work." Marcus knew from experience that it was a big thing for many organizations that were starting with agile development.

To see this in practice, Marcus suggested that the team create a sticky for each work item they were working on right now and then post them on the board.

"Everybody done?" Joakim asked after a minute or two. "Please post them on the board."

Next to the previous six items from JIRA, another eight were posted.

"My God!" Frank cried out. "Is this true?"

"We told you!" Daphne said, throwing her arms out wide. "We get a lot of stuff on the side."

"I know, but I never realized …" Cesar scratched his head. "You've been through some bad, stressful times, people."

"But that's more than the *actual* work in JIRA," Beth said, as she counted the stickies.

"That's what we've been saying all along," Eric said, changing the tone of his voice for once.

The group grew silent and gazed at the board for a while. By creating small notes that represented each work item, they had shown, in a physical way, what they were doing. Joakim and Marcus had witnessed this eye-opener for teams many times before.

"There you have information being picked out of JIRA, the electronic tool—or the 'information fridge,' as you like to call it, Joakim," Marcus said. He looked at Joakim, pausing to have him explain the metaphor.

Joakim picked up the cue and explained: "A visualization on a big visible board can be called an *information radiator*; its information is obvious and apparent to people passing by. Electronic tools are, I think, sometimes more like fridges in that you have to open them and poke around to find what you're looking for." He wasn't too sure anybody heard him, as the team stared at the pile of stickies in front of him.

Joakim

"Looking back at your challenges," Marcus intervened, "we've at least started addressing the confusion of who's working on what and what work the team is actually doing, and we've touched briefly on prioritization."

* We often deliver late
* Estimates are often inaccurate
* Team is swamped with work
* Priorities are unclear •
* Work is coming to the team from everywhere
* Unclear who's working on what •

Beth took in the scene before her with the stickies on the board. After a minute she said, "What do we do with that pile of stickies then?"

"Yeah, stacking them on the wall doesn't help us get more work done and keep the stakeholders satisfied, does it?" Daphne added.

Visualizing work

* Makes hidden work apparent
  - Can be as easy as a sticky for each work item
* Helps you see:
  - Who's working on what
  - What you're working on
  - How much is going on
* Visible work radiates information to people seeing it

1.3 Mapping the workflow

"Well, all those stickies show you that you have a lot of work in progress," Joakim started. "But there is more you can get out of visualizing your work, like letting everyone see the progress of the different work items and what the priorities are. This will further improve transparency and help you to prioritize work as it comes to you," he said, pointing to the list of challenges. "Let's try to map your workflow to the board and put the stickies in the right places." Joakim removed the cap from his whiteboard marker, ready to go at it.

"Map our what to the what, now?" Beth asked.

"Well, the items you work with *flow* through your system from idea, or customer request, to finished feature in production, providing value to the customer, right?" Joakim asked.

"Yes … I guess so." There was mumbling all around.

"Where does the work start?" Joakim asked.

"Hmmm—hard to say," Frank said. "It depends on where you draw the line. Is it when the idea is first conceived? Or when we decide to do it, or get the approval to do it? But I guess something that's concrete is that we register all the stuff we're doing in JIRA, our ticket-handling system."

"But Beth," Cesar interrupted, "you and I have done a lot of work before that, right?"

"Yes," Beth replied, "but that's a bit unstructured, because it goes back and forth a lot before we decide what to put into JIRA. Sometimes it's a big idea, and sometimes it's a little fix."

They decided to start the workflow when the work was registered in JIRA and to end it when the work was in production.

"I can't see why we shouldn't track it all the way," Daphne said.

"OK, let's draw the workflow as columns that the work progresses through." Joakim started drawing columns on the whiteboard, but then he stopped. He had tried too many times to draw the board for a team, and knew that it would make the board *his* rather than the *team's*. Luckily there was a simple solution. "Better yet; you draw them." Joakim threw the marker into Beth's lap.

Marcus

"To indicate that some work is in a certain stage, we put the sticky in the column with the corresponding name," Marcus explained.

"But what are the names or stages, then?" Beth looked confused, because Joakim hadn't written any names.

"Well, that's where you guys come in," Joakim said with a wry smile. "We can't do all the work for you. The stuff you haven't done yet in JIRA—what do you call that?"

"Well … I don't know. Undone?" Frank said. There was laughter all around.

"How about Inbox?" Cesar suggested.

"I don't know," Eric said. "My thoughts go to the mailbox. And I hate email. Can't we try something else?"

"To do," Daphne suggested. "Or is that too simple?"

Nobody seemed to mind, and Joakim said: "That's a great start! Remember, we want it simple and easy. If you see a need to later, you can always change it."

"In fact," Marcus said, raising a finger, "we suggest that you draw the board with a marker on a whiteboard. Don't make it permanent, using tape and stuff for the columns too soon, because that might make you less inclined to change it. And you'll have to change it as you learn."

As Marcus talked, Beth drew a column on the board to the far left. She wrote *Todo* at the top of the column.

Joakim said: "OK, all the stickies that you haven't started working on yet—move them into that column."

The team went up to the board and started to move items around. There were some discussions and questions about what items actually meant, but pretty soon three stickies were posted in the Todo column.

"OK, guys," Joakim called out to the group as they huddled around the board. "Let's make it easier from the outset, and put the items in prioritized order, from top to bottom. This will be helpful later on, because you'll be able to easily see what is more important in each column."

"How do you go about working with the item from there?" Marcus asked. "What is the first thing you do?"

"We often sit down for a design discussion. How should this be built? What can we use from our existing platform? Should we use other teams' components for the new solution? Things like that," Frank said.

"There's some documentation of our findings, as well," Beth added.

"What would you call that?" Joakim asked.

"How's Design as a name?" Cesar asked.

Todo Analyze

"Hmmm, not quite right. There could be a lot of different things to do. Maybe Analyze would be a better fit? What do you think?" Frank asked Marcus.

"I haven't got a clue. It's *your* workflow. Ask your team instead. What do you all think?" Marcus faced the group.

"Yeah—Analyze is better," Daphne said, and the others nodded and murmured in agreement.

"Anything you're analyzing right now?" Marcus asked.

The team agreed to put two items in the Analyze column.

"Continue down your workflow, following the flow to 'in production.'" Joakim thought that Lean terms, strung together, sometimes became poetry. A quick look around confirmed that he still was alone in that belief. He coughed slightly and said, "OK, what happens after that?"

The team continued by creating columns for Development and Testing, and they added the stickies with the current work to the columns. After that, there was a brief discussion about what "done" meant. They decided to add a step in the workflow for acceptance. They settled on Accept as a column name. When asked, Adam also realized that three of the items in the Testing column were tested already and were waiting for Cesar's approval. They decided to move those into the Accept column as well, together with another item that was already there.

Adam went up to the board and moved the stickies from Testing to Accept.

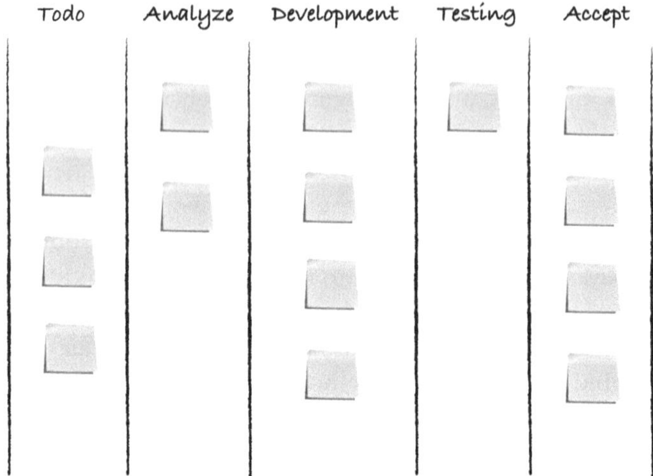

"Then what?" Joakim said. "You have your work analyzed, developed, tested, and accepted. What more needs to be done?"

"Well, we should roll it out in production, dude," Eric said.

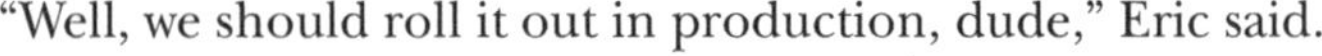

"And by 'we,' you mean …" Daphne prompted.

Eric

"Ops." Eric shrugged, sighing.

"What's that?" Marcus said.

"Well, that's operations," Frank, ever the diplomat, explained. "The operations part of our company has been outsourced to another company. That's increased the time it takes to get a deployment into production."

"And the first thing they did was to revoke all our access to the production servers," Daphne muttered.

"I take it that you have to wait a while before stuff is shipped, then?" Joakim asked.

"Yeah, they do deployments six times a year. And they're not going to change their minds." Eric was disappointed.

"Write 'Waiting for Ops' or something," Adam said.

"Yes, let's go with that," Frank said.

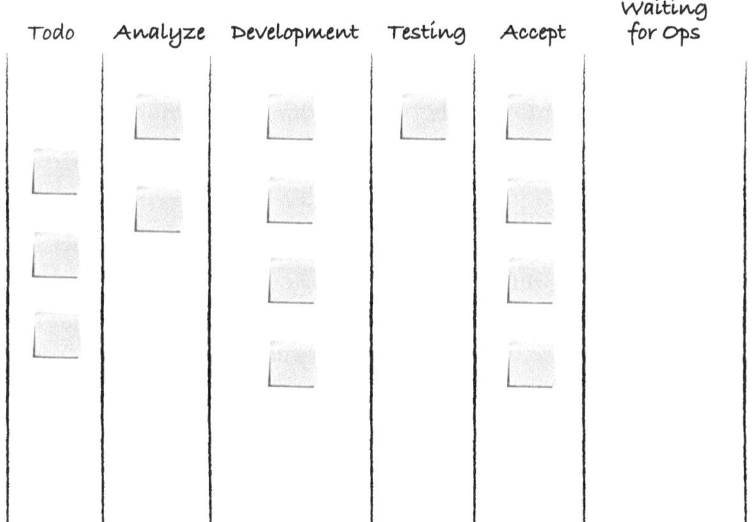

"But it could be called Done or Out of Our Hands, if you like," Frank said.

Frank

"Why?" Marcus asked.

"It's only Ops work that's left, and our hands are tied," Daphne said.

Frank continued, "Yes, we don't do much after that."

Joakim and Marcus exchanged a "Should I do it or should you?" look. It was Joakim's turn, apparently, and he asked, "Who is your customer?"

"What do you mean, 'customer'?" Frank asked.

"Well, who is interested in your work or the features you create?" Joakim explained.

"Well, the stakeholders who wrote the requirements for the system—," Frank began.

"Really?" Joakim said sneakily.

"Hmmm … define 'customer' again for me," Beth said thoughtfully.

When the team gave it some more thought, they soon agreed that the users of the internet bank were the important customers to keep in mind.

"'Done' for them would be when they can use the product," Cesar said.

"What about the Waiting for Ops column, then?" Joakim pressed. "Will that make your end users happier?"

"No, of course not," Beth said. "But that's apparently how things are done, so what can we do about it?"

"If we were to ask you to post all the items that were Waiting for Ops, how many would that be?" Joakim asked the whole group.

"A truckload of them," Eric answered before anyone else had time to say anything.

"Yeah—it's many. The last release was—" Frank stopped and thought for a while. "I think there's one coming up this Wednesday. I'd guess maybe 25 to 40 items."

Marcus faced Cesar and asked, "What good are the projects doing your customers there, in Waiting for Ops?" He pointed toward the column.

"None whatsoever—we want it out," Cesar said. "But as Beth said, it's pretty much out of our hands."

"Can you change that?" Joakim asked.

"Not easily." Cesar sighed. "They're on a different budget, in a different department, and even in a different building, for crying out loud."

Daphne went up to the board and said, "But if we had a Waiting for Ops column with stickies, and the only thing that prevented those items from getting done were the Ops guys. Don't you think we can start a discussion, at least?"

"Yeah, it's much better than saying 'You suck,'" Frank said, looking at Eric, who in turn looked down at the table.

"We might even be able to help them with some of the simple things ourselves." Daphne saw her chance to get back the admin rights to the servers.

"Yes, it's at least worth a shot," Cesar admitted.

"Great work, team," Marcus said. "When you visualize your pain and gather data about it, it's much easier to get the stakeholders' and other teams' understanding. It's not you nagging, it's data." Eric nodded in agreement and looked relieved.

"Here's another excellent example of why visualization is so important," Marcus cut in. "These issues exist right now; you just didn't see them. By making this simple visualization, a sticky for each work item and which stage of the workflow it's in, you were able to see a problem in your process."

"Right—even though I'd rather call it an 'unrealized improvement opportunity,'" Joakim said, smiling at Marcus. "And this is a big thing. Your kanban board will tell you all sorts of things. Items moving slowly, items being blocked, or items not being worked on are only a few examples. They're improvement opportunities from which you can learn how to improve your way of working. Seize these opportunities. Call Ops and do something about this, for example. Maybe they don't even know that this is a problem for you!" Joakim realized he was getting carried away and tried to calm down.

"I sure will," Cesar muttered, but he was also quite happy with the progress they had made so far.

"OK, what happens after that—after Waiting for Ops?"

"Well, then it's over," Adam said. "It's in production. Bugs might turn up, but then they're entered as JIRA tickets, hopefully, and that would go in the Todo column, I guess?"

"If you say so, it's your process," Joakim said. "That leaves us with a final column called Done, or something?"

"Why have a Done column at all?" Daphne asked.

"Why not?" Eric replied. "We want to show that we're amazing, right?"

Marcus agreed. "Yes, by all means do." He paused briefly. "And it's also a great way to collect all the work on the board as it's finished."

"Right." Adam got that. "But why Done? I said that bugs might occur. How about In Production? That says more what it is, I think."

The rest of the team agreed, and there were no tickets to put there at the moment.

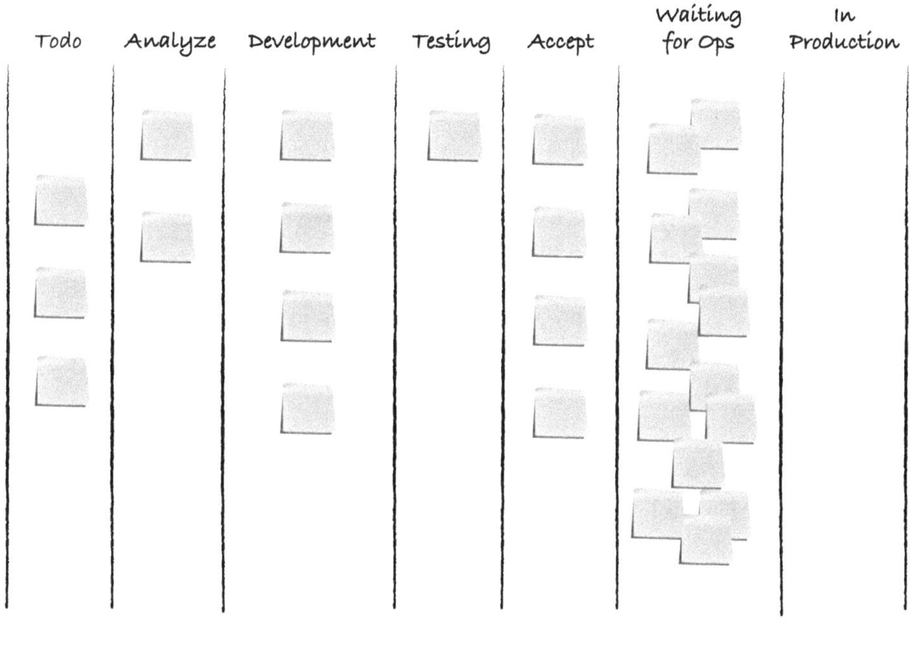

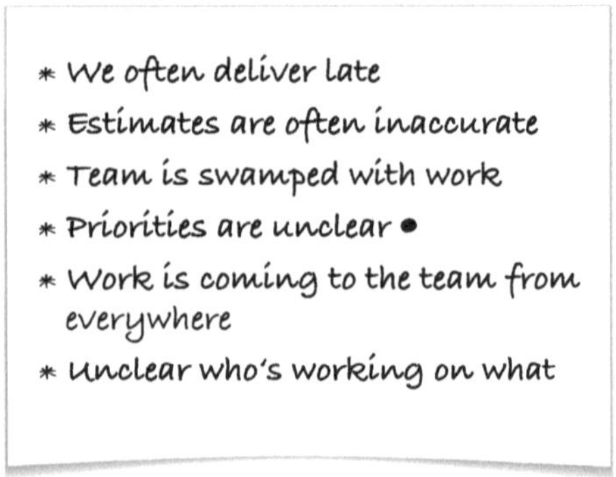

"Looking at this—would you say that it is roughly the workflow your work goes through?" Joakim asked. "Can you see the status of each item more clearly now than when it was locked in the electronic system?" He nodded to the flipchart with their list of challenges.

* We often deliver late
* Estimates are often inaccurate
* Team is swamped with work
* Priorities are unclear •
* Work is coming to the team from everywhere
* Unclear who's working on what

"How about prioritization? That was also one of your challenges," Joakim said, and pointed to the item on the flipchart. "Is prioritization easier for you to see now, when the items are listed in priority order in each column, for example?"

The team looked at the board for a moment. Frank mentioned that it felt a bit simplified and that they couldn't know if it worked until they had tried it.

"That's alright for now," Marcus said. "Two things: first, this isn't final. This is 'best so far.' This board, and everything else we've discussed, will probably be subject to change later on. We should improve it as we go." He paused for a second, trying to avoid going into preaching mode about the virtues of inspect and adapt and continuous improvement.

"Second, let's talk about the different types of work you mentioned. Or in other words—what goes on the board?"

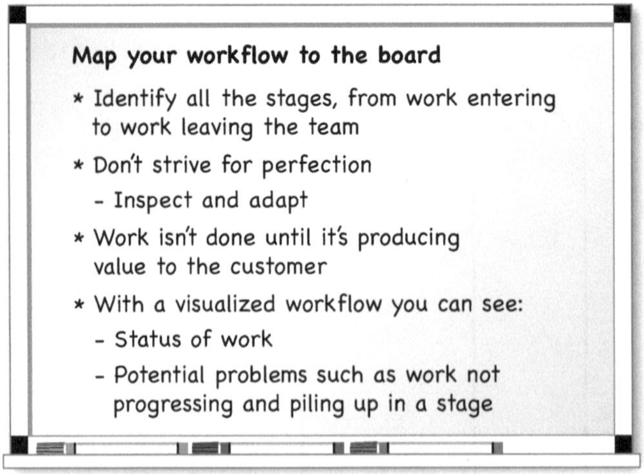

Map your workflow to the board

* Identify all the stages, from work entering to work leaving the team
* Don't strive for perfection
  - Inspect and adapt
* Work isn't done until it's producing value to the customer
* With a visualized workflow you can see:
  - Status of work
  - Potential problems such as work not progressing and piling up in a stage

1.4 Work items

"We now have a lot of stickies on the board, each of them symbolizing a work item," Marcus said. "They each have a short title describing what work item they refer to."

"And the status of each item is clearly shown by which column it's in," Joakim added, sweeping his hand across the board from right to left.

Beth

"Is this enough information for all of you, and for your stakeholders, to understand what you're working on at the moment?" Marcus asked.

"Well, those titles might be too brief at times," Beth said.

"How do you mean?" Marcus asked.

"I'd say that some of them could only be understood by the developers who are working on them, if even by them."

Description

"Maybe you want to write a short description of the work the sticky represents? Not something long-winded, but at the same time not so short that you don't remember what that note was about," Marcus suggested.

"Like a user story, then?" Beth smiled.

"Yeah—you could do that," Joakim answered, "but you don't have to. Any short description that reminds you of what you're doing will do. It's good if it's apparent what the item is about without having to get up close to the board and read for a while. It should be apparent at a glance so you can tell different items apart." Joakim drew a big square on the board and wrote *Description* in the middle of it.

"Is that enough then?" Marcus asked.

"Not always. I often want to know the JIRA number." Eric loved that tool; you could hear it in his voice.

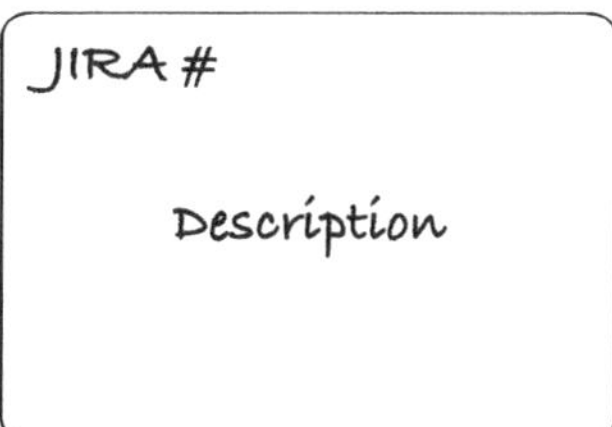

"Why?" Joakim asked, in part because he was not as impressed with JIRA, in part because he thought Eric probably had a point.

"If we're going to have such a short description, we'll need a reference back to JIRA so we can see the rest of the information there. Sometimes there's loads of useful stuff in there. Long discussions, pictures, or what have you," Eric explained.

"Great!" Joakim wrote *JIRA #* in the top-left corner of the square he had drawn on the board.

"Anything else?" he asked.

"Deadlines!" Frank stood up and almost screamed.

"Sure … that seems important to you?" Marcus questioned. He looked at the group: no answer. After a while, Cesar broke the silence. "Yes, they're important to us, but they aren't present on every work item we do. How do we handle that?" He aimed the question at Joakim.

"What do you all think?" Joakim asked the group.

"Let's write them on the notes that have a deadline; it's as simple as that, right?" Eric said from his seated position.

"Yeah, but we want it to stand out, so that we don't miss it." Frank was talking to himself a bit.

"How about using a different color, then?" Beth suggested.

"Great idea!" Joakim went up to the board and added a deadline in the top-right corner. "Another thing that might be useful is to always write them in the same area of the sticky. That makes a connection that the top-right corner has a deadline, if present."

"Great work, team," Marcus added.

"But there's one other thing that can prove useful to add to the work item," Joakim said. "Any guesses?"

No answers.

"How do you know who's working on what?" he asked.

That fact was noted on each item in JIRA, but they quickly realized that they needed to move that information over to the board as well. The first suggestion was to write the name, but that would use up space on the sticky; and sometimes more and more names were added, which would make the sticky hard to read.

"A simple thing would be to have some sort of marker to attach to the work item. A magnet with your name or something," Beth said.

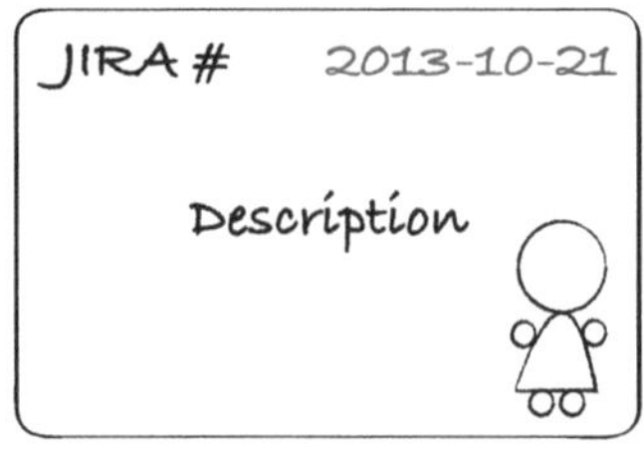

"Right: a simple and common solution is to create what are known as *avatars* of yourselves that you put on the work items you work with," Marcus stated.

"An avatar? A blue guy riding a flying horse? How's that going to help?" Daphne looked quite surprised.

"No, not that kind of avatar." Marcus laughed. "A little picture, or placeholder, that represents you. Like a printed picture of yourself, or a cartoon that looks like you, or whatever rocks your boat."

Frank

"Cartoons? But we look nothing like that!" Frank objected.

"Use something that at least resembles yourself, or make sure to add your name to it, so it's easy to make the connection between the picture and you," Joakim said. He was still burned by the time he chose to use stickers with dogs that were impossible to connect to the right people. He started drawing a sketch of an avatar on the board. His drawing skills caused some giggling.

"You know what would be helpful?" Adam said when the sketch was done. "To know if something is a bug or not."

"How come?" Joakim asked.

Adam explained that bugs were prioritized over other work and probably could skip steps like Analyze in the workflow. They also wanted to track which JIRA ticket the bug originated from. After some discussion, the team decided to indicate that something was a bug by using a different color, writing it on a red sticky instead of a normal yellow one (a pattern common in the kanban community).

"That's really good!" Beth, who always thought of herself as a designer in disguise, was intrigued. "Then those bug items will be easy to pick out even from a distance."

Joakim produced a red sticky and wrote the word *Bug* on it. On a yellow sticky, he wrote *Normal*. He posted them on the side of the board.

"Please come up to the board and change the colors of the items already sitting there," he said, handing out red stickies.

The group discussed some items, but for the most part they were quick to decide the type of work for a particular work item. After a short while, they took a step back and looked at the board.

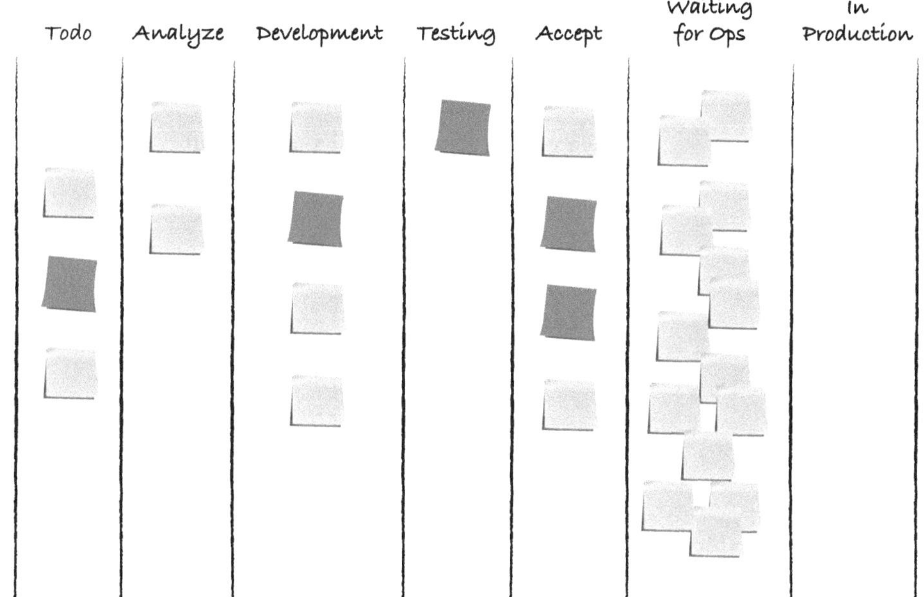

"Now we can see a little more about what we're working on," Marcus said. "Furthermore, if the board starts to be only red stickies, we need to sit down and have a serious quality talk, right? The board is beginning to speak to us, sending us information about the status of our work. Can you see what we meant by *information radiator* before?"

There was nodding all around. It was easy to see the power of visualization and how simple measures, like changing the color of a sticky, could be useful to help important features to stand out, such as the type of work represented by the note.

"Great!" Marcus clapped his hands together. "We now have a board with a workflow and a simple template for what should go on each work item. Let's see how work items should move across the board and what we can learn from that."

"Remember where we started on this visualization journey," Joakim interrupted. "We want the board and everything on it to *radiate* information to us. That information will tell us how our work works so that we can learn from it. The real gain isn't seeing the status of each work item, great as that is. The real gain is to help us make decisions and to improve our process as we learn from how it works. This is only the beginning, and you're never done."

"This is a basic and important principle in kanban: to make work visible," Marcus cut in.

"Right, and the basic reasoning behind that is that you can't improve what you don't see. Do you agree?" Joakim said.

REMEMBER You can't improve what you don't see.

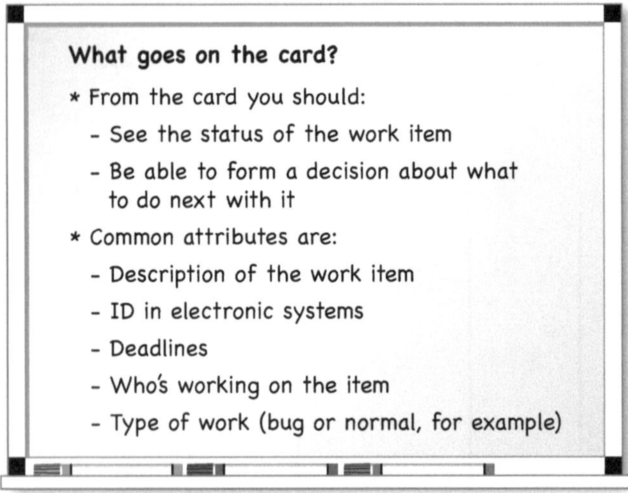

People nodded their heads, seemingly in agreement. "Totally," Cesar said, "and already we've seen the value of this. But what do we do next?"

1.5 Pass the Pennies

"Let's check in with your challenges again," Marcus suggested. "Let's see if we can do anything to overcome your feeling of being swamped with work, shall we?"

"That will take us to another important kanban principle, which teaches us to *limit* the work in process," Joakim started. "That is, to strive to work with fewer items at the same time."

* We often deliver late
* Estimates are often inaccurate
* Team is swamped with work •
* Priorities are unclear
* Work is coming to the team from everywhere
* Unclear who's working on what •

He almost didn't have time to end the sentence before Adam, ever the skeptic, said, "Why? Shouldn't we do as much as possible? Right now we're showing the work we're doing; we can't do much about that. We're going as fast as we can."

"I don't doubt you for a second. But I think you can do better," Joakim said, a mysterious smile on his face. He looked at Marcus, winked, and said, "I think we need some pennies over here." He pulled out a table and four chairs.

"Right." Marcus produced a small coin purse. He emptied it, creating a little pile of 20 coins at one end of on the table.

He turned to Cesar. "How are we doing with time?"

"We're 45 minutes in. An hour and 15 minutes to go. Please go on," Cesar said mechanically, wondering to himself how these pennies would move things forward.

"Four of you please take seats around this table." Joakim invited the group to the chairs. "The rest of you each stand behind one of your colleagues and bring up a timer on your phone. Marcus and I will fill the last two spaces behind you."

He explained that the aim of the game is for each station to flip all coins once and then pass them on. When all workers have flipped all coins, they're done and delivered to the customer. Everyone seemed to be with him so far.

"The people standing behind a 'worker,'" Joakim made air-quotes to emphasize the irony, "are responsible for timing the worker in front of them to see how much time is spent on the task. Start the timer when your worker *starts* working, and stop it when the worker *stops.* Got it? You're timing the entire time your worker is active."

"Finally, we want to measure the total *lead time*, the time it takes from start to finish for the work to flow through our workflow," Joakim said. "I'll act as the customer and will be timing the whole chain. I'll track two things: the time it takes until the first coin arrives to me, the customer, and the total time—that is, when all of the 20 coins have arrived to me."

After a moment of razor-sharp thinking, Daphne spoke. "But working like this, it means that the first coin and the last coin will arrive at the same time?"

"Yes, that is correct," Marcus responded. "In this first iteration at least. We'll see changes to that soon, in the iterations to follow."

Marcus concluded the introduction to the exercise. "We're going to run this three times. The first time every worker will flip all 20 coins and then send them to the next worker in line. Are you with me?"

"Are you ready? Timers, time your worker's effective working time," Joakim instructed a final time. "Ready, set, go!"

There was intense silence as Adam started to flip his coins like a madman. He passed his coins over to Beth and turned to his "manager" Frank behind his back. "Done—stop the watch!"

Beth continued with equal concentration and sent the coins down to Cesar. Cesar didn't even breathe during his turn and drew one big breath as the coins were sent to Daphne in the last station. Daphne tried to flip two coins at once, one with each hand, resulting in even slower progress. The others moaned. "Come on Daphne—don't let us down here!"

	20		
Adam	10 s		
Beth	12 s		
Cesar	11 s		
Daphne	17 s		
First	50 s		
Total	50 s		

Finally she was done and sent the coins to Joakim, who stopped his watch. On a flipchart, Marcus created a small table and wrote down the results.

Joakim went around to each of the "managers" and asked them for the individual times for each worker. After adding up the total, he turned to the group. "As Daphne predicted, the first and last coin came in at the same time."

"Now let's try with five-coin batches," Marcus instructed. "That means—flip five coins and then pass them down to the next worker before you move on to flipping the next batch of five, and so on. Got it, workers?"

The workers nodded and started to focus on the coins again.

"And managers, make sure to time the *whole* time your respective worker is flipping coins. Starting when the first coin comes in and is being flipped and ending when the last coin has been passed over to the next worker."

"Hmmm—I think I know where this is going," Frank said to himself.

"Time waits for no one," Joakim interrupted. "Ready, set, go!"

This time there were more sounds from the coins but still a sharp focus and silence from everyone in the group. When Adam had flipped his last coin, he cheered for the others. “Come on! Put your back into it, Cesar!”

It wasn't long before the five-coin iteration was over and the results added.

	20	5
Adam	10 s	14 s
Beth	12 s	17 s
Cesar	11 s	13 s
Daphne	17 s	15 s
First	50 s	18 s
Total	50 s	34 s

“What? That doesn't look right,” Cesar called out as he looked at the numbers. “You sure you timed that correctly?” he asked, looking first at Marcus and then at Joakim.

“I assure you it's correct. Let's discuss this further after the next iteration,” Marcus responded. “This time we'll do a single coin at the time. Flip it and pass it down. Got it, workers?”

“As before, managers, time the *whole* time your worker works. Ready, set, go!”

Total silence, except for the continuous sound of coins sliding around the table. After what felt like a short time, they were done. Joakim collected the times for each worker and added them to the flipchart.

	20	5	1
Adam	10 s	14 s	18 s
Beth	12 s	17 s	19 s
Cesar	11 s	13 s	15 s
Daphne	17 s	15 s	15 s
First	50 s	18 s	4 s
Total	50 s	34 s	20 s

“I can't believe that!” Frank sounded skeptical and almost as though he felt cheated. “How on Earth can that be right?” The others also looked quite surprised.

“It's correct, all right. Let's discuss what we can learn from this,” Joakim said.

“First, take a look at the time for the first coin to arrive to the customer. What happens with that as we switch to smaller batches?” Marcus asked rhetorically and pointed to the summarized rows.

“It goes down, way down! Fifty versus four; that's amazing!” Frank shook his head in disbelief.

“And what about the total time?”

“Well, that went down too, of course,” Daphne said, not as impressed.

“But not as dramatically as the time for the first delivery,” Frank still could not believe that number. He looked at it over and over.

"And now—take a look at the times for the individual workers," Joakim said, giving them a few seconds to reflect.

"What's the common trend? Not pointing fingers to anyone in particular." He coughed and winked at Daphne. She got the joke and waved him off.

"Well, as strange as it sounds, those times go up at the same time as the others go down. How can that be?" Cesar looked to Marcus and Joakim for answers.

"What we've shown you with this simple exercise is that when you decrease the number of concurrent or simultaneous ongoing work items, the *lead time* decreases," Marcus explained. "Notice that we're doing the same amount of work, but working in a different way—with smaller batches, with less *work in process* at the same time."

"Or WIP, as you'll hear it referred to in the kanban community," Joakim added.

REMEMBER Work in process (WIP) is the number of work items you have going at the same time. Less work in process leads to quicker flow through your process: shorter lead time.

"It wouldn't be much of a community if it didn't have its own strange three-letter acronyms, now would it?" Marcus said, with a big grin on his face.

"As you've seen, this has a dramatic effect on the total time, which in this case went from 50 to 20 seconds." Joakim pointed to the board. "But another thing also happened. When we worked with big batches of 20 coins, we delivered the first and last coins at the same time; but with smaller items, we got the first one in after 4 seconds. Less than a tenth of the time for the first delivery when doing 20-coin batches."

"Smaller batches," Marcus made a shrinking movement with his arms, "with less work in process, will both give you better total speed and let you become more agile, because you can deliver the small, important stuff first. Do see why this could be an advantage?"

"Not only that," Marcus continued "but what if there was something wrong with the way you flipped the coins? What if the customer expected them to be flipped to stand on the edge—what would have been different with different batch sizes?"

"Because we didn't deliver until all of us were done with our individual contributions, we would have to do it all over again," Daphne said. "In the first iteration, that is."

"Finally, we stopped focusing on using each worker as efficiently as possible," Joakim said, directing his comment to Cesar. "In the first iteration there was a lot of waiting until the last worker did any work, but each worker was efficient and worked through the entire batch before handing it down. On the other hand, in the last iteration, when the lead time was the shortest, every worker worked for a longer time, making them less efficient as individuals but more effective as a team."

REMEMBER Optimizing your process for quicker flow can lead to poorer resource utilization.

Adam

"I hate to rain on your parade, but …" Adam leaned back and crossed his arms over his chest. He let out a big breath. "Our work, the 'reality,' is a bit more complicated than this. I hope you realize that?" Adam sounded tired.

"How do you mean? Please explain." Marcus tried to open a discussion.

"For starters, items don't arrive in a continuous flow like that. They go back and forth between us. I do a little testing, then there's some more coding, more testing again, and maybe even changing requirements.

"Second—the items we handle vary a lot in size. The coins and the work are exactly the same all the time."

"Good points," Joakim interrupted, as he saw Cesar checking his watch. "And you're right. This is a simplification, a simulation that aims to show a single principle: that less work in process leads to lower lead times. In reality, there are a lot of other forces at play, and you have to make trade-offs, but the basic principle still holds."

"There are also a lot of other advantages with shortening lead times and limiting the amount of work in process—but we don't have time for that now." Marcus tried to wrap up the discussion. "This exercise is used as a bit of an eye-opener, and for now the important thing is that you understand the principle. Let's get practical again and gather around the board; how can you apply this to your work and to your board?"

Limit work in process

* Strive to work with fewer items at the same time
* Smaller batches means shorter lead times
* Resource efficiency decreases while flow efficiency increases
* Games/simulations like Pass the Pennies can be a great way to teach people abstract concepts

1.6 Work in process

They went back to the whiteboard.

"Where are our pennies?" Adam said dramatically, underlining the fact that he still didn't trust the result fully—not yet, at least.

"What are the pennies on this board?" Joakim asked the group, ignoring Adam's comment.

"They're the stickies," Beth said.

"What about them? What did you learn in the game?" Marcus asked.

"OK, let's see if I understand this," Frank began. "If we want the work to flow fast across the board, we should do fewer items at the same time. Going from 20 coins to 5, so to speak." He looked at Joakim and Marcus.

Joakim

"Do you agree?" Joakim looked at the group. They seemed to agree.

"But how do we do this in practice?" Eric wanted to know. "What do we change?"

"Well, if we all agree that this is a good idea," Daphne replied, glancing briefly in Adam's direction, "that should be enough, right? We agree to work on fewer things at the same time."

"Yes, you could all agree to *stop starting and start finishing*." Joakim mused on this kanban call to arms that he was so fond of, but the blank stares from the audience told him he had to elaborate. "Rather than starting on a new work item, you could help someone on the team finish one already in progress."

"And rather than allowing yourself to be blocked," Marcus added, "for example, by waiting for information or a review from someone, you should try to resolve the situation or work on how to avoid it in the future. These are the unrealized improvement opportunities we talked about earlier, remember?"

"This sounds great in theory," Eric agreed, "but in practice it's not that easy to help someone finish something. I mean, I don't want to bother Daphne by having her explain what she's been doing and how I can help. Isn't it better if she finishes that herself?"

"That's certainly what it's going to feel like at times, especially in the beginning, but you have to start somewhere and use your own judgment," Joakim explained. "In our experience, the path of least resistance is often to start new work, so we have to make a conscious effort to design the work so that it's easier to help each other finish it."

"Which leads us to the next step in limiting work in process," Marcus interrupted, concerned that Joakim was about to go off on a tangent, "which is to use visualization to make the limits explicit and specific. We choose a maximum number of work items that we're allowed to have in progress at the same time."

"This limitation will help us focus on getting stuff finished and help the work to flow faster through the system." Joakim was back on track again. "Limiting your work in process will help you with a couple of the challenges listed at the outset. First, things will start to move along so you'll stop have people breathing down your neck."

Joakim went up to the flip chart and pointed to the first item. "When stuff starts to come out of your system on a regular basis, the demand for accurate estimates and predictions will diminish, in our experience. Second, you won't feel swamped with work because you now have a limit on how many things you'll work on at the same time. If someone wants to add a new work item, they'll have to also decide what gets taken out."

Joakim added dots to the flipchart as he talked.

* We often deliver late
* Estimates are often inaccurate •
* Team is swamped with work •
* Priorities are unclear •
* Work is coming to the team from everywhere
* Unclear who's working on what •

"Which, in turn," Marcus cut in, a happy grin on his face, "will make it easier to prioritize. Fewer items to start with, but you now have something to show and reason about. The work you're doing is right there, on the board."

"But how do we know what that number should be?" Beth said.

"It depends." Marcus opened with every consultant's standard answer, realized it, and quickly tried to move on to something a bit more useful. "In general, a lower limit is better, but too low of a limit could have bad consequences. Imagine that you all work on one single item. That would be great for the flow; the second it's ready for development, the developers could pick it up and start working on it. And Adam is getting ready to start testing it when development is done. Any problems with that scenario?"

After a moment Frank broke the silence. "Seems like there's a lot of waiting in that case, or am I missing something?"

"No—that's exactly right." Marcus gave Frank a thumbs-up. "Low WIP leads to a lot of slack. Which is good for lead times, but most companies are probably not willing to pay for people sitting idle."

"You need to balance those two against each other: fast flow versus people having work to work on. You want a low work-in-process limit, but probably not a limit of 'one,'" Joakim concluded.

"But that still doesn't help us figure out what that limit should be for us," Daphne said.

Daphne

"No, and I'm afraid we can't tell you." Joakim shrugged. "That is something that you must come up with and constantly tune to increasingly get better and faster flow through your workflow."

"Change the limit of the number of concurrent items. OK—we got that. But from what to what?" Frank was losing patience. "You've got to give us something!"

"Start simple," Joakim said. "Start with one item each on the board. Pretty soon you'll see some problems piling up somewhere, where developers have a hard time keeping up, for example."

"What *ever* do you mean by that?" Daphne said half-jokingly, but there was some sting in there too. She was fast, and she knew it.

"Some tasks take a longer time to finish than others," Joakim said. "It's not that important where the flow slows down or stops. The important thing is what you do about it."

"Take this example." Marcus cleared the notes from the board. "Let's say we think that two items are a reasonable amount to be developing at the same time, because there are two devs, right?" he checked with Daphne.

"Sure," she answered a bit defensively, cautious where this would lead.

Marcus wrote the number 2 above the Development column.

"We have two items in there in progress. Now the analysts are ready with their work and want to push it into development. That will break our limit of two items, right?" Marcus drew an arrow and a question mark on the board.

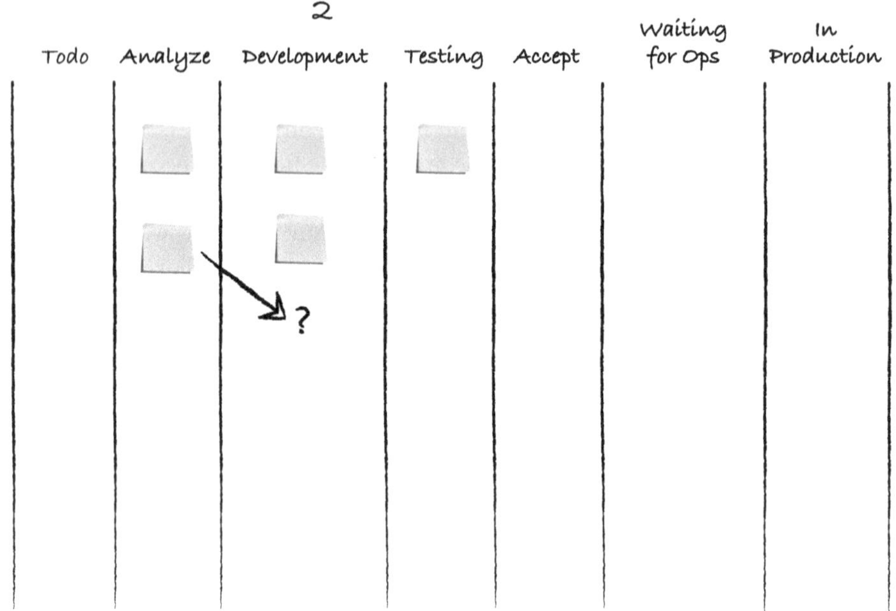

"What do we do now?" Joakim asked.

Frank quickly volunteered his opinion: "Put them in there. They'll get there sooner or later anyway."

"Who else thinks that 'putting them in there' is a good idea?" Marcus asked.

"I sure don't!" Daphne retorted. "Wasn't that the whole idea with all this passing of pennies? Keep the number of items going on to a minimum?"

"Right—but what could we do instead, then?"

"Remove other stuff if what's coming in is more important," Eric suggested.

"Do nothing? Wait? Work slower?" Beth pictured the scene, and it didn't sit right with her.

"See? A discussion is ready to take place," Joakim said. "And that's all the work-in-process limit is: a trigger for discussions. Preferably discussions on how to improve your process so that you can keep the WIP down and have the work items flow faster. It could be a discussion on what specific action to take to avoid bringing more work into the process. Sometimes it will mean a developer helping another developer to finish something, sometimes it will mean replacing something already on the board, sometimes it will mean that developers stop developing to help out with testing—"

"Hold your horses! That will never happen!" Daphne cried; her voice and face told the others she was joking.

"As if I'd ever let you!" Adam was quick to join the joke.

REMEMBER The WIP limit isn't a strict rule; it's a trigger for discussions.

"We often end up doing a lot of testing before a release anyway," Eric chimed in, "so I guess it would make sense to do it all along to avoid the ketchup effect. You know? Nothing, nothing, nothing, and then, all of a sudden, BLAM! Everything comes at once."

"There might even be valid reasons to break the limit from time to time." Marcus tried to get the discussion back on track again. "But if you do it often, you might have to review the limit and see if a higher limit would help the work to flow better. If, on the other hand, you rarely or never reach the limit, you'll never have these useful discussions, and you won't have the tension to improve. Then it's time to lower the limit."

"Now you shouldn't have a problem finding numbers for your limits, right?" Joakim had looked at his watch and realized they had to move along.

"Well, one each is simple, but is it the correct number?" Frank started.

"Think of it as a limit, and not trying to find the correct one," Marcus said, pressing on. "As we said earlier, you'll inspect and adapt with time. If we decide to go with one item each, how can that be achieved in a simple way?"

"Write the number of people doing work in each column?" Adam suggested.

"Yes, great idea! What would that look like? Care to help us out?" Marcus handed a marker to Adam and stepped back.

"Well, I guess, because I'm the only one doing testing right now, we'll end up with a 1 there." Adam wrote a big number 1 above the Testing column.

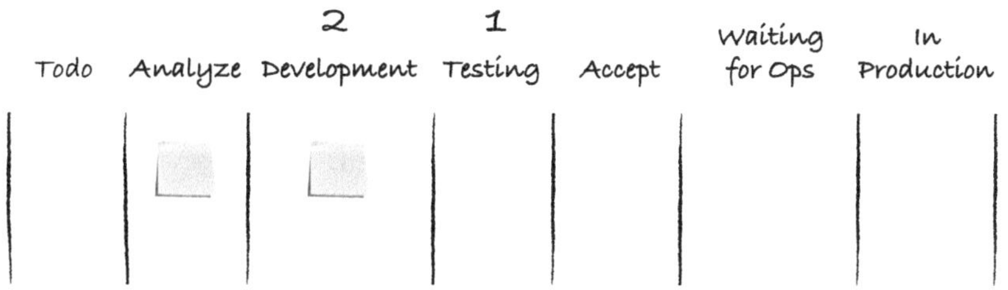

"Hold on!" Beth stepped up to the board. "I do some testing too from time to time. It's a good way to follow stuff up early, and the analysis work rarely takes up all my time because I often have to wait for meetings to take place. I think 2 is a better number."

"Yeah, that's true. Let's go with 2." Adam changed the number.

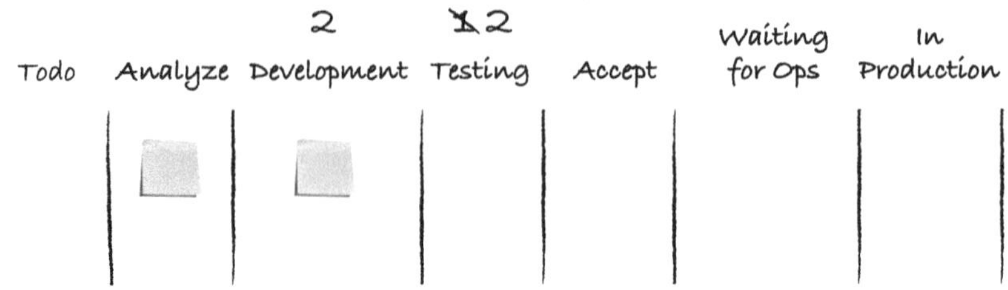

2 ~~1~~2

Todo Analyze Development Testing Accept Waiting for Ops In Production

"OK—how about you devs? What's suitable for you?" Adam threw the pen in the lap of Eric, who instantly passed it over to Daphne.

"Two items seems a bit low to me. Sometimes we need to wait for people, which would mean that we would end up with nothing to do. But four seems a lot as well. What do you think, Eric?"

"I say four items; we do loads more than that today. We'll manage!" Eric said with confidence.

"Hmmm—I'll write 3, and we'll keep an eye out for problems," Daphne said as she erased the number that was there already and wrote 3 instead.

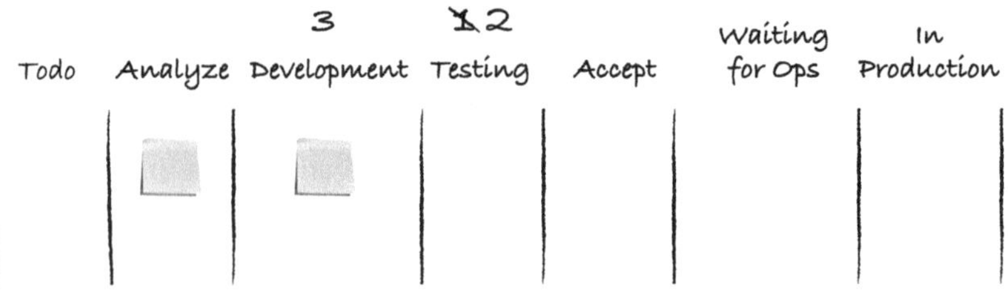

3 ~~1~~2

Todo Analyze Development Testing Accept Waiting for Ops In Production

"As for analysis work, I think a limit of two items seems reasonable," Beth said, and promptly wrote the number 2 above her column. No one seemed to object to that.

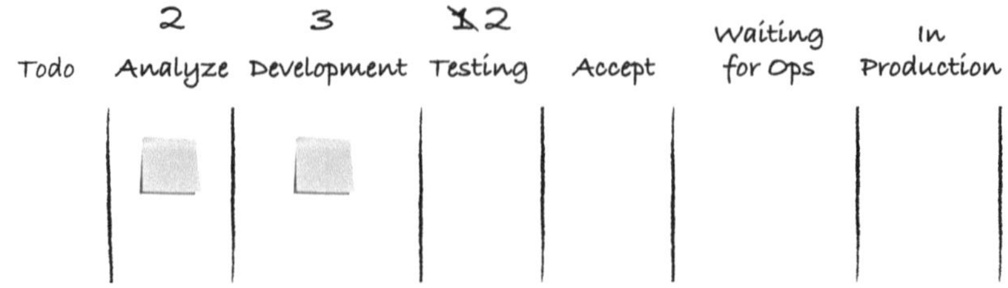

2 3 ~~1~~2

Todo Analyze Development Testing Accept Waiting for Ops In Production

"And the rest of them?" Frank said, turning around. He realized that Marcus and Joakim were nowhere near the board right now. "What should we do with them?"

"What do you mean?" Joakim seemed quite happy to stand in the back and let the team figure it out by themselves.

"Well, the Todo, Accept, and Waiting for Ops columns, and so on. Shouldn't they have numbers on them as well?"

"They could," Marcus answered. "But why? What would you gain by that?"

"Eeeh … I thought that all columns should have a number," Frank confessed.

"As we said: they can have them, but there's no rule," Joakim explained. "Put limits on the columns where you feel it helps you get a faster flow. How about that Accept column, for example? What would a limit of items do there?"

"Let's see." Cesar stepped forward and talked slowly to himself. "Limiting that column to, say, four items means if it's filled with four items, then—" He paused and wrote the number 4 above the column.

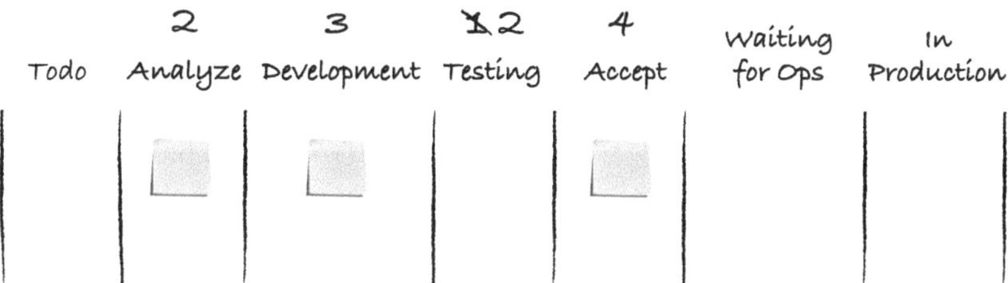

"When the testing team wants to add yet another one, they will be blocked, and things will back up, so to speak. Because the flow is stopped by that limit." Cesar stepped back. "What does that mean?" he mumbled to himself.

"How do you unblock it?" Marcus offered. The others were silent as Cesar continued to think for himself.

"Well, Beth or I check the items out and accept them …"

"Right—so you could see that limit as a signal to you to come and do your acceptance work." Joakim suggested what he thought Cesar was thinking, but translated into the terms they had been using to introduce kanban.

"OK—but why not have a limit of one, then?" Adam asked.

"Because—" Marcus didn't get further before Cesar interrupted him.

"Because then I'll have to run down there the second something is ready to accept, or the workflow will start backing up." A light bulb was turned on for Cesar. "I see. Very interesting."

"Why four?" Frank asked.

"We don't know what a proper limit is. But four seems like a start that we could use and tweak as we see fit. A lower number demands our constant presence, something we often can't handle because we're traveling or are stuck in meetings. A higher number would mean the team would go too long without feedback from us, which might mean rework if something is wrong; and we want to fix that before they're too deep into something else."

"But why should there be a column for stuff that you're waiting to do?" Daphne asked. "I mean, you're waiting for that column to fill up and then start accepting items when it's filled."

"Good point, Daphne," Joakim answered. "This isn't uncommon at all. It's what we call a *queue* or a *buffer* of work. It's usually put in front of a function that is limited in some way, like the Accept column here. Beth and Cesar can't be with us at all times, so when they get here we want to make sure there's work for them to do. Hence we build a little buffer of work for them, and only call them in when it's filled."

"Not sure I'm following you here, Joakim," Cesar said.

"Let's visualize it, and see if it gets clearer," Marcus said, and went up to the board.

Within the Accept column, Marcus drew a Ready column and a Doing column, dividing the column in two. He turned to the group and said, "Now it's apparent what's waiting and what's in progress. When the Ready column starts to fill up, we call on Beth and Cesar."

"Isn't it like that in Testing and Waiting for Ops as well?" Daphne said.

"It could be. You could have queues where you think they fill a purpose: for example, where there's a limited resource or if you want to visualize the difference between waiting and working. If there's a handoff involved, for example from someone doing development to someone else doing testing, a queue would be a good way of signaling that the work is ready to be pulled to the next stage." Joakim looked at his watch.

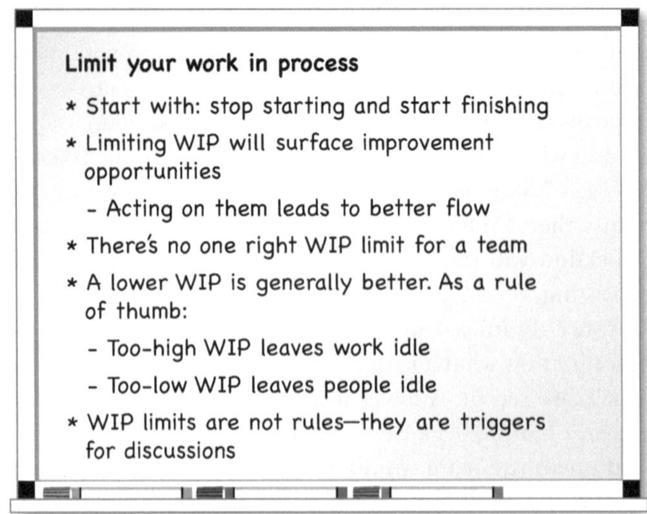

Frank nodded; it seemed he was slowly coming to terms with Cesar's explanation. He looked at the board for a moment. "That's it, then? This is the board, we have our limits, and we're done with it?"

1.7 Expedite items

"Yeah … that could be the board for you." Joakim took a step back and crossed his arms over his chest. "What do you think, people? Is everything up there? Is this how you work?"

Marcus went through the challenges on the flip chart, and said: "Even though we might not have solved every point on this list yet, you should now have tools to tackle most of them, agreed?"

* We often deliver late
* Estimates are often inaccurate •
* Team is swamped with work •
* Priorities are unclear •
* Work is coming to the team from everywhere
* Unclear who's working on what •

There was a moment of silence, and then Adam cleared his throat. "Again—this all looks great, but it's still a simplification," he said, and sighed.

"Everything is not new features and moving stuff forward, you know," he continued. "Sometimes things go wrong in production, and then it doesn't matter what you're doing right now or how many things you already have in progress; you fix it! There and then!"

"That's right," Daphne cut in. "Surely we're not holding off urgent work in order not to break the work-in-process limit, are we?"

"Well—you could, but most teams don't, because that would be bad for business. At the end of the day, your bottom-line result trumps keeping your process perfect. How do you treat urgent work today?" Marcus turned to the group. "If you're happily moving along on your new and cool features, and you suddenly receive an alert that the production server is down, what will you do?"

"I'll drop everything and 'run to the hills'!" Eric said, Iron-Maiden-singing the last part. There was giggling all around, because nobody had seen Eric move fast—ever.

Eric

"Seriously … I'll stop what I'm doing and start to look in to it," Daphne said. "Ah, I get it. We should visualize it on the board. Start where we are, visualize it, and make it explicit, and so on, right?"

"Right!" Marcus gave her a cheesy pistol-shooting sign with his right hand.

Joakim rolled his eyes and quickly moved on. "This is a common scenario. A common solution is to create a special lane on the board for urgent stuff, often referred to as an *expedite lane*."

Marcus, having holstered his imaginary pistol, added a new lane at the top of the board while Joakim explained.

	Todo	Analyze	Development	Testing	Accept	Waiting for Ops	In Production
Expedite							

"The policy you hinted at, Daphne, that you should drop your other work and help resolve the issue, is pretty standard; but it's often implicit and not understood or agreed on by everyone. It can be unclear who should act and do something about it or if everyone is supposed to help out. Should the new item be counted against our WIP limit or not? And so on. There are a lot of implicit policies at play."

"Uh-oh, I know where this is going." Eric threw his arms up in the air. "What's the point of sitting here discussing limits if we're going to have this loophole?"

"What do you mean?" Frank asked, giving him an unappreciative stare.

"You guys," Eric nodded his head to Frank, Beth, and Cesar in turn. "You guys could fill this lane with items all the time. It will be your fast lane into the development queue, and you'll use it like crazy, so that *your* work will get done first! Which makes us hop from one item to another. Again. Like last spring with the big Bank 2.0 release, remember?"

There was a moment of awkward silence.

"OK, there seems to have been some not-so-good things going on with expedite work in the past. What could you do avoid that from happening again, then?" Joakim asked.

More pondering. Eric, putting some extra thought into the challenge, fueled by the guilt of having caused the awkward silence, proposed, "Put in a limit of sorts, I guess."

A short discussion followed in which the team agreed on some simple policies for how to handle the Expedite lane. Joakim summed up the discussion: "Let me see if I've captured your policy correctly. An expedite item should only be used for urgent cases and is not to be used as a fast lane to cheat the system. You'll settle on a limit for how many expedite items you allow per month, OK?"

"Well—I for one am happy with that setup. I'll promise you all that we'll handle the expedite items with respect and not cheat the system," Cesar said and held his hand over his heart for the last part. The laughs that followed were a relief from the slight tension that had crept into the room.

"Let's make sure you understand the implications of this policy. What would happen if you put an expedite item into the system?" Marcus asked.

"It gets done faster. That's what we needed," Cesar said, but realized that he might be walking into a trap. *Two can play that game,* he thought, and asked a question back. "Why are you asking?"

"Well, I meant what will happen with all the other work already in your process? Adam, if you think back to the pennies game we played, what would an expedite item look like there?"

Adam thought for a while and then started to reason out loud. "I guess that would be introducing a new coin that had to be passed around before the others." He paused. "And that would not be great for the flow, because we would have to stop flipping the other coins …" All of a sudden, he got it. "That would make all other coins move slower through the system."

Adam

"Correct!" Marcus said. "Use the expedite lane with care. Sure, it will take that item through the system faster, but it will also increase the work in process, and that in turn will slow down all the work already in there."

Joakim thought that sounded a bit ominous. "That is, make sure you know this and take it into account when playing the expedite item card. There are times when it's the right thing to do to get one valuable or important item out there fast. But it has a cost; make sure you know you're paying it. Like a toll, if you like."

"And we'll make sure the lane isn't misused too." Eric looked happy.

"This could also be a way to handle the work that is handed to you in the corridor," Marcus said, and he made a little dot close to that point on the flip chart. "Sure, you could do it, but is it worth the toll you have to pay for it? A discussion can be had with some real data to back it up."

* We often deliver late
* Estimates are often inaccurate •
* Team is swamped with work •
* Priorities are unclear •
* Work is coming to the team from • everywhere
* Unclear who's working on what •

Expedite lane

* Common way to handle special cases
  - Such as work that is urgent
* Often visualized as a separate lane on the board
* Policies around that lane might be:
  - Only one item can be in the lane at the time
  - Max one expedite item per week
  - Don't count the expedite lane against the WIP limit

1.8 Metrics

Cesar

Cesar went to the board, looked at it, and turned around. He was in boss-giving-speech mode now; they could tell.

"I think I speak for everybody when I want to extend a big thank you for this, and—"

"Now wait a minute," Beth cut in. Cesar looked a bit surprised, but then again, this was Beth. She was worth listening to; he knew that from experience.

"Yes?" he asked, encouraging her to go on.

"I know we only have 20 minutes left, but there's one area that we've left untouched," Beth said. "How do we improve on this?"

"What do you mean?" Frank was surprised. "This will give us better control over our work than we've ever had before. I think it's a fine start!"

"It is! But as I've understood it, this should evolve, right?" She looked at Joakim for support.

Beth

"Yes, but ..." Joakim responded, "as we talked about when we drew the board, and designed the work items, and so on, everything on the board is subject to change in order to improve as we go—"

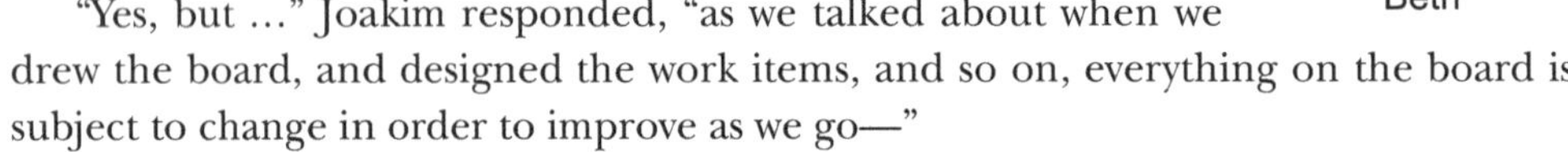

"Great!" Beth stopped him short. "How do we know that we're going the right way?"

Joakim said, "How do you know that you're improving when you make a change?"

"Well, if we're doing better than before," Adam said.

"But against what?" Frank responded. This was his territory. "What does 'better' mean? How do we know? We need some metrics to know if we're improving."

"Here we go," Eric and Adam said together, and others joined in with sighs and despondent voices. Joakim and Marcus looked at each other, a bit surprised by the strong reaction.

The team had apparently been subjected to a company-wide effort to introduce key performance indicators (KPIs)[2] that didn't help them at all. Because the KPIs had to be fulfilled, the productivity of the team had been suffering, as well as morale. Before long, the KPIs were abandoned.

"OK, what do you say about skipping that, then?" Joakim tried to steer the discussion back onto a positive track and waited to get their attention. "We're not talking about metrics like that. These are metrics by *you*, for *you*, to help *you* to find areas in which to improve."

"Yeah, exactly," Marcus said. "Track them on the board, and keep them to yourselves if you like. Or at least only show them to the people you choose."

"But it's drudge work to capture and track," Daphne moaned. "I want to do real work!"

[2] Key performance indicators (KPIs) are a common way to measure performance.

"It doesn't have to be," Joakim said. "With the board in place, you've set yourselves up to easily track at least two simple and powerful metrics: lead time and throughput."

He went up to the board and took a couple of stickies with him. As he spoke, he drew a big brace under the entire board. "*Lead time* is the time it takes for a work item to go from start to finish—from the first column to the last."

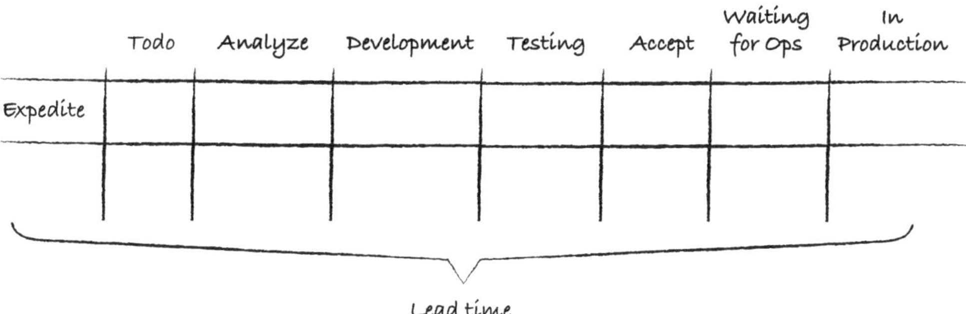

"Really?" Adam cut in. "The time our work takes varies greatly. What could we possibly learn from that?"

"Bear with me for a while," Marcus begged. "Starting to track lead times can be as simple as writing down the date of the sticky as it enters the Todo column and then writing down the date when it enters In Production. Plot that out in a simple diagram, and you'll have a pretty good idea of what your average lead time is."

Marcus quickly drew an example sketch chart on the board.

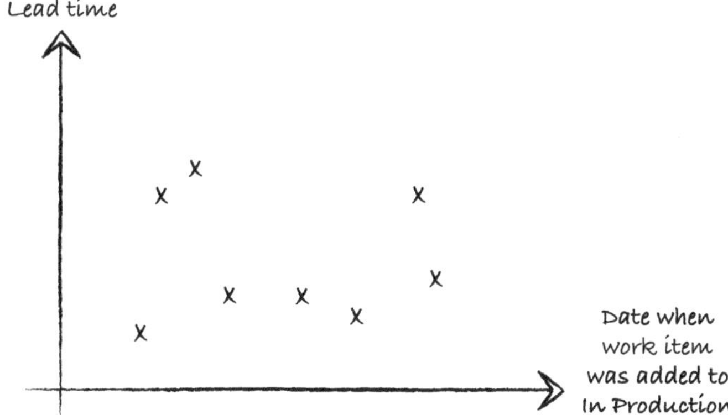

"With a chart like this, you can easily see the differences in time for the different items," Marcus explained. "As always, this is more something to talk about than the solution to your problems."

"But what does that chart help us with?" Adam scratched his head.

"Let's see," Joakim began. "What do you see that stands out to you on that chart?"

They looked at the board, and pretty soon Frank said, "Well, those three." He pointed to the three Xs that scored the highest on lead time. "They seemed to take much longer. Why is that?"

"Why indeed?" Joakim asked. "That might be worth investigating."

"Maybe all of them had to do with a certain subsystem of the application," Marcus offered.

"Or were badly specified," Adam said, looking at Beth.

"Or even lacked testers' input when we did the specification," Beth answered without missing a beat. They both chuckled about it.

"See?" Joakim said. "Another discussion got started. But you could have a discussion even around the general stuff. For example, what would it take to reduce the average lead time by half?"

"Half?" Frank sounded like he thought it was impossible. "It can't be done now. We're waiting so much on Ops and others that—"

"Exactly," Joakim interrupted him, "but what would it take to change that?" He left the question hanging.

Joakim checked his watch and hurried along.

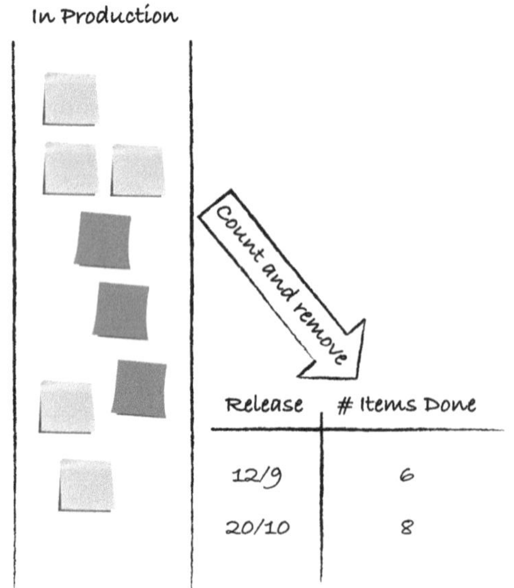

"*Throughput*, the rate at which you complete work, is even easier to track. Count the number of items you finish for a given period of time: for example, every two weeks. Or four, if that suits you better."

"We release the second Wednesday every month," Frank said, "so that would be a great point in time, if you ask me."

Marcus drew an example on the board. "Count the items in the In Production column every second Wednesday, and then remove them from the column. This will give you a simple way to track throughput."

Adam was hesitant. "Again—how will *that* help us improve?"

"Remember before when we talked about lowering work in process to get quicker flow through the workflow?" Joakim asked. "How can you know if you don't track data? Sure, you can go on gut feeling or intuition, but how will you *know*? And will your feeling be enough to convince others if need be?"

"If you've tracked this metric for a while and average out the result, you could even start doing predictions and make promises you can keep around due dates. Wasn't that one of your challenges?" Joakim continued.

"With these simple metrics," Marcus added, "you can start where you are and track your current process. As you change, you can easily see if you've improved or not."

"But isn't that a bit simplistic?" Adam was still skeptical. "We have some sophisticated systems in place today to track and measure—"

Adam

Eric interrupted. "And we didn't like them and didn't use them, remember? I'd much rather use some simple metrics for us that work and that we use than those stupid ones we worked with because someone in management thought it was a good idea. I distrust most forms of metrics, but these I at least feel I can live with."

Metrics

* There to help the team improve
* Let the team choose their own metrics; do not use them for performance review
* Two common and useful metrics are:
  - Lead time—the time for the whole workflow
  - Throughput—how much or how many work items you complete over a period of time

1.9 The sendoff

There was silence again. Not as awkward this time, but silence nonetheless. Suddenly, Daphne turned to Cesar. "Time?"

"There's plenty of time—no, wait, we've gone the full two hours right about now," Cesar said, looking at his watch.

"There's much more we could talk about," Joakim said, "but this is a great start that will get you rolling, we think."

"As you progress and want to know more, you can check out the principles behind Lean and try to apply them in your context," Marcus continued. "That can be tricky, so take hints from other teams and how they have applied Lean in their contexts. You can also check out the kanbandev[3] mailing list, the Limited WIP society,[4] and conferences on the topic."

[3] http://groups.yahoo.com/neo/groups/kanbandev.

[4] http://limitedwipsociety.ning.com/.

"With what you have now, you could start tomorrow and continue to improve from there." Joakim tried to close the discussion.

Cesar

"I won't give a speech," Cesar said and stood up. Immediate cheers from the others followed, and when they settled down, he said, "But I want to say: thank you guys. This was a vitamin injection that we needed. And you were right; we could get up and running in under two hours." He smiled.

"When you get home you might want to know more details, some background, and sooner or later a few advanced techniques." Marcus reached over to his bag. "Then this book could help you." He handed Cesar a draft of their upcoming book, *Kanban in Action.*

"One last question: What should we focus on now?" Frank asked.

"Lead times," Marcus and Joakim said in concert; Joakim continued. "Take the whole process into consideration, and try to shorten the *lead* times."

"And here's a hint: try coming up with ways to lower your work in process to get there," Marcus finished.

"Thank you." Cesar looked them both in the eyes and turned away hastily.

At the door, he stopped and turned around.

"Oh that's right—we never talked about your fee," he said, pointing to the table behind Marcus and Joakim.

They both turned around, and at first they didn't see a thing. They approached the table and found a sticky with some sort of number scribbled on it.

"What's this?" Marcus looked back to where Cesar stood a second ago, only to see the door closing behind him.

"Looks like an account number in a bank," Joakim answered. "But what use could we possibly …"

They both got it at the same time.

"We got paid. I think we better get a login to that internet bank, right?" Joakim looked at Marcus, smiling.

1.10 Summary

We leave our heroes there, and the Kanbaneros team is on the way back home, ready to get started with kanban. This whole chapter was a fictional story, and it incorporated some simplifications and adjustments to get the story to flow better, but it has also shown you how you can get up and running easily.

Maybe your work, team, and context aren't exactly the same as for the Kanbaneros, but you can follow along with the reasoning and adjust it for yourself. You don't need to do everything they did; pick and choose what suits your needs best.

This chapter aimed to get you started with kanban. In the next section of the book, we'll examine all the elements described and more in greater detail, offer variants, and warn you about common pitfalls. We'll also offer some more background on where the concepts originated and how they have been applied in other contexts.

You're more than welcome to try kanban out with what you know now, or you can also continue your journey in the next part of the book. In the next chapter, we'll take a short look at the origins of kanban and dive into the principles on which it's built. We'll also give you a cheat sheet for getting up and running in no time.

Part 2

Understanding kanban

After helping you get to know kanban, this part of the book will go into the details of the theories behind kanban. But don't worry—we'll still keep it practical and go into the theory little by little. The focus of this part is the principles that kanban is built around and how those principles can be applied in your team. The topics will range from the theoretical foundations of Lean all the way to how to properly remove a sticky from its pack.

2 Kanban principles

This chapter covers

- Introducing kanban principles
- Getting you started using kanban
- Defining what kanban is

In chapter 1, we introduced you to kanban through a short story. The purpose of this story was to show you, in a practical way, how kanban can be used to help you improve. We hope you already feel that you could use kanban now; but you probably have a few questions, too, such as

- How did Marcus and Joakim come up with all those ideas? Did they pull them out of thin air, or was there some method to the madness?
- That all sounded good, but my team and its situation don't look much like the Kanbaneros; how can I use kanban in *my* team? What do I need to change?
- Was that all? It seemed a little simplistic, didn't it? How can we expand on this?

All of these questions and many more will be addressed throughout the rest of this book. In this chapter, we want to show you the principles that kanban is based on, by looking back on what we did with the Kanbaneros.

But fear not, this is not a lengthy theoretical write-up on everything kanban. If you really want to, you can always go directly to section 2.2 and skip the theory. We'll still keep the theory part short and practical; this is a practical book focusing on practical needs. That's why we'll keep the theory to a minimum and serve it to you in bite-sized chunks as you need it. We'll also give you a quick recipe in this chapter for how you can get up and running with kanban quickly.

You remember the Kanbaneros, don't you? They will pop back into the text throughout the book to ask questions, challenge us, and present practical problems on your behalf. Here they are again:

Had we introduced another process, such as Scrum, XP, or even Rational Unified Process, the first chapter would have looked different. We would have focused on *how* the process should work, what to do and not to do, how long iterations or sprints are, what the tasks are for the Product Owner role, and so on.

Kanban isn't like that. It doesn't prescribe many things at all; it's more like a meta-process that can be applied to whatever process you're working with today. This is great news, because it means you can start where you are today, without changing anything, and improve from there. No new processes, no new roles, and no troublesome reorganizations needed.

Kanban, kanban, or kanban systems?

If you read the text closely, you might spot that we're spelling kanban with a lowercase *k* in this book. The kanban community is continuously improving and evolving, so things change a lot. We have interpreted the current knowledge as follows:

- *The Kanban method* (capital *K*)—A method to create evolutionary change in your organization, first formulated by David J. Anderson and documented in his book *Kanban: Successful Evolutionary Change for Your Technology Business* (Blue Hole Press, 2010, http://amzn.com/B008H1APTO).
- *Kanban* (sometimes lowercase *k*, sometimes capital *K*)—Sometimes refers to a "visual process management system that tells what to produce, when to produce it, and how much to produce" (last time we checked Wikipedia anyway), sometimes to the actual visual signal.
- *Kanban system*—The system that is set up to track the work in process. An example of this might be a kanban board, the cards, and the policies around your work. All of that is your kanban system.

(continued)

In theory, these things have quite different meanings; but in practice, people in the community often don't distinguish between them. What people typically refer to as "using kanban" is to use some sort of kanban system to manage and optimize kanbans (the visual signals) in order to evolutionarily improve. That is what we mean when we use the word *kanban*.

If that was confusing to you, don't worry—you can read the book and make up your own mind about what kanban is, and we promise there won't be a test at the end.

The Japanese connection

You should probably know something about the word *kanban* itself, if for no other reason than so that you can impress your friends with your knowledge of Japanese. *Kanban* is two Japanese words put together: *kan*, meaning visual, and *ban*, meaning card. Put together, it becomes something like "visual card" or "signaling card."

Kanban as a concept comes from Toyota, where it was invented as a scheduling system for just-in-time manufacturing in the Toyota Production System (TPS). When researchers in the West studied TPS, they called it Lean Production System, later Lean Manufacturing and Lean Thinking.[a] Kanban has its origins in the principles of TPS and Lean, which is why you'll find a lot of references to these concepts throughout this book and in most other texts about kanban for software development.

a. John F. Krafcik, "Triumph of the lean production system," *Sloan Management Review* 30, no. 1 (1988): 41–52. James P. Womack, Daniel T. Jones, and Daniel Roos, *The Machine That Changed the World* (Scribner, 1990, http://amzn.com/B001D1SRRS).

Although kanban doesn't prescribe many concrete rules or practices, you still can improve greatly by using it. How can that be? At the heart of kanban are a few principles that can guide you on how to use kanban to improve. Let's take a closer look at those principles.

2.1 The principles of kanban

Kanban is based on three simple principles:

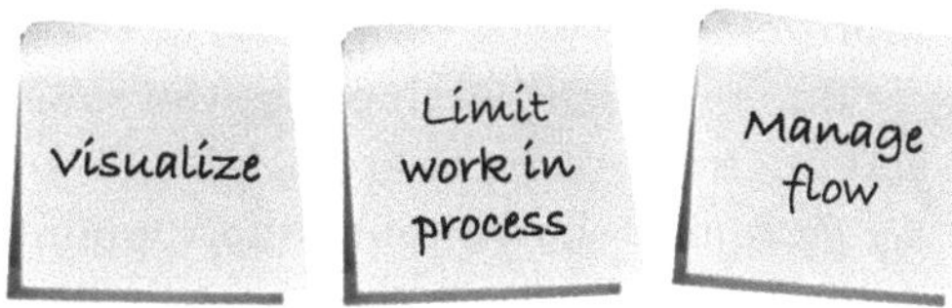

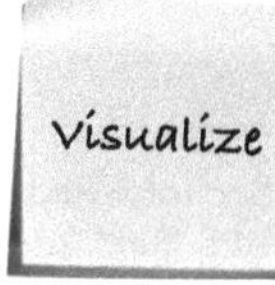

When we got down to business with Team Kanbaneros, we started by *visualizing their work*. To start, this can be as simple as creating sticky notes that represent each work item and a visualized workflow in the shape of a board to track each item's current status. This is a great way to get to know your work, learn how your "work works,"[1] and start seeing improvement opportunities in your workflow.

For many teams that we coach, this creates a big impact right away. Just making information visible that previously was not can help you solve a lot of problems by itself.

There are other underlying aspects of visualization as well, because you're also starting to make implicit policies around the work explicit. That is, everybody might think they know how you work with a feature request; but by showing the workflow on the board in columns, the real process becomes apparent to everyone on the team. By doing this, you make any differences you might have on policies about work more evident. This can lead to a discussion that clarifies the policies you work from, and you can easily capture them on the visual board so that all team members approach the work in the same way.

With Team Kanbaneros, we went through some common ways of visualizing work: the board, the work items, and the expedite lane, for example. There is much more to know about this, and chapters 3 and 4 will take you through it in greater detail.

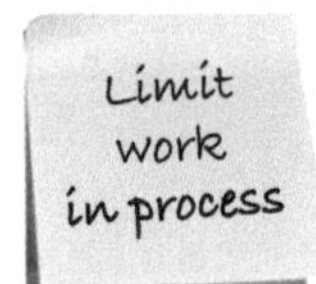

We continued with the Kanbaneros by playing a game called Pass the Pennies (see chapter 13 for more details on this and other games). This showed the principle of *limiting work in process.* Simply put, the principle states that you deliberately establish a limit for how many items you'll work on at the same time. The first apparent gain from doing this is that with fewer items being worked on at the same time, each item will be done more quickly. Chapter 5 will explain the effects of work in process in depth.

But limiting work in process (WIP) is also important for other, subtler reasons. By establishing a WIP limit, you'll create a little tension in your workflow; this is a Good Thing™, because it will expose problems in your system, or, as we put it to the Kanbaneros, "unrealized improvement opportunities." You can read more about limiting WIP, the reasons for doing so, and how you can visualize these limits in chapter 6.

Limiting WIP will start surfacing improvement opportunities. Flow through the workflow will stall (stickies moving slowly over the board), start to back up (a lot of stickies in certain columns), or stop completely (items waiting). These are all indicators that you can improve your system. What you do to fix these problems will determine whether you improve.

But if you want to improve, you should know what the goal is, and this is where the last principle of kanban comes into play: *manage flow* quickly and without interruptions through the workflow.

This is the start of your journey to continuously improve the workflow. The bad news is that you'll never be done with this task. Your workflow can always be improved; there's always a bottleneck

---

1 See John Seddon, *Freedom from Command and Control: A Better Way to Make the Work Work* (Vanguard Consulting Ltd, 2003, http://amzn.com/0954618300).

that slows you down.[2] The good news is that the problems will reveal themselves to you, visually, on the board. Not only that, but often the biggest problem will be revealed first—solve that, and you have made a big improvement to the flow through your workflow.

Team Kanbaneros discovered several improvement opportunities, as you might remember from chapter 1:

- They realized that the way deployment was done was hindering the flow severely. For the Kanbaneros, we could see this on the board with all those stickies in the Waiting for Ops column. You could say they already knew this, but now they have data constantly in their face, demanding action.
- They talked briefly about bugs, which were handled differently than normal items. You could say that bugs are in a different class of work than the other items and maybe should be given precedence over other items in prioritization.
- The Kanbaneros put WIP limits in place to help their work flow smoothly; for example, they queued up four items for acceptance so that Cesar and Beth didn't have to run to the team several times every day. Instead they now have a reasonable amount of work to do, waiting for them when they come by the team.

Help the work to flow faster through the workflow. That doesn't sound so hard, right? You can always find help in chapter 7, so by all means—make it happen!

There are a lot of things you can do to accomplish this. When working with this principle, you can find inspiration in Lean Thinking to help your work flow more smoothly by removing waste in your process. You can also take a look at the Theory of Constraints[3] and identify, exploit, and alleviate the bottlenecks in your system. Practices from the agile software development community movement might help you to improve collaboration and quality and thereby improve the flow of your system. It's up to you which route you take to improve your system. The important thing is that you react to the signals that your work is sending you and improve on it.

In reality, you'll see the principles combined with each other a lot. For example, in order to get a quicker flow, you limit WIP, which is also shown visually on the board.

With a visualized workflow, a limit for the WIP, and a focus on moving work through your workflow, you have set yourself up to easily spot improvement opportunities. How you go about doing that is pretty much up to you, but we won't leave you high and dry. We have packed chapters 3–7 full of tips, practices, patterns, and common solutions to improve the flow in your workflow.

The search for improvements will soon take you outside the boundaries of your own team. In order for you to get a faster flow, you might have to interact with other teams or functions around you in a different manner. A first step toward this is to include teams or functions before and after yours on your board. Or maybe you could

[2] Well, when software—or rather, solutions—materialize instantly when you imagine them, we guess there are no more bottlenecks. It probably won't happen any time soon, though.

[3] Visit http://en.wikipedia.org/wiki/Theory_of_constraints to read about the Theory of Constraints (TOC).

even have a board for all the teams in your department, aggregating the status of the teams there.

It could be the start of a transformation that can ultimately reach the entire company, in an evolutionary way. Soon you'll find yourself teaching kanban to others and being involved in change management on an organization-wide scale. You can read about this in chapter 13.

Three principles? I thought it was five properties. Or was it six practices?

Kanban is fairly young as a methodology used in the software business. There's a vibrant community, and new things are discovered and put into practice continuously. This is something good, and it's very much in line with the principles of Lean and continuous-improvement thinking.

The three basic principles we describe in this section make up the foundation that kanban is based on. Recently, David J. Anderson and others have extended the three basic principles to five properties and later six practices; these are now referred to as the *core practices*.[a] They are as follows:

1. *Visualize*—Described earlier.
2. *Limit work in process*—Described earlier.
3. *Manage flow*—Described earlier.
4. *Make process policies explicit*—With explicit policies, you can start to have discussions around your process that are based on objective data instead of on what you think, feel, and have anecdotal evidence for.
5. *Implement feedback loops*—This practice puts a focus on getting feedback from your process: for example, in what is called an *operations review*, which is a kind of retrospective for the process itself.
6. *Improve collaboratively, evolve experimentally (using models and the scientific method)*—This practice encourages you to use models such as the Theory of Constraints or Lean to push your team toward further improvements.

That's three more practices added to the principles we've talked about so far. Note that this holds true for the Kanban Method of "incremental, evolutionary change for technology development/operations organizations," and in that context the last three practices are important.

As you probably have noticed already, we take a practical and pragmatic approach, and for us the last three practices fit nicely within the basic principles:

- *Make process policies explicit*—Making policies explicit is what much of the visualization of work is about. As often as not, the important step might not be to write it on the board (although that's important too), but rather to hold discussions that allow you to form consensus about the policy you intend to put in place. Although it's great to make this ... umm ... explicit, we feel that it's part of the principle of visualization.

a. See http://mng.bz/EkgB.

(continued)

- *Implement feedback loops*—This is part of the "manage flow" step for us. In order to help the work to flow, feedback loops are essential and should be sought and implemented where needed.
- *Improve collaboratively, evolve experimentally (using models and the scientific method)*—We wholeheartedly agree on the importance of this. But this mindset is so deeply rooted in the Lean principles that underlie kanban that we don't think it's a principle of kanban per se, but rather the environment and ecosystem that kanban springs from.

To further complicate things, David J. Anderson and others are now using "principles" to describe some other principles:

- Start where you are.
- Agree to pursue incremental, evolutionary change.
- Initially, respect current roles, responsibilities, and job titles.

And recently a fourth principle was added:

- Leadership at all levels in the organization.

During our time as kanban practitioners, the principles we talk about have become practices, the practices have gone from three to five to six, the term *principles* has been redefined, and a new principle has been added. We expect and hope that the discussion around these practices isn't over. But from this sidebar, you now understand why we're talking about three principles (visualize, limit work in process, and manage flow) when others are talking about five practices. Or was it six?

2.2 Get started right away

Just like the Kanbaneros, you can easily get started right away, due to the lightweight nature of kanban. In fact—why not start now?

It doesn't take much, and you can start easily right where you are today. Just begin focusing on getting stuff done, really done, before picking up new work. Make that the motto for you and your team: *stop starting; start finishing!* This is a simple way to limit the work in process, but it can be effective.

If you want to be a little more concrete and practical, you can also do an exercise similar to the workshop we ran with the Kanbaneros in chapter 1. Here's a short description of how that can be played out:

1. Start by visualizing your work. We asked the team to create a sticky for each work item they worked on and place it anywhere on a whiteboard.
2. Map your workflow to the board. A simple way to do this is to create a column for each stage in your workflow. Move the tickets that are in the different stages into

the correct columns. At this stage, the Kanbaneros talked quite a lot about how the work worked, and that's something good that increases your knowledge of the process. But resist the urge to optimize your workflow before you can see what's going on. After this exercise, you might end up with a board like this:

A WORD FROM THE COACH Make sure you draw the board *together* as a *team.* Don't let one person do this by herself—especially not you, if you're an external coach. The buy-in from the team will suffer greatly. Trust us; we've made that mistake far too many times already.

A simple way to make this exercise a team effort is to pass the pen around as you draw the board.

3 Make a couple of dry runs with some work that has passed through your workflow to see that the workflow actually matches the way you work. Change as needed. We didn't have time to do this with the Kanbaneros, but we think it's good practice, and it quickly shows you whether you got the workflow right. Remember, at this stage you're aiming to track down how you *actually* work.

But how do we know if that limit is the right one?

You don't! Read more about this in chapter 6, and adjust as needed

4 Decide on a work-in-process limit—how many work items you, as a team, should be working on at the same time. We spent quite a lot of time here as we helped the Kanbaneros, but please don't overthink it. It's better to get something up there and improve as needed. For now, go with two work items per person in the team (six in our example), for example, and spread them evenly across all columns. Or get some good ideas in chapter 6, which is all about WIP limits.

5 For extra measure, create some avatars—small pictures of yourselves—and attach them to the things you're working on now. This will help you more easily see what's going on and who to turn to if you have questions regarding one of the work items.

There—you now have a simple kanban board to improve on. But even this simple tool will help you to spot problems and continuously improve, in small steps. The rest of the book will help you learn how to do that.

2.3 Summary

Kanban is an approach to software development based on simple but powerful ideas. It aims to make the work *flow* fast through the whole value chain, from idea or concept to software in production, delighting your customers. The tools that make this happen are a few simple yet powerful principles: visualizing your work and policies, limiting the amount of work in progress, and helping the work to flow better through the process.

These tools can guide you to continuously improve your process to gain an even faster, smoother flow of work through that process. This is a never-ending quest that will help you and your team to improve, little by little, every day.

There—now you're up and running. As your work progresses, move the items accordingly on the board. Take care of problems that are hindering your flow. When a problem occurs, stop and talk about it; these are your improvement opportunities! Don't waste them; handle with care!

The rest of this book is packed with practical advice about visualizations, how to limit WIP, and different ways of helping your work to flow smoothly and quickly through your workflow. We have put a strong focus on practical matters to make sure you can use the practices, patterns, and tools we describe right away with your team.

Let's jump right in and start looking at visualization—a subject that will get your creative juices going.

3 Visualizing your work

This chapter covers

- Using visualization for transparency and information sharing
- Making policies explicit
- Using information radiators
- The kanban board
- Mapping your workflow to the kanban board

The first thing that strikes you as you enter the Motomachi Toyota assembly plant is how Toyota uses *visualizations* and sound to track progress, display status, and communicate. The company has large signs everywhere explaining what different parts of the plant are for, and big *Andon boards* that show the status of production, including when and where assistance is needed. When you remove a tool from its place, a bright image of the tool is revealed so that everyone knows the tool is gone from its spot and remembers to put it back.

If a worker encounters a problem, he pulls a cord—the famous *Andon cord* or *stop-the-line* cord—and his foreman and coworkers are alerted by a tune playing, unique to that workstation, and by flashing lights on the Andon board that indicate which station is in trouble. At the same time, a yellow lamp lights up next to the station; and if the issue isn't resolved until the vehicle on the assembly line passes a marker for the next station, the lamp turns red and the line stops.

Another big board in this plant is shaped like a car seen from the front; one of its "headlights" is a clock. It hangs from the roof, big and visible to all, displaying information such as the planned number of cars to assemble, the actual number assembled, the plan for the current shift, and the percentage of the target achieved. A light indicates whether a quarter or half an hour of overtime is going to be needed to meet today's target.

These are only some of the visualizations used to help the workers act and make decisions; there are plenty of others all over the plant. Visualization is so important to "the Toyota Way" that one of its principles is "Use visual control so no problems are hidden."[1] This seems to be deeply ingrained in Japanese culture. If you have ever been to Japan, you may have noticed that the Japanese use all kinds of nifty visualizations to help in everyday life. When Japanese use the term *visualization*, or *mieruka* in Japanese (**見える化**), they often mean not only presenting things in an easily understandable visual form, but also the goal of greater transparency and information sharing among employees and stakeholders in order to increase the organization's effectiveness. The term also refers to a series of processes that make use of the visualized results, thinking them over and initiating actions in an appropriate manner.

To us, this is the essence of the principle "Visualize" in kanban: to make all necessary information visible when people need it, enabling effective collaboration and improvement through understanding how the work works. To achieve this with kanban, you have to make policies explicit and use information radiators.

If you remember from chapter 1, when we introduced kanban to the Kanbaneros team, we started by visualizing their work. At first, they created a sticky note for every item they were working on right now. We have seen many teams experience "Aha!" moments from visualizing work like that. Questions like "Are you working on that? Me too. Maybe we should cooperate!" are quickly brought to the surface.

This chapter will show you the best-known visualization tool for kanban practitioners: the kanban board. After reading this chapter, you'll be able to set up and start using a kanban board that is customized to your way of working.

---

1 Jeffrey Liker, *The Toyota Way: 14 Management Principles from the World's Greatest Manufacturer* (McGraw Hill, 2003, http://amzn.com/0071392319).

3.1 Making policies explicit

Often, when people are working together, a lot of implicit assumptions and policies are at play. People make assumptions about everything from how people are supposed to clean (or not) the toilets after using them to what it means to take responsibility for finishing an important piece of work. Sometimes these assumptions are inconsistent or even conflicting, which can lead to misunderstandings and ineffective teamwork, emotional and subjective discussions of problems, and so on.

If you can make these policies explicit—for example, through visualizing your workflow on a kanban board and talking about what the different steps mean—the inconsistencies have to be dealt with and the conflicts can be resolved. Once the policies are made clear, it's much easier to hold a rational and empirical discussion about how to improve them. This provides a good foundation for collaborative process improvements.

> ... the code is more what you'd call "guidelines" than actual rules.
>
> Captain Barbossa in *Pirates of the Caribbean*

Remember that the policies are only that: policies—not rules that *must* be followed. They can, and should, be broken from time to time, but the decision to do so should be made intentionally and often with careful consideration from the whole team.

The Kanbaneros in chapter 1 made a lot of their policies explicit by mapping out their workflow as columns on the board. If you remember, they had a long discussion about how their work behaved in different situations. There was a lot going on in those discussions under the surface, because the team had not formalized the way they worked. In the process of doing that, they got insight into what worked and what didn't.

Other policies that the Kanbaneros made explicit concerned the types (colors) of their work items and how they should be handled, the limits for how many work items they could work with in certain columns, and the expedite lane (an example of a so-called *swim lane*).

WARNING Sometimes transparency can threaten people. If you have grown accustomed to doing things your own way—maybe you prioritized work in your own way, did favors for "your people," and managed to fly under the radar for a long time—making policies explicit may not seem like a good thing to you. Introducing an open and visual way of working can seem threatening. Handle this problem by introducing the visualization in small steps, and let the team decide what to visualize and how.

To us, visualizing the work and making policies explicit are inseparable; but because visualization can be more narrowly interpreted, the official kanban definition has

"Make process policies explicit" as one of its six core practices, along with "Visualize." As you'll see throughout the book, a lot of the kanban practices and patterns are about making policies explicit and using visualizations to do it; the most important and obvious practice is the kanban board itself, an excellent information radiator.

3.1.1 Information radiator

Effective teams have to constantly respond to events together and coordinate their activities. In a fast-paced environment, traditional status meetings often feel dry and dreary, and traditional project documentation feels like unnecessary overhead, inaccurate and incomplete. You want information to be up to date and easily available to all interested parties at the time when it's needed.

> *An information radiator displays information in a place where passersby can see it. With information radiators, the passersby don't need to ask questions; the information simply hits them as they pass.*
>
> —Alistair Cockburn[2]

Information radiators typically take the shape of big and visible displays or charts that you can understand at a glance. They can be big posters with charts showing the progress of a project, walls of index cards detailing the actions from a workshop, or whiteboards with columns showing a workflow, with stickies representing the work items. They're placed so that the team can always see them, but they should also be easily accessible to stakeholders outside the team.

The information radiator should be easy to keep up to date, so that it's constantly updated with the necessary information and worth visiting. This is why many teams prefer hand-drawn charts and low-tech equipment such as whiteboards, papers, stickies, and index cards. Perhaps more importantly, this also makes it easy to continuously experiment with and improve the information radiator to make it fit your particular context.

There are a lot of electronic tools that mimic boards and card walls and that are invaluable to teams who might not sit together or who for other reasons have chosen to use them over a physical tool. Digital tools can be great for a lot of reasons, but you run the risk of having the tool deciding, and putting limits on, how you improve your process. Especially when creating a new information radiator, you want to be able to change your visualizations quickly and easily, because it's unlikely that it will be perfect from the start. Choose a technique (electronic or physical) that isn't difficult to change.

The Kanbaneros created a big board with all their work in a sequence of columns. Each of their work items was represented with a sticky note on the board. From these simple and common visualizations, their current status and workload was easy to see and understand, even for someone who had never seen a kanban board before.

Let's take a look at some of the things to think about when you create your information radiator.

DON'T HIDE YOUR INFO IN THE FRIDGE

Digital tools sometimes become information *refrigerators* in which information is hidden. You have to know where to look for it, you have to be able to use the tool, you have to be authorized, it takes effort to go into the tool, and so on. It's the opposite of radiating information; you don't know if the information is even there, and you have to open the door and dig around before you find it.

This is an important point if you have picked a tool that doesn't naturally become an information radiator. A lot of electronic tracking systems today offer a dashboard or screen that looks a lot like a board of stickies. Make sure you display it on a big monitor near the team or even on the wall with a projector. You can read more about tools for kanban teams in appendix B.

---

2 *Agile Software Development* (Addison-Wesley, 2001, http://amzn.com/0201699699).

Electronic or physical board: pros and cons

There's a lot of debate in teams all over the world about whether a physical or an electronic board should be used. Because there's no one right answer for all, you can only weigh the pros and cons against each other and decide for yourself.

Pros with an electronic board:

- Universally accessible, and hence a great help for teams that not are co-located
- No loss of data, whereas with a physical board, stickies can drop on the floor
- Automatic calculation of metrics
- Can store information and discussions about each item

Pros with a physical board:

- Generally bigger
- Draws people from their desks and becomes a natural place to gather
- Generally easier to set up—you only need a whiteboard or a wall
- Easier to change and adjust to your particular needs

The reason we talk more about physical boards is that they're generally easy to get started with and to change in those early phases. But again, you decide for your team!

CO-LOCATION? LUXURY!

Maybe you and your team don't have the luxury of sitting together. You can try to use a common area or hallway, someplace where you can easily gather around the radiator and where it's easily accessible to others. You could also try to use a digital tool with a projector or a big screen.

Leave it to the team

The decision to use an electronic tool or not should be left to the team. Marcus had the opportunity to do some coaching as a contractor at Spotify, where Joakim works, and found that two out of the three teams he was assigned to used an electronic tool.

That fact in itself was not so surprising, but the team that didn't use an electronic tool was *not* co-located, with a team member in Germany and the rest of the team in Sweden. It was a perfect fit for an electronic tool, but the team felt that using a physical board and sending photos of it once a day was good enough for them.

The other two teams sat not more than 10 meters from each other and still opted for electronic tools, but with big visible monitors that radiated the information to them. That team had strong opinions about using an electronic board, and there was no reason for Marcus to talk them out of that.

There's no right or wrong, only what you think would suit your team best. Make sure your information is visual for everyone in the team to see; that's what visualization is all about.

CAN. NOT. PROCESS.

Avoid information overload. Don't try to fit too many charts, too much info, or too much detail into your information radiator, because this will make your radiator more difficult to understand.

GO BIG

This should go without saying, but experience tells us that it's necessary to point it out at times: make sure the information is big enough to see easily from a few feet away, that text is legible, and so on, so that people can read it without having to get too close and squint.

USE IT OR LOSE IT!

Don't use information that isn't valuable to the team or the stakeholders. There are few things more demoralizing than having to update information that you don't see the point of and that no one seems to care about. Constantly reevaluate whether you should keep the radiator as is or if you should change it in any way.

1+1 EQUALS 3

When you combine the power of making policies explicit with visualization using information radiators, the policy is in your face, and it helps you do the right thing. If this isn't helpful enough, your fellow team members will probably apply some positive peer pressure when they can see that what you're doing, or the visualization of what you're doing on the information radiator, is diverging from the policy you agreed on (see section 3.1).

The ultimate kanban combination of making policies explicit and visualization of the work through information radiators is the kanban board. Let's take a closer look at that in the next section.

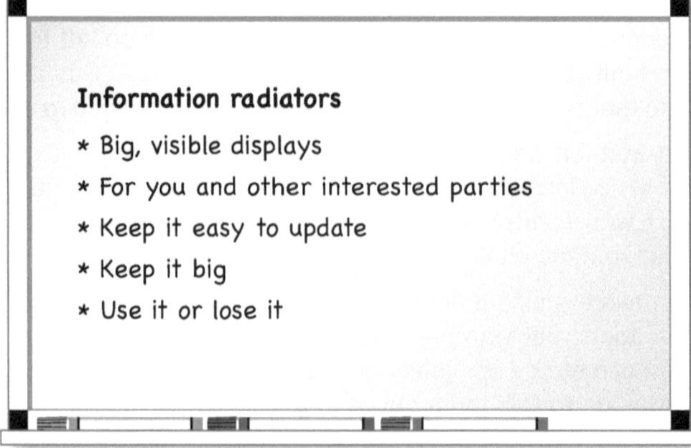

3.2 The kanban board

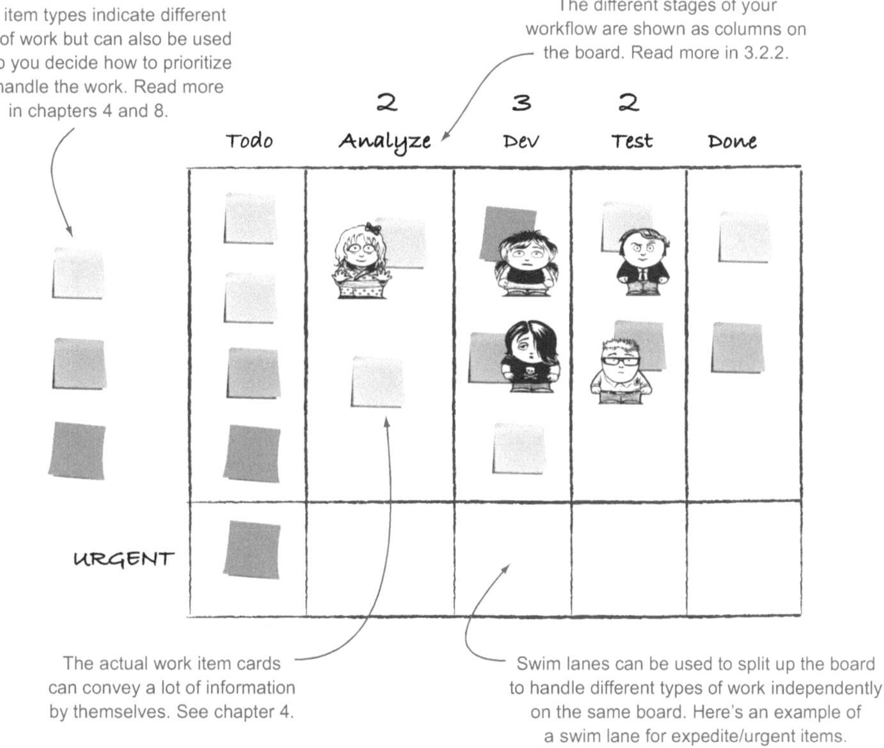

When you're working in a team, there are lots of things you need to know in order to collaborate effectively: things such as who is working on what, whether you're focusing your efforts on the highest-priority work, that blocked items aren't left unresolved, and that work isn't queuing up in front of a bottleneck. You want to be able to track the progress of the work. Not only is this important to the team, it's also important to other stakeholders. Why not create a good information radiator for all of this?

Kanban teams use a lot of information radiators, but one that stands out as the most common and prominent is the board itself.

3.2.1 The board

The basic board is a whiteboard or some empty wall space where you put up stickies or index cards to visualize your workflow and how the work is progressing. Update it frequently, so everyone can see and act on the most current information.

Using a big board not only makes it a good information radiator, but also makes it easy for a group of people to simultaneously move things around, to discuss what is happening, to create new work items, and so on. It's here where you gather around and "tell the stories" of what happened and might come in the future, like a campfire that the tribe gathers around. The board becomes the natural place for gathering and sharing.

To maximize the reach of the information on the board, you should aim to set it up in a location that is easily accessible for everyone and in which you have enough space to gather for daily standups (see chapter 7) to discuss the work.

Sometimes it's difficult to use a big physical board. If the furniture police or a lack of space is the problem, you can always use a foldable board, a board made out of cardboard that you can at least use during standups. If this is too much of a hassle, if the team is distributed in different physical locations, or if something else stops you, there are plenty of good digital boards to go around (see appendix B).

WARNING You should think twice before going completely overboard with electronic tools. Given the benefits of a physical board, you shouldn't use one or two off-site team members as an excuse to strip these benefits from the rest of the team; using both physical and digital versions and doing a little double bookkeeping is usually a lot less work than you imagine, and it's often well worth the investment.

Meet often: daily standups

The board is a great tool that radiates your current status to the team. Another great practice to combine with the board is to gather around it for short but frequent meetings. In these meetings, you'll be able to coordinate, share, and learn from each other. Keep the meetings short and to the point; focus on what has happened on the board. This type of meeting is commonly referred to as a *daily standup*.

A simple recipe for a daily standup can be as follows:

- Decide on a recurring time. The earliest available time in the day that isn't painful for anyone is a good starting point so that you can use the meeting to begin the day together.
- Keep the meeting short: a max of 15 minutes. A smart way to make sure the meeting doesn't run long is to stand up during the meeting, ergo daily *standup*.
- Discussions that don't involve most people are paused and moved to after the meeting.

For many teams we have coached, these two practices make a big difference: visualize your work so that you easily can see what's going on, and meet every day to follow up on the work and share problems or concerns. You can learn more about effective daily standups in chapter 7, section 7.3.

OK, so you've got a board or a piece of wall or other means to create a board. What should you do with it? What makes up a board? How do you create it? A lot of questions are piling up. In the next section, you'll find the answers.

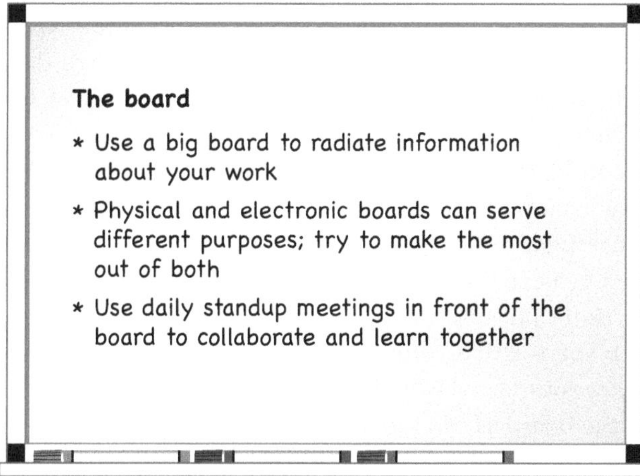

3.2.2 *Mapping your workflow to the board*

If you were clueless about what a kanban board looked like when you picked up this book, you should at least have a hunch by now that it often has a number of columns.[3] The columns represent the different steps the work flows through—but what are these steps? How do you know what to put on your new board?

For starters, you want to capture the *actual* workflow and not the formal, company-standard, on-paper version that you're *supposed to* use. An easy way to get started is to identify one or two of the most typical work items and "walk the stream." You need to find out how the work flows in your particular context.

Getting your workflow correct can be hard; as you recall from chapter 1, the Kanbaneros spent quite a lot of time discussing it. It was time well spent, because it forced them to examine implicit assumptions and gave them a deeper understanding of how they work as a team. Up to the point where they mapped their workflow, there could be many views on how the work was flowing, but making it visual also made it explicit and to the point.

A WORD FROM THE COACH It isn't the manager, the team lead, or some kind of coach who should design the kanban board; the team members who are going to use it should do that. This creates a sense of ownership and increases the likelihood that they will honor the policies and the processes they agree on.

Next, resist the urge to improve your process here and now. The whole idea of visualization is to understand the work and make improvement opportunities more obvious to you. Let the board help you with that. For now, map your workflow. Who knows, the opportunities might not be where you think they are. They might be somewhere else.

Not all types of work go through the exact same workflow, but that's OK. You have to decide together how to handle this. Perhaps a certain type of work skips a column or two; for example, maybe bugs don't have to go through the Analyze column on the board, as the Kanbaneros decided for their bugs in chapter 1.

Sometimes a column's name might be too specific to suit all types of work, but when you consider what it's about, a more abstract name makes the workflow work for all cases. An example is Test, which makes sense for code but maybe not for documentation or investigative types of work. But when you change the column name to Verify or Reviewed by Peer, it turns out that they both have the same workflow.

Finally, don't put too much effort into this up front; rather, be ready to redo the board when you see that your work doesn't flow as you first thought. We recommend that you draw your board with an erasable whiteboard marker. In this way, you can easily change the board as you see fit. Hold off with the electronic tool and the fancy tape until you feel the design is somewhat stable.

---

[3] To be frank, the board can look however you want it to. We've seen examples of spirals, stairs, and other creative solutions. But the column-based board is by far the most common and probably a good place to start.

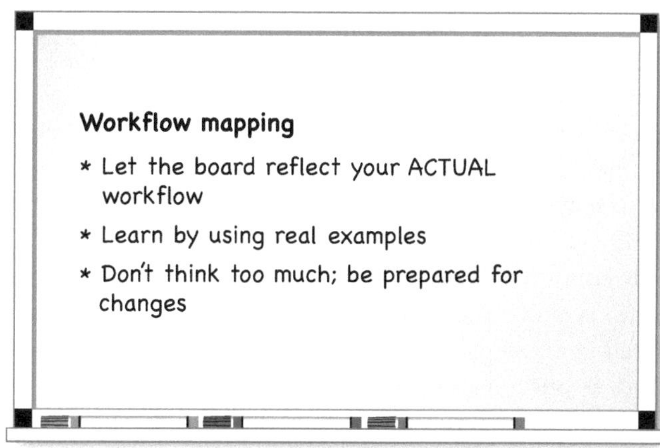

3.3 Queues

Queues can help you to manage handoffs, get a more even flow of work, and give the team members visual signals that work is ready to be started. On a board, this often manifests itself as a separate queue column before or after a column. Here are a couple of examples of queues on a board:

- *Todo*—The first column of the board
- *Ready for Development*—Things that have been analyzed and now are ready to be picked up by developers
- *Development Done*—Items that have been developed and are now ready for testing
- *To Test*—Stuff that is ready to be tested

As you can see from the last two examples, the same state can be expressed in different ways. Development Done and To Test are more or less the same thing. Both of them signal that development is finished, and testers can pick up the items and start testing them. Where you place the queues (belonging to Development or Test, in our example) is entirely up to you. Here's a simple board with an example, to clarify this a bit.

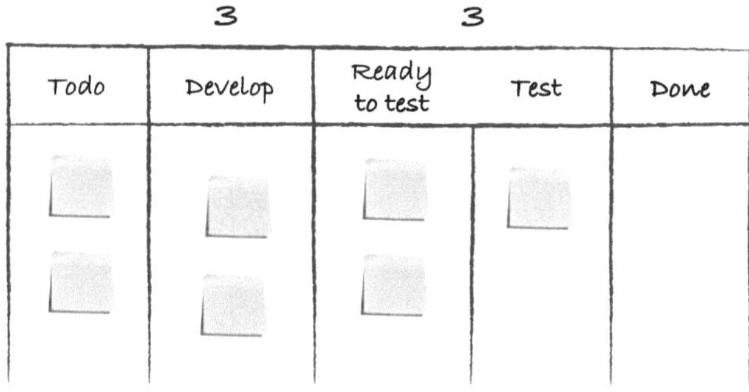

A Done (Development Done, for example) column is the normal case and signals to others in the workflow that this step is finished and someone else can start working on the work item. The person moving it to Done doesn't need to be aware of what's going to happen to it next. For Development Done you could imagine that a tester and a product owner do some kind of quick "triage" together to decide where a work item will go next: maybe into Test, maybe to Stakeholder Verification, maybe to Ready for Production.

A Ready column (like the Ready to Test column on the board we just showed you, for example) is always for a known step, because it's placed in front of a step, ready to be processed by it. Steps like this are used for distinct handoffs, maybe even to other teams. Work is pushed into that step: for example, an Inbox column where work is moved by an event or cadence[4] such as the biweekly planning meeting or when you have three items left in the Inbox column. In our example board, you can see that this team has decided to split the Test column into Ready to Test, and Test. Ready to Test is a queue with work that is ready to be tested. Because the testers allow for three items, you count the items in Ready to Test against that limit.

From this you can see that the testers have two items in the queue (items waiting to be worked on) and another item in the Test column (they're working on that item).

ENTRY AND EXIT CRITERIA

A great way of rooting out misunderstandings and achieving consensus around what the columns, the queues, and the workflow in general mean is to answer the question "Which criteria need to be met in order for me to move a work item to the next column?" These entry and exit criteria can, once they're made explicit, be captured as bullet points or as a checklist and visualized above or below the column they apply to, for example by writing them on a sticky or directly on the board.

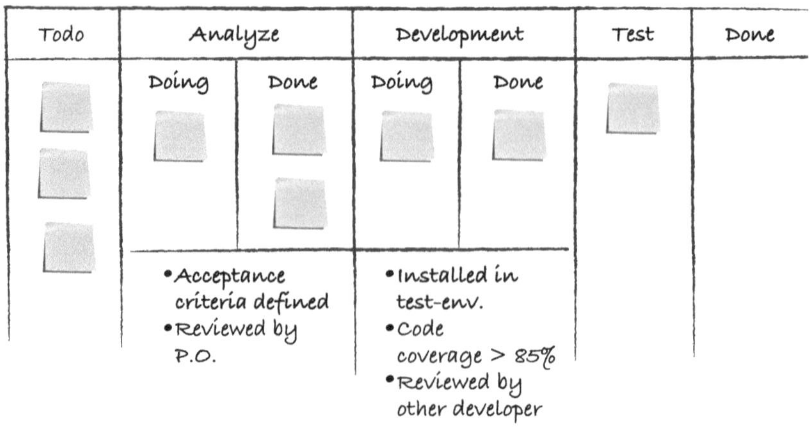

4 The rhythm or heartbeat of your process; read more in chapter 9.

These criteria should then be checked every time you move an item on the board. When you have new or modified criteria, it can be good to use them as a checklist against every item discussed during the daily standup, maybe even adding the policy that at least two people have to agree that the criteria are met before you're allowed to move the item. The policies are continuously discussed and incrementally changed and improved. Just as with the columns, you could have entry or exit criteria, or both, depending on how and what you want to check as each work item moves through your workflow.

A WORD FROM THE COACH We often find it useful to revisit the entry and exit criteria when something related to the workflow comes up: for example, in conversations during the standup, in team retrospectives, or when doing root-cause analysis for a defect. You ask, "Did we follow the criteria?" If you did, is there anything you could add to the criteria that would help you avoid this issue in the future? If you didn't, you should examine why you're not following the policies you've agreed on together.

3.4 Summary

This chapter talked about visualizing your work—making work and the policies around it visible where previously they were not:

- Visualizing your work is ultimately about creating the transparency and information-sharing needed to understand how the work works and to collaborate effectively together.
- The process of visualizing work means making information visible that previously wasn't, making implicit knowledge and policies explicit, and, in doing so, resolving inconsistencies and conflicts that surface.
- The kanban board is a great way to visualize your workflow and share information about priorities, who's working on what, the progress of individual work items, and so on.
- By using a big, visible board, the information radiates to everyone interested instead of being hidden in people's brains or inaccessible tools.
- Creating a kanban board is easy: you map the workflow of your work items—that is, the steps they typically go through in order to be completed—to columns you create on a whiteboard or a wall.

The next step is to create the work items, which is the subject of the next chapter.

4 Work items

This chapter covers

- Work-item cards
- Design principles for work-item cards
- What to keep on work-item cards and how to use this information to gain better knowledge about how your work works

Work in the software business is often not visible. Most of the work takes place in our heads or inside the computer. In order to get a better overview of who's working on what and the status of the work, you visualize the work—thereby making information visible that previously wasn't.

By far the most common way to track work items is to create a small card that represents the work that is being done. It can be an index card or a sticky note[1]: anything that is easy to work with and move around on a board, such as a white board. Cards on a board are a simple yet powerful way to see progress, bottlenecks, and queues happening in your workflow—and to make it in-your-face apparent to everyone what is happening.

1 For example, a Post-it® Note.

Using a physical card gives you some advantages over an electronic representation. A physical card can easily be annotated and customized with avatars, blockers, progress bars, tracking IDs, and other things that we'll look into in this chapter. Also, because cards are tactile, they're easy to use for collaboration, to move around, and even to take with you if needed.

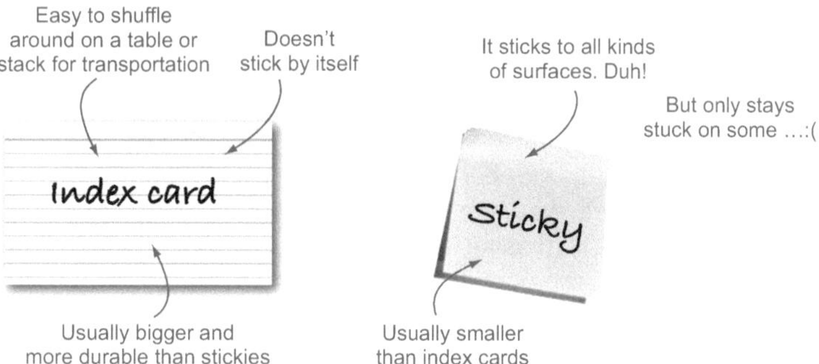

This tactile concept holds some other secrets. By moving stickies on a board, you involve more of your senses in the process and thereby create a stronger connection between you and the work items. It's more likely you'll remember that you took responsibility for an item that you moved with your hands from one column to another.

This chapter is dedicated solely to those cards. What goes on them? How do you show that a work item is blocked? Who's working on this item? These questions and more will be answered in this chapter. As always, don't limit yourself to only our suggestions; you should probably not use all of them at once, and there are probably other things that could go on a card that we haven't thought of.

Use your imagination to solve workflow issues, and use our suggestions as inspirations to improve on. The topics we discuss in this chapter are common ways of visualizing the basic information of a work item. Make sure your card contains all the information needed to help your team make decisions regarding each work item.

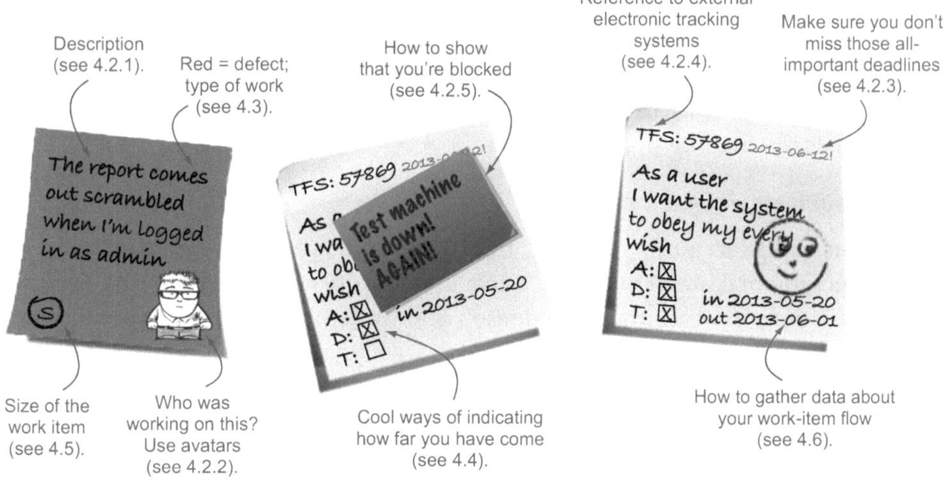

How to remove a sticky note from the pack

Yes, this might be the geekiest sidebar in history.

But it's here to protect you from a plague that haunts a lot of teams using stickies as work-item trackers. Picture the scene: you enter the office and see a board with a lot of stickies lying on the floor beneath it. You happily realize that it's not your board; your stickies are securely attached, thanks to this sidebar. With a wry smile on your face, you visit the poor team whose board is missing its stickies to educate them in the noble art of "how to remove a sticky correctly."

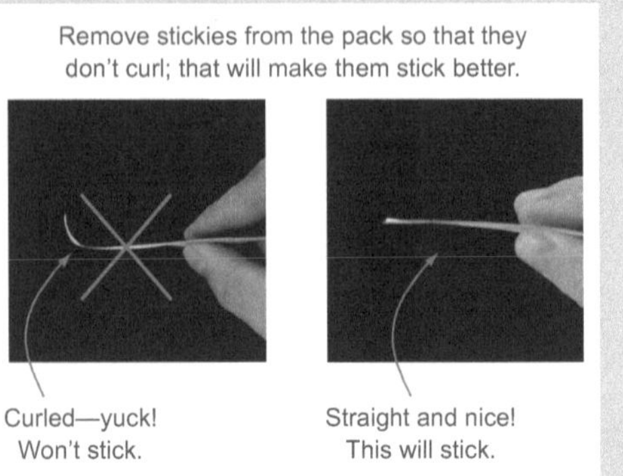

The trick is to be careful that the sticky part doesn't curl. Slide your finger under the note up to the sticky area, and then lift it from right to left, slowly but firmly. That will make the sticky part straight and nice, and thereby increase the sticky area of the note.

Now you know and can pester all your friends with the proper way to remove a sticky. Not only is this a geeky party trick, but it will also, more seriously, save you problems with work items falling off your board.

Instead of a physical work-item card, you can use electronic systems that represent the work. There's nothing wrong with that, and many of the systems nowadays are great, especially for gathering data and reporting metrics. But remember that you're giving up some of the benefits of a physical, tactile card. When in doubt, start physical and then move to an electronic version later if you see the need. Or even better—use both!

4.1 Design principles for creating your cards

The work-item card can be represented in a lot of different ways, and we'll soon dive into some of the common patterns for doing so. You will undoubtedly find other ways that suit your needs better, so please change and elaborate as needed. But there are a couple of design principles that you should keep in mind when you're deciding what to put on your cards and what to annotate them with. Let's take a look at some design goals for creating work-item cards.

4.1.1 Facilitate decision making

First and foremost, you want the design and information on the card to facilitate decision making in the team. Strive to help yourselves self-organize. You want to avoid situations in which the team doesn't know what to do next and they have to ask someone in order to continue. Equally bad is a team in which people respond differently to the same situation because of lack of information. This is one of the main reasons for having explicit policies and clear ways of working in the first place.

These goals are easy to state, but it might take some time before the team knows them by heart. Meanwhile, strive for simple, obvious rules, and make them visually apparent to everyone on the card. An example could be to show with an avatar who is working on an item so that you know who to talk to for more information or which items don't yet have someone working on them.

4.1.2 Help team members optimize outcomes

The design of the card should also help team members optimize the outcome when it comes to matters such as risk, customer satisfaction, and economics. If a work item is high risk, you need some way to show that to the team members, so that risky actions can easily be avoided. An example of a high-risk work item is one with an explicit deadline for when a new law goes into effect. Missing this sort of deadline could be associated with a fine of some sort. Therefore, you want to make sure you all know about the deadline and prioritize accordingly.

The same goes for customer satisfaction or economics; make it apparent if one (type of) customer is more important than another. An example of this is a work item with new functionality that greatly benefits new users. Maybe you want to complete that before any maintenance work items.

How to treat the work item is governed by policies (explicitly articulated or not) and often associated with the type (for example, normal features, defects, and maintenance work items) and class (for example, work items that are particularly urgent or have a fixed delivery date) of work. We'll be talking more about work-item types in section 4.3 and in chapter 8. Help the team to follow the policies by clearly showing what type and class of work they're picking up.

As you can see, there's quite a lot to think about, but let the guiding star be *simplicity*. There's no use adding too much on the sticky, if you stand the risk of forgetting what it was about. Start simple, and experiment with more information as you see the need. You want the information that the work item is radiating to be easy to see and understand. Along those lines you also want changes and *smells* (see the sidebar "Process smells") to be apparent and clear. You want to act on things that are outside of normal operation, and it must be easy to spot them as they happen.

Process smells

We borrow the *smell* concept from Kent Beck and Martin Fowler, who talk about code smells (*Refactoring: Improving the Design of Existing Code,* Addison-Wesley Professional, 1999, http://amzn.com/0201485672). A smell could mean trouble, but it isn't necessarily trouble because it smells. Much like the smell from a toddler's diaper, if it smells, you should at least check it, but it doesn't mean you'll always find something there.

If one of your stickies has a smell to it—for example, that it has been sitting idle in a column for a couple of days—you should check on it. It might be that you need to take action. But there might be perfectly natural reasons for it to be stuck there.

A WORD FROM THE COACH Keep these design goals in mind as you read the patterns on work-item design, and see if you can come up with other ways of articulating the goals in your team and on your board.

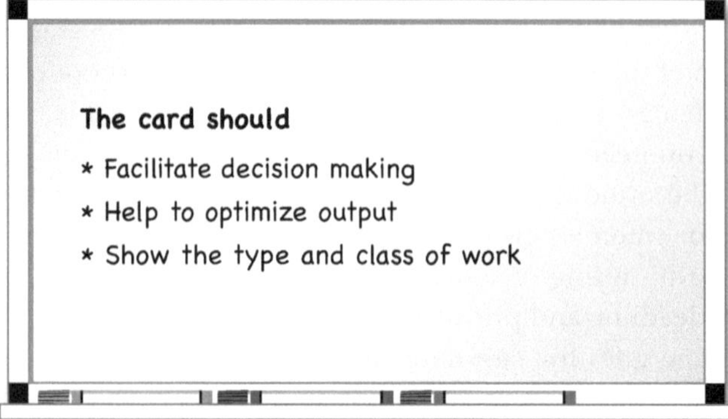

What about the size of the card?

As you soon will see, there can be quite a lot of information on a work-item card. Be sure to choose a card size that allows you to fit all the information you need on the card. Stickies come in different sizes, so experiment with sizes that suit you.

We've also seen a lot of teams that create cards of their own with custom-made structure and form. Here you can see a refined work-item card;[a] the team has laminated the card in plastic so that it can be wiped clean and reused over and over:

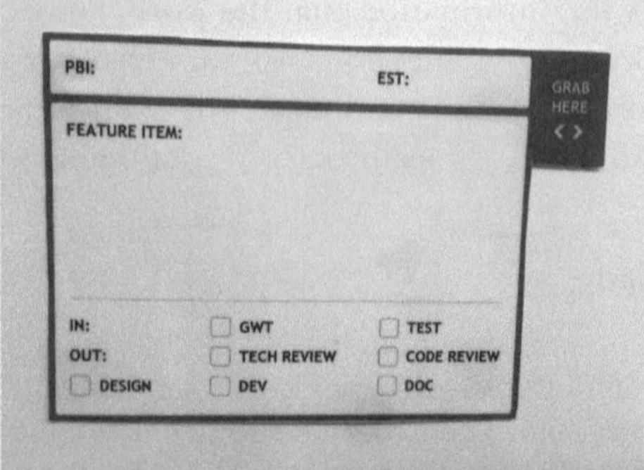

There's no right or wrong. Just pick a size and form that suits your needs, and change it as your needs change.

a. One of Marcus's clients, Tradera (Swedish eBay branch), had these cards on a board when Marcus visited. They're some of the most elaborate cards we've seen.

4.2 Work-item cards

A lot of things can be on a card, and in the following sections we'll examine some common attributes, starting with the most obvious one: the description of the work item.

4.2.1 Work-item description

To many of you, this might sound like a no-brainer; *of course* the work item has a description. But this is one area in which we see that many teams have room for improvement. We can't count the number of times we have seen teams argue over what an item is about because the description on the card is inadequate.

In order to more easily talk about the item and its content, the description needs to be terse, to the point, and easy for everyone on the team to understand. What does that mean in practice?

USER STORY

A user story is an example of a description that is short and terse and can prove useful.[2] It says *what*, for *whom*, and *why* the work item is being worked on.

---

[2] Beware of relying too much on the user-story template format and its merits. It's just a way to structure your description of the work at hand and not a silver bullet that always works. Some (including Joakim) have been known to call them an antipattern from time to time.

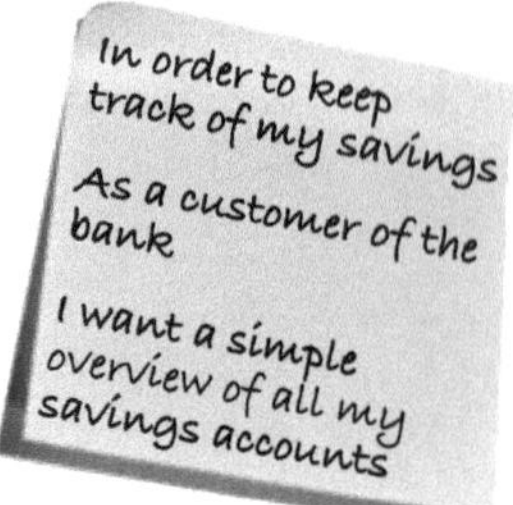

We won't dwell on the user-story subject here, because it's not in the scope of this book.[3] For now, we can simply say that it's a Card with a little text that is a reminder of a Conversation you're going to have later. In the conversation, you'll flesh out the details and write down your Confirmation as acceptance criteria. That can easily be remembered with the acronym CCC: Card, Conversation, and Confirmation.

A common template for a user story is

As a [role], I want [feature], so that [benefit]

Or maybe

In order to [benefit], as a [role] I want [feature]

Use a format that feels natural to you, but make sure to include the Why (benefit), the Who (role), and the What (feature) in the description.

TITLE

If the description tends to be longer than you care to repeat every time you talk about the work-item card, you could benefit from adding a title to the card. A short sentence that is easy to remember and to refer back to can help you remember what the work item is all about.

"THE ONE WHERE ..."

User stories are one way to write descriptions, but sometimes they don't sit right with the team for the item at hand (like bugs, for example). You still need to have a good description, and a simple mnemonic that we've used is the *Friends* naming convention: *in your mind,* put "The one where" before the description on the card. (All the titles of the episodes of *Friends* started this way, such as "The one where Ross and Rachel think they're in/out of love again.")

Using this little reminder will put the focus back on why this work item is up on the board in the first place. Make the title easy to refer to in a conversation, like these work items, for example:

- (The one where) the name field allowed too many characters
- (The one where) you were missing the administration rights, if you logged in as administrator

A WORD FROM THE COACH Remember that "The one where" doesn't need to go on the card. It's a little lead-in, there to get you focusing on the real reason behind the work item.

---

[3] See more in the excellent book *User Stories Applied* by Mike Cohn (Addison-Wesley Professional, 2004, http://amzn.com/0321205685).

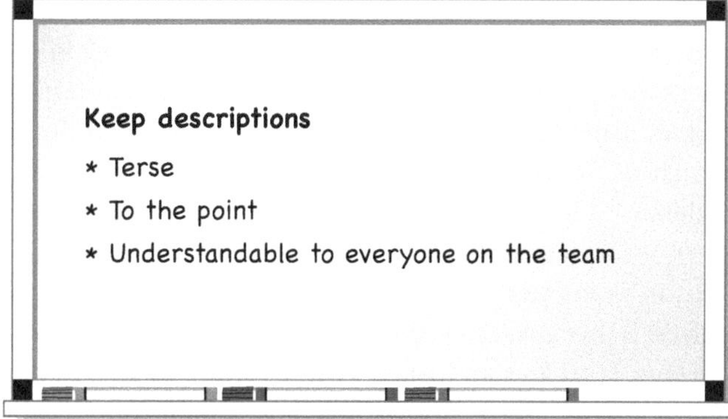

Here are a few good (and some bad) examples of what to put on your card as a description:

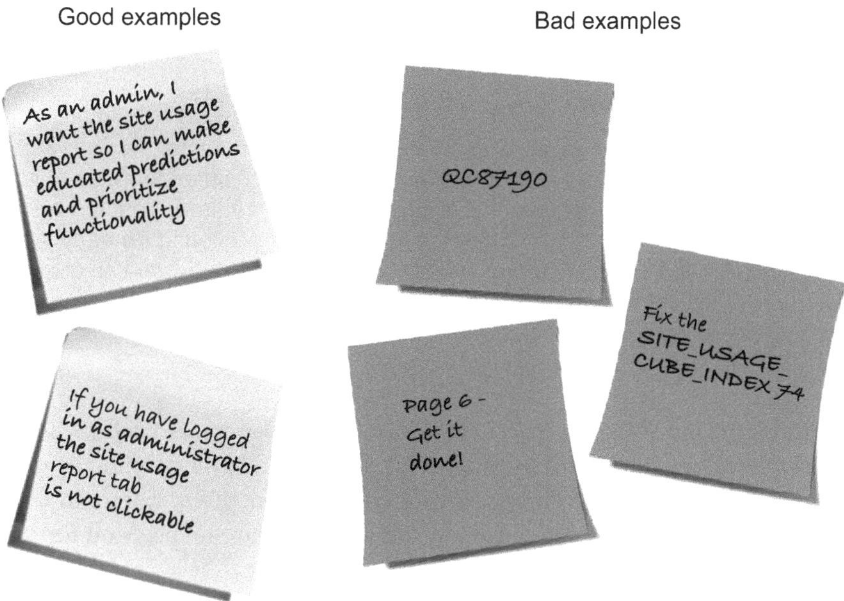

After learning what the work item is all about, the next problem to address is probably who is working on it now. Let's check out a common solution to this problem.

4.2.2 Avatars

You want information about who is responsible for a work item to be as clear as day, so you know where to go with your questions, suggestions, and praise. Many teams indicate who is working on what by attaching an *avatar* to the work-item card. In this context (see the sidebar "What's an avatar, anyway?" for the real meaning of the word), it's a clear indication of who is working on what.

The reason many people use pictures, cartoons, or drawings of themselves is because it's easier to identify a person using *pattern matching*. It creates an instant connection if you compare an image to a person, as opposed to looking at a scribbled name or signature that might need some translation to read and then to associate with the right face.

This means you should use avatars that resemble your team members or are caricatures with features that are easily recognized. Of course, you could add a key or legend on the side of the board, but that means people would have to look up which avatar belongs to whom. With avatars that resemble the team members, you don't have to do that lookup.

> **What's an avatar, anyway?**
>
> In computing, an *avatar* is the graphical representation of the user or the user's alter ego or character. It may take either a three-dimensional form, as in games or virtual worlds, or a two-dimensional form, as in an icon in internet forums and other online communities. It can also refer to a text construct found on early systems such as MUDs. It's an object representing the user. The term *avatar* can also refer to the personality connected to the screen name, or *handle*, of an internet user, such as the user icons on Facebook, Twitter, and other social media sites.

Some teams use avatars to limit the work in process for each person. This can be an effective self-constraint for hoarders[4] who have a habit of being involved in every item on the board. For example, giving each person three avatars to put in play on the board is a visual and effective way to make sure no one takes on too much work.

A WORD FROM THE COACH You might think having cute animals or cool cartoons as avatars is the thing and will spice up your board. Our experience tells us you're probably wrong. One team that Joakim coached decided to use dog avatars. This caused confusion when they had to try to remember who the poodle was, why the Dalmatian had not completed those tests yet, and what on Earth the schnauzer was doing with that analyzing task all that time. Use avatars that at least resemble the person in question!

---

4 Nickname for people who often end up collecting a lot of stickies.

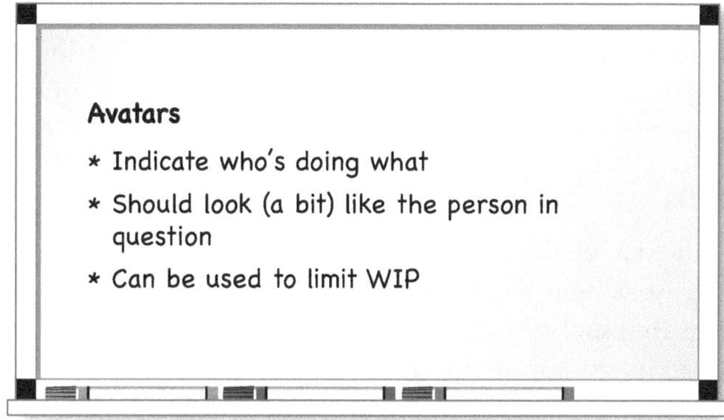

By using avatars, you can easily see who's working on the item in question. We now turn our attention to deadlines, which help you know when the work item is due to be completed.

4.2.3 Deadlines

Deadlines can exist for a number of reasons; there can be features that need to be done for a campaign, a new law kicking in on a certain date, or a new customer coming to the office next week, for example.

To clearly show the date when the work needs to be done, you write it directly on the work-item card, maybe even with another color that stands out. Deadlines are *risk-management information* and help the team prioritize and self-organize; you don't want to miss seeing them, so make sure they're clearly visible.

Some teams even use different colors of stickies for fixed-date-delivery types of work items in combination with the deadline date. Make sure you use the same visualization every time to create a pattern or habit. Always use the upper-right corner of the sticky for deadlines, for example.

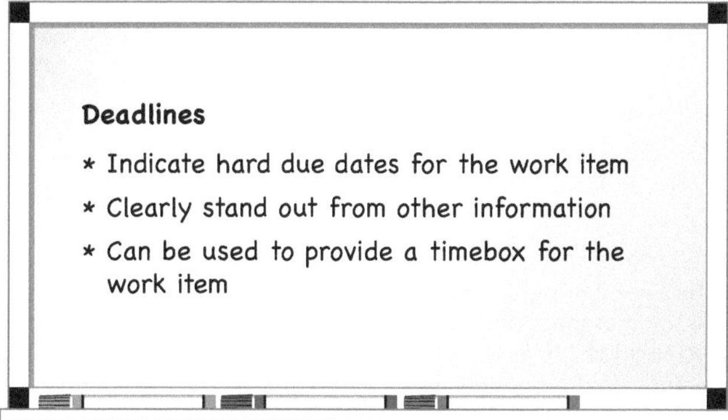

There—you now have deadlines on the work item too. They're another piece of important information. Continuing down this road, putting all information on the card, you'll soon run out of space. What do you do about information that you cannot fit on the card? That's the subject of the next section.

4.2.4 Tracking IDs

We have talked a lot about the good things that a physical board with work-item cards on it brings, but there are some things that such a setup doesn't do well. The limited space[5] on a sticky might not hold all the information needed in order to complete a feature. There might be a lot of other documentation that simply isn't feasible to try to attach to the sticky or keep near the board. Or you might be required to track your work, the number of hours, and the progress in an electronic system.

In these cases—and there are surely other cases too—you need to easily know which item in the electronic system represents the one on the board. You can think of it as a "more information here" link.

A simple solution to this is to write down the electronic tracking ID in a corner of the sticky. Similar to the deadline, make sure to use the same corner on every sticky, which creates a good habit. Or you can prefix the tracking ID with, for example, *JIRA:*, *TFS:*, or *Git:* to make sure it's not confused with other numbers that might be on the note.

WARNING Beware of falling into the trap of putting all the information about the sticky into the electronic tracking system, regressing back to work-item cards with no easily understandable description (see section 4.2.1).

Astute readers will now begin to worry about the "double bookkeeping" this will make you do and how to keep the board and the electronic system synchronized. To handle that, you could first decide on a master—preferably the physical board, because it's "out there" and the one on which your work is most visible.

Update board.
Update JIRA.
Update team at standup.
When will it end?

[5] Limited space can be a good thing, forcing you to work with smaller items and divide larger items into many smaller ones. This is the reasoning behind writing user stories on a small card, for example. If you feel that a big index card is too small to hold your information, try an even smaller one to force yourself to express it briefly.

In the electronic system, you can then make a simplified version of the workflow: Not Done, and Done, for example. This will make the updating much more lightweight and not create a lot of extra work. Also, on the work item in the electronic system you can now attach documents and links to other important resources.

Of course, you can go the other way around and use the electronic system as the master; but then we recommend that you try to get a projector. Or why not use a large touch-screen display and a board-like plug-in for the system in question?[6]

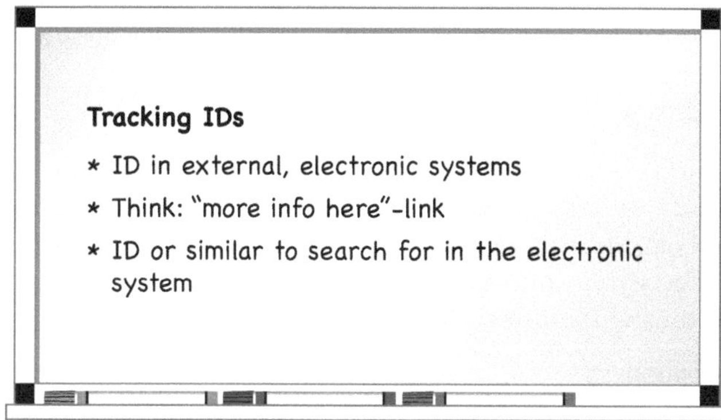

Until now, we have considered the evenly paved road of success. That's not the road we all travel in reality. What happens when things don't work out as planned? Let's investigate that next.

4.2.5 Blockers

Even though the goal is that your work flows quickly and smoothly through your workflow, sometimes things happen: you have to wait for someone else to complete their work, someone is sick, or you run into questions that hinder the work from being completed.

BLOCKED ITEMS

In these cases, you want the item to stand out and show that it's *blocked* from further progress. When you do so, you get a signal and a reason to focus on the blocker (at your daily standup, for example). Eyes are drawn to the items that are different from the normal items, and this helps you to focus on those deviations. A blocked item should be a visual *smell*, to use the terminology we introduced earlier (see section 4.1.2).

To accomplish this, many teams attach another sticky on top of the blocked work item. This is a good idea because you also can write the reason why the item is blocked

[6] There are loads of these plug-ins, but a few that we like are Kanban for TFS, JIRA Agile, and HuBoard for GitHub.

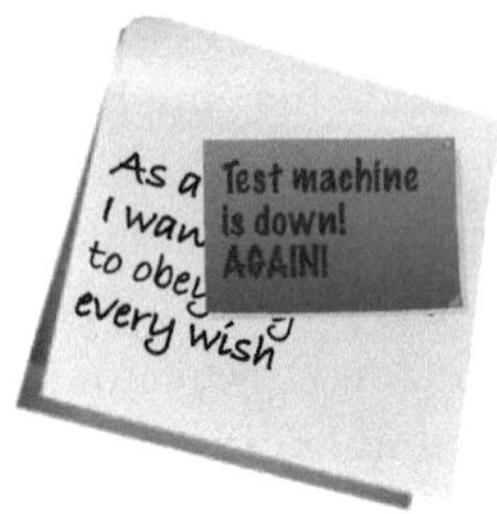

on the blocker sticky. In this way, you get not only a signal that the work is blocked, but also some information about *why* it's blocked, which in turn helps the team focus on resolving the blockage.

There are many other common alternatives to signal that an item is blocked: magnets put on top of the blocked work item, turning the work item on its side, or moving it into a blocked "parking lot" on a separate part of the board. If you decide to move the card, make sure you have some way of remembering its previous location, so you can move it back there once the blockage has been resolved.

A WORD FROM THE COACH Although keeping a separate "parking lot" for blocked items might seem like a good idea, we advise against it. It's basically the same thing as saying that it's OK to be blocked—"Look, we even have a dedicated area on the board for it!" Keeping the blocked item in its column keeps it in your face, affects your amount of WIP, and forces you to constantly have to consider it during standups.

BLOCKAGE PROGRESS

Some teams also write a simple form of progress indicator (see section 4.4) on the blocker sticky, to put further focus on resolving it rather than to leave the item blocked. For example, a blocked work item with three dots on it means the sticky has been blocked for three days, and that needs your attention, right? Some teams use more elaborate policies for this: for example, after three days they contact the person or team blocking them in person, and after five days they escalate to management or another support function.

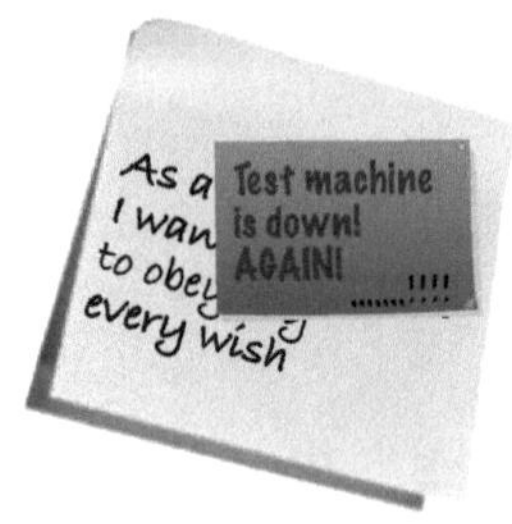

When choosing which blocker design works the best for your team, remember that you want the item to stand out from normal work items and preferably radiate some information about why and for how long the item has been blocked.

Taking smells to the next level

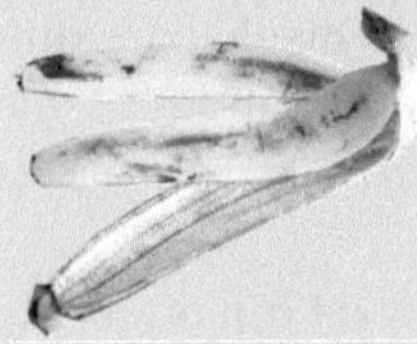

During the Lean Kanban North America conference in Chicago 2013, we learned about a team that has taken visualizations and smells to the next level. Instead of adding a small sticky to the work item to indicate that it was blocked, this team staples a real banana peel to the index card.[a] As the days go by and the blocker isn't removed, the banana peel gets darker and darker, and an unpleasant smell starts to spread. That's a call to action for you!

a. Image courtesy of Gualberto107/FreeDigitalPhotos.net.

> ***(continued)***
>
> Their next idea was to use actual bugs to indicate software bugs. We don't know about you, but we would certainly beef up our code quality to avoid having to nail real bugs to the board.
>
> Some teams love to get creative with these things. If you're in a team like that, you should by all means go bananas with the visualizations ...

With blockers, you can now handle situations in which the work doesn't flow as planned.

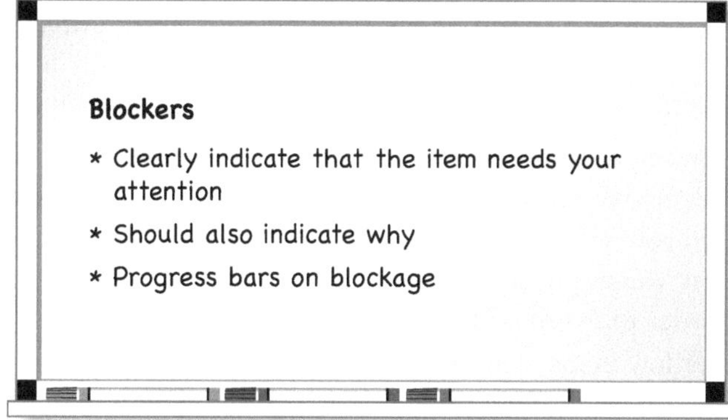

Up to now we have used the generic term *work item*, but work items are of different kinds or types. Let's see how you can visualize that.

4.3 Types of work

Work items can be of different types, such as bugs, technical items, or maintenance or feature requests. Work of different types should often be handled and prioritized in different ways. You want the team to be able to easily distinguish different types of work from each other and be able to prioritize work items on their own.

To help the team self-organize around how work should be handled and prioritized, a common practice is to let each type of work have its own color. In this way it becomes easy to distinguish a defect from a normal feature, for example. These types can also be used to set up policies on how work should be treated, commonly referred to as *classes of service* (see chapter 8).

Here are a few common examples of types of work. Some of the colors used here have grown into a convention in the kanban community. But, as always, make sure the colors make sense to you and your team. (Although the stickies are shades of gray in the printed book, they're green, yellow, and red in the eBook and on the kanban board.)

The choice is up to you, but you should take care to make sure that not everything on the board looks the same. You don't want to end up in the yellow sea of stickies, which makes it hard to know how to prioritize between different types of work items or to see any kind of patterns.

Making work of different types apparent—by using different-colored stickies, for example—can help you see what's going on. Simply by glancing over the board, you can get a feeling for the overall status of the team. For example:

- If you see a lot of red stickies (bugs and defects), you can see a problem with quality in your system. You should probably make an effort to improve quality.
- When you note that there are no green (maintenance, technical) items on your board, you might not be paying off your technical debt as needed, which makes it harder to maintain the system over time.
- No yellow items (features) means you're not adding new features to your system. This might be what you want, or not. The board gives you a simple visual signal that tells you how it is, either way.

If you only used yellow items, you would have to read each and every one of the notes to know the overall status of all the items on your board.

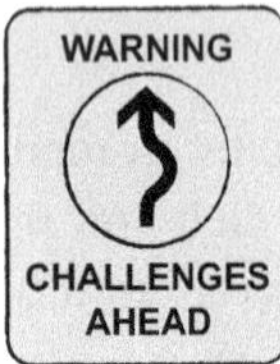

WARNING Don't fall into lazy mode and grab any colored pad of stickies you have lying around. Mixing colors of stickies on the board for no reason causes confusion. The best thing is to pick a limited number of common types of work, assign each one a color, and then use that color all the time for that type.

If you have a hard time remembering what type of work each color means, a legend can be posted on the board to rule out any misunderstandings. This can also be helpful for stakeholders and others who don't work with the board on a daily basis.

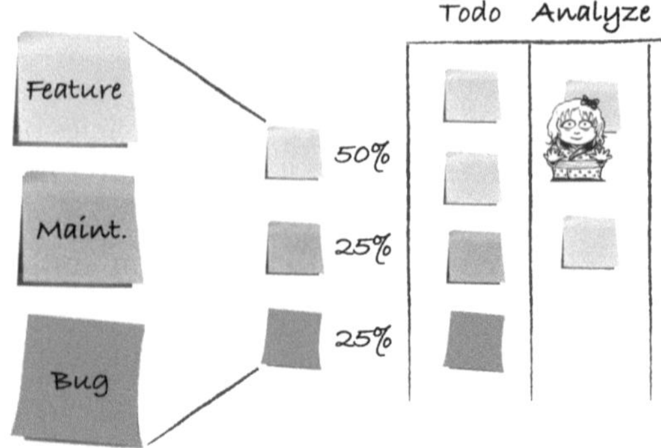

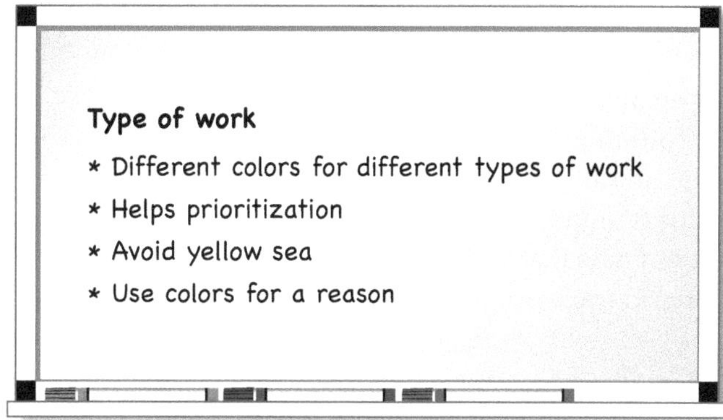

Let's now turn our attention to seeing how far you have come. In the next section, you'll get a simple tool that will help you track that.

4.4 Progress indicators

A card in a column on the board is a great visual cue and gives you a lot of information, but the history of the work item isn't as easily tracked. For how long has this card been sitting here? Is this a normal lead time for the development stage? Questions like these aren't easily answered by looking at the card where it's sitting today.

A *progress indicator* is a simple tool that helps you track this information and shows "how much done" the item is. It can be as simple as marking each sticky in the workflow with a dot for each day it's been worked on. If you're a bit more advanced, you might use different colors of dots for different states in your workflow.

In teams we've coached, we have also seen the expected timeline drawn as boxes, which are filled in as the work progresses. This gives you a hint as to how you're doing compared to what you usually do or the expected outcome. You could even talk about using a simple form of service-level agreement (SLA) here: "You can expect items that you classify as 'small' will be done within three days."

For items that don't follow a linear flow,[7] each state in the workflow could have its own box to tick when work there is done, and that will show what's left to do.

GOING GOOFY: COUNTING DOWN

Instead of counting the number of days you've spent, you can instead count down by tracking the number of days left before the item needs to be completed, based on its deadline, for example. Then at the daily standup you can update this figure to reflect the number of days that still remain. If you have been doing Scrum, you know this is a common way to track progress against the estimate on a burn-down chart.

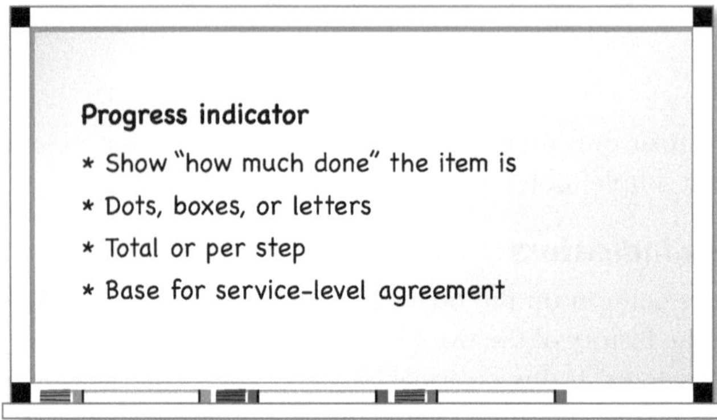

By using progress indicators, you've now started to collect and track data around how your process is working. In order to do that with any accuracy, you'll soon need to know how much effort goes into each work item. Let's take a look at one way of doing that.

4.5 Work-item size

The size of a work item can provide valuable information to help you manage the work item on the board. The only problem is that the exact size of work in your business is often not known until you're done.

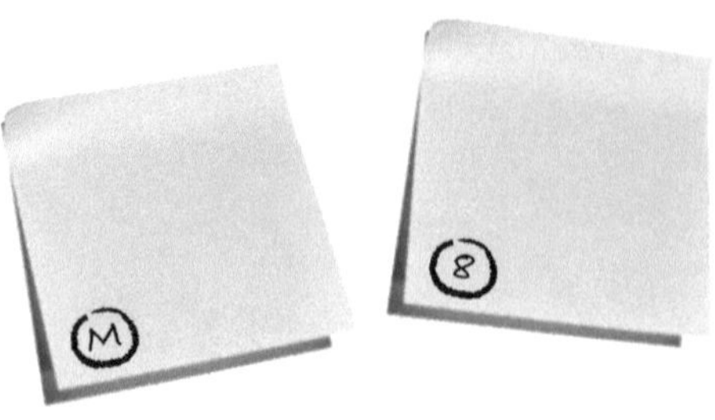

We'll talk more about estimation later (see chapter 9), but briefly, we can say that giving a number for how many hours a certain item will take is hard and often ends up being wrong. A much more compelling approach is to instead compare that work item to other work items. The question is then, does work-item A require more or less work to complete than work-item B?

[7] Where the process doesn't follow a natural sequence of steps, so that the steps to complete the work for the work item can be run in any order.

By doing this for all of your tasks at hand, you can assign equally sized work items a number—what are known as *story points*—or even T-shirt sizes (S, M, or L). These numbers only show your *relative estimates* of how much effort is needed to complete the task. This approach isn't exact, but it's probably more useful anyway, because exact measurements (104 hours, for example) are also guesses.

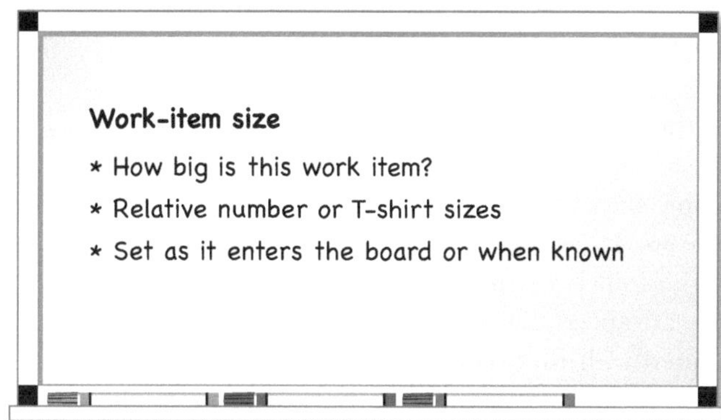

However you have come up with your estimate, you want to write it clearly on the work-item card, so that it's plain and easy for everyone to see.

4.6 Gathering workflow data

The last few sections have talked about adding information to the work item that can help you collect good data about how your workflow is behaving. This can be useful information for improving your process going forward. Let's take a closer look.

4.6.1 Gathering workflow metrics

When the workflow is set up in a detailed way, you have an excellent opportunity to gather data about how well your work flows and to measure and track trends in your work. In short, you can learn even more about how your work works.

Some of these metrics can be captured quite easily at almost any time, and others must be done as the work progresses through the flow because some of the data cannot be captured in hindsight. Many teams track a couple of easy-to-get metrics, such as the lead time of each work item and throughput (number of items completed per week, for example), in order to learn about their work. In chapter 1, you saw the Kanbaneros setting up such metrics for their process with a few simple steps.

This section isn't about metrics and how to use them. You can read more about metrics in chapter 11. Here we want to suggest a couple of simple ways that you can customize your cards to catch metrics.

In the simplest form, you can "stamp" the card with the date it enters the board and the date it enters the final stage of the workflow. This will help you track the lead time for that item.

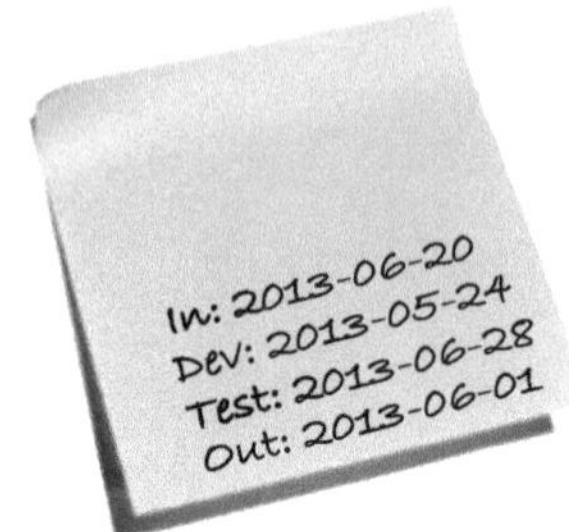

Stamping the arrival date for each new column (that is, each new step in your workflow) can extend this idea. You can now start to see trends in cycle time for each step of the workflow, where your bottlenecks are, and where work often is waiting. You need data like this to build more advanced diagrams (see chapter 11).

Combined with the work-item size we talked about before (see section 4.5), you can now start to make some predictions, such as these:

- "If you put a small work item into the inbox, it will be out the door in three days, tops."
- "A medium work item will be handled in five to eight days, in 9 cases out of 10. We have statistical evidence to back that up."

Remember—you're gathering this data for the *team* to approve. Don't overdo it. Start with a metric that is simple to track, and then make it more advanced as the need arises. You don't want to add a lot of extra work to catch and handle the metrics. Just jot down a simple date on the card—that's about it. Change it when that simple metric doesn't suffice anymore.

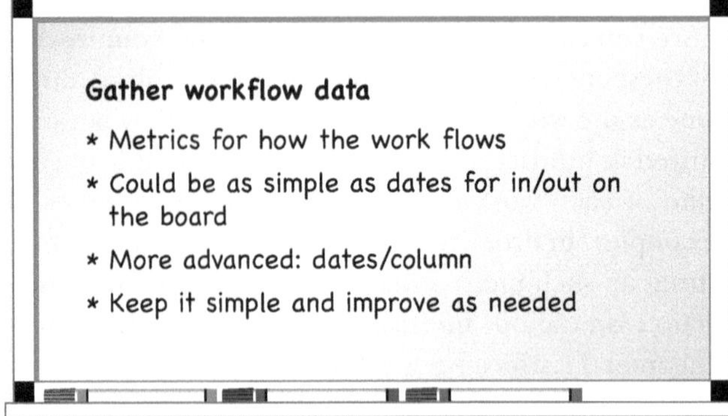

This section talked about gathering hard data about how your work items move through your workflow. We'll end this section with a softer and cozier tone: talking about emotions.

4.6.2 Gathering emotions

Some teams use the work items to keep track of how happy the team is with the work they're doing. You can too; simply draw an icon, such as a smiley, an angry face, an indifferent face, or something else indicative of your emotion with regard to the work, on the sticky when you finish it. This little icon indicates how you felt at the time.

Because the card is about to be moved off the board, you don't have to worry about messing up the sticky. Just draw the icon over the existing information as a quick reminder of how you were feeling.

Anyone on the team can capture the "emotion" of the card as it moves off the board. One way to do it is to have a quick vote at the morning meeting. You could also decide that the last team member that touched the work-item decides. In teams in which one or a pair of developers moves the work item through the entire chain, they decide the status at the end.

At regular intervals, you examine the data together to see if it tells you anything about the team and the work. Can you see any trends or patterns? Maybe work of a certain type, or for a certain customer, seems to make the team sadder than other types of work. Could you do anything about that? Examining the data can be triggered by having a certain number of finished items (for example, after every 10 items); or it can be scheduled with a particular cadence, such as every two weeks; or it can be done in retrospective meetings if you have such meetings (see chapter 10).

Fun and maybe useful practices

We have heard about a lot of other practices—too many to list them all in this book. But here are two practices that are fun and a bit different that you may find useful and that might inspire you to try something different:[a]

- Split an item in two parts (literally, with scissors) when you have concurrent activities/parallel lanes that merge together again. For example, a work item goes to security and software review in parallel, and each has its own workflow/column before they come together again
- Use different-sized work items for different sizes of work, so that large is a really big sticky (the roughly A5-sized ones), medium is a rectangular sticky, and small is a square one, for example. You could even have physical WIP limits (by width and height on the board) for these instead of a number.

a. If you do, please tell us about it.

4.7 Creating your own work-item cards

Now you've seen a lot of tips about what *could* be on the card. It's time to get practical and start thinking about what your work items should look like.

We suggest that you do this as a team exercise. Start small and simple, and expand as the need arises. Here are a few things your team can discuss:

- What information is needed for you to know what to do with the work items? Remember the design goals from section 4.1.
- What information may be interesting to other people who aren't working with the work items every day?
- Do you have different types of work? Do you benefit from distinguishing between different kinds of work?
- Do you need blockers? If you do, what are your policies around that? What should happen with items that are marked as blocked? Who is responsible for unblocking them?

As a final little fun exercise, create your own personal avatars. Remember not to go completely overboard with creativity, though; you want avatars that at least resemble yourselves.

4.8 Summary

This chapter was all about the work-item card and the information it radiates (communicates) to you as it sits on the board. A work item should contain all the information the team needs to be able to know how to work with it. We discussed the following:

- *A description*—So you know *what* the work is about
- *An avatar or other marker*—So you know *who* is working on the item
- *Deadlines and other important dates*—So you know *when* you need to have the item done
- *Tracking IDs or other references to an external system*—So you know *where* to find more information
- *Blockers*—So you can pick out items that are blocked and therefore *hindered* from further progress
- *Type of work*—So you know the *type* of work for each item, which is important so you can prioritize the work items against each other if needed
- *Progress indicators*—So you know how much of the work you have *done so far*
- *Size*—So you can see the differences in *size* and effort
- *Flow data, emotions, and other data accumulated during the flow through the board*—So you know how the *work behaved and how the team felt about it*

If you find this list daunting—stop! Don't do all of it; we haven't met a single team that does all these things at the same time. Start with what fits your current needs, and don't overdo it. Add features as needed.

If you find that something is missing from this list, you're probably right, and that's how it should be. Don't limit your work-item cards to this list alone. This is a starting point. Feel free to elaborate with your creativity and come up with amazing things.

Here are examples of work-item cards that use some, but not all, of the features we've talked about:

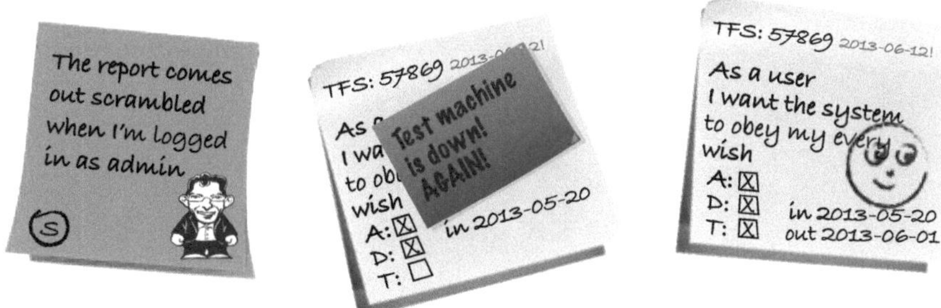

Now you have the tools you need to create a lot of work items; but you shouldn't. You should create small amounts of work. This is the topic of the next chapter.

5 Work in process

This chapter covers

- Introducing the concept of work in process (WIP)
- The effects of a lot of work in process
- How to limit work in process

Work in process (WIP) is a phrase that you'll hear a lot in the kanban community or when reading about Lean. WIP seems to be something that you don't want or at least want as little of as possible, so you often hear kanban aficionados talking about "limiting" WIP.

This chapter will help you to understand what WIP is, what could happen if you allow a lot of WIP in your process, and, finally, some ways to help you to limit work in process.

5.1 Understanding work in process

In this section, we'll dissect the concept called work in process. First let's talk a bit about the abbreviation WIP and how it can be interpreted. WIP has at least two different meanings:

Work in pro*gress*
Work in pro*cess*

Both of these meanings are widely used in the Lean literature. We happened to pick up "in process" from the literature we read as we learned about Lean and kanban. Throughout this book we're using *work in process*, but you can exchange it for *in progress* if you like.

5.1.1 What is work in process?

Work in process means all the work that you have going on right now. That includes work you're actively working on right now, work items waiting to be verified or deployed, and also the work sitting in your inbox that you haven't started yet: all the unfinished things you need to do in order to deliver value to the end customer.

WORK IN PROCESS AND LEAD TIME

Limiting WIP is one of the core kanban principles. It doesn't mean you should do less work, but that you should do less work *at the same time*. Limiting your WIP will help you complete more work in total more quickly.

If you remember, back in the introduction we played a little game with the Kanbaneros—Pass the Pennies (see chapter 13 for details on how to run the game). The objective of this game was to show how different amounts of WIP affect your *lead time*, the time it takes for an item to go through your complete process. When the Kanbaneros were asked to flip 20 coins each before continuing, the total lead time was high; the WIP was 20 items at this stage. When the WIP was lowered, or limited, first to five (each worker flipped five coins and passed them on) and then to one (each worker flipped one coin and passed it on), the lead time went down—way down. The simple game showed you that the bigger the batches, the more WIP you take on, and the longer lead times will be.

A WORD FROM THE COACH If you want some more concrete examples of what a lot of WIP can mean before moving on, we can give you one from when we were writing this book. At one point we grew impatient and started to write a lot of chapters simultaneously, before finishing the ones we were working on. We had about eight chapters going at the same time, and some of them were closing in on being done. We then decided to restructure the table of contents and ended up moving a lot of stuff around. That change was considerably harder to do, took more time, and caused more pain with a WIP of eight chapters than, for example, two chapters.

This relationship between WIP and lead time has been expressed as a law in mathematics—in queuing theory, to be more precise. It's called Little's law; let's take a closer look at it.

LITTLE'S LAW

When talking about limiting WIP, Little's law often comes up. The law is a mathematical proof by John D.C. Little that says that the more things you have going at the same time, the longer each thing will take. It's a formula that looks like this:

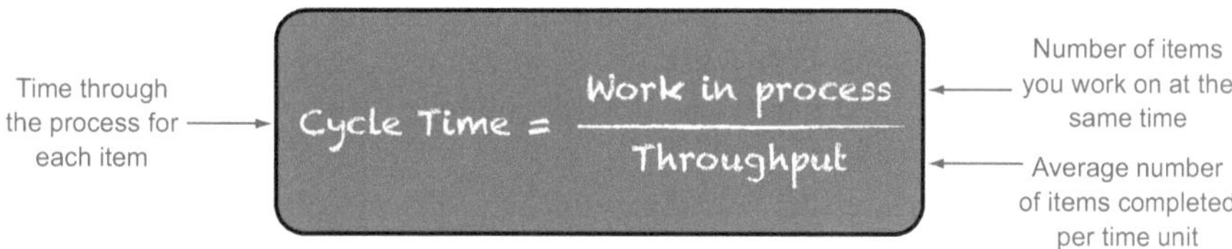

As always, the first time you see something like that, the correct response is "Eh … what?!" If you're anything like us, it didn't make you go "Aha!" Let's throw in some real numbers and see if that makes it clearer.

Imagine that that your team takes on 12 items for a month and works on them all at the same time, resulting in a WIP of 12 items. They also typically finish 12 items per month, giving them a throughput of 12 per month. It's now trivial to calculate the cycle time for each item: 1 month.

1 month = 12 items at the same time / 12 items / month

Let's do an experiment and—without changing anything about the way people work, the number of people on the team, or the work items—work with six items at the same time. That gives you a WIP of 6, still a throughput rate of 12 per month, and a cycle time of half a month. Wow! That's quite an improvement just by doing less stuff at the same time; don't you agree?

1/2 month = 6 items at the same time / 12 items / month

For completeness—the reverse is also true. Double the number of items you work on, and the cycle time is doubled to a whopping two months. This is provided that the other conditions (way of working, item size, people on the team, and so on) remain the same.

2 months = 24 items at the same time / 12 items / month

By handling fewer items at the same item (or limiting your WIP), you're lowering the cycle time and moving stuff faster through the process—without changing anything else! You can *probably* do it now and have your work items flow much faster through your workflow. This in turn gives you feedback faster and helps you to learn about your process faster, which in turn gives you an opportunity to improve your process to move even more quickly.

WARNING Did you notice the small "probably" there? If your WIP is already pretty low, chances are you can't lower it and expect the other variables in Little's equation to stay stable. It might prove difficult to parallelize the work and have two people working on a task with the same efficiency. Decreasing WIP can have a negative impact on the average completion rate.

This isn't necessarily a bad thing; in fact, it's one of the strengths of kanban, because it will pose an improvement challenge. What do you have to change in your way of working to keep up your completion rate, even though you lower the amount of WIP? You can read more about this in section 11.1.2.

You now know a little about the concept of work in process and the theory of why you want to limit it. Let's be a little more concrete and take a look at how WIP can manifest itself in the software development industry.

5.1.2 What is work in process for software development?

In chapter 1, the coaches helped Team Kanbaneros understand what their WIP was. WIP in Lean manufacturing is obvious because it often manifests itself physically: items piling up in front of a machine waiting to be processed or finished items on the floor waiting to be moved to the next step in the processing chain. Once you learn that it can have a negative impact on your work, it's pretty easy to spot, because it often involves physical things.

WIP in knowledge work isn't visual, and this is the driving force behind wanting to visualize work, to make work apparent and obvious where it previously wasn't. This is one of the main reasons to create boards and stickies that show your work items and their status, as described in chapter 3. The work is there even if you don't use a board; you just don't see it as clearly.

But there's more to WIP than the number of items you're working on at the same time. Considering only the *number* of things you're doing at the same time is a simplification. In this section, we'll look at a couple of ways that WIP can manifest itself in the world of software development.[1]

SPECIFICATIONS NOT BEING IMPLEMENTED YET

If you think about it, specifications have a "best-before" date. You could say that they rot if they're left lying around.

---

[1] See Mary and Tom Poppendieck, *Implementing Lean Software Development* (Addison Wesley Professional, 2006, http://amzn.com/0321437381), for more on this.

Imagine that today you write a specification, and then you leave it. What are the odds that anyone could pick it up in six months and start coding from it? Even after only two months, there's only a slim chance. Things in the business environment change, and the system for which the specification was written has probably also changed during the waiting time. At the very least, you have to go through the specification again to be sure it's still valid.

A specification that is written and lying around waiting to be implemented is work in your process.

CODE THAT ISN'T INTEGRATED

Continuing along a stereotypical development process, the next thing that might increase your WIP is *implemented code that you haven't checked in and integrated* with other people's code yet. That's also WIP, because you don't know how much work there is still to do before you're done with the work item.

If you've ever heard the phrase "It works on my computer," you know what we mean. If you haven't yet integrated the code with other people's work, you still don't know if it works at all. It works on your computer, with your settings, and in your environment.

Checking in and integrating your code often is a good way to not accumulate loads of integration work and to get quick feedback on the quality of the work you have done so far.

UNTESTED CODE

So is the report printing done yet?

Yeah sure ... I haven't tested it yet, but it's 95% done.

Untested code is another way that WIP manifests itself in software development. To write code without having a quick way of finding out if it works or not is an excellent way to build up a stock of unfinished work.

Automated testing is one way to handle this problem. By using automated unit testing or test-driven development (TDD), you get quick feedback that you're not introducing defects into the existing software. By doing automated acceptance testing or specification by example, you get feedback that you're building the right application.

A WORD FROM THE COACH Test-driven development (TDD) is a design and development practice in which you start by writing a small test for the code you're about to write. It's a micro-specification for the next little chunk of code you need to fulfill your task. As a side effect of working this way, you get a suite of test cases for all of your code. TDD is all about developing *things right*!

ANOTHER WORD FROM THE COACH Specification by example is also known as behavior-driven development (BDD) and is a powerful way to, in essence, write your specifications as executable test cases. Specification by example is about communication and making sure everyone understands each other. Doing this badly, in our experience, takes a lot of time, because you then have to go back and forth and anchor the information around the feature to build. By using concrete examples early in the process, as you specify the functionality, you increase the likelihood that everyone means the same thing when you talk about the feature. In essence, specification by example is all about developing the *right thing*.

CODE NOT IN PRODUCTION

You're done?! Great—I'll log in and try it out right now.

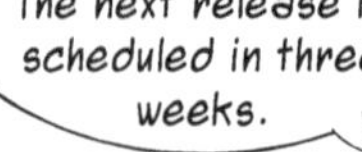

Finally, code that has been developed and tested but *has not been taken into production* is also WIP. You still have some work to do, and you still don't know if the feature is functioning or if it will have a bad effect on other parts of your system. Above all, it's not yet providing any value to the user—it's still WIP.

If you think about it for a while, code in production might also be WIP. The work isn't necessarily "done" just because it's in production. Having the code in production, working, isn't what matters—it's how the users receive it, whether they benefit from it, and whether your software accomplished the (business) impact that you intended. If the user behavior isn't affected, are you really done?

We have now examined what WIP is and how it manifests itself in our industry. Let's dive in and look into the effects of too much WIP.

5.2 Effects of too much WIP

You might now think, well, a lot of work in process is a bad thing, I know. But how bad can it be? What happens if you have too much WIP? This section examines the answer in detail. It's demoralizing reading, but keep your head high. You already know how to tackle this: limit your WIP!

5.2.1 Context switching

If you were Adam in the preceding cartoon, do you think you'd have to struggle to remember what you were doing when you came back? You probably would, right? This happens due to something often referred to as *context switching*.

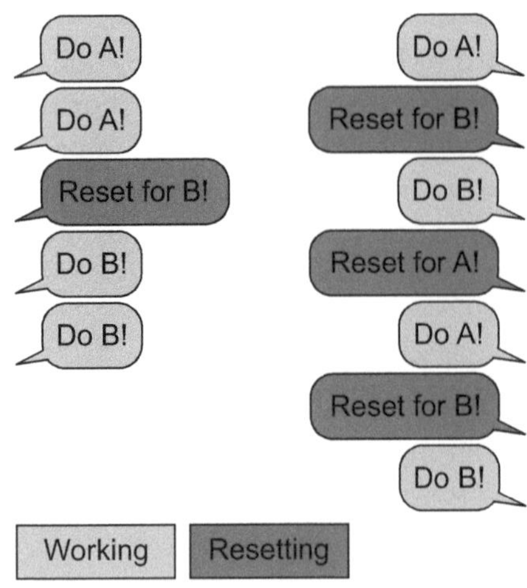

Context switching was originally a concept from computing that describes how the computer stores and retrieves state for one process as it switches to another. This is the basis of multitasking several processes on one CPU. The feeling of "trying to get back to whatever I was doing" is the same thing, but for humans. When switching between several tasks, you need to set up in your mind the "state" of the task you were doing earlier. Think of it as human context switching.

You can compare this with the setup time for a machine in a factory. If the machine is rigged to produce Model A, it will take some time to readjust it to produce Model B. It's then easy to understand that if every other piece is alternating between Model A and Model B, a lot of time will be lost due to setup.

That's exactly what you experience when doing context switching in knowledge work. You lose time and focus for every task you're trying to keep in your head at the same time.

One study[2] showed that as much as 10% of your working time per project is lost to context switching. This means if you're running two things at once, you have only 40% of your available working time per project to spend. With five tasks going at the same time, you have only 5% per project left.

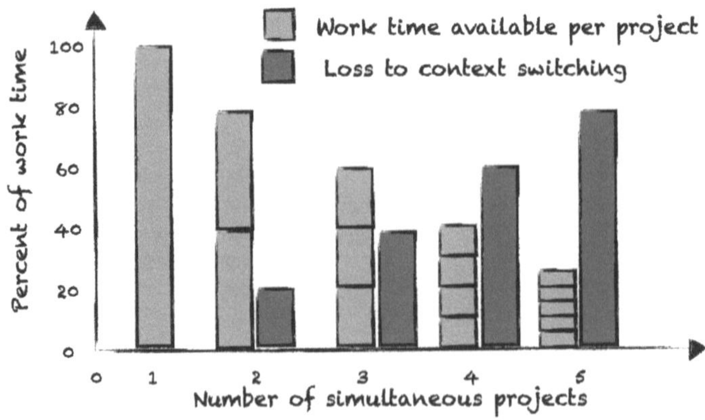

[2] Gerald Weinberg's book *Quality Software Management: Systems Thinking* (Dorset House, 1991, http://amzn.com/0932633226) is often referenced as the source of these numbers, although we haven't been able to find them there. But Weinberg has confirmed that he's the source in private correspondence with us.

Interestingly, another study also showed that context switching represented a 10-point drop in IQ. That's more than twice the number found in studies on the impact of smoking marijuana (!). So if you have to choose between the two, you know what to do.[3]

What can you do, then? These projects and tasks are part of your WIP—the WIP for you. And by now you know what to do with WIP: limit it! Keep it to a minimum. If you have to keep several tasks going, at least try to have as few as possible at once. Try to complete one before starting another. Doing this will help you avoid context switching and complete each task more quickly (according to Little's law).

Now you know something about the problem with context switching in our type of work. Let's continue and take a look at another of the problems that a lot of WIP causes: more work.

5.2.2 Delay causes extra work

Imagine that you happen to introduce a bug in the application you're writing. If you're notified about it immediately, within minutes, it's simple to fix, and nothing bad will have happened.

Now consider the same situation, but suppose it takes two months before somebody finds the bug and notifies you. It's now considerably more work to fix the bug. You first have to remember what the feature is, what you did about it, and how to fix it.

---

3 We want to be clear that the last part was meant as a joke. We wouldn't want anyone to think that we're proselytizing for using marijuana. Marcus, a member of the Salvation Army, particularly wants to underline this. The study is no joke, though: "'Infomania' worse than marijuana," BBC News, http://mng.bz/HjcX.

Then you might have to set up the system in the state it was in at the time to be able to reproduce the bug. Finally, the rest of the system might well have changed since then, making the bug much harder and more complicated to fix. And that is only considering you and your situation. You might have to involve others to be able to reproduce the defect (testers, system admins, or DBAs to set up the system in the correct state, for example).[4]

All this extra work is caused because of the *delay* from the time you introduced the bug until when you were notified of its existence and could do something about it. You get more work (in process) due to the delay itself.

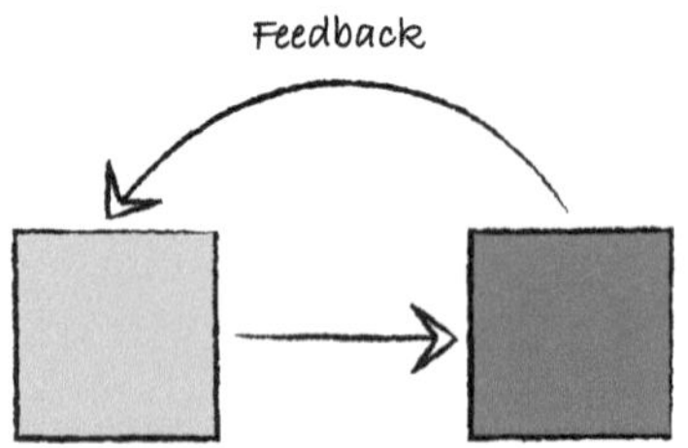

This problem boils down to the feedback loop being longer. Not only does a lot of work going on at the same time make each item go more slowly, but feedback on how each work item was received and behaves in production takes a longer time to get, too.

And that is a bad thing.

Feedback is an essential part of every agile process. Feedback is the creator of knowledge. It tells you about the quality of your work and the quality of your workflow. What works? What should you change? What shouldn't you change?

The more quickly you can get feedback, the more quickly you can change a bad process into a slightly better one. So you want to fail fast if there are any problems. Delayed feedback makes it difficult to connect the effect to its cause, making learning very difficult or even impossible.

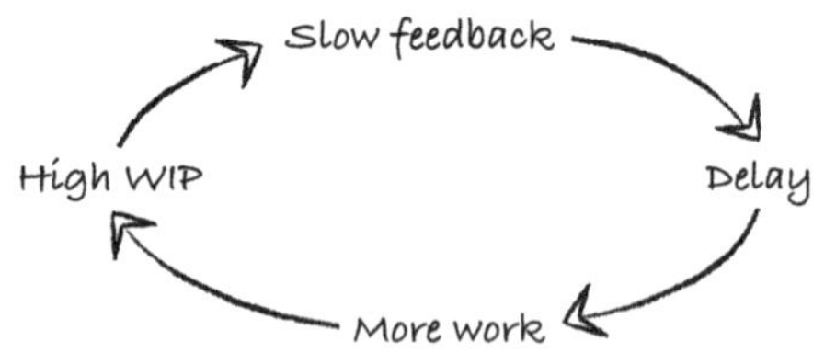

As you've seen, higher WIP causes feedback to become slower and slower. And the slow feedback itself causes even more work to be created, which causes even higher WIP, which prolongs the feedback loop, and … well, you see where this is heading, don't you? By lowering your WIP, you can stay on top of this problem and get feedback quickly on the small work items that move rapidly through the complete workflow.

But more WIP, longer lead times, and prolonged feedback loops: are those such as big deal? Yes, and the next few sections will show you examples of how they can haunt you.

[4] At one client, Marcus had a meeting cut 30 minutes short because the other person had to read up on a bug they were about to discuss in the next meeting. "I filed it one and a half years ago" was the understandable reason for her need to go and read up on what she wrote back then.

5.2.3 Increased risk

With more work going on at the same time, you're increasing risk. This has to do with not being able to change quickly and hence be more sensitive to changes in the world around you.

For example, let's say that you have a process with long lead times. If your customer requests a change in a feature, it will take a long time to build and take into production. During that time, the feature may become obsolete, or a competitor may pick up that request and implement it first.

An example of such a feature could be integration with social platforms such as Twitter and Facebook. Many online services now give you the ability to log in using credentials from these platforms. If you have a long lead time, say a year, someone else might have already created a copy of your service with the social media integration in place.

Other places where the ability to change fast is important are within technology, as well as in the environment in which your company operates (trends, laws, and other regulations, for example). If you can't change fast and get new features or changes to your customers fast, you stand the risk of losing relevance for your customers, your service becoming obsolete, or even being outmaneuvered by someone else.

5.2.4 More overhead

A really nasty thing about a lot of WIP is that more work will be created from the need to coordinate all that work. It's a vicious circle that quickly can spin out of control and in which you end up only doing coordination. This resembles the situations we described in section 5.2.2, in which we talked about delays creating more work. The delay we talk about here is that you have longer lead times with a lot of WIP.

Imagine that you're taking part in three different projects at once. Not only does that mean a lot of context switching for you, but those involved in the three projects will also likely ask you to do reporting, time tracking, and planning for all three projects. Because you're moving in and out of the projects, you probably need to do a lot of hand-overs and coordination, too. Much of this extra work is created because you're doing several projects at the same time. If you were assigned one project only, you wouldn't be asked to do a lot of the tasks required to coordinate your work among three projects.

This kind of situation often occurs in organizations with a strong focus on using "resources"[5] to the full. If you instead have a focus on keeping lead time short for the things you produce and smoothly flowing items to the customer, a lot of these extra tasks will be considered wasteful, and you will strive to eliminate them.

---

[5] Often the word *resource* means people in these organizations, too.

A WORD FROM THE COACH We have both worked as contractors for quite some time. In this business, time reporting is of the essence, because that is our product: as contractors, we're billing the customer for hours. Without fail, the time-reporting system in contracting companies is typically a mess, is complained about, and takes a lot of time to use. More often than not, you'll hear this at any contracting firm: "So who should we bill for the time it takes me to do the time reporting?"

At Marcus's employer, Aptitud, he's tried to resolve the problem of this wasted time by reporting deviations from a norm. If he's assigned to one project for 60% of his time, and that's the number of hours he worked for that client, he does nothing and Aptitud will bill the client for 60% of his time. If he, for some reason, is two hours short of 60%, then he reports those two hours as a deviation.

5.2.5 Lower quality

If you're a developer, the quality of your code may suffer from long lead times. This has to do with the prolonged feedback loop that lasts from the moment you write code until you know how it was received and how it functions in production.

Imagine that you happen to cause a bug to be introduced; you assumed that the customer had one name, but there should be both a first and a last name. The error passes unnoticed, because all the customers in your system up to that point were companies and used a single name field.

Then one day, several months later, your first "private" customer tries to log in and gets upset because he can't enter his first and last names as he is used to doing. Correcting this bug isn't easy; a lot of code that depends on customers having a single name property has already been written. You have worked around the bug without noticing.

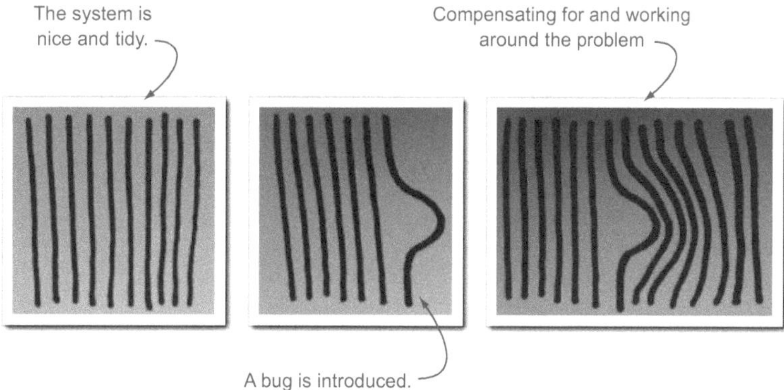

Scott Bellware[6] once compared this situation to introducing a hernia in the system, and he illustrated that with the preceding pictures. At the outset, your system is nice and tidy. When you introduce the bug, one line gets distorted. Until you're informed about the bug, you'll work around the problem, creating bad code that compensates for the bug in the system. It's not until you fix it that you can get back on track and have a well-aligned system again.

Compare that situation to one in which you're immediately notified about the bug you introduced and are able to fix it within hours of writing it. No hernia, no fuss: simple and quick.

The difference between these two situations is lead time: lead time from when you introduced the bug until you're informed of it. During that time, your code has suffered in quality, which means fixing the bug will take longer and will be more difficult.

5.2.6 Decreased motivation

Long lead times can decrease the motivation of your team, too. It's not hard to see why, because stuff ending up in another queue isn't a motivation booster.

---

[6] See Scott Bellware, "Design Flaws, Hernias, and Anemic Quality," February 9, 2009, http://mng.bz/f2x1, for more.

Take Daphne in the preceding cartoon. She has been slaving away on that feature that Adam has asked her to complete by today. It even took her part of the night, but she knew that it needed to be ready for Adam. He demanded it, because the last three times he had to wait on her. Making Adam happy this time provided the sense of urgency (or motivation) that Daphne needed to go the extra mile and finish the item today.

But when Daphne arrived in the morning, she found out that the item was the last in a long array of work items that needed to be tested. Her motivation to deliver on time took a severe hit.

In this example, it was Adam who had a lot of things going on at the same time. Because of that, he couldn't give Daphne feedback on her work until two weeks later. That in turn resulted in Daphne's motivation dropping; and when Adam finally came back, she couldn't have cared less about the testing result. He was interrupting her at that point, because she had moved on to other work.

What should they do about that? Well, herein lies the real reason to strive for lower WIP and hence shorter lead times. It will expose problems[7] for you: problems that, if you try to fix them, will make your flow even faster, even smoother. Sadly, kanban doesn't say much about how to fix these problems. You have to find out for yourself by seizing one unrealized improvement opportunity at a time. We have devoted chapter 10 to practices that can help you find and implement process improvements.

5.3 Summary

This chapter talked about work in process and specifically discussed limiting WIP in order to get shorter lead times:

- WIP is a common abbreviation, and it has at least two meanings: work in pro*gress* and work in pro*cess*. We prefer *work in process* and use that throughout the book.
- Little's law tells us with mathematical certainty that the more WIP, the longer the cycle time for each work item will be. You should limit the WIP to get faster flow and shorter lead times.
- WIP can take many forms, and we looked at some common ones in software development:
  - Specifications that haven't been implemented yet
  - Non-integrated code that "works on my computer"
  - Untested code, which may or may not live up to your standards
  - Code not in production, which sits and wait for the next release
- Problems and bad things can follow from having a lot of WIP:
  - More context switching
  - Prolonged feedback loop, which in turn causes extra work for you

[7] Sorry—"unrealized improvement opportunities" is much better.

- And we mentioned some ways that WIP can manifest itself:
  - Increased risk
  - More overhead
  - Lower quality
  - Less motivation

You now have solid knowledge of what work in process is and why too much of it is a bad thing, and you have a theoretical understanding of what to do about too much WIP. The next chapter will be much more practical, and you'll start setting WIP limits for your team.

6 Limiting work in process

This chapter covers

- Principles for finding suitable WIP limits
- Common ways that teams limit WIP
- Common ways to visualize WIP limits
- Answers to some frequently asked questions regarding WIP limits

From the previous chapter, we hope we have now convinced you that a lot of good things come from limiting your work in process (WIP). By now you're probably full of questions: What is the right limit for you? How do you go about finding the WIP limit? Are there some good starting points that can guide you?

As you soon will find, there are no hard rules here. Finding a suitable WIP limit is not only contextual and dependent on what you want to achieve, but also like hitting a moving target. The WIP limits can and should change. At the outset of this chapter, we can already reveal a secret: *the goal is not to limit WIP.* WIP limits are only a means to drive you to improve. Improve to achieve a better flow, which is the theme of the next chapter.

That's why you'll see a lot of "It depends" and "You can do this, that, or the other" in this chapter. It's not a sign of us not knowing; it's that you need to find what works best for you and your team.

No need to worry, though; we have packed this chapter full of guidance and principles for finding a suitable WIP limit, as well as practical ways many teams go about visualizing and setting their WIP limits. Let's dive in and see how you can reason your way to finding a WIP limit for your team.

6.1 The search for WIP limits

Searching for a suitable WIP limit for your team can be tricky business. What is right for you and your team right now? The answer is the old-favorite answer of consultants worldwide: "It depends."

And it does. It depends on

- How much pressure there is to continuously improve the organization
- The number of people on the team and their availability
- The shape and size of the work items you're working with

And the list goes on.

To find a WIP limit for your team, here are few basic rules of thumb, but be prepared to change the WIP limits as you learn more:

- Lower is better than higher.
- People idle or work idle.
- No limits is not the answer.

Let's examine these approaches in detail.

6.1.1 Lower is better than higher

A lower WIP limit is generally better than a higher one because you want to limit the number of items you work on as much as possible. This will give you better lead times and faster feedback and force you to remove impediments. These are all things that help you improve the flow of work items in your process.

Setting the WIP limit *too* low, however, could make your process come to a grinding halt, because it will quickly bring out any problems in the process. Imagine that your entire team is working on a single work item, and all of a sudden you need an answer from a customer in order to continue. Because that work item is the only thing you were doing, you have come to a complete stop.

Problems are symptoms of things that will have to be changed in your process to improve your flow. Finding many problems can quickly become a painful experience for teams that aren't equipped to handle a lot of issues like these at once. Instead of feeling encouraged to improve and solve their problems, a common reaction is to give up and stop caring that they're breaking the WIP limit on a regular basis.

You want to search for a low WIP limit, but not too low. There are signals to guide you, as you'll see in the next section.

6.1.2 People idle or work idle

Tuning the WIP limit can easily become something that is talked about forever: striving to find the one true limit can result in a lot of discussions in which no one is able to decide what is best. This isn't time well spent; it's better to try something and then adjust.

A simple method to help you adjust the WIP limit up or down is the following:

If your *WIP limit is too high, work will become idle.* There will be work items that no one is responsible for. This might be a good time to lower the WIP limit.

With a *WIP limit that is too low, people will become idle.* All items are being worked on, and there are people without work. You can now collaborate to get items done or raise the WIP limit.

6.1.3 No limits is not the answer

Be sure not to fall into the trap of not setting a WIP limit at all! This is one of the most common mistakes we see in teams starting with kanban. Kanban involves three simple principles; don't remove one of them too soon.

The risk is that you'll end up with a board flooded with work, as you see in the figure to the right, showing your inefficiencies and your failure to move work through your process. Eventually, the board will end up not being used, because you can't see the work items for all the work on the board.

Office spaces around the world have unused boards covered with stickies. Don't add your board to that sad bunch; instead, make the board a tool that helps you improve.

Also, as we'll discuss further in chapter 7, removing the WIP limit will remove your incentive to improve. With no WIP limit, nothing pushes people to do better. If you allow an unlimited number of items on your board, nothing will force you to complete the ones on there before starting new work.

This is because (if you remember from chapter 5 about work in process) the more stuff you have going on at the same time, the longer the lead time will be for all the work in your process. You want a constraint that pushes you toward finishing work and toward improvements in your process. We'll dive much deeper into this in chapter 7.

Let's turn our attention to some principles of how to decide on a suitable WIP limit.

6.2 Principles for setting limits

Finding your WIP limit depends on your context and particular situation. In this section, we'll take a look at some common ways that teams we've coached and heard about have agreed on their limits.

Remember that it's not so much about finding *the* WIP limit, but rather, visualizing your current WIP limit; it's the best so far. You *should* change it as often as needed. Embrace change; it's good for you.

As always, use the examples here as inspiration, and expand on them to suit your needs. Let's start with a simple principle, one that might already be stuck in your head from previous chapters: stop starting, start finishing.

6.2.1 Stop starting, start finishing

A simple yet powerful starting point to limit your work in process is agreeing to *strive to complete current work before starting anything new.* This will keep your WIP low, because you only start new work when something else is finished.

An easy way to begin doing this is to adopt this slogan for your team:

Yes, you have to think hard when saying it the first few times, but then it sticks. A good idea might be to put this statement above your board, where you'll meet each morning; or why not use it as the opening or closing phrase of your daily standups?

Hill Street Blues—roll call

To beat that sound bite into your head, you could use the *Hill Street Blues* roll-call ending. As people leave the standup, say:

"Oh, one more thing. Stop starting, start finishing, everyone."

Wait a second. And then add the famous ending:

"And let's be careful out there."

By using a reference to *Hill Street Blues*, we have probably dated ourselves pretty well. It was a police series in the 1980s that was a big hit in Sweden. Every person who has seen it remembers the ending of the morning roll calls at the police station; everyone rose, and the sergeant called out, "One more thing ... let's be careful out there."

There is great power in this simple slogan, because it pushes you to a lower WIP. It also sums up a basic pattern of kanban: to prefer to finish work before starting something new. Doing so will help you not only to limit the number of work items you work on at the same time, but also to shorten lead times, take work through the whole value chain, get feedback, and improve your process.

Let's finish this section with an inspirational quote to help you remember what's important:

> *It's not "the more you start, the more you finish," it's "the more you finish, the more you finish."*
>
> —David P. Joyce

Soon you may need a bit more control over your WIP limit, and at that point this principle might be too coarse grained. But it's a great start to emphasize a principle.

6.2.2 *One is not the answer*

Striving for a low WIP limit is desirable because it gives you better flow (see chapter 7), but setting it too low will probably be too disruptive for your flow. For example, if you have a WIP limit of one, any disturbance in the flow—such as handoffs, people out of the office, and so on—will cause all work to stop. Most organizations aren't ready to handle all those improvement opportunities (you remember that's what we call problems, right?) at once, so you probably should go with a WIP limit higher than one item.

Mob programming

Mob programming is an interesting and novel approach to system development pioneered by a team coached by Woody Zuill. The basic concept of mob programming is simple: the entire team works as a team together on one task at a time. That means: one team, one (active) keyboard, one screen (projector of course). It's just like doing full-team pair programming.

A team doing mob programming has a WIP limit of one. That's very effective when it comes to completing the work being worked on as fast as possible. Any question, any problem, will be tackled immediately; and all the people needed to solve the problem are present in the room and have time to solve any issues right away.

But this approach is very inefficient when it comes to utilizing the people on the team to the fullest. Not every person on the team is actively typing code.

The question is, are you selling keystrokes or completed features?

For many organizations, mob programming is too extreme; a WIP limit of one is probably not suitable for everyone. But for the organizations that can handle it, work flows very fast indeed.

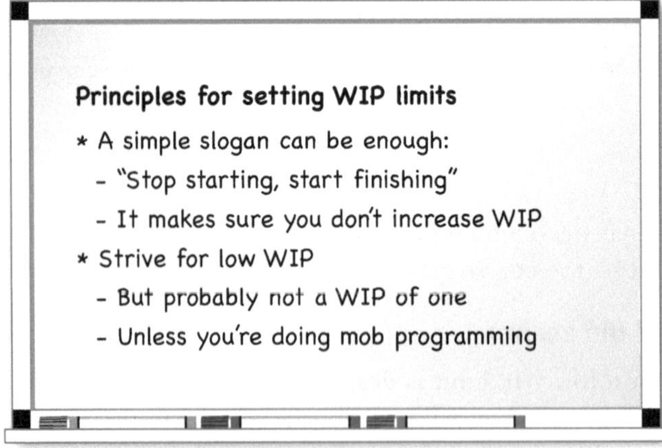

Summing up this section on guidance for setting your WIP limits, we can say that in most cases, setting the WIP limit to one isn't a good idea. You should strive for a low number, but not necessarily one.

By now you're probably longing for some practical advice on how to set WIP limits using common practices, visualizations, and methods that other teams have found helpful. Well, let's get to it. You'll start by setting a single WIP limit for the entire team.

6.3 Whole board, whole team approach

In this section, we'll take a look at a couple of ways to limit the total number of work items on the board for the whole team. This can be a simple way to get started and may be all that's needed for your team.

Remember that there is no true WIP limit to be found. WIP limits are tools that you use to improve. You might ask questions like "Will this WIP limit help our work to flow better or make our flow worse? Will this WIP limit render a lot of people idle? Will a lot of work be idle? Is that a problem, and what can we do to resolve it?"

6.3.1 Take one! Take two!

Many teams that we have coached have gone through a similar journey to reach a suitable WIP limit. Their experience illustrates the kind of reasoning that we think is necessary concerning WIP limits, and we want to relate that reasoning here. Learn from this, and then pick a limit that suits you.

Let's assume you have a five-person team. You could, for example, start out boldly and decide on a WIP limit of one per person, making the total WIP limit equal to the number of people on the team.

Pretty soon, you'll find out that this approach creates some problems; if you become blocked, you can't pick up new work without breaking the WIP limit, for example. You may decide it seems more reasonable to allow for a maximum of *two* items each, so people have something to do if one item is blocked. That makes the total WIP limit equal to the team size times two.

But that setup might not be reasonable either, because it allows for situations in which every person on the team can be blocked on one item and still keep working on another without breaking the WIP limit. That's a perfectly valid situation with a WIP limit setup like that, but in many instances this isn't pushing the team enough. You want the WIP limits to push you into resolving problems, not allow you to work without noticing them.

To push the team, you can back off from a WIP limit of 10 items and decide on maybe 8. If all team members are now blocked on one item, you'll start to break the WIP limit if everyone picks up another one to work with. You get a gentle nudge to do something about the blockage, because you exceed the WIP limit earlier with 8 items than you would with 10 items. If you want to get this warning even earlier, lower the WIP limit a bit more.

Note that the numbers in our examples aren't that important, but the *reasoning* (what happens if you're all blocked, will this improve flow, and so on) to find your WIP limits is. Remember—there is no right WIP limit that can be calculated. You must find the one that suits your team and your situation the best. The most rational thing is to try a WIP limit and then change it as needed.

Also, think about what kind of behavior you want the WIP limit to drive. It's the mechanism that drives improvements.

6.3.2 Come together

The previous section allowed every person to have at least one item going on at the same time. If your team is using collaboration practices like pair programming, you should probably lower the WIP limit even more. In such cases, you could set the WIP limit to a number lower than the number of people in the team. You could take the number of people on the team *divided* by 1.5 (or some other number you see fit) to yield a low WIP limit.

For our example five-person team, this will add up to roughly three items total to work on.

With a WIP limit of three for a five-person team, people will quickly end up with nothing to do, if everyone works alone. To be able to handle a WIP limit of three and still engage people in the process, the team members will have to cooperate on items to finish them by using pair programming, writing the specifications together, or testing in pairs: exactly the kind of collaboration that agile teams seek. As a nice side effect, the work items will move fast across the board.

This might be a big change for some teams that aren't used to collaborating closely. As always, don't set the WIP limit too low to start, but rather lower it little by little and improve your process at the same time.

6.3.3 Drop down and give me 20

One technique to set a suitable WIP limit was introduced by Don Reinertsen.[1] He proposed that you first observe what a normal level is in an unconstrained system. That means: what is the normal load of work items in your system? Start where you are: visualize the work items, and count them to learn what your current WIP is.

Then double that amount of WIP and use that number as the limit, allowing for twice as much WIP as you have normally. You double the WIP limit because it can be statistically deduced that with normal variation, almost no teams will reach the limit. It's safe to say that this limit will have no effect at all to start with—everyone should be able to pull it off. From this new limit, you can then incrementally go down by 20–30% decrements—say, every month or every two weeks—until you start to experience problems, queues build up, or you see people idle between tasks.

Let's see this in practice. Say that a team usually has roughly four to five items going on at once. Following Mr. Reinertsen's reasoning, you should start by allowing for 10 items on the board. You then back off that number by 20% at regular intervals. The first iteration you're down to 8 items, and then 6, and then 5, and so on.

As you do this, you're not only lowering the WIP limit, which will flow items through your system faster. You're also starting a trend of continuous striving to improve: a mindset that characterizes Lean thinking.

This approach puts the focus on an important aspect of WIP limits; they're cheap to implement. You pick the number and don't take on more work than that. If that doesn't work out for you, if too many work items are idle, you can go back up to the level you had before. This makes WIP limits excellent for use in experiments.

[1] Presented at a keynote at the Lean Kanban Central Europe conference 2012. See www.lean-kanban.eu/sessions/reinertsen/ for more information.

What happens if you lower the limit by 20%? Try it and see; if it doesn't work out, go back and think about what happened. What would you have to do differently to be able to lower the WIP and still keep items flowing through your system?

This approach teaches the team to continuously evaluate the limit to improve the flow. Because the initial WIP limit is high, decreasing it the first couple of times won't cause any big problems. This helps the team get into the habit of evaluating and changing their limits regularly.

Although we used a whole-team WIP limit approach in this example, it makes perfect sense to apply the same thinking with a column-based WIP limit approach (as discussed in section 6.4). You could stop decreasing the limits for the columns where you feel pain and keep decreasing them for other columns.

6.3.4 Pick a number, and dance

If you don't know what a suitable WIP limit could be, pick a number out of the blue. Yes—you read it correctly. Pick any old number!

Or rather, make an educated guess of what could be smart, but don't think too much. This number, as we've said many times, could and should be changed as you progress and as you see fit.

Use the principles for finding a good limit, as described in section 6.1, to guide you toward setting your WIP limit.

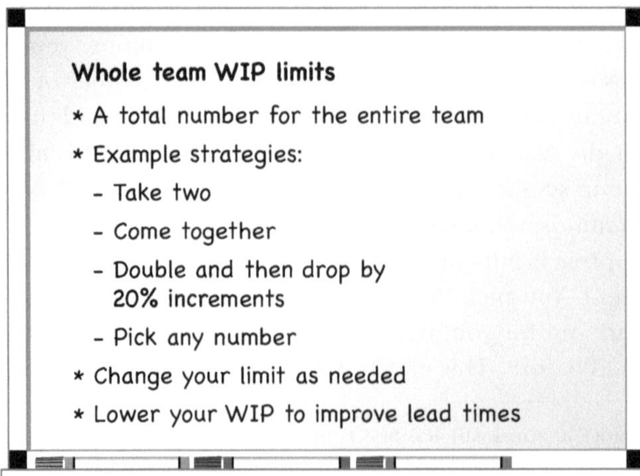

Until now we have considered WIP limits for the whole board and whole team. Doing this, you don't concern yourself with how the work is distributed among the steps in your workflow (the columns on your board). Setting one single WIP limit, like the examples we've considered up to now, is sometimes referred to as a system with a constant WIP (also known as CONWIP).

Let's now take a look at some other approaches for how to limit WIP. Could you limit WIP for only parts of your workflow? Why would you do that? And how could that be visualized?

6.4 Limiting WIP based on columns

Most teams that we have worked with set WIP limits per column instead of for the entire team. This gives them a bit more fine-grained control over how their work flows and an opportunity to handle bottlenecks and uneven flow. That said, setting a WIP for the entire board could still be useful and, if you don't know where to start, provides a good starting point.

In this section, we'll dive deeper into common ways of limiting WIP per column, some things to consider when doing so, and what you can gain from a WIP-per-column approach.

6.4.1 Start from the bottleneck

All workflows always have a bottleneck somewhere, which sets the pace for the entire workflow. Increasing throughput upstream from the bottleneck will just pile up work in a queue in front of it, and trying to increase throughput downstream from the bottleneck is futile because there won't be enough input to work on. If you can identify the bottleneck in your workflow, it makes sense to use WIP limits to help resolve it. For more on bottlenecks and how to discover and manage them, see section 7.5.

Let's look at an example, in the board to the right. Here we have a workflow where work items are piling up in a queue in front of a bottleneck: the Test column. If you do nothing, work will keep piling up, and WIP and lead times will increase. If you instead put a WIP limit of, say, 3 on the whole Development column, the developers will have to stop doing Development work when the queue starts to build. What should they do instead? They could help the testers finish their work. Whatever they do, they shouldn't pull in new work, because that will only build more WIP.

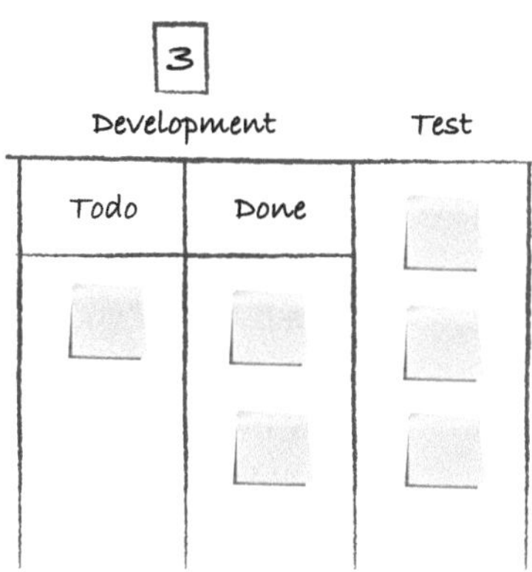

As you can see, putting a WIP limit on the step feeding the bottleneck will stop the bottleneck from being flooded and drive behavior to resolve the bottleneck, thus improving the entire flow.

Start from bottleneck

* A bottleneck is a step in your workflow that slows your flow down
* Limit the step feeding the bottleneck to keep it from being flooded
* And drive the team to resolve the bottleneck

6.4.2 *Pick a column that will help you improve*

Why did you buy this book? What is the reason you think kanban will help you improve? Most teams already have a pretty good idea about where (some of) their problems lie. A common scenario is to use kanban in order to collaborate together on fewer work items in order to complete them faster. In a team of mostly developers, it might make sense to put a challenging WIP limit on the Development column, where most of the active work is being done, in order to drive collaboration.

Many teams start with one of the "whole team, whole board" approaches described in section 6.3 and distribute numbers over different columns. You can also apply the total to just one column: for example, putting 1.5 times the number of developers as a WIP limit on the Development column.

6.4.3 *A limited story, please*

There are as many ways to limit WIP as there are teams in the world, but we'll mention one that sometimes comes up as a question: can you limit your work in process based on estimated size of the work item—for example, by using *story points*?[2] (You can read more about story points in chapter 9.)

As we've said, you'll probably have to experiment to find a WIP limit that is suitable for your team. Start with your gut feeling and adjust the limit up or down, as described in section 6.1. This goes for estimated effort size of your work item (for example, in story points) as well as for work items. Many teams using Scrum do this already, because when they're planning their next iteration, they look at how many story points they typically finish and pull that amount of new work into the iteration.

[2] Story points are a way to estimate effort for a team, using relative measures; they're used in many agile methods such as Scrum and Extreme Programming (XP).

Limiting WIP by estimated size means you only pull new work as long as it keeps you under an agreed-on limit: for example, under 10 story points. The next figure shows an example of a simple board where the developers have a WIP limit of 10 story points.

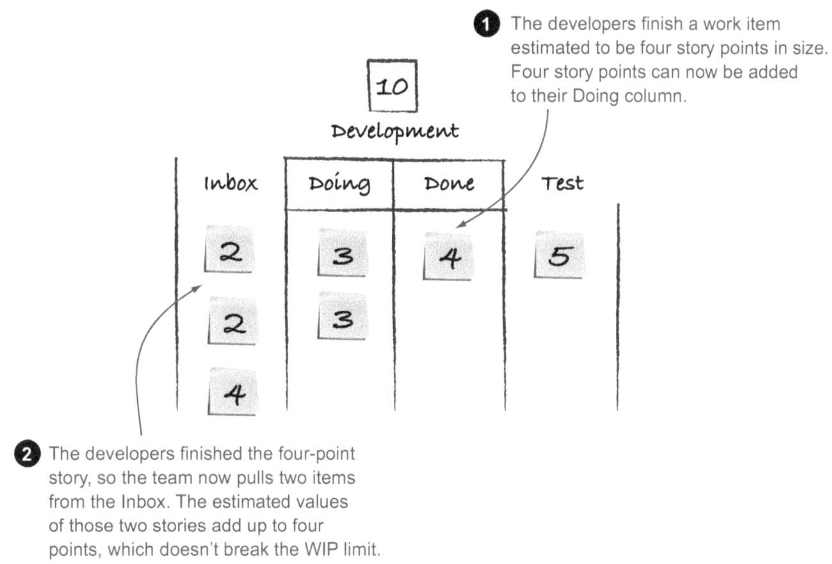

This WIP-limiting approach is often more suitable to decide per column, rather than for an entire team, because the size of a work item may change the more you work with it. For example, when you start analyzing an item, you might find that it will take less effort to implement than you first anticipated.

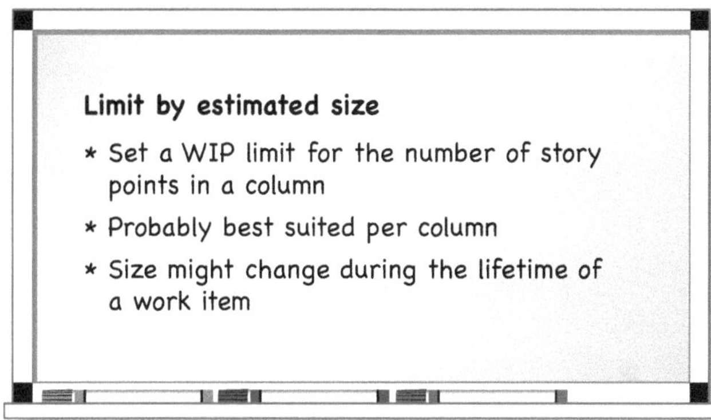

6.4.4 How to visualize WIP limits

Column-based WIP limits are often visualized by drawing them above each column of the board. But variants of this are plentiful.

2 3 2

Analyze Dev. Test

Some things we've seen while working with teams are as follows:

- *Boxes for each work item*—This will make it apparent when you break the limit, because you have to put your work item outside of a box or on top of another work item.

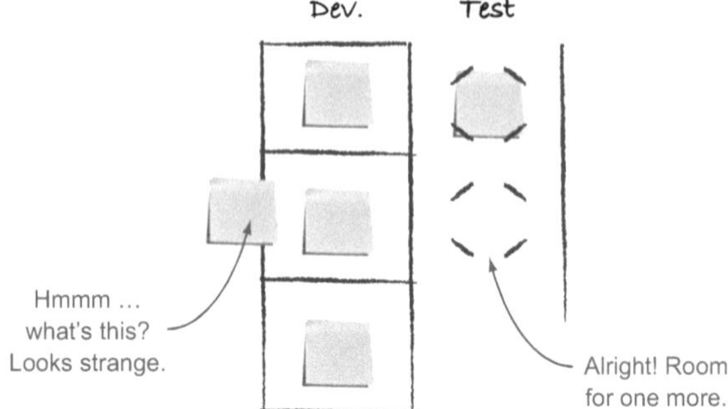

- *Plastic folders or other physical placeholders for each allowed work-item card*—This is similar to the drawn boxes and is also a good visual indicator that helps you to keep track of how you're doing against the established WIP limit.

What you use is up to your imagination and what suits your team. Don't be afraid to experiment. Try something new, and fail, instead of being content with a suboptimal setup.

As you can see, there are lots of ways to use WIP limits on the columns on your board to help you find problems, bottlenecks, and other things that slow down flow in your process. What will work best for you is left as an empirical exercise: experiment. Try something, and change to improve.

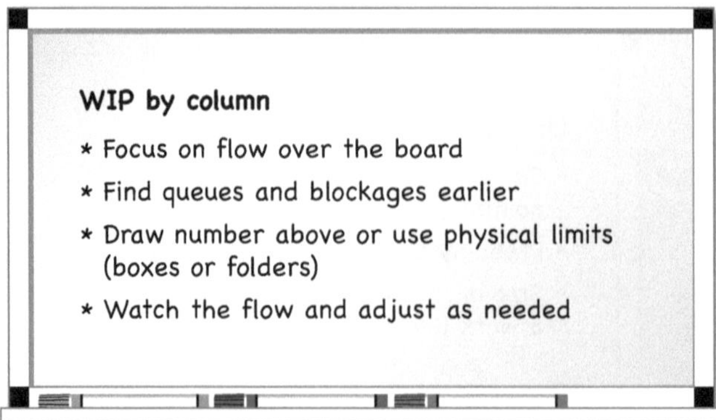

Let's now turn our attention to another way of limiting WIP: by person.

6.5 Limiting WIP based on people

Some teams might have a situation where people take work from start to finish, and it's not common or feasible to hand over the work to someone else. The workflow can still be a sequence of steps that the work goes through. In fact, this can be valuable to show what state the work is in right now, even though the same person is doing the work throughout the process.

A typical example of a team like this is in first-line support, in which you get a case from a customer in dire straits and you stay on it until it's solved. Such a case might go through the following phases: finding a workaround for the customer, filing a bug, testing a new release of the system with the bug fix, and finally closing the case. All these stages are probably handled by a single person on a support team.

This calls for another strategy: some teams choose to limit the number of work items for each person. You focus not so much on optimizing for flow through the workflow, but rather on ensuring that no one takes on too much work and that everyone has things to do.

Another situation where limiting WIP per person is suitable is for fighting multitasking on all levels in the team. In this case, a WIP limit per person can help visualize that some people are involved in many work items,[3] which might be a driver behind the whole team having too much WIP. You can have conversations about how to prevent that, with a limit per person made explicit.

6.5.1 Common ways to limit WIP per person

We'll now take a closer look at some common ways to visualize people-based WIP limits.

THIS BOARD ISN'T BIG ENOUGH FOR ALL THESE AVATARS

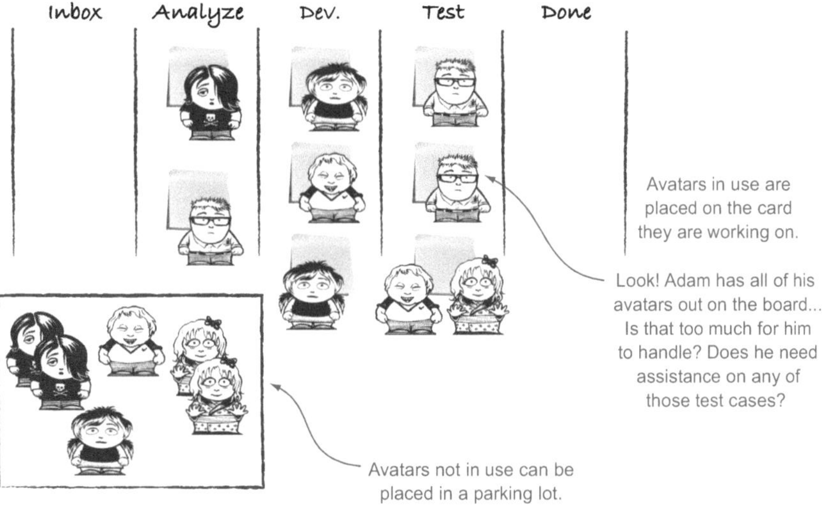

[3] Such people are known as *hoarders* (see the next sidebar for a real-life example).

If you're using avatars to indicate who is working on what, a simple measure is to limit the number of avatars each person can have "in play" at the same time. You could, for example, print three avatars for each person, effectively setting the WIP limit per person to three. Now it's easy to see who's doing what and how many items each person is working with right now.

Poor Sean, he had too few avatars

On one team that Marcus coached, there was this guy: let's call him Sean. Sean had been involved with this application since before you were born. He practically built it himself. Every decision was in one way or another routed through him. You have probably met Sean a couple of times, or at least his type of person.

This slowed the team down considerably, because the team was quite big (eight people) and every work item had to be routed through Sean in order to be completed. When we created the kanban system, we printed only three avatars per team member to put a finger on this pain point.

And indeed, the first morning meeting took about 35 minutes, most of them spent waiting for Sean to place the three ("Only three? Can I have five more? Please?") stickies with what he should work on during the day.

After letting him sweat for a while, we had a discussion about the problems this situation caused for the team and the flow of items. To Sean's big surprise, it turned out that when he was on vacation or was sick, the team still got stuff out the door.

Maybe there were work items in which Sean didn't have to be involved? Maybe not having Sean involved in everything could increase the feeling of autonomy and mastery for other people on the team? Maybe that could free up Sean's time to do the complex stuff that he, in fact, was the only one on the team who knew?

It all ended well, but it was a bit shocking to poor Sean at first.

SWIM IN YOUR OWN LANE, PLEASE!

Another common way to limit WIP per person is to give each person a swim lane through the process. Then you can decide on a WIP limit for each swim lane, effectively allowing a certain number of items in any column of the board for that swim lane.

This approach can also be used to limit work per team on a multiteam board or for *teamlets* (parts of a team).

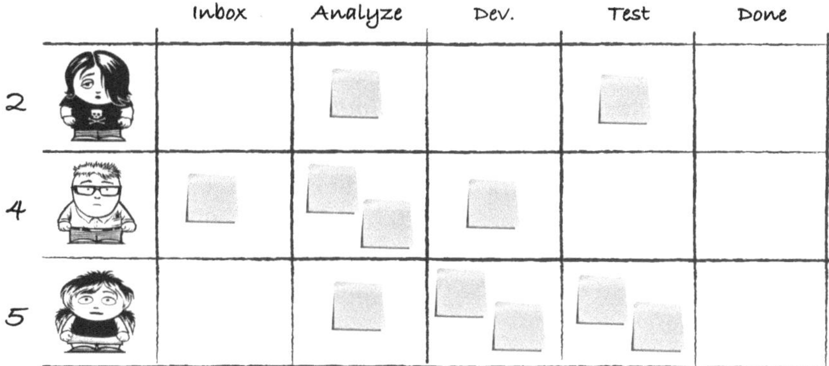

WARNING Remember that these strategies focus on making sure every person has enough to do; they don't help you much to get the work flowing to a finished state. You could start like this, but it's worth questioning the effectiveness of this approach to limiting WIP. After all, your customers seldom care if you're kept busy; they only want you to deliver stuff.

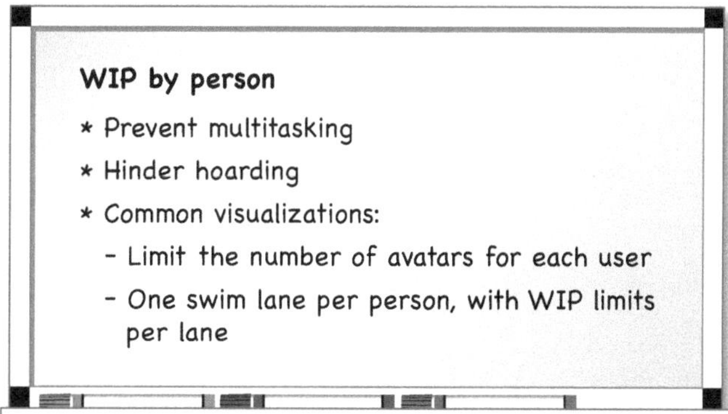

We have now given you a lot of principles, ideas, and practical tips for how to go about setting your WIP limit. The main point is that this is contextual and depends on your needs and situation. There are often a lot of questions around setting WIP limits, and we'll address some of the more common ones next.

6.6 Frequently asked questions

It's not strange that WIP limits trigger some questions, because the limit you select is something that depends on what *you* need and your situation. Sometimes, when WIP limits are described, they come across as something definitive; this adds to the confusion, because WIP limits should be moving targets.

6.6.1 Work items or tasks—what are you limiting?

Quite often, teams split up work items into tasks for certain steps in their workflow. For Development, it could be tasks like "implement data access," "write HTML page," and "complete business logic." In a Testing column, they could be tasks like "prepare test data," "write report," and "perform manual tests." Tasks are part of a work item and can be thought of as all the things you need to do to complete the work item in a given column.

Not until every task is completed in Development are the work items moved to the next step of the workflow. Some teams even divide the columns into subcolumns, forming a mini-board for the tasks.

Here you can see two work items going on (one in each row), and each work item has been split up into several tasks. The team counts the WIP limit against the work item, not the tasks that compose the work item.

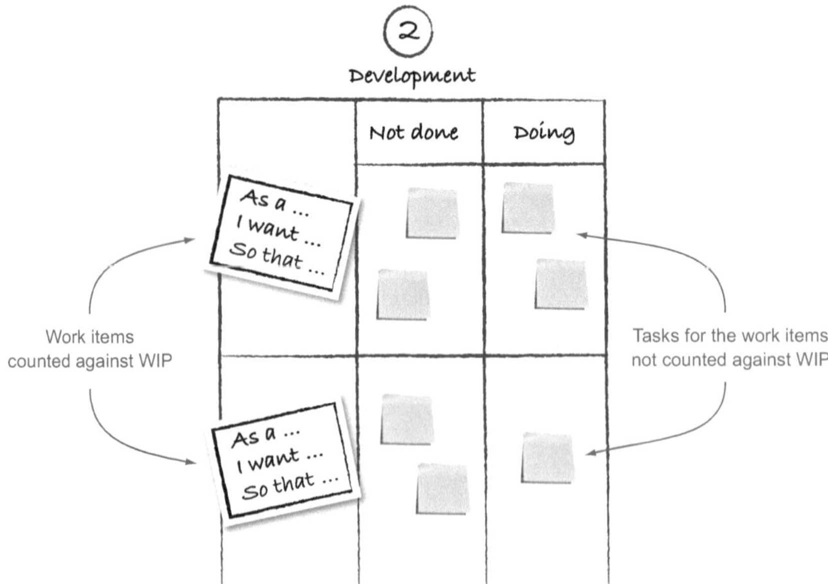

Most teams seem to work this way, counting their WIP limits against the work items. The tasks are only for tracking what you need to do in order to complete the work item and often aren't delivering customer value. It doesn't really matter how fast they flow across the board, if the customers still have to wait for anything useful to be delivered.

There could be times when, in certain columns, you might want to limit the number of tasks. For example, you may want to limit the level of multitasking or make sure you're always cooperating on certain tasks.

6.6.2 *Should you count queues against the WIP limit?*

Queues are often visualized as a column within another column. Ready for Test in the Test column is an example that we have used before.

In the figure at right, you can see a WIP limit of 4 for the Development column. The column is then split into two sections: Doing and Done. The developers are working on one item and have three items completed, which keeps them at their WIP limit.

Another way of visualizing this queue could be to have a Ready to Test queue column in the Test column instead. That would then count against the WIP limit of the testing step.

How you visualize this on your team depends on what you want to achieve: that is, on who should "own" the tickets that wait to be tested. Does it help the team if the developers get the signal in their area, or is it more useful for the testers to count the items in the queue against their WIP limit? The choice is something that needs to be discussed with the team, but the practical function of the queue column is the same in either case: items stuck there will stall and hinder the flow, and people can't pull new work into columns before the queue. With this setup, you can easily see which items are done and which items the developers are still working on.

Finally, if you remember, back in section 6.4.1 we showed another way of doing this, where the queue column is a column by itself with its own WIP limit, as shown at right. In this case, the column has a WIP limit of its own, and it's not counted against anyone's limit. Maybe this is another technique that can help your team. The limit doesn't "steal" capacity from "your" column, but, again, the function of the queue is the same.

That way of visualizing the queue prevents the bottleneck that the single tester has become. A buffer is built before him to make sure he doesn't get flooded and yet always has work to do, which he can pick from the buffer (the testing queue) in front of him.

There are times when a queue should be counted against the WIP limit or even *is* the WIP limit itself (as in section 6.4.1 with the standalone queue column, for example). At other times, the distinction made between a queue and an *execution column* is a way to visualize detailed steps.

The answer to this section's question, "Should we count queues against the WIP limit?" is also, "It depends." For example, let's say you have noticed that testing is a bottleneck.[4] A queue might be a great way to ensure that the tester always has work that is ready to test. A WIP limit on the queue helps you make sure the queue doesn't get too long. With a WIP limit in place, you won't be able to flood the queue with work without breaking the WIP limit. When you see a queue filled to its WIP limit, it's time to discuss how to clear the blockage that is building up.

6.7 Exercise: WIP it, WIP it real good

The time has come for you to start discussing WIP limits. Again, this should be a team effort. Remember that there's no optimal WIP limit for your team; it's a tool that you can use to help you improve your work.

If you don't have an obvious WIP limit that you can come up with, first discuss the points in sections 6.3, 6.4, and 6.5. Here are some questions you can focus on:

- Should you have a single WIP limit for the complete board? Why would that be good for you?
- Can you start by limiting work in some columns? Which ones? Why?
- If you limit work per person, what kind of behavior would that drive or give you?
- Would swim lanes with WIP limits per lane help you in your situation?

If you don't know how to answer these questions, you should try something that seems appropriate, pay attention to what happens, and learn from that. When you come up with a good strategy and a number, start to discuss how this policy should be treated in your daily work:

- What kind of behavior are you encouraging by the way you've set up your limit?
- What should you do when you end up in a situation in which you're breaking the WIP limit?
- Should you count blocked/queued items against the limit?

As always, strive to start simple and make your approach more advanced as you see the need.

6.8 Summary

In this chapter we talked about finding and visualizing good WIP limits:

- There's no one right WIP limit for you and your team.
- Limiting WIP isn't the goal; improving flow is. WIP limits are merely a tool that helps find problems that hinder a better flow.

---

[4] Discovering and managing bottlenecks deserves a complete book on its own. But briefly, you might have a bottleneck if you see work accumulated before the bottleneck and if steps after the bottleneck are starved for work.

- A lower WIP limit will move your work faster and also bring problems to your attention more quickly. You want a low WIP limit, but not too low.
- When setting out to find a WIP limit, start simple—maybe as simple as the slogan "Stop starting, start finishing."
- You can limit the WIP for the whole team/workflow:
  - This approach can help you improve collaboration.
  - It helps you keep focus on finishing work items before taking on new ones.
- You can limit WIP based on column:
  - This puts focus on flowing items through the workflow.
  - It can help to manage bottlenecks.
  - Maybe you already have a hunch about what you need to improve and can start limiting WIP for that column.
  - Work can also be limited by estimated size (story points, for example).
- You can limit WIP based on people:
  - Limiting the number of avatars that can be in play is one way to easily accomplish this.
  - Using swim lanes is another.
  - This can help you prevent too much multitasking and people being involved in every item on the board.
- Most teams have a WIP limit on the work-item level, not the task level.

WIP limits are ways to improve the flow of your workflow, but what is that? It's one of the main concepts of Lean that we haven't yet talked about. And it's the topic of the next chapter.

7 Managing flow

This chapter covers

- What continuous flow is and why you want it
- Eliminating waste to achieve flow
- Managing flow with kanban
- Using daily standups to help the work flow
- Choosing what to work on next
- Managing bottlenecks using the Theory of Constraints

Flow, or rather *one-piece continuous flow*, has been the cornerstone in Toyota's[1] production vision for decades. A one-piece continuous flow is a system in which each part of work that creates value for the customer moves from one value-adding step in the process directly to the next, and so on until it reaches the customer, without any waiting time or batching between those steps. Instead of building up inventories *just in case*, things are produced only when needed, *just in time*—at the right place and in the right quantity: no more, no less.

[1] Toyota is the company that pioneered the Toyota Production System (TPS), which Lean is based on.

This continuous flow turns every process into a tightly linked chain in which everything is connected. There is nowhere for a problem to hide, no inventory of other work or products to work on if something stops or breaks; so when things break, you immediately know what's happened, and you're forced to solve the problem together. It forces people to think, and through this they become better team members and people.

In this chapter, we'll take a closer look at the benefits of the flow approach to organizing your work. You'll learn about waste elimination and cycle time, but also how to actually manage the flow by keeping the work moving and by using models such as the Theory of Constraints to improve your process. We'll take a look at some common practices that can help you focus and improve the flow in your process, such as reducing waiting time, removing blockers, and using cross-functional teams. There are some practices that many teams use that can further help you focus on flow, such as daily standups and policies around what to work on next; we'll check into those as well.

But let's start at the beginning and see why flow is something that's worth striving for and focusing your attention on.

7.1 Why flow?

Toyota is by no means the only, or even the first, company to chase the continuous-flow ideal. People and companies have been striving toward this vision for centuries. And why wouldn't they? If one-piece continuous flow is achieved, you have no delays, no queues, no batches, no inventory, no waiting. You have no over-production; you only deliver what is actually requested and needed by the customer, and you deliver it immediately when it's needed.

You've seen in previous chapters that this gives you flexibility and responsiveness, better risk management, faster feedback leading to improved quality (building the right thing and building it right), increased predictability leading to increased trust, fewer expedite requests, and faster continuous delivery of value.

As if that isn't enough, flow also exposes improvement opportunities and provides you with a vision for your improvement efforts: faster flow.

What can you do to get a faster flow, then? Let's look at a strategy that has helped Toyota for a long time: eliminating waste.

7.1.1 Eliminating waste

Toyota has spent more time perfecting, and has come closer to the vision of, one-piece continuous flow than any other company. An important part of that journey has been a focus on eliminating waste.

> *All we are doing is looking at the time line from the moment the customer gives us an order to the point when we collect the cash. And we are reducing that time line by removing the non-value-added wastes.*
>
> —Taiichi Ohno[2]

Another way of expressing this is to ask, "What's stopping the work from flowing?" Applying this perspective, you examine your processes from the customer's point of view. What does the customer want from this process? The customer can be the end customer or the internal customer in the next phase of production. What the customer wants has value. Everything else is waste. Some steps in a process add value, others don't. This is true for all processes.

---

[2] Taiichi Ohno, *Toyota Production System: Beyond Large-Scale Production* (Productivity Press, 1988, http://amzn.com/0915299143), p. ix.

Early on, Toyota identified seven categories of waste that applied to manufacturing; and later the company applied the same thinking to other areas, such as product development. Different industries have since then made similar categories of waste for their particular contexts. Mary and Tom Poppendieck did this for software development through their seminal works *Lean Software Development: An Agile Toolkit* (Addison-Wesley Professional, 2003) and *Implementing Lean Software Development: From Concept to Cash* (Addison-Wesley Professional, 2006).

7.1.2 The seven wastes of software development

Let's take a closer look at the seven different kinds of wastes that Mary and Tom Poppendieck have identified:

- *Partially done work*—Work that isn't completely done is in reality just work in process. It lies around waiting for you to complete it and adds to your WIP. See chapter 5 for more on this.
- *Extra features*—Taiichi Ohno famously said, "There's no greater waste than overproduction." A lot of the software being produced in the world isn't really used or valued by the customer. According to the famous CHAOS report performed by The Standish Group in the early 2000s, 45% of the features of software applications were never used. This suggests that a lot of waste could be avoided with better understanding of what the customer needs: that is, building the right thing. On an individual level, if you've ever thought "This may come in handy" or "Maybe they want this to be configurable," you know what we mean.
- *Relearning*—Software development is, to a great extent, learning. Failing to remember mistakes you've made before and having to redo them (and relearn the solution) is a great waste. This can happen both in teams and for individuals.
- *Handoffs*—When you hand work from one person to another, a lot of extra work is created in order to convey necessary information to the next person. Even with that extra work, a lot of information will be lost in the handoff.
- *Delays*—Delays create extra work, remember? No? Go read section 5.2.2, "Delay causes extra work," without delay.
- *Task switching*—We talked earlier about context switching (see chapter 5) and the wasteful effect it can have on your focus and capacity.
- *Defects*—Defects are work that comes back to you because you did something wrong the first time around. Not only does this create extra work, but typically that kind of work comes at a bad time, slowing down the things you're working on right now. See section 5.2.5, "Lower quality."

A WORD FROM THE COACH Some people in the kanban community think there has been an unhealthy obsession with waste within Lean software development and that waste is a red herring. According to them, you should instead be focusing on reducing time to delivery and risk management; waste will be identified and removed as a part of this process. We're not sure we see the conflict, but you should of course avoid unhealthy obsessions and heavily faith-based approaches in general. Part of the confusion comes when people look to see if certain actions are waste.

For example, is a daily standup meeting to coordinate team activities adding value, or is it waste? If it's a value-adding activity, why don't you do more of it? Why not just meet all day long? The answer is that the activity in itself isn't a value-add or waste; it's the return of time invested (ROTI) to help you improve your understanding or deliver customer value that determines if it's waste or not.

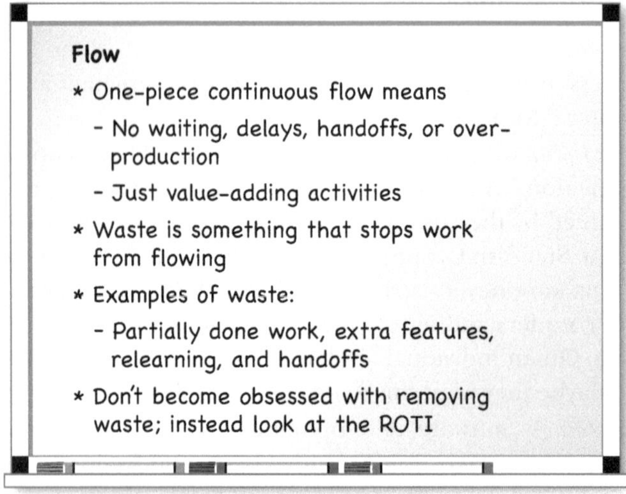

Eliminating waste and limiting WIP are different ways of achieving flow. But how do you apply these principles in practice to help the work to flow?

7.2 Helping the work to flow

One of the core practices of kanban is to manage the flow of work through each state in the workflow. This means monitoring and measuring how the work flows, but also keeping the work moving. You can take several different approaches to help the work to flow.

7.2.1 Limiting work in process

Limiting WIP is of course an essential practice when it comes to keeping the work moving. The fewer things in process, the faster the work will flow and the more improvement opportunities you'll discover. You might remember Little's law, which states that the more WIP you have, the longer the lead time for each item is. You can read much more about this in chapter 5.

Flow vs. resource utilization

Limiting your WIP gives you better flow. But is that what you want? Optimizing for flow is a strategy decision. That decision is a trade-off; to achieve better flow, you might end up with people sitting idle from time to time. Is that acceptable in order to get better flow through your process?

There are types of work and situations for which the opposite is true: you strive to use your *resources* optimally instead. One example is a mill for aluminum. That kind of equipment operates at extreme heat and takes a long time to heat up. It's expensive to turn off the mill. You want the melting furnace to be running all the time, and you want to have a lot of material ready for the furnace to handle (lots of WIP). You might even want it running when no customers are waiting for the aluminum. You're optimizing for resource utilization.

In the other case, optimizing for flow, an example is the fire department. They have a lot of slack (waiting, preparing, and training) in order to be ready to go immediately and put out a fire when it happens. We, as a society, accept that and are paying firefighters to sit idle, because we don't want them busy when we call and ask them to put out a fire. To optimize for flow, we're accepting the fact that they're not busy all the time. That kind of behavior is typically found in high-risk environments.

Optimizing for flow over resource utilization is a strategy decision, but by focusing on flow efficiency you can reduce a lot of superfluous work and waste and actually improve resource efficiency too. In the book *This Is Lean: Resolving the Efficiency Paradox* (Rheologica, 2012), researchers Niklas Modig and Pär Åhlström define *Lean* as an operations strategy that aims to increase resource efficiency through focusing on increasing flow efficiency.

7.2.2 Reducing waiting time

Do you have work items sitting in the board's Done columns, waiting to be pulled to the next state? Are items sitting in states like Waiting to Deploy or Todo? It isn't unusual to see work spending more time waiting to be worked on than actually being worked on. How can this waiting time be reduced?

If you don't already have an explicit way of showing that work is done in a particular state and ready for the next, this should be your first step. This makes the waiting visible and signals to others that the work item is ready to be pulled. It also makes it easier to track and measure the amount of time spent in waiting. Collecting this data and analyzing it may give you insight into what can be improved. If you have a hard time convincing others that time is wasted in waiting, measuring it like this can serve as an eye opener.

Do you start the work from scratch, or is it started or prepared somewhere else (what we typically call *upstream* from the kanban board)? Maybe the work is sitting there, waiting for you to start it. Are you the last people to touch the work before it reaches the customer? In order to reduce waiting time, it's often necessary to go outside of your own workflow and your kanban board.

ENSURING THAT WORK IS READY

An excellent way to avoid waiting is to take steps to make sure the work is always ready for the next state. This can be done by planning and breaking work down to minimize dependencies, maybe having external people or resources prepared and standing by so that you don't get blocked, or designing the work for collaboration so that team members who have finished something can easily chip in on what you're doing instead of waiting or pulling new work.

Being clear on the expected outcome and making sure it's communicated clearly to everyone before work starts go a long way toward avoiding misunderstandings and confusion that result in delays and waiting.

> **Specification by example**
>
> One of the best ways to make sure you understand each other is to practice specification by example.[a] This means you write your specification in the form of acceptance criteria or concrete examples (real numbers and real data used) of how a feature will be used. The feature will be complete when the example is fulfilled: nothing more, nothing less.

a. Read more in *Specification by Example: How Successful Teams Deliver the Right Software*, by Gojko Adzic (Manning, 2011, www.manning.com/adzic/).

Sometimes it actually makes sense to increase the amount of WIP in a queue, particularly in front of a bottleneck (see section 7.5.1), in order to avoid unnecessary waiting.

MAKING THE WORK ITEMS SMALLER AND SIMILARLY SIZED

Another way of designing and preparing work to reduce waiting is to make the work items smaller and similarly sized. Smaller work items reduce lead times and lower the amount of WIP. Large work items are often harder to estimate and sometimes hide issues that will be visible once you start breaking them down. Instead of creating a full use case (like buying books, for example) you could try user stories (such as put book into basket, fill out checkout information, and perform checkout).

If you can make the work items more similar in size, you'll get a more even flow and increased predictability, which in turn can help you build trust and avoid needing to expedite "special requests." In practice it also removes the cost part of the equation because all work now is of the same cost, at least time-wise.

A great way of reducing waiting is of course to limit WIP: the lower the WIP, the faster you'll be able to pull work items to the next state. A lot of waiting is caused by being blocked, a kind of waiting that demands a section of its own.

7.2.3 Removing blockers

Blockers belong to a special class of waiting. They're things that block you but that are outside of your immediate control, such as third-party dependencies, waiting for external code reviews, or waiting for information. In our experience, blockers like these are often accepted as the natural order of things as something "we can't do anything about," but more often than not the opposite turns out to be true.

Never be blocked—the prime directive of agile development

Robert C. Martin, a.k.a. Uncle Bob, the guy who called the meeting that produced the Agile Manifesto, claims that to *never be blocked* is the prime directive for any agile developer:[a]

> *Like a good pool player who always makes sure the shot he is taking sets up the next shot he expects to take, every step a good agile developer takes enables the next step. A good agile developer never takes a step that stops his progress, or the progress of others.*

The main idea is that all the areas that interface with other systems should be handled in such a way that you can continue with your work even though the other parties aren't done with theirs. For coding, for example, this could mean creating an interface to code against for external systems. If the other parties don't deliver on time, you can always supply your own implementation—a *stub* or *fake* as it's called—and continue to work until the real implementation is completed.

But the prime directive isn't just for the individual developer:

> *The prime directive extends to all levels of the team and organization. Never being blocked means you set up your development environment such that blockages don't happen.... If the core group is building a reusable framework for us, and we need some function that isn't ready yet, we'll write it ourselves and use the core team's function later, when (and if) it arrives. If the enterprise architecture supports our needs in such a convoluted and obtuse way that we'll have to spend days just understanding, then we'll avoid the enterprise architecture and get the features working in a simpler way. We won't be blocked.*

For other types of work, you can make sure you do all the work you can to not end up waiting for others.

a. "The Prime Directive of Agile Development," http://mng.bz/NT5s.

That you've filed a ticket in the support system or sent an email to someone doesn't mean you've done what you can to not be blocked. Could you give them a call, or maybe even walk up to them and talk to them? Did you explain how this is affecting you and how it would help your work advance if you could get assistance? Is there someone else who could solve the problem for you? Maybe there's a workaround you can live with for now. Try to be creative and find a way to not be blocked.

If you've tried everything and still find yourself blocked, avoid starting new work. Picking up new work will increase your WIP and result in a slowdown of all your other work, as you'll recall from chapter 5. Maybe there is something that you can help finish while you wait to be unblocked. Are there any bottlenecks or other problems in your workflow that you can help to resolve? More on this in section 7.5.1.

You can save some tasks that are useful to do when you're blocked. Some teams even create special classes of services for this (see chapter 8): that is, special work that you as a team see as important, but that may not be immediately important to other stakeholders. It could be things like upgrading a build server or automating some manual work—things that will improve your future quality and speed. This kind of work can be picked up when you're blocked and dropped quickly as the blocker is cleared.

A blocker is also an opportunity to learn how you can improve your work. What caused the blocker? Is there anything you could have done to foresee and work around it that you can apply to future situations? Can blockers be avoided completely if you change how you work? Or if someone else changes how they work? Some teams create the habit of always applying root-cause analysis to every blocker or issue that stops the flow, to learn and improve from the root cause of the problem (read more about root-cause analysis in chapter 10).

TRACKING BLOCKERS

Tracking blockers and how they affect you is often a good start for reducing them. If you put start and end dates on the blockers, or put a dot on their stickies for every day they sit there, you can see how much of a work item's total cycle time is spent being blocked, just as we suggested with waiting time in the previous section. Use this data to understand how blockers affect you and what you can do about it. The data can also be useful to explain to the people blocking you how it would help you if you were unblocked.

Tracking how the number of blockers varies and what the average time to remove them is can also drive improvement. For more on tracking blockers, see section 11.1.3.

SWARMING

A behavior that emerges in many kanban teams is what has been referred to as *swarming*. The focus on limiting WIP and helping the work flow leads the team to act together when a WIP limit is reached, when a difficult blocker arises, or when a work item is too big, too late, or too complex to be handled by a single person or a few team members. People swarm around the issue to resolve it more quickly[3] and to get back to the normal flow.

Some teams make this an explicit policy when they get blocked, or even when they find a defect. Every time they encounter a blocker or a defect, everyone swarms in to remove it. Swarming can also be a policy assigned to a specific class of service (see chapter 8).

Swarming can also be used to describe the general behavior of working outside your specialization to help high-risk or high-value work get done faster or to reduce the total amount of WIP, a behavior held in high regard by many kanban teams.

---

[3] Of course, sometimes more hands can slow you down rather than help you. The key here is that people are available to help you, like an "all hands on deck" situation. Maybe you don't need everyone to solve the problem, but for starters everyone is there to help analyze the issue and propose a solution. Implementing the solution might engage only a few people.

7.2.4 Avoiding rework

Sometimes a defect will escape from one state of the workflow, only to be found in a later one. This causes the work item to move backward in the workflow, which increases the cycle time both for that item and for other work items, because it increases the amount of WIP. Avoiding rework can have a big effect on flow and cycle time.

It's no coincidence that one of the key principles of Lean software development[4] is to *build quality in from the start.* A good way to accomplish this is to invest in technical practices such as pair programming, test-driven development, continuous integration, and test automation.[5]

Another important practice for building quality in is to minimize the time between introducing and fixing a defect. If the code is tested as soon as it's developed, and any defects are fixed immediately after they're found, you'll save time logging defects and won't have to spend so much time figuring out where they were introduced. This is of course easier the fewer things you work on at the same time and the smaller they are: that is, if the amount of WIP is low.

VALUE DEMAND AND FAILURE DEMAND

Defects aren't the only things that cause rework. John Seddon has introduced the concept of *failure demand* to describe "demand on a system caused by failure to do something or do something right for the customer."

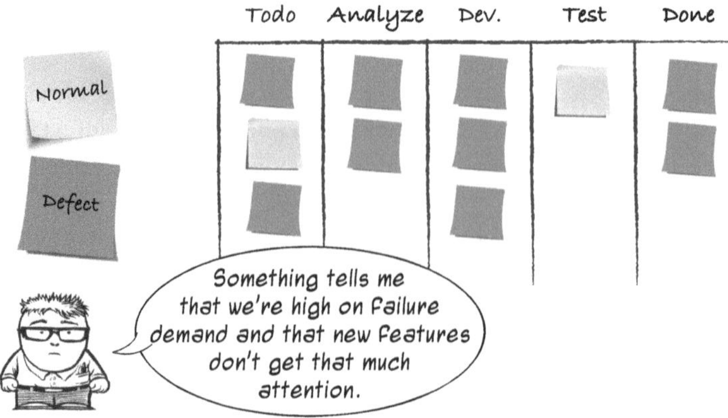

[4] Coined by Mary and Tom Poppendieck.

[5] More on this in the excellent pair of books *Clean Code: A Handbook of Agile Software Craftsmanship* (Prentice Hall, 2008, http://amzn.com/0132350882) and *The Clean Coder: A Code of Conduct for Professional Programmers* (Prentice Hall, 2011, http://amzn.com/0137081073) by Robert C. Martin.

All requests coming in to your workflow that aren't requests for new things, but rather requests generated because something isn't working the way it was expected to, because something is too difficult to understand, because something is missing, and so on, fall into the failure demand category. Examples in software development are faulty design that doesn't take user experience into account, bad requirements generated without real user involvement or feedback, and rework because of misunderstandings and miscommunication.

You don't gain much by making failure demand flow faster; instead you want to eliminate as much failure demand as possible to make room for more value demand, which is what you're (hopefully!) here to produce. Finding out what the customer needs and values and delivering just that also builds quality in.

Failure demand in call centers

In the book *Freedom from Command and Control: A Better Way to Make the Work Work* (Vanguard Consulting Ltd., 2003, http://amzn.com/0954618300), John Seddon tells the story of a call center for which about 40% of calls were questions about invoices.

The *failure* to create a clear and understandable invoice caused a lot of *demand* on the system that easily could be avoided. And sure enough—when the company changed the layout and structure of the invoice, the failure demand went down, and the call center got a lot fewer calls in total.

A WORD FROM THE COACH One simple and useful practice is to start tracking and visualizing the failure demand. This can be done by putting a little red dot on each sticky that represents failure demand as it enters the board. When it exits the board, you can do a root-cause analysis (see chapter 10) on how to avoid that in the future.

7.2.5 *Cross-functional teams*

A *cross-functional team* is a team with different functional specialties or multidisciplinary skills. When a team has all the skills and resources needed to fulfill the requests put to it, it's said to be truly cross-functional. This means it's less dependent on handoffs with other teams and less likely to be waiting for others or to be blocked. If, for example, a product owner or business analyst is on the team, what to build can be decided just in time instead of work not being ready or work to be done piling up; if the team is skilled in both coding and testing, code won't have to be handed over to someone else to be tested.

Striving to make teams cross-functional helps reduce waiting, makes avoiding and removing blockers easier, and can help avoid rework. It's also likely to reduce WIP. In other words, it's a great way to make work flow faster.

The world's greatest cross-functional team

When we think about cross-functional teams, one in particular stands out: The A-Team!

This has to be the best cross-functional team ever assembled. They have all the skills for any job:

- The leader and the brains of any operation: Colonel John "Hannibal" Smith
- Mr. Good Looking: Lieutenant Templeton "Face" Peck
- The muscle: Bosco "B.A." Baracus
- And finally, what every good team needs: a mad helicopter pilot, Captain "Howlin' Mad" Murdock

Although they're all specialists in their own fields, they always end up working together to solve the tasks at hand.

FEATURE TEAMS VS. COMPONENT TEAMS

A common way to organize a cross-functional team is to make it responsible for a feature. Some refer to this as a *feature team.* The team takes responsibility for a certain feature from start to finish. To complete a feature, the team might need to do a vertical slice of the complete system, touching all the parts of the system and, therefore, needing to have a mix of competencies within the team in order to be able to complete the feature.

Consider, as a contrast, a *component team* that creates just the data-access layer or just the user-interface layer. When structuring teams like this, you run the risk of having teams waiting for each other to be able to complete features. A complete feature might involve several teams: the UI team, the business-logic team, and the data-layer team. If any of them are late, the complete feature is delayed. Information is lost, and miscommunication happens in handoffs between teams. Hence it's a greater risk to the overall schedule and quality of the result.

A WORD FROM THE COACH One giant project organization map that Marcus briefly looked at had about 250 people layered in a big five-level-deep hierarchical map. The teams at the lowest level were called things like Integration, Data Access, UI Mobile, and so on. From this it was easy to conclude that the project (which was running well into the second year already) was set up in a way that no one could be *done* until *all* the teams were done. The slowest team was dictating the speed for the whole project—just by virtue of the project's organization.

Organizing your teams by feature sits well with a kanban flow and can even be visualized on a common board as separate swim lanes.

7.2.6 SLA or lead-time target

Some teams find that their service-level agreements (SLAs) give them a clear target to strive toward, and other teams like to set a target themselves—for example, average lead time (or why not a little less?)—to track their progress against. This helps foster a mindset that time is of the essence, to flow the work faster. It can also give you the benefits of timeboxing.

Timeboxing is a simple technique that is used in many agile software development methods to manage risk and to focus on doing the things that matter most first. These methods often use iterations of a set length (for example, two weeks) to plan and review work. When the size of the team and the time allotted are both fixed, scope needs to be flexible, and you have to prioritize and build the most important things first. See chapter 9 for more on using iterations with kanban.

Using a timebox also makes you aware of how much time you're spending on a task and helps you avoid *gold plating*: continuing to work on a task past the point where the extra effort is worth the value it adds.

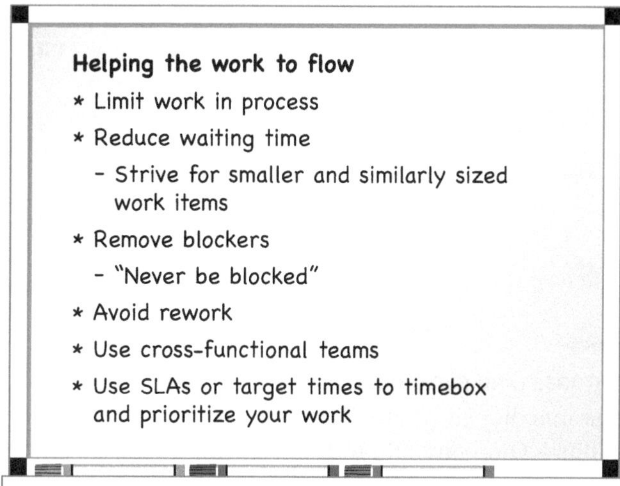

7.3 Daily standup

One way to help the work to flow is to talk about, and do something about, the problems that hinder the work to flow—daily, or even more often. The daily standup meeting (a.k.a. morning meeting, daily, morning call, or standup) was made popular in the software development community in the early agile years with methods such as Scrum and XP. Scrum has the daily standup as a core meeting that's called Daily Scrum. We think that a daily standup meeting is a great tool to get everyone in the team up to date with the current situation in the team and the status of your work.

Just because the agile methods we mentioned made this practice popular doesn't mean it's only when using those methods that a daily standup can prove useful. Many teams use some sort of daily standup even when not using agile methods. It's one of those practices that just seems to make sense to everyone. Together with visualizing your workflow on a board, it's probably the practice that many teams get the most immediate effect from when they start using it.

7.3.1 Common good practices around standups

Running a daily standup doesn't take much; running a *good* daily standup is harder. But in a great standup, you can help the work to flow more smoothly and handle things like blockers and other problems that hinder flow. There are a few general tips on how to succeed with standups, and in this section we check out a few of them.

A STANDUP IS SHORT

Keep the meeting short; 5–15 minutes seems to be the norm. A short timeboxed meeting pushes you into talking about what is important and makes you think about what can be discussed elsewhere. The exact time limit isn't what's important; keeping the meeting focused and the energy up is.

The "standup" in standup meetings is there for this reason. You stand up to keep the meeting short and energized rather than yet another status report in the conference room. Stand next to your visualized workflow (your board) to be able to see and talk about your items (more on this later).

A STANDUP STARTS (AND ENDS) ON TIME

Keeping the meeting short also means it needs to start on time. There are all kinds of ways to try to get people to be on time,[6] but for most teams this doesn't seem to be a problem as long as the things that are discussed in the meeting are important and engaging.

How you get the meeting to start on time will probably vary in different organizations. For some teams, just deciding on a time is all that's needed; but others might need a booking in the

[6] Including fines, people standing silently to wait for latecomers, and other things that feel pretty awkward when you think about it. We're most likely dealing with adults; why not talk about the pros and cons of coming on time and pick a time that suits everyone, instead?

calendar system to make sure the time slot isn't taken for other meetings.

A STANDUP IS FOCUSED

Make sure you talk about things that are important for the team attending the meeting. If a discussion starts to drag and it's only engaging two people, kindly ask them to continue after the daily standup.

There's no point in having a person stand around waiting for others to talk about things that aren't interesting. Make sure your precious time together is well invested for everyone who comes to the meeting.

A STANDUP IS REGULAR

Conduct the standup at the *same time* and the *same place* every day. This creates a rhythm to the day and will soon be second nature to the team.

Many teams start their days with a daily standup (it's often referred to as a *morning meeting*) because it gives a good and focused start to the day, but that's not mandatory. Run the standup at a time that feels appropriate for all team members.

We think starting the day by getting together and checking what's up is great, but you might disagree. Ask the team.

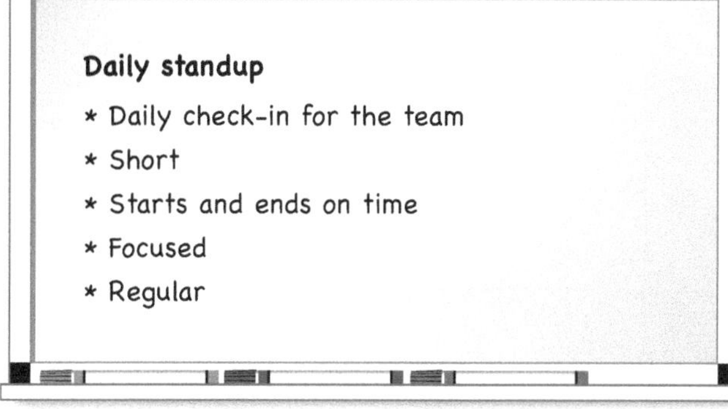

7.3.2 Kanban practices around daily standups

As kanban teams have started to practice standups, a few practices or ideas have emerged that differ from how standups traditionally have been done.

FOCUS ON THE BATON—NOT THE RUNNERS

The first thing that often differentiates a daily standup in a kanban team from other standup meetings is that a kanban team tends to focus on the *work* on the board rather than on the individual people in the team.

This can be contrasted with focusing on each person in the team, as in the Scrum practice of letting each person answer "the three questions":

- What did you do yesterday?
- What are you going to do today?
- Do you have any impediments that hinder you from doing that?

This is a good practice that makes everyone talk at the meeting, and you get a great status overview for each person in the team. But you might miss the opportunity to talk about the work at hand. Maybe there's one item that's blocked, and it could be worth spending the entire meeting talking about how to clear it up. Or maybe nothing is blocked, and work is flowing along as expected; then you can close the meeting early and not drag it out more than needed.

Finally and maybe most importantly, the focus isn't on what individual people have or haven't done but rather on whether there are any problems in the flow, in your process, or with individual work items. It helps you understand that you're a team whose members help each other get the work done together.

WALK THE BOARD

Kanban teams often enumerate their work from right to left, starting from the Done column and moving upstream. This is to emphasize the *pull principle*: you're pulling work to you, pulling features into production, not pushing work over to the next state.

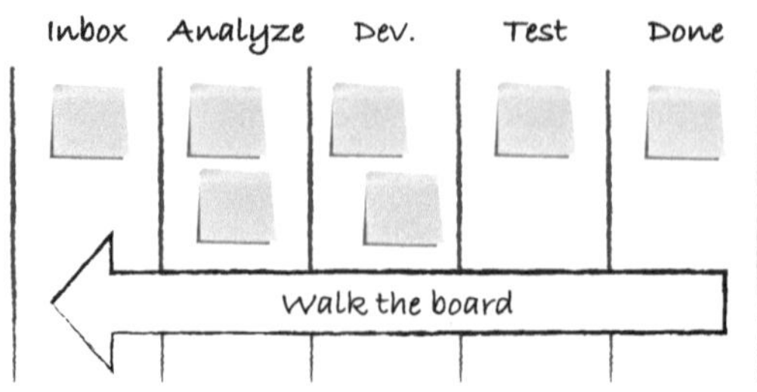

We make sure to honor the good practices around standup meetings and hence keep to our timebox of 15 minutes, for example. This means we might not be able to run through all the work items on the board. By enumerating the work on the board from right to left, this means we might not have time to talk about the far left. This might be OK because that work is also the furthest from being done.

To further increase the focus on progressing the work toward Done, you can ask two questions for each work item:

1 What do we need to do to move the work item closer to done?
2 Who is going to do it?

If you end up missing part of the board often (the leftmost columns when working from right to left, for example), due to the timebox, you might look into another strategy, such as focusing on things that don't follow your policies, or things that smell, for example.

FOCUSING ON SMELLS

Many of the visualizations we have talked about in the book help you see when work isn't behaving as expected, is blocked, or breaks some of your policies. These indicators and visualizations can help you see the work items that are not following your policies—the *smells* (see the sidebar "Process smells" in chapter 4)—on the board.

Here's the Kanbaneros board at one daily standup. It has lots of things that don't follow the visual, explicit policies for the team. Can you spot them all?

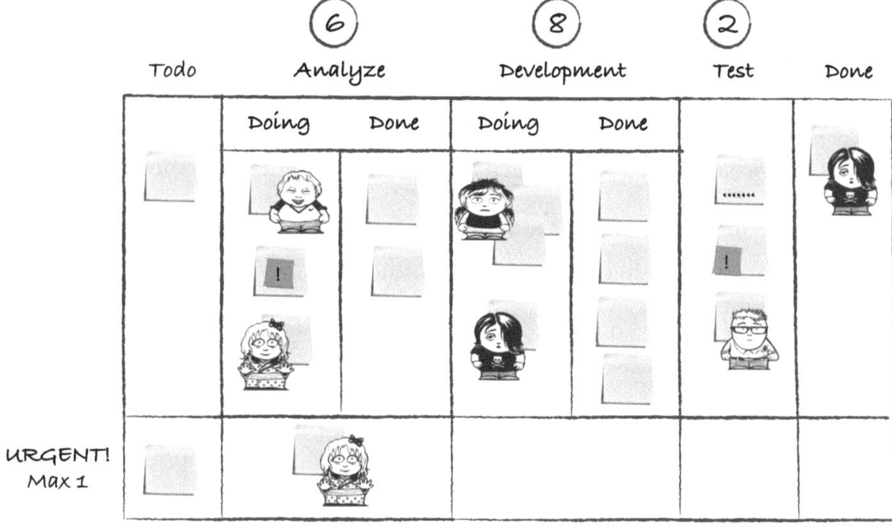

Here are the things that the team saw and talked about in their daily standup:

- We have two items in the Urgent lane. Didn't our policy state that there could be only one in there? What should we do about the second item? Does that urgent item have our full attention?

- In the Done column, Eric is still working on work that is completed. Unless he is still working in a parallel universe, we probably need to talk about that. Is that work done? If not, what kind of work is taking place, and should the sticky be moved? Maybe we're missing a column like Deploying.
- In the Test column, we have *exceeded our WIP limit* of two, because we have three items in the column. That might be OK, but in this case the team didn't notice that it happened. Breaking the WIP limit should at least trigger a discussion: Could Adam help out somewhere else instead of pulling new work? Are we ready to pay the toll of higher WIP? Does this happen a lot? Do we need to change the way we work or maybe change the limit?
- In the Test column, there's work that has been waiting a long time that no one is working on. This is indicated with dots, one for each day in the Test column. Why is Adam testing other stuff? Is there a blocker we should escalate?
- Take a look at all that work that is ready for test, in the Development/Done column. There's a bottleneck building up before Test. Maybe it's better that the developers stop working to put more stuff into that queue and start helping Adam to test instead. Creating a big pile of untested work doesn't make the untested work any more complete.
- Daphne is *hoarding* a lot of items in the Development column. Is that OK? Why is she doing that? Will that be a problem? Does she need help?
- In the Analyze column, there's some sort of Important *indicator* on the only work item that no one is working on. Why? Is that item important, then? Who will start looking into that? What happens with the other work in that column?

You probably found more as well (we've left a few for you to discover), but we hope that we've shown that by focusing on the things that deviate from your normal flow, you can spend the daily standup time on the work items that need your attention. The use of visualizations and explicit policies helps you to find these things pretty easily.

7.3.3 Get the most out of your standup

Here are some other things worth considering if you want to get the most out of a daily standup.

QUESTION OF CONSCIENCE

"Is there anything you're working on that isn't on the board?" This is a great question to ask each other during a standup meeting. It's quite easy to have a "little work on the side" that you need to do. This not only takes time from what you were supposed to do, but also has a tendency to become a habit, which in

the long run means the board becomes less relevant. Before long you might end up with people having private backlogs and maybe even a private board with their on-the-side tasks. Try to make the board reflect reality as far as possible.

WORKING ON THE WRONG THING

"Are we working on the most important things right now? How do we know that? Is the prioritization clear?" We often hear of teams working hard on items that might not be the things that are giving the most value right now. This of course has to be balanced with long-term work such as paying off technical debt. One way to handle this is with different classes of service (see chapter 8).

If you start hearing people say that they don't know what to do next or they feel that they're working on the wrong things, you might have to revisit the policies around your prioritization. This could be a trigger to make them more explicit; can the prioritization policies be visualized, or can they be clearer?

NOT UNDERSTANDING THE WORK

As the board evolves, a lot of policies and enhancements are added to the board with the best of intentions. But after a while, these policies can be hard to understand and see, even for people in the team. For outsiders, the rules to which the work adheres can be difficult to follow.

Try to always find simpler ways to describe your work. Remember that your visualization can also inform others around you who might pass by your board. Would an outsider understand how this works? Do you?

SPONTANEOUS KAIZEN

Just focusing on smells, deviations, and problems on the board isn't useful, of course, if you don't try to do something about them. When the daily standup ends, you'll sometimes see some people linger around the board, forming groups and starting to talk about the work that you mentioned during the meeting. This has been called *spontaneous kaizen* by some, as in, spontaneous improvement meetings. The team is starting to discuss and improve their work.

This kind of behavior should be encouraged, and you can trigger discussions and conversations like this by postponing discussions under the standup until afterward.

When a couple of people start going off on a tangent during the standup, you could, for example, say

- "Can we meet right after this meeting and talk more?" (See the sidebar "Sticky questions" for one example.)
- "Let's find a solution for that work item right after this meeting. We'll do it here at the board."
- "Could you guys work out a better way to solve that problem after the meeting?"

Offer help, and encourage them to involve the people needed to clear out the problem or improve the situation if they want to.

Sticky questions

At Spotify in New York, one team came up with a great way to visualize that a question should be talked about more after the standup. The topic was written down on a small sticky and stuck onto the person who wanted to talk about it. She kept the sticky on her until the discussion was held, which usually took place directly after the meeting.

Another, more formalized way to create a constant improvement focus is to use the Kanban Kata[7] (see chapter 10) in the standups. By using the kata, you get help on how to approach the improvement work and a guide that helps you ask the right questions.

When the team has taken policies and ways of working and made them their own, you'll often find that the daily standups don't have many smells like the ones described in this section. The daily standups can then go by pretty quickly, or your focus can change to an improvement mindset, which you can see in section 10.3.

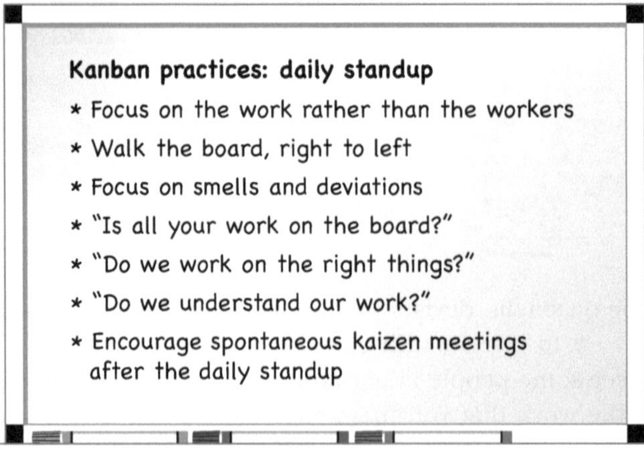

[7] Kanban Kata is a way to apply formal steps around doing improvement work to help you make small experiments that guide you toward a better future.

7.3.4 Scaling standups

The daily standup is, as we wrote at the outset of this section, a practice that is easy, often highly appreciated, and rewarding. This is the reason that many teams pick up this practice, even though they might not be doing XP, Scrum, or any named method at all.

A question we have encountered more than once is how to scale daily standups. That is, "We have more than one team working together on the same product or project, and we need a way to coordinate the group of teams as well. How have other teams used kanban to do that?"

WHY?

It's much more difficult to keep a big meeting with a lot of participants short, focused, and energized, especially if it happens daily. That is why the first question you should ask yourself is, "*Why* do we want to do a multiteam daily standup?" What is the reason for having these meetings? What kinds of problems do you solve with these meetings? What should you *not* talk about at these meetings?

Big Daily → Daily Sync → Release Sync

At one client, Marcus was brought in as they split a big team (about 40 people) into five smaller teams. The big team had met each morning, and hence it felt natural to meet not only in the smaller teams but also in a "Big Daily" with all the teams. All the teams had a lane on the bigger board with copies of their work items underway, often in a coarser form than on their own board.

(continued)

Pretty soon they realized that they had already talked about status in the smaller teams, so it felt strange to recap that at the Big Daily. Keeping the big board and the local team boards' statuses in sync became a hassle. They therefore decided to tweak the Big Daily into Daily Sync, in which they only talked about things that needed to be synced around more than one team. They also removed the swim lanes for the teams and just had them report orally about what they were up to.

After a few weeks of doing that, they realized that they mostly talked about deploying and releasing, and the meeting became Release Sync with a single focus: "What are we releasing today?" They created a simple board with just a Release queue to which each team brought their items to be released, and that was what they talked about. Most days that meeting was over in about two to three minutes.

We always ended the meeting with the question, "Anything else that all teams need to know?" to leave room for other information. More often than not there was nothing to inform everybody about, but when information needed to be shared with everyone, this meeting was a good opportunity to do so.

TIPS ON DOING MULTITEAM STANDUPS

Here are a few things to consider when you create a daily standup for more than one team (let's call it *big daily* for lack of a better term):

- Should the big daily be run before or after the team standups? If you run the big daily before the team dailies, you can send information to the teams, but you might miss out on the latest status from the teams. Running it afterward gives you the status of the teams, but you miss the opportunity to send information to the team daily standups.
- Who is attending the big daily meeting? You probably want at least one person from each team in your group in order to make the meeting interesting. That person needs to be able to make decisions if required (for example, if some extra work should be added to the team backlog). We suggest that you let anyone interested attend the meeting, but require at least one person from each team.
- What kind of visualization should this meeting have to support its decisions? Are you going to have a board for your big daily? What kind of information do you want to show there? What kind of questions, statuses, and progress do you want to show on the board? Whom are you creating the board for?
- Are you displaying the status of each team on the big daily board too? If you have a board for all the teams, how do you communicate the status of each team? Beware of putting too much detail on the big board, because that means duplicating information and that the teams have to keep their work synchronized over two boards. An aggregated status is probably better.

As you can see, there are a lot of things to consider when you set up a big daily meeting. But if you start out thinking about what you, as a group, want to get out of this meeting, you can often start narrowing it down and focusing on those questions. A big daily standup can be a great boost and information-sharing opportunity, but you have to balance it carefully, or you might run into some of the problems we've talked about in this section.

BOTTOM UP OR TOP DOWN?

The approach we've just described is suitable when you have teams that feel the need to synchronize their work to an aggregate board. But the reverse can also be true: you may have a big team that splits out into smaller teams (or *teamlets* as some companies call them) that need to synchronize their work.

You can use a coarse-grained board, without the details, and focus on the baton/work, using all of the good practices we've described around the daily standup. If there are small teams within the team that need to exchange detailed information and coordinate after that, they can have their own boards and/or standups where they focus on a smaller part of the workflow and their smaller tasks.

A good kanban board and the practices described here make it possible to scale a kanban daily beyond a small single team. And taking the practices a bit further (coarser-grained board, and so on) makes it scale a little more.

If you get everyone to meet often, you also foster collaboration that is needed in a bigger group. You get to know who works on what, who to talk to, who is waiting for you, and so on. This increases the likelihood of resolving blockers, minimizing waiting time, and sharing valuable information, because everyone is involved in the same workflow.

Just as with almost all practices, constantly asking yourself if this meeting is providing value for the time you put into it is one way of making sure that you don't fall into those traps. If not, find other ways to keep everyone synced among the teams; great team visualizations might be one way, frequent demos might be another. Make the tool work for you—not the other way around.

Scaling standups

* A recurring standup for more than one team
* Start with WHY?
  - What do you want to get out of this meeting?
  - Share team-to-team information, don't just report status again
* Consider having a board for the big daily as well

Let's leave the daily standup meeting for now and instead focus on a question that often arises in the meeting: "What should I do now?" Several of the kanban practices we have described so far can help you and your team to answer that question. Let's dive in and see how.

7.4 What should I be doing next?

If you want a fast and smooth flow of work, you don't want to be blocked by not knowing what to do next. A common question that comes up quite often around the board is what someone should be doing next. It's a fair question, of course, but also something that you as a team want to be able to answer yourselves. You don't want your flow to be slowed down by having to wait for someone else to tell you what to do next.

Many of the visualization techniques and our discussion of explicit policies in this book try to move you toward being more and more self-organized, to get a smoother flow in the process: for example, ordering the columns for prioritization, using classes of service with different colors, using blocked or urgent indicators, adding swim lanes for work that is to be expedited, and having WIP limits. All these small things help you answer the question "What should I be doing next?"

Let's look at a concrete example of these practices at work. Here's a situation that Adam, the tester, found himself in a couple of days ago:

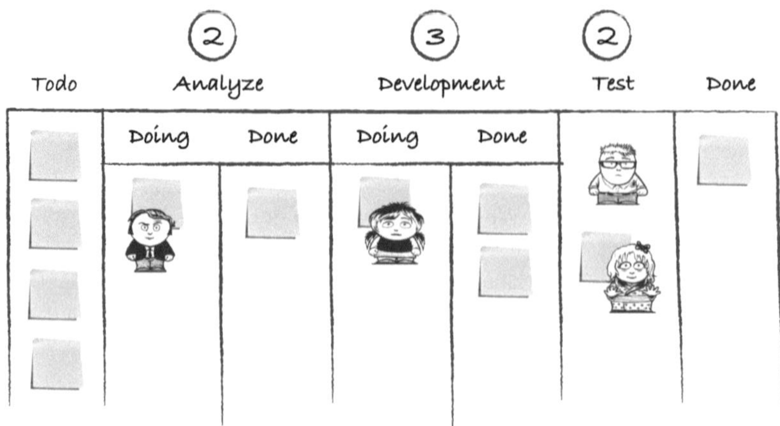

In order to keep the work flowing along, what is a good choice for Adam to do now?

First he should check whether there's any work going on in the Test column (his column) right now. To achieve a better flow, this should always be at the top of your mind: "Can I help finish work in progress?" You might remember the Kanbaneros' motto: "Stop starting, start finishing." Here's a situation where this is put into practice.

Adam can practice this opportunity right away because Beth is testing another item. He helps her to finish that item and thereby clears the Test column. Good for them.

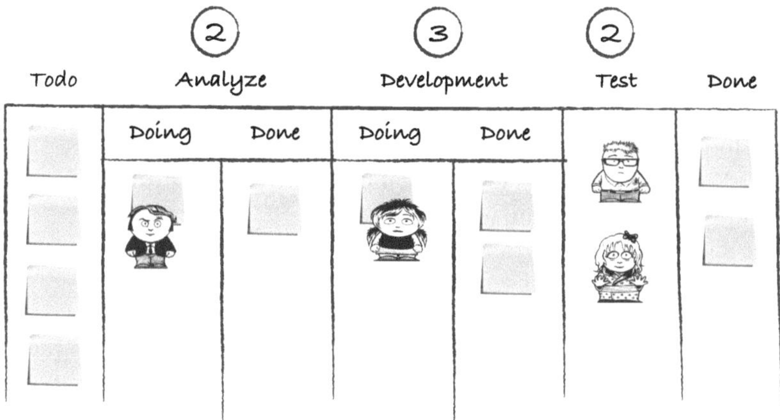

Now what? There's no more work in the Test column, but there are two items stacked up in the Development/Done queue. What should Adam (and Beth) do now? They could pull both of those items into testing. There's room for that, according to the WIP limit, so it seems like a good idea. Or maybe they want to take the top-priority item (at the top of the Development/Done column) first and work together to keep the WIP down and finish that faster. Which item they go after is up to the team and the policies the team has for how they work. In this case, Beth and Adam each take one item and finish it.

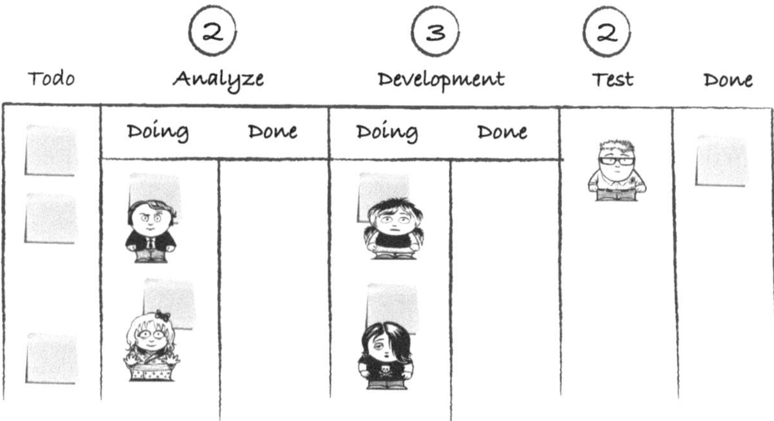

Next, consider the situation that happens a couple of days later. Adam is now the sole tester,[8] and he finds himself in a situation in which there's no other work to be worked on in his column. Not only that—there's no new work to pull in and start working on. What should Adam do now?

The first knee-jerk reflex might be to suggest that he help one of the developers. That would ensure that their items are completed and moved into the Development/ Done column, from which Adam could pick them up and start to test them. Sadly, Adam totally lacks the development skills needed for this particular work item, so he wouldn't be helpful writing code.[9] Not all people can do all tasks, no matter how much we want that to be the case.

So what should Adam do, then? If you look in the earlier columns on the board, you can see a little situation starting to build up in the form of a step that is starved for work (a bottleneck, if you will). It's in Analyze; can you see it?

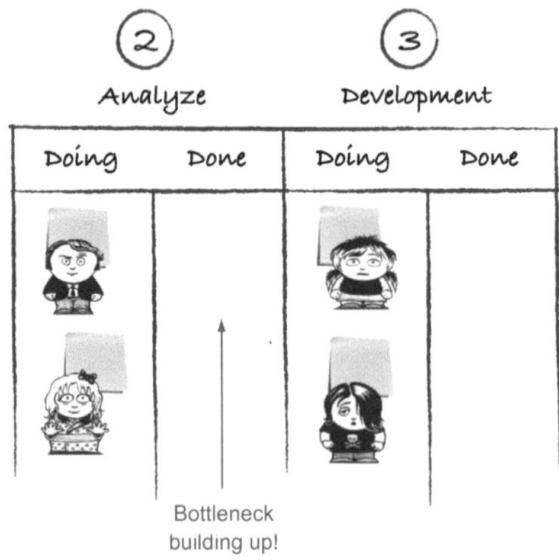

Both Frank and Beth are working on one item each, but nothing is finished. Not only that, but as the developers finish their work, they won't have any new work to pull because the Analyze/Done queue is empty. This is a bottleneck that needs your attention. Maybe Adam can help out there. In fact, a tester's view can be valuable in analyzing features. He goes over and asks Beth if he can help out, and together they finish the feature.

Let's say for the sake of argument that Adam couldn't (or wasn't allowed to) help out with analysis. Maybe those work items weren't suitable for sharing. What should he have done then? He should resist the urge to pull new work that increases WIP and instead try to find other interesting work, something that can be dropped when new work is available on the board: when new work is ready to test, for example. This kind of work can be one of those things that you've postponed for so long: getting that new test server upgraded, cleaning up the databases in the staging environment, or finally updating the documentation of the old API. It should *not,* however, be work that needs to go through the normal workflow that would increase WIP and slow down everything in the process.

This could be an excellent opportunity to work on improvements or invent or learn new things that help you move faster in the future. Yes, this is slack time when

8 Beth is first and foremost a business analyst, you know.

9 Let us be the first ones to object to that statement. A tester is often excellent to pair up with as you write code. It's a great way to produce high-quality code. This is just an example in which we allowed ourselves to make Adam impossible to work with in development. It's rarely the case in real life.

you're not producing value for your customer, but that is needed in order to be able to improve.

> *Without slack there cannot be improvements.*
>
> —Dr. Arne Roock (@arneroock)

SUMMING UP: WHAT SHOULD I BE WORKING ON NEXT?

Let's leave the example that we've been following for a while, and try to sum up how you could reason around what you should be working on next:[10]

1. Can you help finish work that is already in process? Do that.
2. Do you not have the skills needed for that? Look for bottlenecks or other things that slow down your flow, and help resolve them.
3. Do you not have the right skills to help resolve a bottleneck or remove a blocker? Pull new work into the system, as long as you don't exceed your WIP.
4. If you still find yourself without work, find something interesting that you think will help the team, and do that.[11]

A WORD FROM THE COACH These guidelines for what to work on next are rules of thumb that will help a team new to kanban and a flow focus to understand the principles. They aren't to be used as rules. You may have other policies in place that take precedence over these guidelines. Depending on the context, it might, for example, make more sense to try to resolve a bottleneck before helping someone complete work.

What should I be doing next?

* Help the team members know what to do next to make the team more autonomous
* Use explicit policies and visualizations
* Rule of thumb:
  1 - Finish work in process
  2 - Look for bottlenecks and help to resolve them
  3 - Pull new work, if WIP limit allows
  4 - Find other interesting work
* Slack is not bad—slack enables improvements

[10] This list was suggested by David Joyce.

[11] Ok—you can't allow yourself to be idle forever, of course. Just doing "other, interesting work" won't pay the bills. If that happens often, maybe you could see if you can start to cooperate more, or design your work so that it can be split in smaller pieces.

7.5 Managing bottlenecks

The queues and the WIP limits work together to create a leading indicator of the problems in your workflow while you're experiencing them. They tell you where the bottlenecks are and also show you where they're building up even before they happen. Let's look at an example. At the beginning of the day, the board looks like this. All of the steps are filled with work, and people are working away.

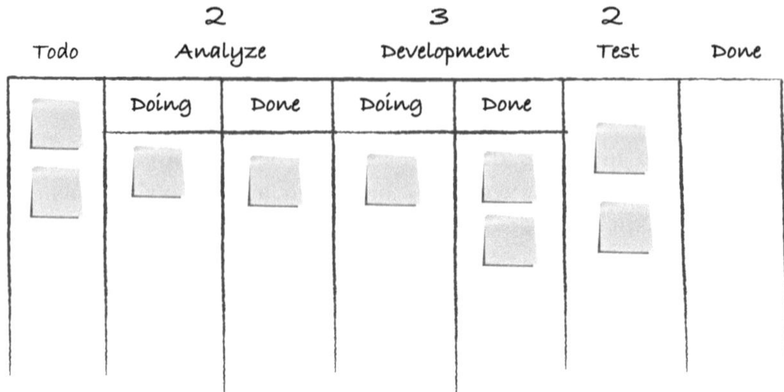

After a little while, the developers want to pull in new work. There's only one item in Development/Doing. The developers pull a new work item from the Analyze/Done column; it's just sitting there waiting.

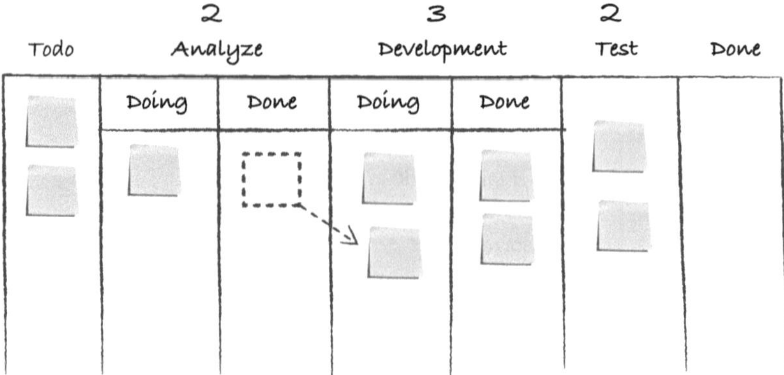

But wait a minute; the Development column is already at maximum capacity. Items are apparently not moving fast enough from the Development column and through Test; we have a bottleneck in testing. What should we do about it?

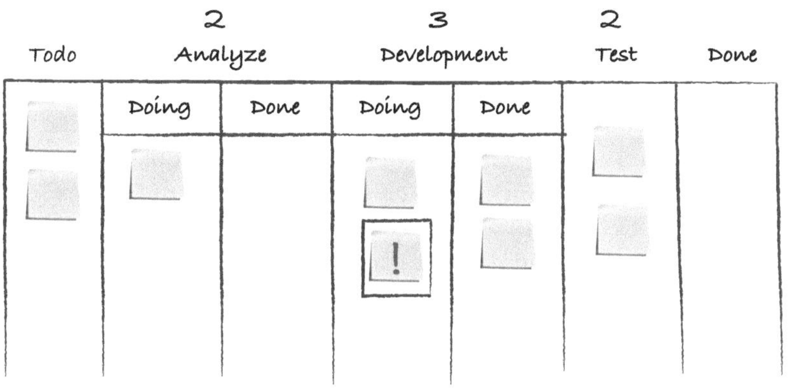

If we do nothing and just keep pulling new development work—that is, ignoring the WIP limits—Test will be flooded with work sitting there waiting. This will increase the lead times of everything in the workflow and result in all the bad things associated with a higher WIP that we talked about in chapter 5.

We need to free up people to fix the problem, and fortunately the developers that were about to start new work apparently have capacity to spare. In many cases, this will only be a short-term solution; for example, testing might require special skills that make it difficult for a developer to be as efficient as needed. If Test is a recurring bottleneck, it makes sense to work on a long-term solution such as hiring more testers or perhaps automating more of the testing.

7.5.1 Theory of Constraints: a brief introduction

The Theory of Constraints[12] is a management philosophy that is based around the idea that the throughput of all systems is limited by at least one constraint: a bottleneck that slows production. With no constraints in a system, the throughput would be instant and infinite; the car would appear in your driveway at the same time as you clicked Buy, or a new software feature would be in production the moment you said you wanted it.

That also means the constraint slows down the whole system. Any improvement you do to help work to flow better through the constraint is an improvement for the whole system. Any improvement you do to another part of the system isn't really an improvement because the bottleneck constraint is what is setting the pace for the entire workflow.

The Theory of Constraints, as an advanced theory of managing bottlenecks, would classify these solutions as elevation improvements because they focus on elevating, or increasing, the capacity at the bottleneck. This is the solution most people intuitively think of when faced with a bottleneck: adding more people or machines, more

[12] Eliyahu M. Goldratt and Jeff Cox formulated the Theory of Constraints in the excellent business novel *The Goal: Excellence in Manufacturing* (North River Press, 1984, http://amzn.com/B0006EI69C).

training, better tools, and better technologies. These solutions are often difficult because they require an expensive investment that takes time to produce results.

According to the Theory of Constraints, you often have another, simpler, and less expensive, option: to exploit the bottleneck. This means you first make sure the bottleneck is used to its maximum capacity. Are the people working at the bottleneck doing other kinds of work than the bottleneck activity? Could someone else do that work instead of them? In our previous example, maybe the developers can fill out the testers' time reports and do their expenses for them. Any idle time in the bottleneck, any time where they can't do bottleneck-activity work, reduces the output of the entire system.

DISCOVERING A BOTTLENECK

Bottlenecks often reveal themselves by having work piling up in front of them and steps after the bottleneck being starved for things to do. In the board below, you can see that there's a lot of work waiting to be tested and nothing that is ready to be deployed.

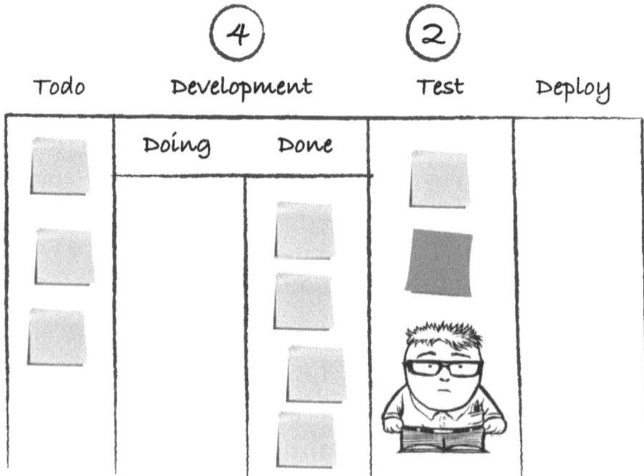

In this example, the developers are blocked from pulling new work because that would break their WIP limit of four. All four development items are waiting to be tested. The testing step in turn is up to its WIP limit of two and should not pull more work either. Finally, we see that the step after testing (Deploy) has nothing to do because no work is flowing from the testing step.

With the queue the team has put in front of the testing step, you get a leading indicator of a problem happening: you can see it build up over time. This gives you an opportunity to react and start doing something about the bottleneck before it becomes a real problem.

EXPLOITING A BOTTLENECK: THE TESTER

Of course, testing[13] is just used as an example because it's common and easy to understand. The bottleneck could be anywhere: yes, even with the developers!

> **The Five Focusing Steps**
>
> In *The Goal*, Mr. Goldratt also teaches the Five Focusing Steps as a way to continuously improve the throughput of your system:
>
> 1. Identify the constraint of the system: for example, a single machine that all the parts in a factory need to pass through.
> 2. Exploit the constraint to get the most out of it. For example, make sure the machine is running all the time.
> 3. Subordinate all other work to support the exploitation of the constraint. For example, make sure you don't send faulty parts to the machine; that would be a waste of time for the constraint.
> 4. Elevate the constraint. For example, buy another machine to share the workload.
> 5. Rinse and repeat. Go over your system again, and see if the constraint is still the biggest constraint in the system. You don't want "resistance to change" to be the constraint; we're continuously learning and improving.

Here are some things you can do to exploit a bottleneck:

- Make sure the people/role that constitutes the bottleneck resource (the testers in our example) always have work to do: for example, by building up a queue of work in front of them.
- Build in quality to minimize the workload.
- Remove or at least limit interruptions.
- Remove impediments that hinder them in their work or leave them waiting.
- Carefully prioritize the bottleneck's work so that they always work on the most important tasks. You don't want the constraint to be wasting time on unimportant tasks, now do you? Remember that the constraint is slowing production for the entire system.
- Let them work at a steady pace by evening out the arrival rate of work.

---

[13] Adam is a great tester, and we love him dearly. He's not always the bottleneck but rather is used as an example in this section. Sorry, Adam.

EXAMPLES

To make sure the testers always have work, try to divide the work items into small deliverables that can be tested individually so that work is quickly ready for them and arrives at a steady pace, rather than in spikes.

Have the testers work closely with the developers and other upstream people (product owners, analysts, designers, and so on) early to build in quality and better understand the work they're testing.

WARNING A common antipattern we have seen is that testers working in non-agile environments expect to do the testing in batches at the end of iterations or releases. A lot of time is spent on preparing, planning, administration, and similar activities. They even get involved in other activities like planning the next release or another project. This increases their WIP and decreases the amount of time they can spend on the bottleneck activity.

ANOTHER WARNING As you make changes to your system, the bottleneck might move. That's the last part of the five focusing steps ("Rinse and repeat") and should be evaluated continuously; where is the bottleneck now? Are you working on the right bottleneck? Remember that an improvement to a non-bottleneck step in your process isn't really an improvement.

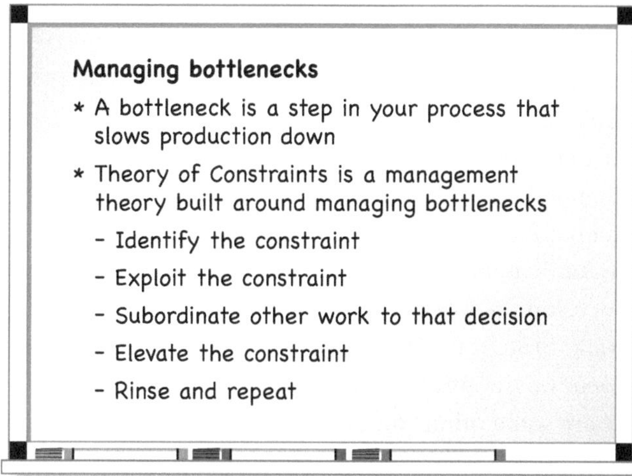

There's a lot more that can be said about and learned from studying the Theory of Constraints, and this has only been a short introduction to the topic. Read more about the Theory of Constraints in *Tame the Flow: Hyper-Productive Knowledge-Work Management* by our friends Steve Tendon and Wolfram Müller (Leanpub, 2013, https://leanpub.com/tame-the-flow), which deep-dives into the subject and its applications.

7.6 Summary

In this chapter we talked about ways to manage your work flow:

- Flow (or continuous flow) is an ideal state that describes a process in which every step in the process creates value, with no interruptions or waiting time.
- Pursuing this ideal state is a never-ending quest that will help you not only get a smoother, faster flow but also find problems in your process.
- Everything that isn't value in the eyes of the customer is waste. Eliminating waste leads to better flow.
- "Managing flow" is one of the principles of kanban, and there are a lot of things you can do to help the work flow:
  - Limit WIP.
  - Reduce waiting times in your process: for example, by ensuring that the work is always ready for the next step or by making the work items smaller so that they move faster through the process. Remove blockers as fast as possible. Or why not strive to "never be blocked"?
  - Avoid rework by building quality into your process from the start. How much of the demand you have in your system today is failure demand? How can you have less failure demand and more value demand?
  - Create cross-functional teams that can minimize waiting times.
  - Use goals and targets like SLAs to get clear timeboxes and objectives to strive toward.

- Many teams use the daily standup to collaborate well together. Here are some practices to help make a standup great:
  - Keep it short and energized: never more than 15 minutes (that's why you stand up).
  - Keep it regular: same time and place every day.
  - Keep it disciplined: start and end on time.
  - Keep it focused: complete discussions afterward.
- Many kanban teams have some practices that they follow:
  - Focus on the work, not the workers.
  - Walk through the items on the board from right to left.
  - Focus on deviations—the smells in your process.
- Here are some other things to think about to get the most out of your standup:
  - Is all the work visible on the board?
  - Are we working on the right thing?
  - Do we understand the work?
  - Encourage spontaneous kaizen meetings after the standup in which small improvements are made every day.
- Standups can be scaled to more than one team, but make sure each layer adds value and isn't just another reporting instance. Think about the following:
  - Run before or after smaller team standups?
  - Who attends?
  - What kinds of visualizations are needed?
  - How will statuses be synchronized between local team boards and other boards?
- "What should I be doing next?" is a common question at standups. With explicit policies on how to handle that question, you minimize the risk of hindering the flow of work.
- A bottleneck is something that slows down production. With queues, you can get leading indicators and discover the bottlenecks.
- The Theory of Constraints is a management theory built around finding and eliminating bottlenecks in a process.

Part 3

Advanced kanban

So far in the book you've read about the foundation of kanban, the principles it's built on, and a lot of practical techniques that help you apply those principles in your context.

We now turn our attention to more advanced or peripheral practices that many teams using kanban are using or picking up. These practices and tools may help you in certain situations but aren't necessary to use kanban. And don't let the "Advanced" in the name of this part scare you; nothing advanced is required in order to apply these practices, and we'll continue to hold your hand in a very practical way. But applying some of these practices may take you further and help you reach beyond the scope of your own team, so you can start to transform your organization.

8 Classes of service

This chapter covers

- What a class of service is
- Putting classes of service to use for you
- Examples of commonly used classes of services

In the previous chapter you learned different ways to manage the flow of work. One thing all those different principles, rules of thumb, and good practices didn't address was that not all work items are of equal importance. Some types of work may need to flow faster through the workflow than others. This is where the concept of *classes of service* comes in handy. Let's start with an example of a pretty standard case.

8.1 The urgent case

The case of a particularly urgent work item is a well-known one to many teams; there's often a need to be flexible with your process to allow for important and valuable exceptions to your normal rules and policies. It could be a production issue, a fix needed to comply with a regulation or a contract, a business opportunity you have to act on fast—anything that makes it reasonable to drop what you're doing to drive this work item to completion as fast as possible. A common way to visualize this is to add a special lane on the board to make it clear that it's a different class of item with special policies attached to it. Be explicit about what these policies are—here's an example we've seen:

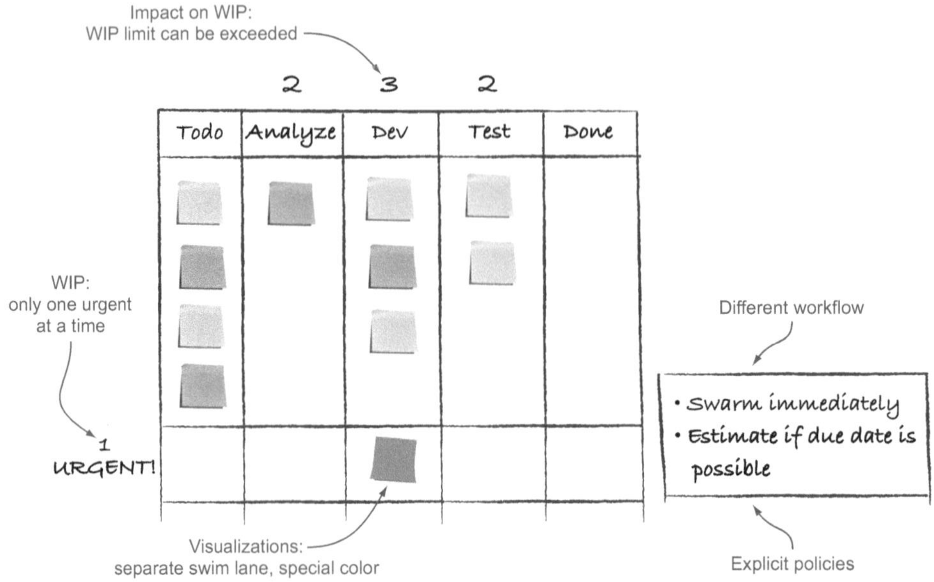

Urgent items:

- Have their own swim lane
- Are written on pink stickies
- Don't count against the WIP limits
- Should be prioritized *above* regular items; in fact, everyone should drop what they're doing and help fix this issue (also called *swarming*; see section 7.2.3)
- Only need a rough estimate to see if they can be delivered in time for a particular due date
- Should be exceptions; for example, only one urgent item in its lane at any given time, and a maximum of two per week

The last point can be of particular importance in environments in which the cost of expediting the item isn't immediately apparent to the people pushing the urgent work items through the system. If you remember Little's law (from chapter 5), you might recall that adding more work will cause longer lead times for all the work in your process. Using kanban to visualize this may help people understand this and avoid unnecessarily expedited work.

Kanban helps you point out that urgent items are, and have to be, exceptions.

A WORD FROM THE COACH To make sure the Urgent class of items doesn't get overused and to help us improve and learn from this exception, we have recently started to introduce an extra activity that is done after every urgent item: a short retrospective or root-cause analysis. Because such items are exceptions, you should treat them as holding nuggets of knowledge that you need to harvest to improve your process. Hence, after every urgent item is completed, you get together for a retrospective:

- What in our process made this urgent item occur?
- How can we prevent this from occurring again?
- Did our handling of this item work out as planned?

We've also found that some stakeholders reclassify their urgent items when they're informed that we intend to discuss those items in a retrospective meeting after we're done with them. Maybe it wasn't that urgent after all! And that was what we wanted; Urgent is for urgent things only. It isn't a fast-lane access to the team to get "my items" done faster.

Urgent, sometimes also referred to as *Expedite*, is just one example of a class of work items with different policies from regular items. You could say that these work items have a different class of service.

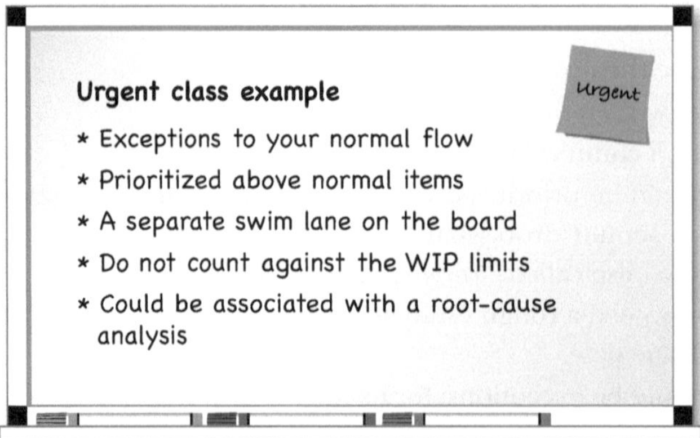

8.2 What is a class of service?

What you do with the Urgent class is to explicitly state that *a certain class of work items gets certain service*. As it turns out, not all work items necessarily have the same level of value or time pressure. You want this to be reflected explicitly on your board and in other work policies. This is why classes of service have become an important concept in the kanban community.

Assigning different classes of service to different work items is an easy way of creating a simple and transparent approach for the team to self-organize around the work and to meet the needs of the business by making work-item value, risk information, and policies explicit—maybe even visualized on the board. It also helps increase customer satisfaction by using different service levels for different types of work.

Let's take a look at some aspects to consider when capturing and visualizing different classes of service.

8.2.1 Aspects to consider when creating a class of service

As you can see in the example of the Urgent class of service, there are many aspects of a work item's behavior that you can consider when capturing or creating a class of service. Here are a few examples of aspects that a class of service can affect.

VISUALIZATION

In order to easily see a work item's class of service, you want to make it *visual* to all members of the team as well as other people who might be interested. One way is to use a swim lane, as in the Urgent example. You can also use a special color for the work item's sticky or indicate the class of service on the work-item card somehow—for example, with a sticker or an icon.

IMPACT ON WIP

Does the class of service have an impact on the WIP limit or not? Does the class of service impact WIP in some columns and not impact WIP in others? If the class of service has its own lane, does that lane have a WIP limit or a maximum number of items? A minimum?

PRIORITIZATION

How is the class *prioritized* compared to other classes? Should work items of this class be pulled before other classes? Does it have a swarming policy so that other work should be dropped and everyone swarms to pull this through the workflow as fast as possible? Maybe a First In, First Out (FIFO) type of queuing would be a suitable policy for this type of work.

Risk information such as cost of delay, special skill requirements, and technical impact are typical considerations to make explicit, to empower and assist team members to make good risk decisions just in time.

DIFFERENT WORKFLOW

Should the class follow a different workflow than other classes? Maybe it skips a column: for example, no analysis is needed for items in the Defect class of service. Maybe it has a different policy for one step of the workflow: for defects, a non-QA developer may do the QA work. Maybe it needs less-detailed estimation than other classes.

Change the workflow for your classes of service to optimize the outcome of items by the class of service. For urgent items, you could optimize for speed, whereas items that are classified as intangible might have code quality as their primary outcome.

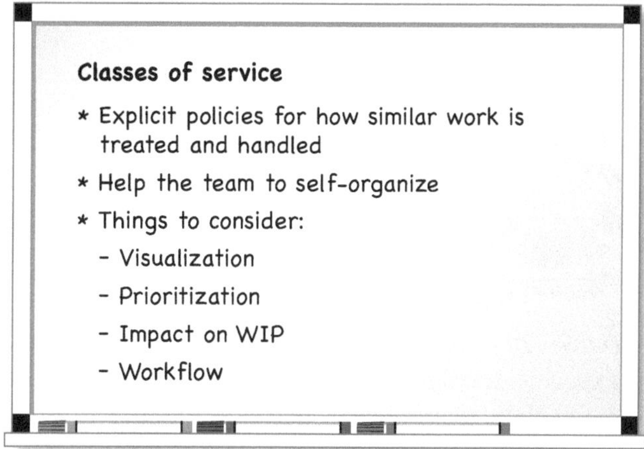

With these aspects in mind, let's take a closer look at a number of classes of service that are commonly used in the kanban community.

8.2.2 Common classes of service

In addition to the Urgent class, which we mentioned already, there are a number of other common classes of service. Among the most widespread are the classes of service that David J. Anderson describes in his book *Kanban: Successful Evolutionary Change for Your Technology Business* (Blue Hole Press, 2010): Expedite (which we call Urgent), Fixed Delivery Date, Intangible, and Regular (Anderson uses Standard, but we prefer Regular to avoid confusing it with the Lean concept of standard work). In our description of the different classes, we have also added a class for Defects because it's a common class of service in many organizations.

This section takes a closer look at these classes of service. If you don't find them fitting for your specific situation, please elaborate and change them as needed. Use the guidelines here as an inspiration, and make them suit your situation better.

FIXED DELIVERY DATE

The *Fixed Delivery Date* class of service is used when something has to be delivered on or before a specific due date. The work item must be prioritized and pulled through the workflow in time for this date, because a failure to do so typically is met with increased costs or missed opportunities. Contractual or legal obligations are examples that easily come to mind, but there can also be technical reasons such as discontinued support of a third-party service on a certain date.

With a Fixed Delivery Date class, you need to schedule the items in time for the due date—but not too early, or the items will delay other, more valuable work.

Fixed delivery date items could have these properties and policies:

- Are written on purple stickies
- Have the due date clearly stated on the card
- Will be pulled in preference to other, less risky classes: for example, in preference to everything except Expedite

2013-06-12!

Fixed date

- Should be considered for promotion to the Expedite/Urgent class if the due date is threatened

WARNING Don't overuse this class and turn your work items into tasks in a traditional plan-driven Gantt chart.[1] Use it sparingly for external due dates and similar constraints, or you'll mess up the workflow for the normal items.

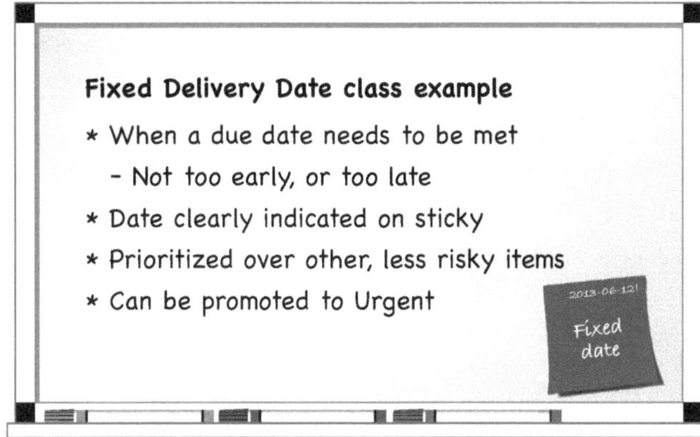

REGULAR ITEMS

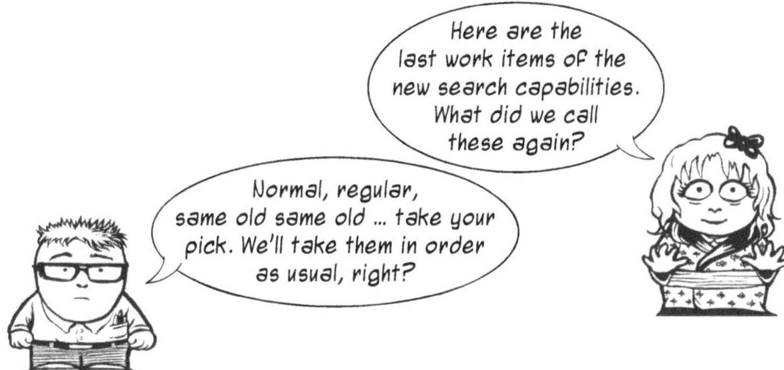

The Regular class of service contains the bread-and-butter work items that fill up the workweek. Flow and focus will move these as fast as possible through the system and with reasonably predictable lead times.

[1] A Gantt chart is a type of bar chart that illustrates a project schedule and the dependencies between the different tasks in the project. The agile community shies away from Gantt charts because they make guesses and estimates about the future look like they *are* the future. Dan North even says, "Newborn children only fear two things: bright lights and Gantt charts."

Another term we've heard[2] of for this class of service is Increasingly Urgent. Typically these items aren't urgent right now, but as time goes by their urgency increases.

We have often seen regular items used with the following simple policies:

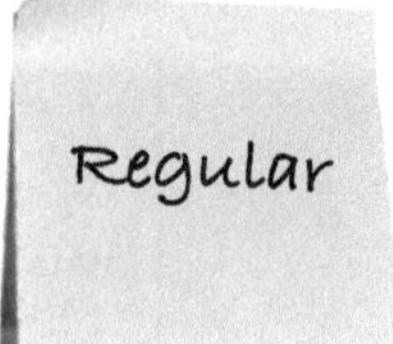

- Are written on the ubiquitous yellow stickies
- Are pulled based on FIFO order: First In, First Out

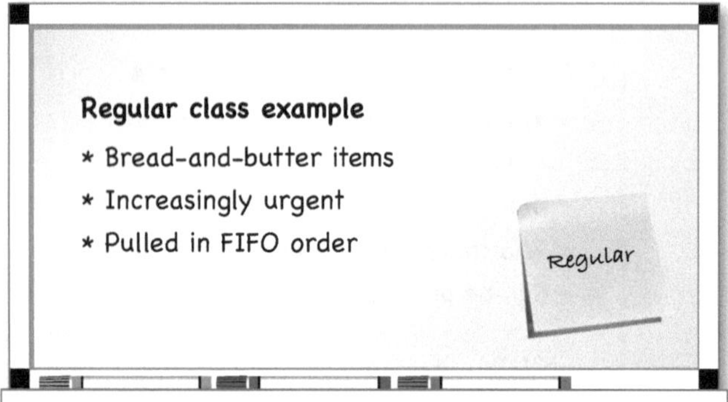

INTANGIBLE ITEMS

Items of this class are those that don't have a tangible, concrete business value, or at least not one that is easy to estimate, but which are still important. This includes things like low-priority defects, small usability improvements, and design changes.

[2] Read more at http://mng.bz/P6M4.

This class also covers what Stephen R. Covey (author of *The 7 Habits of Highly Effective People*) calls *important but not urgent tasks*. They're ones you're likely to neglect but should focus on to achieve effectiveness: improvement work, removing technical debt, increasing medium or long-term capacity, and other things that will help you reduce future costs or create future options.

The low cost of putting off these tasks creates a temptation to put them off indefinitely, a day at a time. One way to avoid that is to ensure that there is always some capacity for this class of work. An added bonus is that doing this creates slack in the system that can be used to flow other classes through the system faster: for example, by pulling other classes before this one, if needed.

In organizations in which a product owner or external stakeholders select the team's work, it isn't uncommon to use the Intangible class as a way for the team to select items at their own discretion: for example, for reduction of technical debt and improvement work.

Items in the Intangible class could have these properties:

- Are written on green stickies
- Will only be pulled if there are no other class items available
- Might be limited in some way by number of items on the board (see section 8.2.3). For example:
  - Should always be two of them on the board
  - Should make up 20% of the story points for the iteration
  - Should have a rate of three items per month

The Intangible class of service can also take other forms, such as the famous Google time that allocated certain days for intangible work. Other forms we've seen are technical or improvement cards that the team creates: for example, the team may be allowed one "improvement card" on the board at all times. Some people call these *technical gold cards*, because it's those golden nuggets of improvements that developers often long to tackle but never have time to work on.

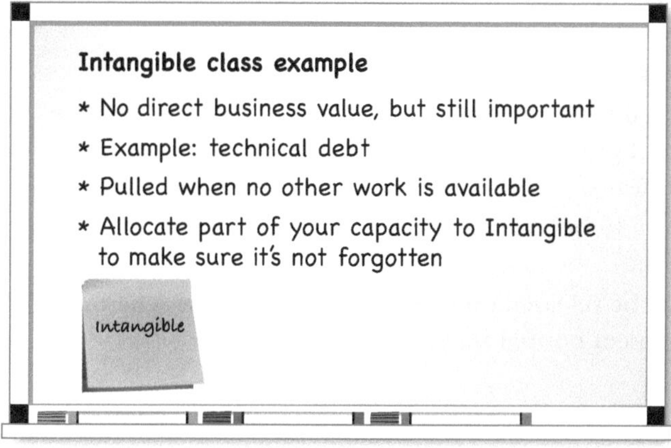

DEFECTS

Defects are the class of work that you don't want to see. A defect is often a sign of some lack of quality in the work you did the first time around. In this form, it's rework that is introduced and added to the work you're already doing.

Defects can be other things as well, such as production bugs or a server failure that you need to handle immediately.

Here are some example policies for defect items:

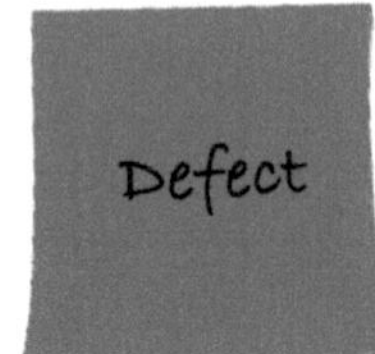

- Are written on red stickies
- Skip the Analysis step and go directly to the Development column
- Don't have to be estimated
- Should be subjected to root-cause analysis on how to avoid similar defects in the future before being pulled to Done
- Have to be managed in the bug-tracking tool: closed and assigned to QA, and so on
- Can be released outside the normal release schedule: they don't have to wait for the next normal release

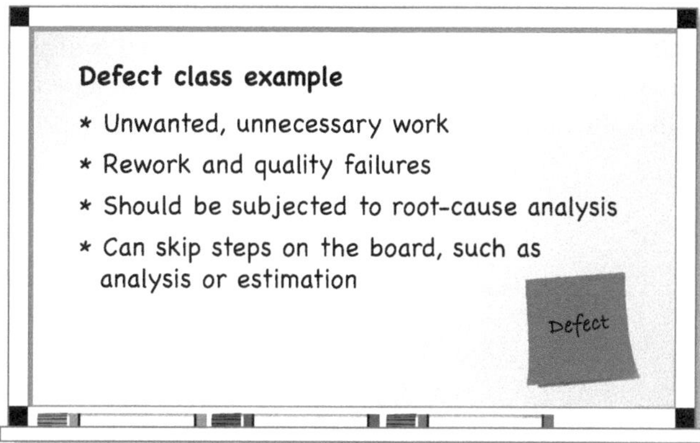

By now you've seen a lot of uses for classes of service and examples of commonly used variants; but why go through all this trouble to classify work items? What use can you get from classes of service?

8.2.3 Putting classes of services to use

Classes of services can help with a lot of decisions that you, as a team, will be facing. It's all about making policies, work-item value, and risk information more explicit (see chapter 3), thereby helping the team to self-organize and pull the right work items. This in turn helps the work to flow more smoothly and quickly through the workflow, because you don't need decisions or approval from others at every question or decision point.

One way to use classes of service is to decide how much of a team's capacity should be used for different classes: for instance, by deciding on a number (or percentage) of work items per class that will always be on the board. Let's see an example in action:

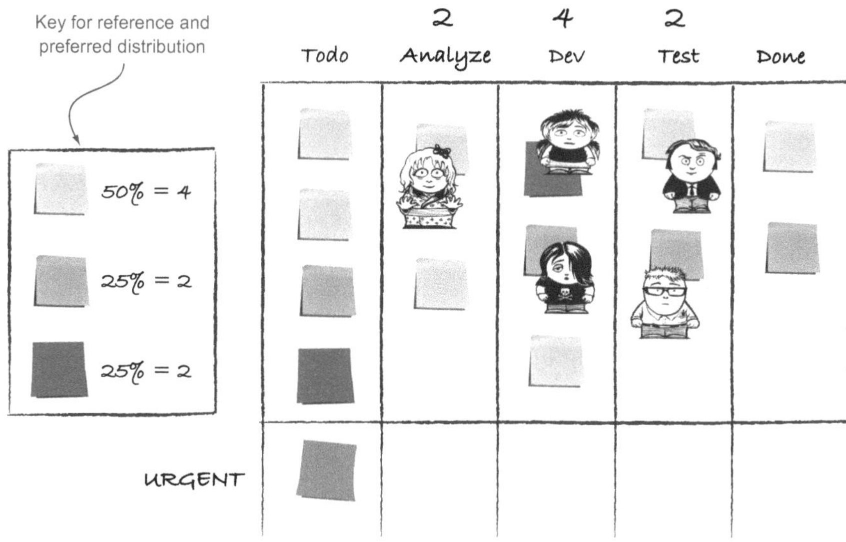

On this board, to the left, the team has posted a legend and the preferred distribution between the classes of services. You can see four classes of service in action here: Regular, Intangibles, Defects, and, finally, an Urgent swim lane for work items that have to be expedited through the workflow.

A percentage number and a concrete number are written beside each class of service in the legend. They indicate how you strive to have the work distributed. When you finish one work item, you can easily look at the board and see which card to pull next from the Todo column to keep the distribution as the team agreed.

From this example, you can see an explicit policy at work to help the team self-organize. With the help of the preferred distribution (percentages of each class of service), Beth could easily conclude what kind of work she should pull next. Using different colors for each class of service made this easy to see; Beth finished analyzing a yellow sticky, and to keep the proposed distributions of colors, she could count the work items and see that a red one was the one to pull.

But also, and maybe more important, this system made sure work was prioritized in a proper manner. The defect card that was waiting in the Todo column was prioritized over the others, ensuring that the team attended to defects, even though it might be more fun and even more important to the business stakeholders to work on new features.

Used like this, classes of service can also help you make sure low-priority work is at least getting done to some extent and not constantly deferred to "later." In this example, the team is guaranteed to always have at least one intangible ongoing at all times. Because the intangible has a lower priority to be pulled to the next column while it's in the workflow, it also creates some slack for more important work to move to Done faster.

The distribution of different classes can of course be continuously modified to allow for changing business needs. For example, if there is a perceived quality problem with the product, you may want to increase the ratio of defects until that is resolved. Or if the team has had to sprint to reach a deadline, maybe it's time to dial up the number of intangibles and pay off the accumulated technical debt.

Everything is miscellaneous

At one client Marcus coached, a review showed that they had been spending about 70% of their budget on work classified as miscellaneous—even though they put aside money for three main investments that were to be prioritized over other work.

How can this be? First, this is common and probably reflects the industry standard in which a large portion of the budget is spent on patching stuff. Second, in the heat of the moment it's hard to turn down "this quickie that we need by Friday."

If a clear prioritization with a distribution of classes of service had been in place, they would have more easily and quickly seen that they were going off track.

You're aiming to get a better flow for the work items on the board. On many teams, the flow can be stalled for a simple reason, such as people not being present when needed for prioritization, for example. If you've ever experienced the need for a product owner to know what to work on next, and being stalled because she's only present for a half hour each week on Tuesdays, you know what we mean.

Transaction and coordination costs

Transaction cost is a term from economics that represents the cost incurred in making an economic exchange, such as search and information costs, cost of drawing up and enforcing contracts, and so on. Applied to the world of software development, transaction costs mean setup and cleanup activities associated with the delivery of value, such as planning, estimation, budgeting, integration, and deployment. All these costs are really waste (see section 7.1) because the customer would prefer to get the value you deliver without having to pay any of these transaction costs. This doesn't mean

(continued)

you should stop doing them; it's just the cost of doing business. But you should always try to eliminate as much as possible of these costs.

Coordination costs are the specific costs incurred as soon as you need to cooperate with others to achieve your goal. All the meetings, phone calls, emails, and so on needed to coordinate your activities are part of the coordination costs.

For example, getting hold of an absent business stakeholder has a lot of coordination costs connected to it: the stakeholder needs to be summoned and take time out of his schedule; meetings have to be set up; and the team must stop what they're doing and get together with the stakeholder for the meeting.

All of this can be contrasted with being able to walk over to a business stakeholder who is present at the next table and ask him about the priority of the work items.

With explicit policies in place, the coordination costs for selecting work are much lower. You have the principles for how to select work from the backlog in place already, often visualized on the board. The team is more self-organized and can do the selection just in time instead of batching up work in advance, just in case, as they would need to do with a stakeholder who is hard to get hold of.

The process of selecting the right thing to do, in the right order, at the right time, is called *scheduling*:

> *Scheduling is the process—and it's an ongoing and dynamic thing—of producing economically optimal results from the sequencing of work items. It's a big responsibility; so let's try to do it in a robust and transparent way.*[3]
>
> —Mike Burrows (@asplake on Twitter)

You'll learn more about planning and scheduling work in chapter 9.

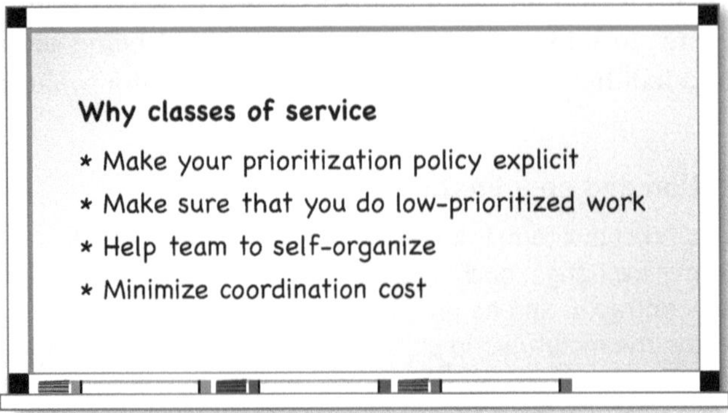

[3] Read more at http://mng.bz/avnN.

If you strive to have a quick flow with small batches (small-sized work items) through your workflow, you'll minimize both transaction and coordination costs. This will happen through an ongoing and dynamic selection of work items to work with, rather than making plans for a future that might change. The tool to accomplish this is transparent, explicit policies, such as limiting the number of items that can be in a certain class of service on the board at the same time.

8.3 Managing classes of services

If you run into situations like the one the Kanbaneros are asking Joakim about, you're not alone. Although the different classes of service might be clearly defined and agreed on by everyone, the work might not always fit your classification. For example, work items might consist of several tasks, each of which belongs to a separate class of service; or you might handle work items differently depending on where they come from. This section talks about a couple of common methods and practices that can help you handle these situations.

DIVIDE AND RECLASSIFY

Sometimes a single work item might be a mix of different classes of service, particularly if it's a big work item. This might result in you having a hard time deciding which class of service the item's in, and thereby being unsure how to handle it. It might feel like both a bug and an intangible at the same time. Try to break down big items like that into smaller ones, and see if the new items belong to other classes and should be treated accordingly.

Reasons for dividing work items and reclassifying the new work items are contextual and depend on the way you work, in the team and with your clients. Following are some common reasons that we see from time to time.

SIZE MATTERS

Sometimes you can't break big items down due to the nature of the work item or the dependencies in the technical environment or the organization. Other times, teams end up with some items that are an order of magnitude bigger or more complex than others.

It goes without saying that lead times for such big items will be different, and perhaps other policies apply. This can be a reason to consider a special class of service. Maybe you can allow a big item to be on your board for a long time and during this time always allocate a certain amount of work to it.

SOME CLIENTS ARE MORE EQUAL THAN OTHERS

Different clients can be more important than others, as typically represented by a different service-level agreement (SLA). You might want to favor a certain customer while securing the new contract with them, or perhaps one department or a specific product has been given priority over others in the company.

If the difference implies a different policy for how you treat work, a new class of service might be the solution.

SLICING IT DIFFERENTLY

Another way to differentiate between classes of service that could prove to be useful is to classify work based on its origin or the source of demand. In this way, you may end up with classes like Marketing, Customer Support Issues, and Developer Requests.

This is yet another way to classify the work items and make the policies around each class explicit. Which policies you associate with each class will vary depending on your context. But from the prior examples (see section 8.2.2), you can extract some common patterns that are easily applied to the classes of service that you find useful in your context.

WARNING Don't overcomplicate things. A rule of thumb is to not use more than five to seven classes of service, because more than that makes it difficult for everyone to understand and remember them and to use the policies in daily decision making. Having said that, don't be afraid to be imaginative and explore in order to understand how your work works.

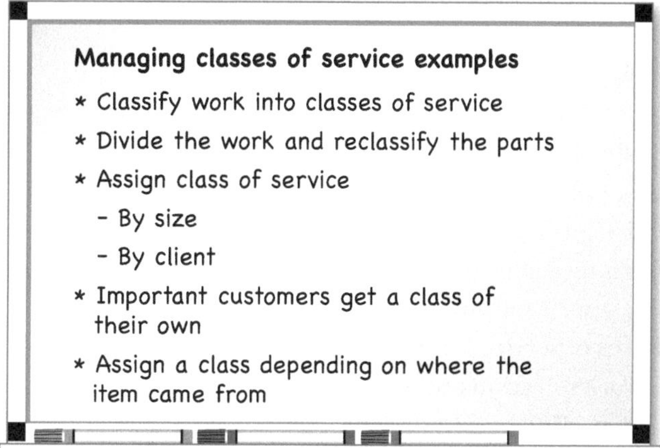

ZOOM IN, EXPLORE, AND SIMPLIFY

With a lot of different ways to slice, divide, and change your classes of service, an obvious question is, how detailed should you get? We would like to quote a friend of ours to help explain that:

> *Zoom in (more columns/classes), explore, and then simplify is a pattern I've seen work.*
>
> —Jabe Bloom (@cyetain on Twitter)

What Jabe Bloom means in the quote is to first detail and add stuff: more columns to your board and more classes of service, for example, to your policies and workflow. This forces you to explore and try different ways of applying these until you feel you have something that works for the team. Now try to simplify what you've created: what can be removed, which classes could be grouped together, and so on.

8.4 Exercise: classify this!

Sit down with your team, and start thinking about how classes of services can serve you:

- Should you use an Urgent swim lane? What kind of policies should surround that class of service? How do you make sure not everything is urgent? Can there be only one urgent item active at the time?
- Think about the different types of work you do; maybe you already have different colors for some of the work (bugs, for example). Are there any implicit policies that "everyone knows" that you could benefit from by discussing and writing them down?
- Do you have work that often is forgotten or that frequently gets low prioritization? Could a class of service and a policy around that help you get low-priority work done? Can you formulate that policy in words? What kind of visualizations can help you remember your policy and help you "fall in the pit of success"?
- What kind of policies do you have in place today that you could simplify?

8.5 Summary

This chapter talked about ways to associate explicit policies with certain types of work—a concept called classes of service:

- Classes of service are a powerful way to make your policies explicit around the service level for certain type of work.
- Assigning a class of service to a work item can influence the work item: visualization, prioritization, impact on WIP, and workflow.
- Classes of service help the team to self-organize around
  - Work selection and scheduling
  - Work distribution
  - Making sure the work capacity is distributed as decided
- Common classes include
  - *Urgent (or Expedite)*—Prioritized over other work
  - *Fixed Delivery Date*—Needs to be completed on or before a certain date
  - *Regular*—Normal items, increasingly urgent, pulled FIFO-style
  - *Defects*—Rework produced by bad quality (you want as few of these as possible)
  - *Intangible*—No tangible business value now, but later: paying off technical debt
- You should use classes that suit your needs and situation, using the examples in this chapter as inspiration. There's no one right answer for everyone.

In the next chapter, we'll take a look at another concept that is important for any process: planning and estimating. How does planning go together with kanban? Are estimates still important? Are there some common ways of estimating?

9 Planning and estimating

This chapter covers

- Planning, scheduling, and ways to plan at the right moment
- Estimating, story points, and other relative estimation techniques
- Cadence: the heartbeat of your process
- Do you need plans at all?

The need for planning arises from the need to inform others around you and yourself about where you are and where you're going. You should raise your eyes and consider not only your own board but also the context around your team. There are sometimes other teams or people who come before you, and you want to keep them informed about your process and let them know how it's going for you.

Consider a team with the board at right.

There are only two items left in the Inbox column; how will it be refilled? Who do you need to talk to in order to know what to do next? How often can you meet with them and talk about what they want done next? This is the kind of planning you need to do in order to understand what to do next and to inform upstream processes that you're ready to accept more work. *Upstream* means the work that takes place before you; it could be other departments or other people doing the work, or tasks that are performed before yours but at another stage in the process. This could be visualized with separate boards, as shown here:

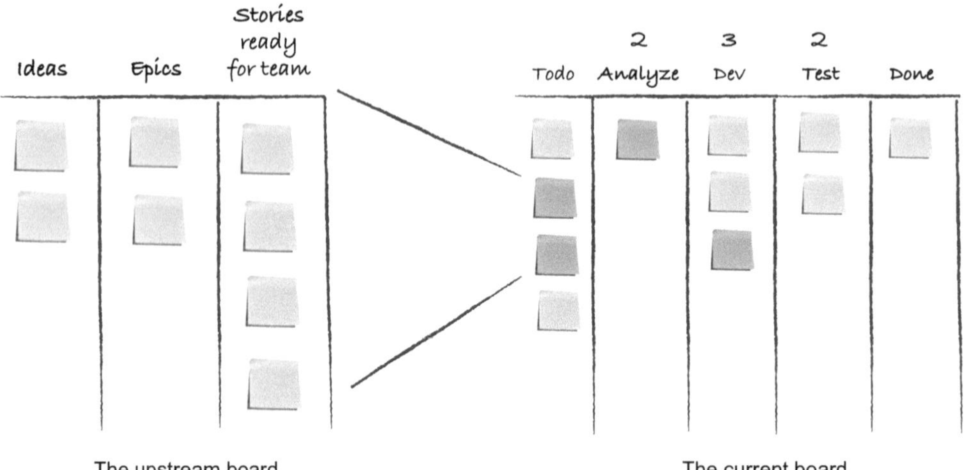

At the other end of your board, you might have to plan for and interact with *downstream* processes that help you move your work into production, for example. At both ends, where your process touches other processes (where you bump into the up- or downstream processes), some sort of synchronization or planning is often needed.

Another reason to plan is that you need to synchronize your work with other teams around you. Imagine you have two teams working on the same product and that they have the following boards to visualize their work:

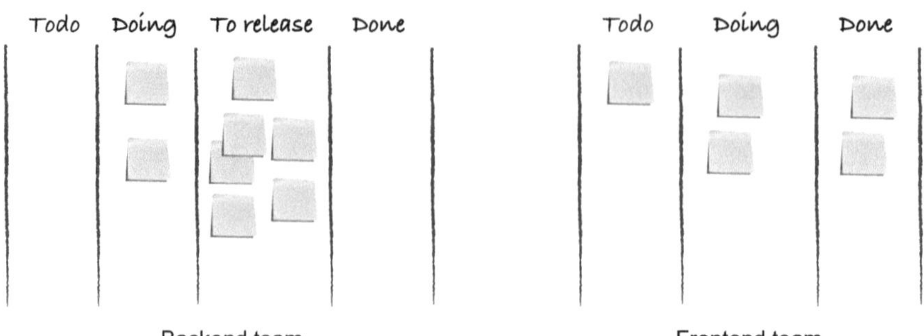

The backend team has made a major change in their system during the last couple of weeks. This will have an impact on the frontend team, so the release of the reworked backend service needs to be closely monitored and coordinated as it's moved into production.

This chapter will show you several ways to handle these kinds of needs for planning and synchronization in kanban. We'll go through some common visualization techniques and ways of thinking about planning.

In order to plan, you often need to have a hunch about the effort that the work ahead will require: that is, some kind of estimation. We'll take a look at a number of estimation techniques that can help you make quick estimates and get good enough material to start planning.

When you estimate, you start to dig into the work ahead and uncover some of the uncertainty. Therefore, estimation can be seen as risk management; you try to learn about the things that you don't know, that feel risky and that might cause problems later, as early as possible.

Let's start from the beginning and see when and how often you should plan. Can kanban help you to *schedule* planning and visualize the process, to get cues for when planning is needed—just in time, instead of doing it up front, just in case?

9.1 Planning scheduling: when should you plan?

Planning is by definition an activity that is done in advance, but not too early, because you then stand the risk of having the things you've planned for changing, and needing to do it all over again later. On top of that, planning for more work is in fact creating more work in process (WIP), because you've started work that will lie around waiting for you. On the other hand, you don't want to plan too late, either, because then planning becomes pointless. If you plan too late, the future is upon you already.

You may wonder when the right time for planning is and how you can be informed about when that moment occurs in your process. Ideally, you want to plan at the exact right moment—not too early and not too late, but just in time.

9.1.1 Just-in-time planning

When you're planning, you're creating a little stock of work items to work from. This can be a good thing because the team now knows what they're going to start working on the next time capacity allows pulling new work. But it can also be bad. A stock is more WIP, and as you learned in chapter 3, more WIP makes each item go slower through the workflow.

You also become less agile with a long list of work items piling up and being committed to by the team. If a new urgent work item needs to be prioritized, you must take that into consideration and prioritize it against all the other work you've planned for.

What you instead want to do is to plan for new work just in time for you to start working on it, keeping the stock of preplanned work to a minimum. But that poses another problem, because there are often costs associated with planning: for example, holding a planning meeting. Often the customer can't be with you at a moment's notice. Maybe there's considerable preplanning to be done before you know what the next prioritized work item is. (See the sidebar "Transaction and coordination costs" in chapter 8.)

One way of balancing the cost of planning while striving for a small buffer of work is to use event-driven planning. This means events in your process tell you that you have capacity to take on more work. Event-driven planning can be achieved by building a simple signaling system that alerts you to plan for more items. Such a signaling system can easily be created in your workflow and visualized on the board.

In contrast, you might instead plan each month, whether the need for planning existed or not. The risk of scheduling your planning at intervals is that you might hold planning sessions at a time when no more work is needed because you haven't finished the work you're doing right now. Another risk is the opposite situation: the next planning session isn't for two weeks, and you don't have anything more to do because you've completed your work earlier than planned.

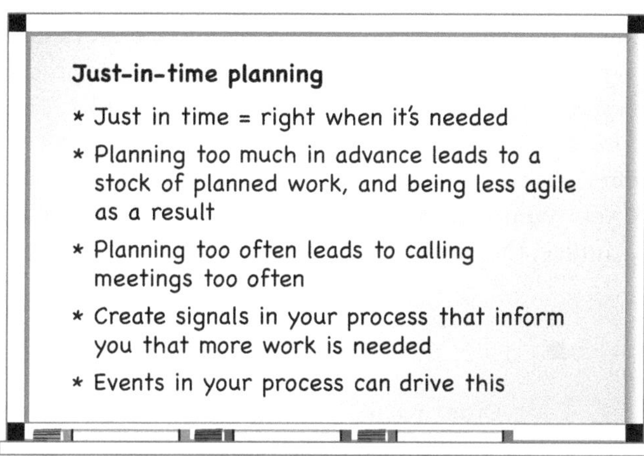

9.1.2 Order point

By introducing an order point, you can pull new work from the stakeholders when you reach a certain number of items left. It's quite simple in action. In fact, we already talked about this in section 6.4.2.

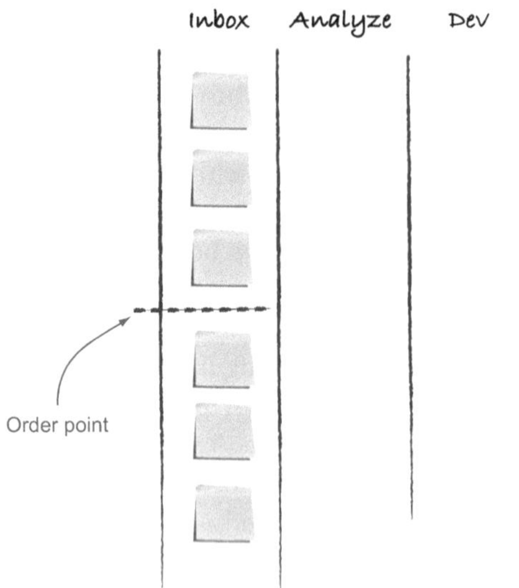

On the board to the left you can see that the Inbox column contains six work items, and under the third one a line is drawn. The team picks stuff from the top of the column, working their way down toward the dotted line drawn under the third work-item card. This line is the *order point* for the team.

When the Inbox has reached this level, the team contacts the stakeholders for a meeting to get more work to do. They know that getting that meeting in place will take some time, and that probably some other work needs to be done before the work can be ready for them to work on. Because of this, they've created a little stock of work—in the form of the three items *below* the order point. This will make sure they have items to work on while the meeting is coordinated and held.

By introducing this simple visualization and mechanism into their workflow, the team has created an *event* that signals to them when more work needs to be planned for. They have also ensured that they're planning just in time, when a need for more work is imminent, rather than creating a big stock of work items, just in case.

As always, you need to be watchful and change your process as needed in order to suit you best. If your stakeholders are hard to get together, or if you need to do a lot of work before you can know what you're going to work on next, you should have a larger buffer of work items. This is a situation in which your coordination costs are higher. If your coordination costs are lower, and you can call your stakeholders at a moment's notice, then you can have a lower order point. Experiment and improve.

Order point

* Signals when more work is needed
* Drawn as a line in your inbox
* When you pass the line, you call a meeting to plan for more work
* Balance the work left in the inbox against the time it takes to plan for more work

9.1.3 Priority filter: visualizing what's important

But how do you know what's important and how to prioritize between the work items? Have you ever encountered a list of features in which everything is priority 1?[1] Or does your company have more than one project that is highest priority? Prioritizing your features in the right order is a hard task, and in many organizations considerable time and effort is spent on prioritization.

Corey Ladas[2] introduced a technique called *priority filter* that simplifies the prioritization process and makes it visual. It also puts the focus on the right things; you should strive to work only on items with priority 1, because by definition they're the most important things right now.

The visualization is simple to set up and is best introduced with an example:

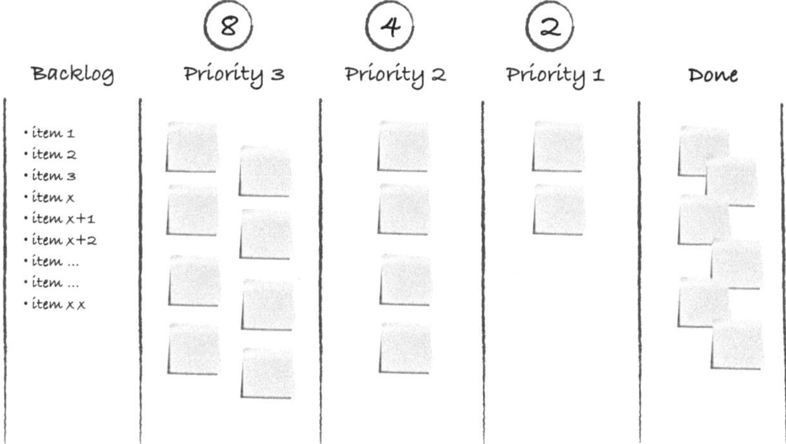

This prioritization board has columns with increasing priorities: priority 3 is the lowest, and priority 1 is the highest. That translates to: priority 1 items should be worked on now (because they have the highest priority), or at least as soon as possible. The number of items in this column is limited by your current capacity; these items are the actual input to the Inbox column (or similar) of your kanban board.[3] Priority 2 items are the items that are coming up next, ready to be moved into Priority 1 as soon as you have capacity. Priority 3 are things that you'll work on later.

Each column has a WIP limit that adds up to your capacity. In this case, the team has decided to work on two Priority 1 items at the same time. The WIP limits are then

---

1 We've encountered clients that had priority 1, 2, and 3 but felt the need to add priority 0 as well, because there were so many items that were the "highest priority." We're not sure that kind of prioritization helped them, though.

2 Visit http://mng.bz/8cDm for more information.

3 You could add these Priority columns to your regular board. In practice, this can be difficult if the board isn't big enough or if the people in charge of planning and prioritizing aren't on the team but are sitting somewhere else.

increasingly higher as you continue to Priority 2 (WIP = four) and Priority 3 (WIP = eight) items. This reflects the fact that you have an increasingly higher uncertainty of the items being worked on soon, the lower the priority they have.

There's also a Backlog, or pool of ideas, column with items that you might start to work on later, but right now you don't know if or when it will happen. As an illustration of this uncertainty, the Backlog items don't even become work items until it's

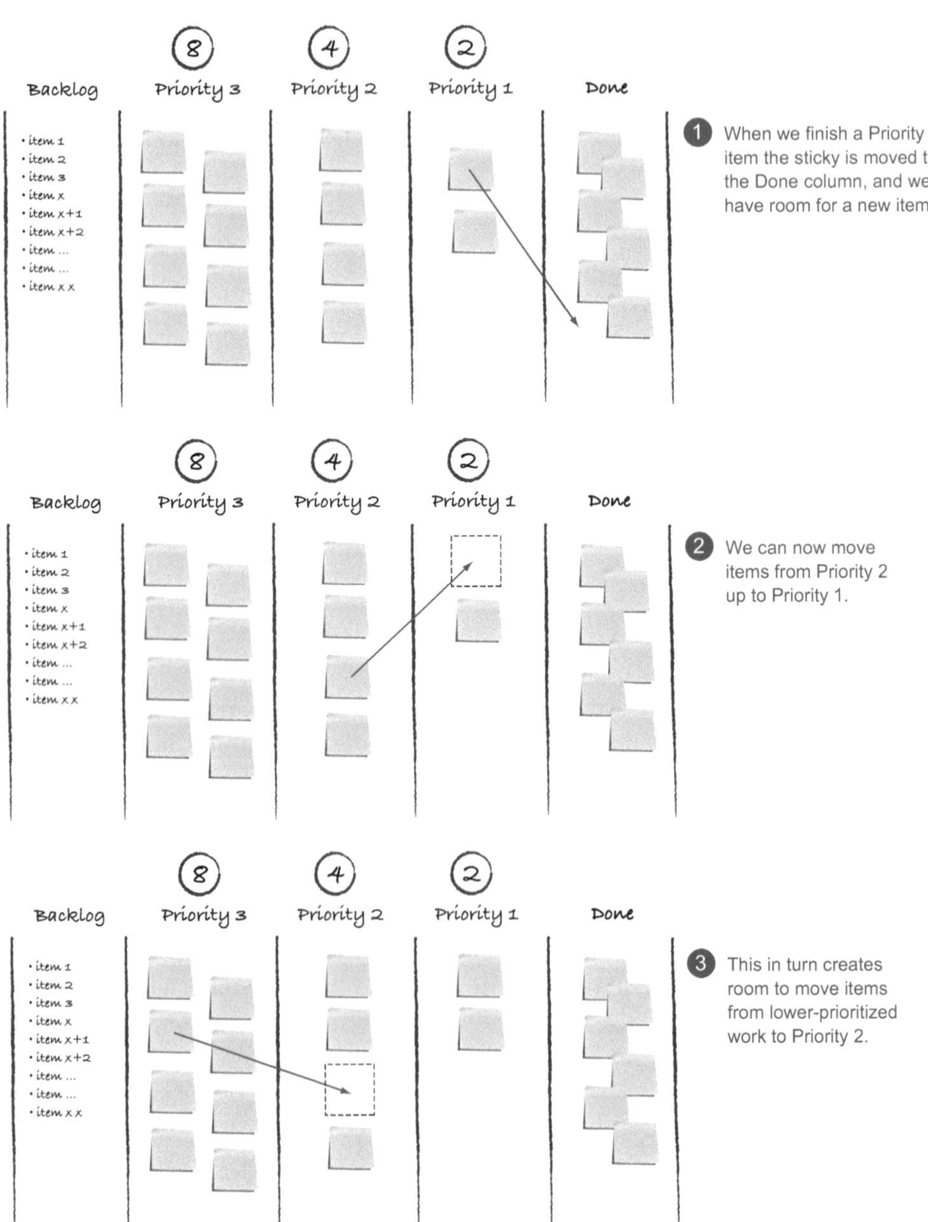

important (or pressing) enough; only when an item is promoted to Priority 3 will you create a sticky for it. Until then, it's written on the board. We've seen teams that have visualized their backlog as a mind map and put it next to the priority filter board instead of creating a backlog list.[4]

Remember that this is just an example. Some teams we've worked with only use P1 and P2; and some call the columns other things, more meaningful to them, such as Upcoming or Next.

One thing that the priority-filter approach highlights is that priority is tightly connected to time. You need to care about what "the next most important thing to work on" is when there's room for more work—that is, after you've finished a Priority 1 item. In fact, you don't need to have the Priority 2 and 3 columns in order. It's not important that a work item has priority 34 or 35, right? Not until it's time to pull a new item into Priority 1 do you have to spend time on prioritization, and then you only have to consider which one item in each column to promote to the next column: which item goes from Priority 2 to Priority 1, which item goes from 3 to 2, and which item goes from Backlog to Priority 3. Instead of spending time prioritizing things against each other that you may never end up implementing anyway, you defer decisions until they're required.

With this simple visualization, the prioritization is easy to see and follow for everyone in and around the team. It's another example of an implicit policy made explicit; because prioritization seems to cause headaches and take a lot of time in many organizations, this approach can come in handy.

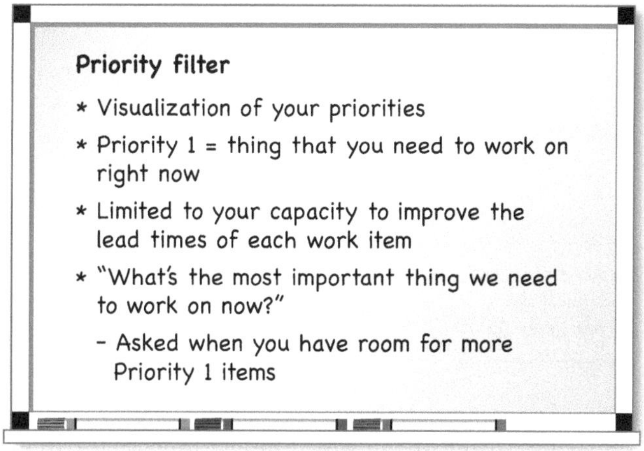

Priority filter

* Visualization of your priorities
* Priority 1 = thing that you need to work on right now
* Limited to your capacity to improve the lead times of each work item
* "What's the most important thing we need to work on now?"
  - Asked when you have room for more Priority 1 items

[4] An excellent example of this is found in a blog post where Marcus describes a client that uses a priority filter to gain better focus and speed. See http://mng.bz/32q3.

9.1.4 Disneyland wait times

Your estimated waiting time from here is: 8 min.

Imagine that you are at an amusement park.[5] You're waiting in line for that amazing roller coaster that your kids have been nagging you about all year long. In fact, you're looking forward to riding it yourself. Sadly, but unsurprisingly, there's a long line that you now have waited in for about 35 minutes. You take another step forward, and in the distance you see a sign like the one to the left.

You think to yourself, "How on Earth can they know that? Well, in any case, good to know." Now you have something to plan with, a prediction that seems reasonable. "I can take eight more minutes," you conclude, and you hand the kids yet another candy from the bag in your pocket.

The roller coaster staff can know how much time is left because they've tracked data and measured the flow of the process: *x* number of coaster cars leaves the platforms per minute, carrying *y* passengers in each car. Then it's a matter of counting the number of people in line and doing the math. Showing the result to the waiting customers is a way to give them a prediction of how long it will take, on average, before it's their turn to ride the roller coaster.

This is a metric that you can achieve too, pretty easily, on your board—which is great, because it'll send your stakeholders the same waves of comfort that you got by knowing you had only eight more minutes of waiting. This is sometimes referred to as *Disneyland wait times*, modeled on the way Disneyland (and other amusement parks) indicate waiting times for their popular attractions. An example could look something like this:

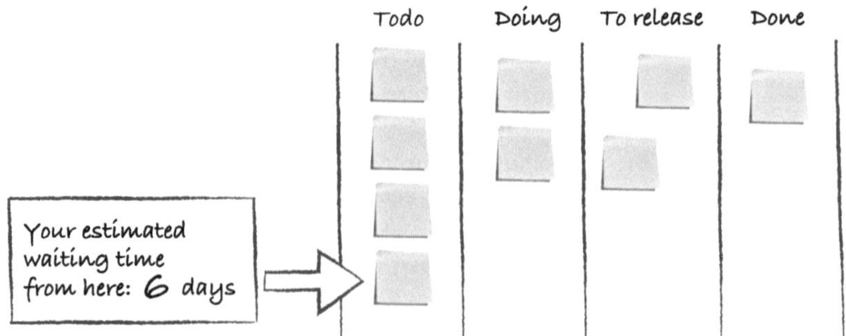

Not only does this comfort the stakeholders waiting for their favorite feature to be deployed, but it also builds trust between the team and the stakeholders. You, as a team, have tracked this data and can confidently say that this is the estimated waiting time: six days.

---

[5] The park might have an association with a big film company. Or not. It's your imagination; don't let the heading push you in any direction.

Finally, because six days isn't that long of a time, the stakeholder is pleasantly surprised when she adds her feature at the bottom of the column. "Six days!? I used to have to wait for a month or two."

A metro is not a train: building trust

When we talked about the order point in section 9.1.2, we suggested that you should strive to have few items under your order point. There are some apparent flow advantages to that, having to do with lower WIP, but there are also advantages related to collaboration and trust between the team and the stakeholders around it. The closer the collaboration and the more regularly you deliver, the more trust the stakeholders will have in the team.

Imagine that you're going to travel for several hours by train. You'll probably want to buy a ticket online well ahead of time, to make sure seats are available. In order to be sure you don't miss the train, you get there early, and maybe even check with websites before you go in order to see that the train is leaving at all.[a] When you go to the station, you make sure you get there in good time. You don't want to miss your opportunity.

Now consider the situation in which you're going on the metro. How much planning and checking do you do then? None, probably. You go down there and hop on the next train.

The difference between these situations has to do with the *cost* associated with missing your train. In the case of a long-distance train, that cost is quite high; there might not be another train today, or even this week. If you miss it, you can't easily get to your destination any other way.

In the case of the metro, if you miss the one you intended to take, it's only a couple of minutes' wait for the next one. If there's mayhem in traffic, you could get out of the metro and walk, or take a taxi instead.

A stakeholder who leaves his work to a team that he meets every six months will be inclined to get good estimates and accurate plans. He wants to make sure his stuff gets delivered, and he wants to know when and in what order. A stakeholder who has a team that she meets every Monday and Wednesday isn't as inclined to ask for detailed estimates and plans. If one item isn't delivered as expected, it will be soon, for sure.

What you're doing here is lowering WIP in the form of the number of items you're planning for. With a lower WIP of planned work, you'll meet the stakeholders more often and hence build trust with them.

a. In Sweden, there's a long period of the year when the high risk of snow on the tracks has a big impact on the likelihood of trains leaving or arriving.

An obvious question and objection is that it can be hard to come up with a trustworthy number of days for your Disneyland waiting time. The answer is that you measure your lead time to come up with a good target number and your *due date performance* against it: that is, the percentage of your items that succeed in meeting the date. Many teams find this hard to do because the lead times vary a lot. Here are some ideas for how to solve this:

- *Use time spans for different sizes.* For example, on average, your small items take 1 to 3 days, medium items take 2 to 6 days, and large items take 5 to 20 days.
- *Use the due date performance.* Measure your lead times over time and say that in, for example, 80% of cases, you're done in *x* days. You could also study the data and try to find the typical characteristics of the items that didn't meet that performance (work that depends on third parties, certain types of work items, or certain classes of service), to increase the predictability for your customer.

Disneyland wait times are a way to increase predictability. You give your stakeholders a way to know when the work will be done. In our experience, we can often see that this is more important than speed. To deliver often and with predictability builds trust, as we discussed in the previous sidebar.

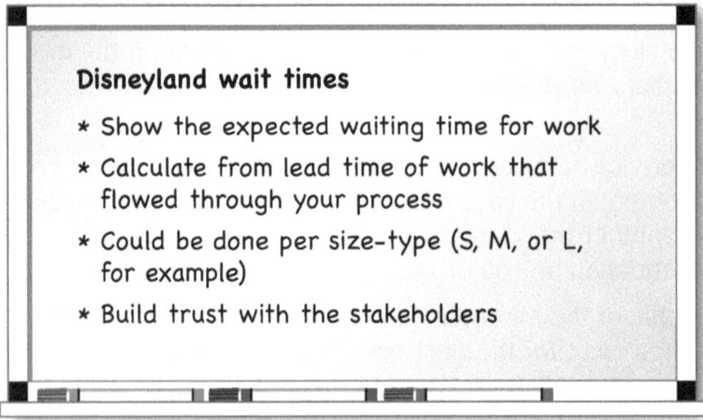

9.2 Estimating work—relatively speaking

Closely related to planning is the task of estimating how much effort you'll spend on completing the work ahead. This is difficult because you're trying to predict the future, and history has often shown that we, as an industry, often miss our estimates—by a lot, in many cases.

Estimates are often wrong, but *estimating* (the process of coming up with the estimates) can still prove useful. Estimating gives you a chance to start managing the uncertainty that lies ahead. It can be used as a risk-management tool that allows you to discover misconceptions, inconsistencies, and areas that need further investigation early on.

To be able to make estimates, you need to start digging into the work that lies ahead, in order to understand it well enough to know what you're up against. Doing so as a team helps you create a shared understanding of the work. But you don't want to do too much estimating either, according to the law of diminishing returns. You can come up with a quick estimate now that has a low probability of being accurate (or covers a big span: 70–130%, for example), or you can spend a little time investigating it and get a better, more accurate estimate in place. But it's not useful for you to spend days figuring out the *exact* number of hours. Somewhere in between a WAG[6] and a fully specified system is the sweet spot; find yours. The rest of this section and the next give you tools to help you do estimates.

9.2.1 Story points

One reason that estimates are tricky is that you're trying to predict the future and be sure how it will play out. The future is by definition unknown. In order to give precise and accurate estimates, you need to know quite a lot of details about the work you're estimating, and this is asked of you at the beginning of a project: the time when you know the least about the work you're about to do.

On top of all that, we, as humans, aren't good at estimating in exact terms. You can easily test this yourself by looking at a tall building and trying to guess how tall it is off the top of your head. That isn't easy.

It's better to ask a simpler question, like "Of those two buildings over there, which is taller? In relative terms, how much taller is one than the other?" These questions are much easier for people to answer and are probably ancestral to humans since the stone ages, when it could be useful to know which of two mammoths was the bigger.

This has led agile teams around the world to do their estimations in *relative* terms rather than with exact numbers. The best-known agile tool for estimating like this is called *story points*.

Story points were first introduced in agile methods such as Scrum and Extreme Programming. This technique is a way to indicate *relative* sizes between work items. The name *story points* has to do with the things that you're estimating, which often are user stories.[7]

You've probably been asked, "When will this feature be done?" The most common answer would be a number of days or hours, often with a span—because you don't know at this point. This resembles the hard question of how tall a building is (the illustration is a couple of pars earlier, in this section).

Story points are a response to that problem, in which you instead focus on the relation between the individual work items. With a relative measure, you're not stating how big a story point is; you're saying that something you've estimated to be five story points is about double the size of something you've estimated to be two story points. And it's about a third the size of something that you've estimated to be 14 story points.

[6] Wild Ass Guess (WAG) is a term coined by Robert C. Martin, a.k.a. Uncle Bob. It's named for the great estimation capabilities of wild donkeys, we presume …

[7] User stories can quickly be described as small increments of functionality that give value to a user—hence the name.

If the *story* part of story points refers to user stories, the *point* part is only a name. The "relativeness" between the numbers is the important thing—not the number itself.

A WORD FROM THE COACH Try to avoid using "days" or "hours" in estimates because it might confuse you and others into thinking that you're referring to real days. Some teams use the term *relative days*, for example, which sends that kind of signal.

Fibonacci series

The Fibonacci series is a famous number series discovered by Leonardo Fibonacci that is often used for estimating story-point size. The series starts with 0 and 1 and is then constructed by adding the two previous numbers in the series, which produces the following numbers: 0, 1, 1, 2, 3, 5, 8, 13, 21, 34, 55, and so on.

The reason the Fibonacci series is often used when doing estimates is not only out of pure mathematical geekiness. The idea is that by only allowing ourselves to use Fibonacci numbers for our estimates, the precision in our estimates automatically decreases, the bigger the items are. This reflects the fact that our ability to relatively estimate decreases when one item is an order of magnitude bigger than the other. If you're discussing whether an item is a 12 or a 13, you're probably fooling yourself that you have more information and better precision than you do.

HOW IS THIS USEFUL AGAIN?

By now you might be wondering how this can be useful. Relative estimates: what use can somebody possibly have for those?

First, they convey that an estimate isn't exact. You have *not* said, "It will take 258 hours to complete this feature." The only thing you've said is that this eight-story-point work item is about twice the size of that five-story-point work item you completed last week.

Second, a relative estimate can be useful because you can follow up the estimates against your real performance. Say that a team has been working for a month, and during that time the team has delivered work items estimated to be 34 story points. You can then make a prediction that during the next month, given the same team and the same kinds of tasks, the team can probably deliver features estimated to be 30–40 story points.

THE PROBLEMS WITH STORY POINTS

The relative nature of story points is a great tool for doing estimates, but herein lies the problems with story points: they're relative and hence not exact. This is uncomfortable for many people, and it's easy to fall into the trap of trying to convert story points to days or hours. A manager for a team that did 34 story points in a month could make the generalization that a story point means roughly one day of work. But he would be mistaken. It's a relative effort between the stories that you estimated at the time.

The same manager might also think that because *this* team did 34 points in a month, and he has three other teams at his disposal, he can count on 136 points being delivered from all four teams each month. But again, he would be mistaken. The estimates are only valid for a certain team: two teams that are asked to estimate a number of work items might come up with different results. The same story that one team decides is five story points can be eight for another team, because the first team started by having their smallest story be one story point, whereas the other team chose two, and everything is related to this story.

Estimates can also be affected by team dynamics and who is more prominent in the discussions, or by teams having different strengths, weaknesses, and experiences. Things that are hard to do for one team can be dead simple to another.

In short, story points are relative; they estimate the relative size of things and are relative to the team and setting they were made in. This relativeness is good because it conveys that you can't give an exact estimate but can still use a tool to reason about the size of the work.

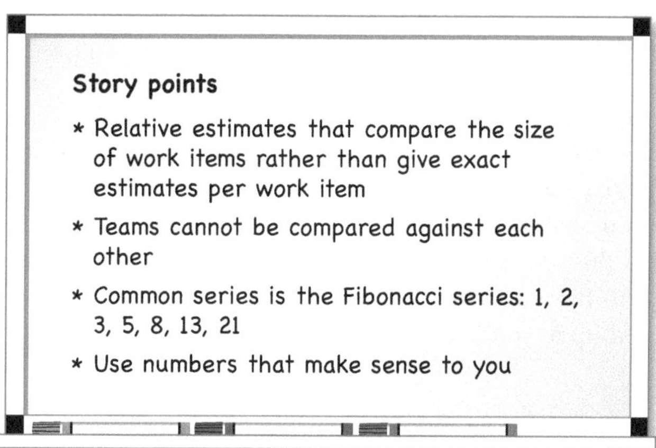

The fact that story points are numbers can be bad because numbers convey exactness where you really just want to show the relative size of the estimated work. To solve that, let's look into the subject of the next way of doing estimation: T-shirt sizes.

9.2.2 T-shirt sizes

The problems with story points have led many teams to abandon them and go with something that doesn't use numbers at all, like T-shirt sizes, for example. This means you estimate by picking one of the following: S, M, L, or XL.

Keep the system as simple as possible. This is a rough estimate of a work-item size, and the only thing you're indicating is that an S is about the same size as all the other

S items you've done. More values indicate higher accuracy in your estimates, and the whole idea is to just indicate the relative sizes of the work.

Quite often, we have encountered teams that use S, M, and L; anything bigger than that, they break down into smaller work items that they can estimate as S, M, or L. An XL work item would take up too much of their capacity and be cumbersome for the team to manage.

You could add sizes to this series if needed (such as XS and XXL), but in most cases we haven't seen a need to do so. Remember that a work item estimated to be XL would hide a lot of uncertainty and risks. It's not uncommon to split an XL item and end up with … two or three new XL items, because the team didn't know what was hidden within that big work item.

A WORD FROM THE COACH Agree on always breaking up items estimated to be XL until they're L or smaller. This is a great way to manage uncertainty and reduce risk as well as limit your WIP.

As with story points, the benefit of having relative estimates like this is that you can start to make predictions based on real data from the team's performance over time. If the team normally uses two to five days for a small work item, and has been doing so for the last 30 work items estimated to S, chances are that the next S item will take about two to five days. Based on that knowledge, you can predict that the 30 S items you've lined up in your backlog will take the team about 100 days to complete.

Other than the fact that T-shirt sizes use letters, whereas story points are numbers, there's not a big difference between the two in the way they're intended to be used.

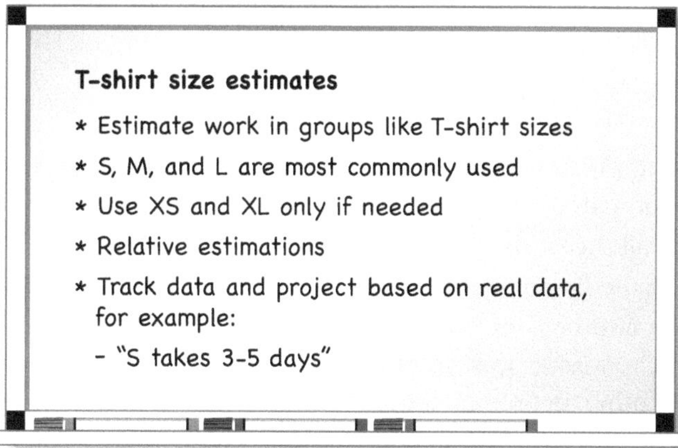

Let's see how relative estimations can be used in practice with a couple of estimation techniques.

9.3 Estimation techniques

There are a number of common ways that agile teams come up with estimates. What they all have in common is *collaboration*, and in all the practices we're suggesting in this section you'll see another underlying theme: they strive to be good enough. You don't want to invest too much time in estimating.

We strongly advise you to estimate in groups and preferably include people in the exercise with different competences, skill-sets, and roles. Estimating and planning can be seen as a knowledge-gathering exercise in which you're uncovering information as you remove uncertainty.

Let's go through some common techniques, starting with a quick way of estimating the effort for an entire project or a complete backlog.

9.3.1 A line of cards

Let's say that you have 50 work items for which a stakeholder asks you to estimate the size. This is the dreaded "How long will this project take you?" question. We have had great results from this simple exercise that can be run quickly in a group. For about 50 items, this can be run in 10–20 minutes.

The exercise goes like this:

1 Write the descriptions of the work items on separate index cards. They should be prepared before you start.
2 Put all the cards in a pile on the table.
3 Pick the first one, and place it on the side of the pile of cards.
4 Pick another one, and ask: "Is this bigger or smaller than the first one?" To be able to answer this, you might need to discuss what the work item is about with the other people in the room. Take time to do that, but not too much time. Remember, this is a quick estimate.
5 When you've decided whether it's bigger or smaller, place it above or below the card on the table so that the cards form a line.

6 Repeat steps 4 and 5 until you're out of cards. The question will now be "Where should this card be placed in relation to the card already on the table?" and then place the card in the right slot depending on its estimated size.
7 Now you can group the cards together—which is stage 2 of this technique. Start from the bottom (smallest) part of the line of cards on the table, and declare that the first group will be estimated as small.[8]
8 Continue upward, and decide where the cards get bigger and when a new value (medium, for example) should be used. Have the team call that out.

[8] You could use story points instead. Use the scale and measurements that work for you.

9 Pretty soon you've walked the entire line of cards. You can now summarize the values (five cards estimated to be small, four cards estimated to be medium, and so on) and get a total for the entire line of cards. This is the estimated effort for the work items.

A WORD FROM THE COACH We have used this as a repeated exercise after each release (every second week) to estimate the remainder of the work items in the backlog. We never spend more than 10 minutes on it.

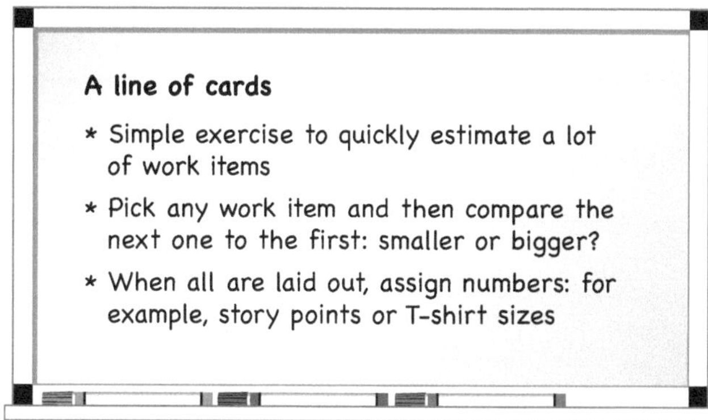

A more formal and detailed way of doing this is through Planning Poker, which is the next exercise we have coming up.

9.3.2 Planning Poker

Planning Poker is another way to do estimations in a group, using the wisdom of the crowd and some playfulness to produce great discussions and help you estimate the work items in the process. The name Planning Poker was coined by James Grenning (one of the signatories of the Agile Manifesto[9]), and the only connection with poker is that some sort of playing cards often are used during the game. The game is simple to play:

1 Hand out playing cards (discussed later in this section) to all participants of the game.
2 Pull a work item to estimate, and describe it briefly to the group.
3 Talk about and answer any questions about the work item.
4 When everybody feels comfortable enough about what the work item is, go to the estimation.

[9] Visit http://agilemanifesto.org/.

5 Each person picks a card that represents the points they think the work item should be estimated to be. Don't show it to the others.
6 On the count of three, everybody shows the card with their estimate to the rest of the group.

7 This step is the interesting part. If you all are more or less in agreement, then you've found the estimate and can move on to the next work item. If you have wildly different estimates (2, 3, 8, and 13 for example), you should ask yourselves why:
   - What did the people estimating 2 and 13 story points think the item meant?
   - What did the 8- and 13-story-points people think the work item meant?
   - Go back to step 5, and have a new vote.
8 Repeat until you reach agreement on the size of the estimate. Some smaller variations in estimates can be accepted, but you should be pretty close to each other.

The main point is the discussion, which is apparent to anyone who plays Planning Poker more than once. Only by talking to each other can you understand what everybody thinks about the effort it will take to complete the work item. Asking the group to do the estimates is a way to provoke such a discussion to happen.

Another way to do Planning Poker

In the book *Agile Adoption Patterns: A Roadmap to Organizational Success* (Addison-Wesley Professional, 2008), Amr Elssamadisy describes planning in a different manner than we did. For each requirement:

1. Have a domain expert explain the requirement in question to the team, to ensure that everyone understands what it's all about.
2. Perform the following estimation rounds, and only continue to the next round if you aren't in agreement of the size of the estimate:
   - Round 1—Conduct silent voting using cards. No discussion, but cast votes: on the count of three as described earlier, for example.
   - Round 2—Let people think for a minute or two before doing a new silent vote, still without discussion.
   - Round 3—Let the team members explain why they voted as they did, and then vote again.
   - If you're still not in agreement, then park that story for a separate session, and continue with the next requirement.

With this approach, you focus on producing good-enough estimates quickly. There's no point discussing each and every one of the requirements in detail when you're already in agreement.

For teams who haven't worked together before, this exercise might be hard, because you don't have a norm for what your relative estimates are. What does two story points mean to you? In cases like these, you should pick a small story and try to agree on an estimate for that. All other work can now be estimated in relation to that work item.

Another way is to estimate with the line of cards (see section 9.3.1) a couple of times before you, as a team, start doing Planning Poker.

A WORD FROM THE COACH The discussion is the goal—not the estimates. We can't emphasize this enough. Make sure you encourage questions and discussions: this is where the learning takes place, new ideas are discovered, and old "truths" that we might carry around get challenged and maybe discarded. Coming up with no answer because of too many unknowns is a valid and useful result. Not many stakeholders would start a project under those conditions. For a good and effective session, make sure you have the people present who are needed to answer questions that might arise.

WHAT CARDS SHOULD YOU USE?

A lot of companies[10] create their own Planning Poker decks, and if you get your hands on one, it will work fine. If you don't have one, you can easily create some cards on

[10] Not that there's anything wrong with that; we were both eager proponents of creating cards for a consultancy where we both worked.

your own with pen and paper; it'll take you 30 seconds. These are some cards you could include:

- Numbers 1, 2, 3, 5, 8, 13.
- ?—This means, "I haven't got a clue. Give me more information before I can even guess."
- A break or coffee cup symbol—This means, "My brain is toasted and I need a break, preferably with coffee, before we go on."

There are also a number of smartphone applications[11] that can help you with this. Don't spend any money on one: use your hands if nothing else works. The estimate isn't the important thing, so don't go to great lengths to have a nice way of showing the numbers.

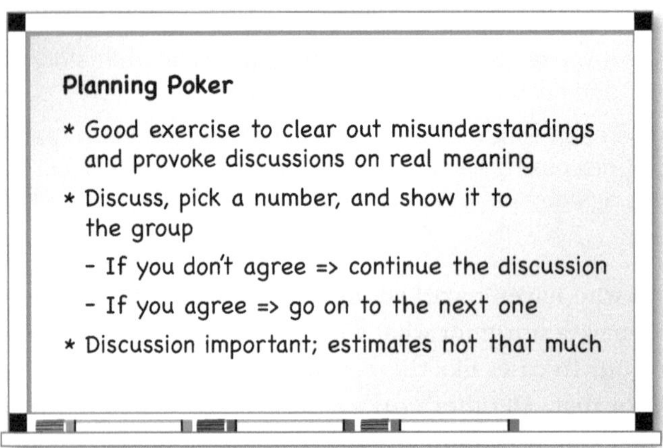

The first exercises we've discussed are all about estimating work items, but there's another way. What if you instead tweaked the work items into something that suits your estimates? Let's get help from a fairy-tale figure to do that.

9.3.3 Goldilocks

Instead of estimating the work-item size, you can change the work item *into* a suitable size. It's a bit like the old saying, "If the mountain won't come to Muhammad, then Muhammad must go to the mountain."[12] This technique[13] takes its inspiration from the children's story of Goldilocks and the three bears.

In this story, the heroine, Goldilocks, walks through the woods and finds the three bears' house, inhabited by Papa Bear, Mama Bear, and Baby Bear. Papa Bear is the

---

[11] Search for "planning poker" in your application store, and you'll find a long list of applications.

[12] See http://mng.bz/0l2M for more information.

[13] Joakim first picked this up at a workshop led by Johannes Brodwall and Lasse Koskela at the Oredev conference a few years back.

biggest bear, Mama Bear is next in size, and Baby Bear is the smallest of the three bears. The bears are out when Goldilocks enters the house. She is tired and wants to rest. Goldilocks tries the bears' chairs (among other things …) for comfort. Papa Bear's chair is way too big, Baby Bear's chair is way too small, but Mama Bear's chair is *just right.* Goldilocks sits in that chair and rests.

Before we lose ourselves totally in children's stories: with the Goldilocks estimate technique, you change your work items so that they're *just right.* Not too big, not too small. Instead of assigning different estimate values to each work item, you divide and merge work items to make them roughly the same size and *just right* for your convenience.

You can run this as an exercise if you want to, by splitting up a stack of work items into three smaller stacks: too small, too big, and just right. Describe each work item, and have the team vote for placement. After this, you split the work items in the "too big" stack into smaller "just right" items. Vice versa, you merge the items in the "too small" pile into "just right" work items.

This simple exercise can be beneficial to you and your predictions. You now have equally sized items that you can start to track and measure. After a few weeks, you know how many "average-sized" (or *just-right* sized) work items the team can cope with each week, for example. Because all work items are the same size, it makes predictions easy to make.

In section 7.2.2, we talked about making work items smaller and similar in size to increase the flow. The Goldilocks estimation technique is a direct application of those ideas that can help you estimate as well as improve the flow.

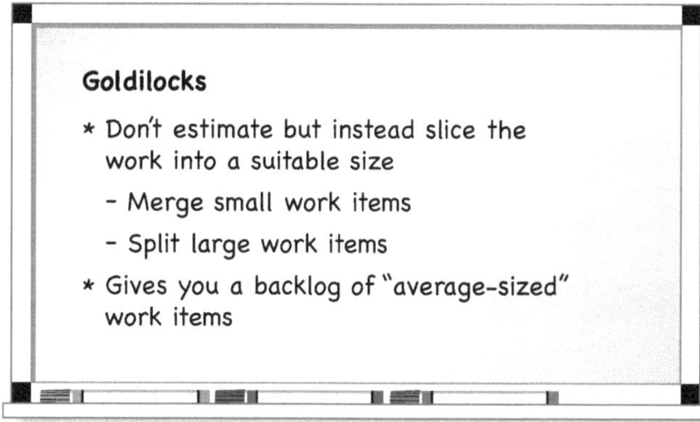

Now that we have investigated a couple of techniques for doing estimates, we'll turn our attention to something that can help you split up the work ahead into manageable pieces.

9.4 Cadence

Cadence roughly means beat or rhythm, and you're probably wondering why we're starting to talk about musical terms this late in the book if we want to introduce you to music theory. But the rhythm that Lean practitioners mean when talking about cadence is the rhythm of the work, like the heartbeat of your process.

This isn't as strange as it first sounds; you have a rhythm in your process today. A simple example is iterations found in many processes. In Scrum, for example, work has a natural heartbeat in iterations called *sprints*. Each sprint starts with a planning session, in which the team takes on as much work as they think they'll manage during the next sprint. After two weeks the sprint is over, and the team can look back on the sprint with a review, demonstration, and retrospective.

A cadence gives you a foundation for predictability. With a regular cadence, you can start to measure and predict how you're doing against a goal. You could say that your goal is to deliver four to six work items every other week. When two weeks have passed, you can look back and see how you did against your goal. The two weeks' cadence you now have introduced is for review purposes.

Timeboxed iterations like the ones we described previously are only one kind of cadence. Cadences can take many forms, and in this section we'll examine different ways that they can manifest themselves in kanban and the gain you can get from using them.

ITERATIONS AND KANBAN

An iteration typically starts with some sort of planning or assessment of what you're getting ready to do; you do it, and then you're done—preferably you end by looking back on what you've done during the last iteration and seeing if you can improve. The cadence for the sprint is, for example, two weeks, and a new "heartbeat" in your process is started when the next iteration begins.

As you can see, iterations are like timeboxed, small projects with a clear start and goal. As an example, you can see an iteration in action on a board like this:

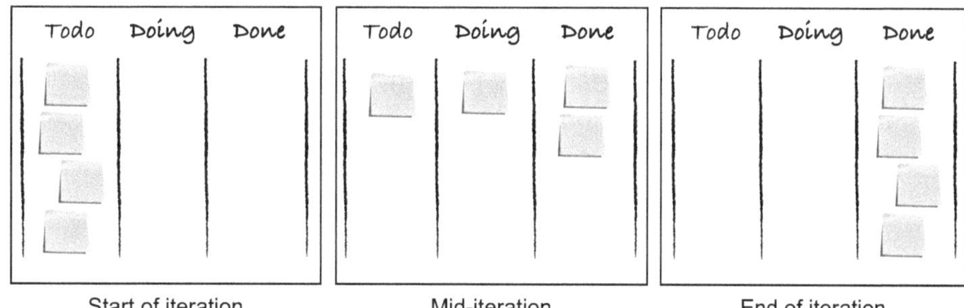

Start of iteration Mid-iteration End of iteration

In the first picture, the team has lined up all their work for the next iteration in the Todo column. In the mid-iteration picture, some work items are being worked on, others are done, and there's one that hasn't been started yet. At the end of the iteration, hopefully all of the work items have been moved into the Done column. The board is reset, and the team starts over by planning for the next iteration.

TRANSITION FROM ITERATION-BASED PROCESSES

You could also map the iteration flow more explicitly on the board, as suggested by Eric Willeke,[14] with a board looking something like this:

Product backlog | Ready for planning | Sprint backlog | Building | Accepted | Demo complete | Done

This gives you a smooth transition from Scrum (or other iteration-based methods) to kanban (which is flow-based) because nothing has changed, other than that you've started visualizing your entire workflow. The current cadences of Scrum (planning,

---

14 See "Switching from Scrum to Kanban – Huh?" http://mng.bz/j6UJ.

daily standups, retrospectives, and demos) can be left untouched and run with the same regularly as before.

THE KANBAN APPROACH TO CADENCES

Kanban doesn't say much about cadences like those you've seen examples of up to now. The main focus is the work items and how they individually flow over the board. This gives you the freedom to decouple the iteration (like planning and review) from the work.

That means you plan at regular intervals—every week, for example—and maybe have a review and retrospective every third week. Or you might use events in your process to signal you to do planning, review, and so on, as we talked about earlier. That would be like applying the Lean principle of *pull* for those events. This approach makes sure you plan just in time when you need more work, not just in case by creating a stock of planned work.

Even though kanban doesn't say anything about iterations, you could still do iterations in kanban if you wanted to. Remember that kanban is three simple principles (make work visible, limit work in process, and help the work to flow) and doesn't say anything about your cadences or iterations. Many Scrum teams adopt the kanban principles and move slowly away from an iteration-centric cadence, toward a more flow-based process without iterations. You can read more about this approach in the book *ScrumBan* by Corey Ladas (Modus Cooperandi Press, 2009, http://amzn.com/0578002140).

All the benefits we have talked about in this book regarding visualization, limiting WIP, and helping work to flow would still apply to a team using iterations. The only difference would be that the impact of the kanban principles would be limited within the scope of the iteration.

Iteration- or flow-based: which is better? There's no way to tell. If you have a backlog of items that are the only things you work on, then an iteration-based approach would be suitable. This would give you great focus, and you could push work that comes to you during the iteration to the side until the next iteration. If you, on the other hand, manage items that might come to you at any time (doing support and maintenance of an application that you also are developing, for example), you might be better off with a flow-based approach, without the start and stop of iterations.

DON'T GO LAZY ON ME

Finally, if you transition from an iteration-based process, like Scrum, into a flow-based approach, don't go lazy (as we'll talk about in chapter 12). Use the practices that make sense to you; keep having planning sessions to break down work, keep doing retrospectives to improve, and keep doing demonstrations for your stakeholders at suitable cadences.

9.5 Planning the kanban way: less pain, more gain

In this section, we want to step back and take some time to ponder *why* you're planning and estimating—and maybe think about the alternatives. In addition to theoretical and logical reasons to try to do less planning and estimating, many kanban teams find the need for planning and estimating diminishing the more they use kanban and the principles we discuss in this book.

A WORD FROM THE COACH Don't stop doing planning (and other practices that help you do great work) because kanban doesn't tell you to. Far too many kanban teams hide behind this "excuse" and stop planning because "There's no planning in kanban." Don't be that team! You're better than that.

On that note, there's not a single word about code quality in kanban, either. Or writing code, for that matter. Or about doing testing. Or that it's a good idea to deploy your code at all.

9.5.1 The need diminishes

Teams that use kanban gradually find the need for planning and estimates fading away. The need for estimates and plans is based on an urge to manage risk and uncertainty. Plans are there to give you some feel for what you have in front of you, how far you've come, and how to handle unforeseen circumstances. In order to make plans that are trustworthy, you need to have some estimates of how much effort is needed to complete the work you have lined up. The more things you have going on at the same time, the more planning is often asked of you (which causes more work: more planning, more estimating, and so on; see chapter 5's discussion of Little's law, page 95).

With kanban, you strive to minimize WIP and help the work you have going on flow faster. This means there's not a lot of work to plan for, and because you want the work you take on to be small and fast, the planning and estimating should go by pretty quickly. Estimating and planning the effort for a single new feature is much easier to do accurately than if you're asked to estimate 25 features, right?

When teams are pulling new work often, maybe several times a day, estimating each work item quickly starts to feel cumbersome. Pretty soon you start to question the value of doing these estimates in the first place. This is a signal you should act on. Why not go and ask the stakeholder what the real need is? It's not unlikely that after some time using kanban, the stakeholder has also seen the need for detailed estimates and plans diminish, as you have. At least you could do an experiment, and try to go a month without or with much more lightweight planning and estimating: trying out T-shirt-size (see section 9.2.2) estimates, for example.

Kanban teaches you to visualize as many aspects of your process as possible for people on the team and others around it. That means the current status is obvious for anybody to see: right in front of you on a whiteboard, for example. If there's data that some stakeholders are missing, you should add that data and make it visual, too. Printed backlogs on which you strike out the items that have been completed, and simple graphs of the number of items you've completed each week, are examples of ways to visualize information that might help the stakeholders to see what is going on and the progress of the team's work.

"The best reporting we ever had!"

Marcus helped a client to convert a critical system from an outdated technology (VB6) into something a bit more modern (VB.NET). The system was a big monolithic Windows application with literally hundreds of forms. Naturally, the inevitable questions came in the first week: "How long will this take you?" "When will you be done?"

Because the team didn't have a clue, quite naturally (they had never done it before, they didn't know the code, they had not decided on what the end result should be), we decided to use simple reporting—to calm people down.

We listed all the code files (VB6 forms) by size in KB, with the simple assumption that the larger the file, the more code to convert. Everything less than 20 KB was classified as small, 20–50 KB was called medium, and 60–100 KB was large. Above 100 KB was called XL.

We threw everything into a spreadsheet in which the developers reported the date they started and stopped development on the form.

From this it was simple to do a diagram stating the current status of the project. And with the dates, we could do projections of how much time was left for the rest of the forms. "We have done three small that took on average four days. There are 60 small left in the backlog. 60 × 4 days = 240 days left until all the small ones are done."

The developers were happy with this lightweight reporting. But what surprised Marcus was that the steering committee of this high-risk project called this "the best reporting we have ever seen in the company."

We think that it has to do with two simple facts: it was transparent and simple for everyone to see, and it was kept up to date on a daily basis. That built trust, and the predictions were on a good-enough level for everyone to feel secure about the progress of the project.

9.5.2 *Reasoning logically: the customer's plea*

Let's step back a moment and think about why you're here. The main goal of any IT department or project is to help the business to work smarter, easier, or better. To paraphrase Gojko Adzic,[15] make business impact—not software.

This means software is a means to an end; software in itself isn't the point. There's someone out there who wants to be able to get her work done better, more smoothly, in a more fun way, or not to have to do it at all. Let's call that person the customer, shall we?

[15] *Impact Mapping: Making a Big Impact with Software Products and Projects*, by Gojko Adzic (Provoking Thoughts, 2012, http://amzn.com/B009KWDKVA).

A WORD FROM THE COACH Yes, there's always a customer who needs your work, even if you don't see it. We've worked with teams that couldn't name their customers or didn't think about them, but they're always there.

If you have a hard time knowing who they are, follow the money. Who is paying your bills? On which budget do you work, and how does that person get his money? That's your customer—and you should care about him.

The customer is the reason you're here. And customers don't care about plans or estimates. Yes, we said it. When was the last time a *customer* phoned you and said, "Thank you for the great and accurate estimates and plans you made for the last project"? Exactly: never. That never happened, and it never will, either. The customer wants capabilities that she can use to do business in better, faster, or new ways.

You know that you "need" plans and estimates to be able to do your work or to keep doing it consistently and accurately, but it's ultimately not adding value to your product. Again, you can run a litmus test in the form of this question: "If you think that estimating is value-adding, do much more of it. It's adding value, right?"[16]

That said, as long as you see value in planning and estimating, keep doing it, but enough of it to improve the flow of work through the team. For example, you can learn quite a lot about a work item when estimating, but after a while more estimating isn't uncovering new knowledge, and then you shouldn't keep on doing it.

Plans are worthless, but planning is everything.

—Dwight D. Eisenhower

9.5.3 #NoEstimates—could you do without this altogether?

By Torbjörn Gyllebring

One way to further illustrate the points from the last section comes from the No Estimates movement. We've invited our good friend Torbjörn Gyllebring[17] *to write about that, because he's well acquainted with the subject. Torbjörn, the stage is yours.*

Few ever stop to question estimation and estimates; rather, most consider them a given. Questioning that assumption and finding ways to work effectively without them is the core question of #NoEstimates.

WHAT IS #NOESTIMATES?

The idea is that in many contexts, it's not only possible but also beneficial to forego estimation in favor of alternative ways to manage work. Following are a few alternative strategies to solve different aspects of the benefits ascribed to estimates.

---

[16] This excellent way of determining whether an activity is adding value was introduced by David J. Anderson.

[17] Known as @drunkcod on Twitter.

Studying the nature and type of demands on the system enables the use of probabilistic forecasting and simulation to create robust plans based on historical data. One pioneer in this field is Troy Magennis, with his work on the Monte Carlo simulation.[18]

Others reach a point where they don't estimate but rely on what I've dubbed The Law of Average Averages. This law states that

On average, an average work item will take average time to complete.

The observation is that assuming requests are similar enough, or that the team has learned to instinctively break work down into "right-sized" chunks, you can skip estimation and consider them all average. Some items will take longer, some will take less time, but over time things will even out.

Suppose you work in small chunks and that a high degree of stakeholder involvement enables using a very fine-grained drip-funding model. You start working in the direction of "the next most valuable thing." When value is realized or you discover you're spending more than it will be worth, you stop investing.

This requires a honed ability to always be in a deliverable state and requires embracing uncertainty at a low level. High-level direction and vision are managed by tracking overall investment.

You can also reverse the estimation question. Instead of asking, "How long will it take to complete all these things?" and essentially aggregating a set of guesses, you can pose a different, more powerful question: "Given that I'm willing to invest this much, what is possible?"

WHY #NOESTIMATES

The driver behind #NoEstimates is that estimation can drive dysfunctional behavior, such as estimates turning into commitments, plans, or deadlines. By engineering out the need for estimation, you remove these problems and their associated time and resource costs.

Estimation becomes problematic not because estimates are inherently evil, but because they tend to be used for multiple purposes, and their purpose morphs over time as the numbers assume a life of their own. Working without estimates forces you to think deeply about what different functions estimates play in your process, inviting you to find more focused solutions. Coordination, discovering differing assumptions, long-range planning, go/no-go decisions, and costing can all be solved in ways that don't muddy the waters. #NoEstimates is hard and requires discipline and skill, but the opportunities are exciting.

FURTHER #NOESTIMATES READING

We invite you to join us and explore the topic. A good starting point is the following list:

- Follow the discussion on Twitter: search for #NoEstimates.
- Read Neil Killick's blog entry "#NoEstimates Part 1 – Doing Scrum Without Estimates," http://mng.bz/7wvp.

[18] http://en.wikipedia.org/wiki/Monte_Carlo_method.

- Read Woody Zuill's blog entry "If You Found Estimates Bring No Value – What Would You Do?" http://mng.bz/3a85.

Thank you, Torbjörn! #NoEstimates is both inspiring and thought provoking. It's also a great way to end our chapter on planning and estimating: by looking ahead and challenging ourselves to try new and better ways and never stop learning.

9.6 Summary

In this chapter, we talked about planning and estimating:

- We first talked about *when* to plan and different approaches to find the right time to plan: not too early nor too late—just in time:
  - We took a look at event-driven planning and talked about order points, one way to run event-driven planning.
  - Planning more often involves stakeholders around you more and builds trust, but it can also be costly. You need to balance it so that you plan with the right frequency.
  - Using Disneyland wait times is a way of showing expected delivery times.
- Plans and estimates are often requested by others around you, and we talked briefly about extending the workflow upstream and downstream.
- Estimating in exact terms is much harder than giving relative estimates, so we prefer doing relative estimates:
  - Story points and T-shirt sizes are two common ways of doing relative estimates.
- We looked at a couple of estimation techniques:
  - A line of cards
  - Planning Poker
  - Goldilocks
- Cadence is the natural rhythm or heartbeat found in your process. In iteration-based processes, there are natural cadences when iterations start and stop.
- With kanban you can have the cadences you see fit for activities: reviewing, planning, demonstration, and retrospectives. You don't have to tie it to the flow of your work.
- Finally, we stepped back and pondered the need for plans and estimates:
  - Teams that use kanban see the need for detailed plans decreasing with the tightening of feedback loops.
  - Customers don't want plans and estimates; they want business capabilities.
  - Estimating and making plans is useful as long as you're uncovering new information.
  - The #NoEstimates movement talks about abandoning estimates altogether and finding effective ways to work without estimates.

In the next chapter, we'll look into process improvements, which is how you can use all the tools we have presented so far to help you continuously improve.

10 Process improvement

This chapter covers

- Continuous improvement—the real purpose of kanban
- Respect for people—putting people first
- Retrospectives, root-cause analysis, and Kanban Kata

Since it is people who manufacture things, manufacturing is impossible unless people are developed.

—Display at Toyota Technology Museum in Nagoya

"Developing people first" is a core principle in Toyota's philosophy, and its two parts, "respect for people" and "continuous improvement" (or *kaizen*), are often referred to as the two pillars of The Toyota Way management system.

This philosophy of improvement is a mindset that can be found throughout Lean organizations like Toyota, from the CEO and overarching strategies to the janitorial staff and how people place their tools on the workbench in order to be more effective. There's a deeply rooted aspiration to do better, to improve, and to be more effective in the heart and soul of a working Lean organization. It's the respect for people—respecting, developing, and encouraging everyone in the organization—that makes this possible.

With its roots in Lean thinking, kanban is all about continuous improvement and respect for people. Visualizing the work is an easy but effective way of enabling self-organized improvement work. Limiting WIP and helping work to flow make bottlenecks and improvement opportunities visible to the team, allowing team members to come up with ways to improve.

Unfortunately, kanban doesn't solve the problems for you, and it doesn't automatically improve things. Kanban exposes improvement opportunities, but it's up to you to find out how to improve. In this chapter, we'll look at a few different practices that will help you with that. There's no better way to start this chapter, and get your attention, than to paraphrase the demanding dance coach Lydia Grant from *Fame*:

> *You've got big dreams. You want to improve. Well, improvement costs. And right here is where you start paying: in sweat.*[1]
>
> —Lydia Grant, *Fame*

1 See www.imdb.com/title/tt0576603/quotes for the original quote.

10.1 Retrospectives

The *retrospective* is an important practice in most agile methodologies. In fact, one of the agile principles[2] states, "At regular intervals, the team reflects on how to become more effective, then tunes and adjusts its behavior accordingly." In the retrospective meeting, you analyze your process and progress during the last period and try to find areas in which you can improve.

Agile retrospectives are a big area, and several books have already been written on the topic. This section is by no means an attempt to provide complete coverage of the topic; rather, it'll show you how the practice of retrospectives can be put into action in a kanban setting. If you want more information about a lot of different ways of running retrospectives and the thinking behind them, we recommend *Agile Retrospectives* by Esther Derby and Diana Larsen (Pragmatic Bookshelf, 2006, http://pragprog.com/book/dlret/agile-retrospectives) and *The Retrospective Handbook* by Patrick Kua (CreateSpace Independent Publishing Platform, 2013, https://leanpub.com/the-retrospective-handbook). Both of these are great and have a nice practical and pragmatic touch to them.

10.1.1 What is a retrospective?

A team retrospective is run at regular intervals, with a preference of doing them more often rather than seldom. Typically, teams set aside a few hours every one to four weeks for retrospectives. This can be seen as the team investing time in improving how they work together.

The aim of the retrospective is to come up with a few improvement actions (preferably no more than three) that can be changed before the next retrospective. This ensures that you, as a team, take on only as much improvement work as you can handle. You're doing small improvements often. ("Limit your WIP," remember?)

A retrospective usually consists of five distinct parts:[3]

1. *Set the stage.* This first step is when you kick off the retrospective and set the mood for the meeting. A great way to do that can be to inform everyone about the retrospective prime directive (see the following box) or use some sort of icebreaker exercise (see the next Word from the Coach).

> Regardless of what we discover,
> we understand and truly believe that
> everyone did the best job they could,
> given what they knew at the time,
> their skills and abilities, the
> resources available, and the
> situation at hand.

[2] Check out the principles at http://agilemanifesto.org/principles.html.

[3] From the excellent book, *Agile Retrospectives* (http://pragprog.com/book/dlret/agile-retrospectives).

A WORD FROM THE COACH A great trick is to use some sort of exercise that ensures that everyone says something, if only a single word such as "yes" or "no." For example, go around the room and ask, "Do you agree with the retrospective prime directive?" Research has shown that if someone says something in the beginning of a meeting, there's a much higher probability that they will speak again later in the meeting.

2. *Gather data.* At this stage, the team looks back (hence *retro*spective) at the past period and gathers data about what happened. Different retrospective exercises focus on different events, on different moods, or on the progress of the team, but the main idea is the same: gather data for analysis.
3. *Generate insights.* Here you analyze the data you gathered to learn what conclusions you can draw from it. Why did these events go down the way they did? There are a lot of different ways to do this: for example, root-cause analysis.
4. *Decide what to do.* The main effort next is to find a suitable set of actions that you know you can complete during the period up to the next retrospective, which often is a nice timebox for improvements. Typically it's better to choose fewer actions than more; more actions stand the risk of ending up not being done.

   Sometimes you might not have actions come out of the retrospective. Maybe the team solved the problems during the retrospective, or maybe they had to sit down and talk for a while. This is OK, too.
5. *Close the retrospective.* A good practice at this point is to do a mini-retrospective of the retrospective.[4] It can be as simple as asking people what they thought about the form of the retrospective and how it can be improved.

In order to stay focused, we suggest that you timebox the meeting to, for example, an hour and that you also timebox the different parts of the retrospective.

10.1.2 How does it work?

The outline we just described is pretty generic and doesn't tell you much about what to *do* during a retrospective. There are a lot of different ways to do this, and we often mix different approaches to keep the team alert and keep the retrospectives from becoming boring. A good tip is to invite someone from another team to facilitate the retrospective for you; that gives you fresh ways of running retrospectives, and someone who isn't involved with the team can be neutral, focusing on the facilitation of the retrospective without feeling a need to participate.

You can find a lot of good exercises and complete plans for retrospectives online. Here are two sites that we've found useful:

- Agile Retrospective Resource Wiki, http://retrospectivewiki.org
- Gamestorming, www.gogamestorm.com

[4] But don't do a retrospective of the mini-retrospective on the retrospective, because then you might be drawn into a recursive loop of retrospectives ending in the inception of the universe.

In the following sections you'll find a basic retrospective that we think is a good representation of how a retrospective can be run.

SET THE STAGE

1. Start by showing or reading the retrospective prime directive, and ask the people attending the retrospective if they can adhere to this for this retrospective. If not everyone agrees, you should underline that the goal of the retrospective is to find improvements, not to end up in a blame game.
2. Gather data. Ask the team to write down all the great things that have happened during the period since the last retrospective:
   - Instruct them to write each thing on a separate sticky.
   - Allow three to four minutes (use a timer) to brainstorm ideas. When the team is done, have them post the items on part of a whiteboard in any order they want.
3. Do the same thing again, but this time, write down things that you want to improve. Remind the team of your focus: you don't want to find bad people, but rather improvement opportunities that you haven't yet realized. Follow the same instructions as before.
4. There will often be a lot of similar ideas; ask the team to group them to identify common themes. If you want to, you can have them do this in silence.[5] That brings out a different kind of dynamic in the group and is often quite quick. This should be done in a few minutes.
5. Do the exercise one more time, but this time focus on an ideal future. You could say. "If you had a magical wand and could do anything—what would your situation look like at the next retrospective?" Use the same patterns as for the good and bad items.

GENERATE INSIGHTS

1. You should now have a lot of ideas of good things that have happened and some areas that the team can do better in or would like to experiment with to improve. This is usually a good basis for a discussion.
2. Ask the team to vote for the one or two (maybe even three) things that they would like to change during the next period.
3. Decide what to do. During the discussion, help the team to focus on things that stand a chance of being implemented during the next period and that have a concrete outcome. You could, for example, ask them, "How do you know when

[5] Of course you can talk if you can't read the stickies. The silence part makes everyone equal in that anyone can move a sticky without being interrupted. Watch carefully for stickies that move back and forth a lot, because those are things that people don't agree on how to group. Those might be interesting to discuss separately or maybe to split into two stickies.

that's done?" Using SMART goals[6] for your improvement actions is another good practice.

Make sure to set aside a good portion of the retrospective timebox for this, because this is usually an important (and hopefully fruitful) discussion. Allow at least 15 minutes, if you're running a one-hour timebox (25% of your time, in other words).

4. Close the retrospective. Ask the team to vote with a "fist of five" on what they thought about the retrospective. On the count of three, each person raises the number of fingers corresponding to their rating of the retrospective: one is worst, five is best.
5. Ask them to write down one thing that can be improved before the next retrospective and post that sticky on the door on their way out.
6. Thank them for their participation.

These instructions should be viewed as a starting point. You can elaborate on this by using other forms of retrospectives as you see the need: for example, to address a specific area or to mix it up a little.

WHEN SHOULD YOU RUN RETROSPECTIVES?

For methods that are iteration focused (Scrum, for example), the retrospective comes naturally at the end of the sprint or iteration. Many teams that are using kanban use a flow-based approach, and there's no "end of iteration" in your process. Our suggestion is that you decide on a suitable cadence (see chapter 9) for your team. A suggestion could be to have retrospectives every other week and keep them timeboxed to one hour. As you start to get more used to doing retrospectives, you could experiment with what a suitable cadence for your team would be.

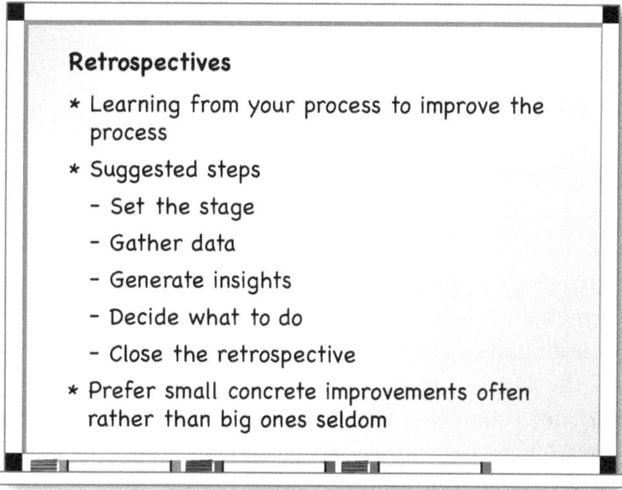

[6] SMART is an acronym that stands for Specific, Measurable, Attainable, Relevant, and Time-bound goals. This makes sure you end up with a very clearly expressed goal, and in the discussions you'll also clear out misunderstandings and misinterpretations of the goal.

A retrospective can help you come up with a couple of improvement points that you want to implement. To understand why this is important or where the root of the problem lies, you can do a root-cause analysis, the topic of the next section.

10.2 Root-cause analysis

Imagine that you're working on a team and that lately a lot of bugs have appeared. You have metrics in place and see that the trends are clear: the number of defects has gone up, and the total lead time has increased quite a lot. The team has decided to do something about this trend. They want to have fewer defects and shorter lead times.

What do you do? Where should you start? What is the problem at hand? Should you tell the developers that they should get their act together? Has the quality of the specifications degenerated? Are the testers not on their toes? Do you need more testers, to keep quality under control? Everyone is doing the best they can, right?

Root-cause analysis is a structured approach to reason around a problem so that you get to the bottom of the issue: the real, underlying reason that the problem occurs. The idea is that there's no use in fixing the symptoms without also looking for the root cause, because that will only make the same, or similar, symptoms resurface somewhere else later. You want to fix the *real* problem,[7] to make sure it doesn't happen again and that all the problems that follow go away.

[7] "The problem, the real problem, and nothing but the problem, so help me God," if you want.

You might also have heard about the *five whys*. Root-cause analysis is based on the same thinking. You keep asking "Why?" until you hit the root cause of the problem. Strangely enough, teams often hit the real problem after five "Why?" questions and answers; hence the *five* in the *five whys*. Let's see that in action.

10.2.1 How it works

Root-cause analysis can be used to solve problems on all levels, both big and small. You could ask questions to find the root cause (the five whys) or, if it's a more complicated problem, run a workshop. If you run a workshop, we suggest that you have all the people in the room who you think might help you find the root cause. Keep the workshop timeboxed to focus on the important questions and discussions, and don't wander off topic. Decide on a start and end time for the workshop, and tell everyone attending that the goal of the workshop is to find the root cause of the problem at hand.

WHY DO WE NEED TO FIX THIS?

Start by writing down the problem you're discussing on a sticky note, and post it in the middle of a whiteboard. The first part of root-cause analysis is finding the *consequences* of not fixing this problem. This is done to gain a deeper understanding of why it's important to fix the issue:

1. Starting from the "problem sticky," ask "So what?" to generate ideas.
2. Post each new idea on the board, and continue upward until the "So what?" questions don't make sense anymore.
3. You'll probably generate several different paths or branches of ideas. Follow each branch, and keep asking "So what?" to follow the reasoning in each branch.
4. Indicate how the stickies relate to each other by drawing lines and arrows between them.

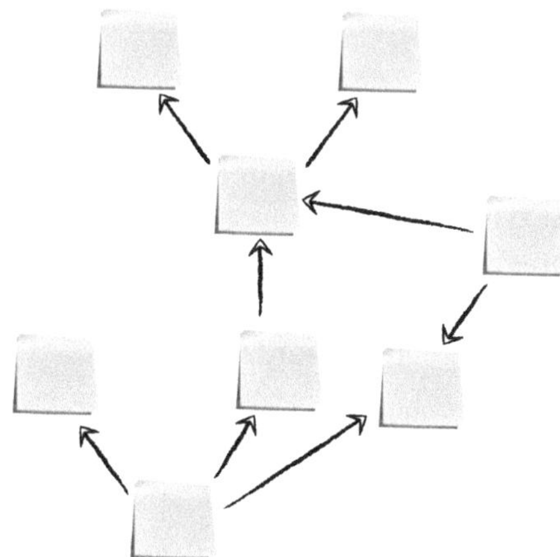

Here's one example of a dialogue:

Marcus: We have a lot of bugs; so what?
Daphne: Well, that takes time away from developing new features.
Beth: Yes, and it will also make our product look bad.

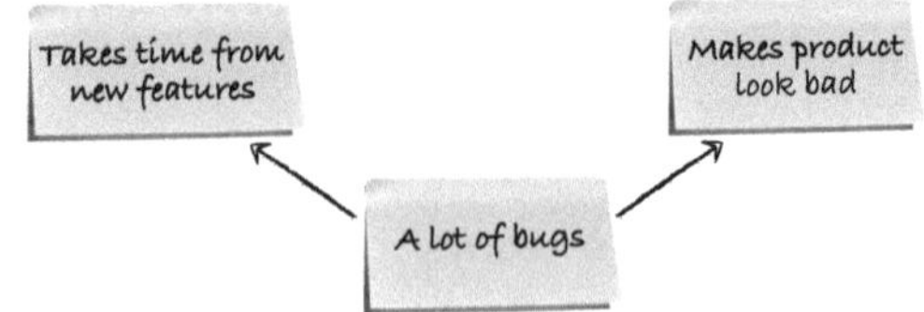

Marcus: Ok, our product looks bad; who cares?
Beth: Are you crazy? We may lose users.
Adam: And the net promoter score, NPS, goes down.

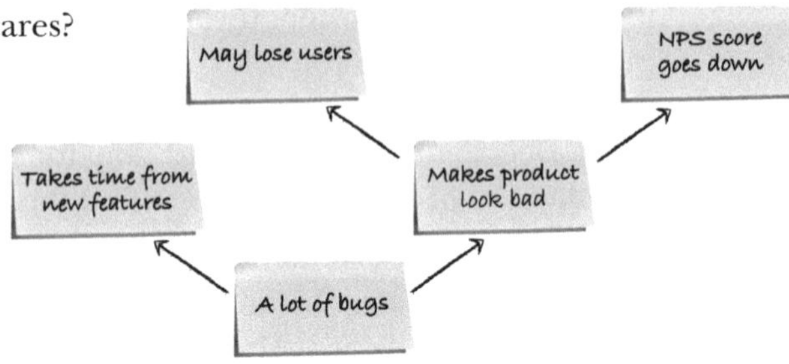

Marcus: What about the NPS, why is that bad?
Beth: Well, that's what our investors are looking at. In fact, they care about the number of users as well.

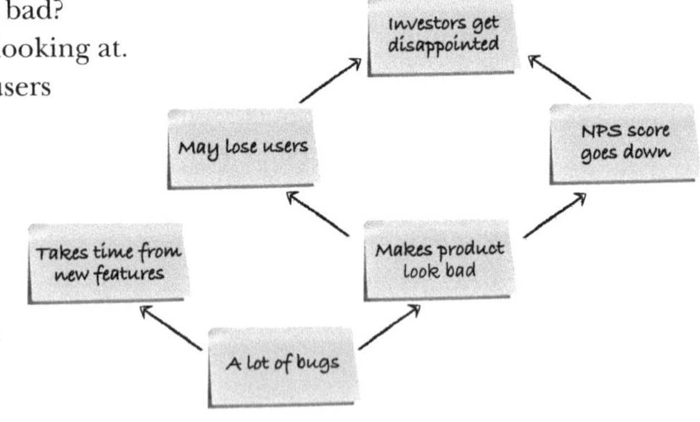

Marcus: Why is upsetting the investors bad?"
Beth: They may cut back investments—ultimately stopping the product development. That's why.
Marcus: So what? Who cares about …
Daphne: Marcus, come on … I think we've reached the end of the road for this one. It's bad. We end up unemployed, alright?

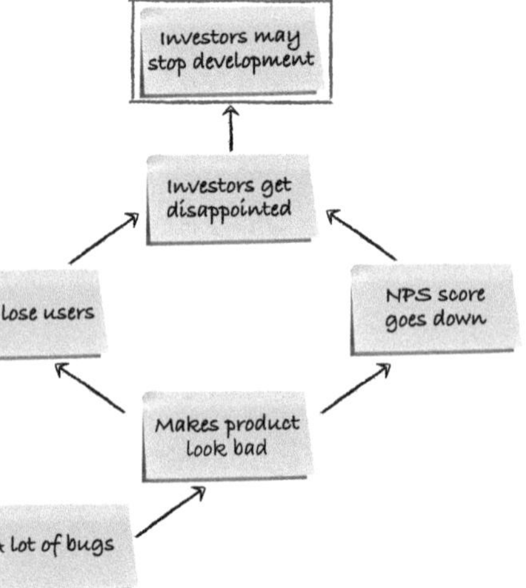

Marcus: You're right. Let's go back to the fact that bugs take away time from developing new features. Why is that so bad, then?
Daphne: It means we can't build new features. There's no new stuff added to our product.
Marcus: So what?
Daphne: Well, that would also make us lose users.

Beth: But that also means there's an opportunity for our competition to catch up.

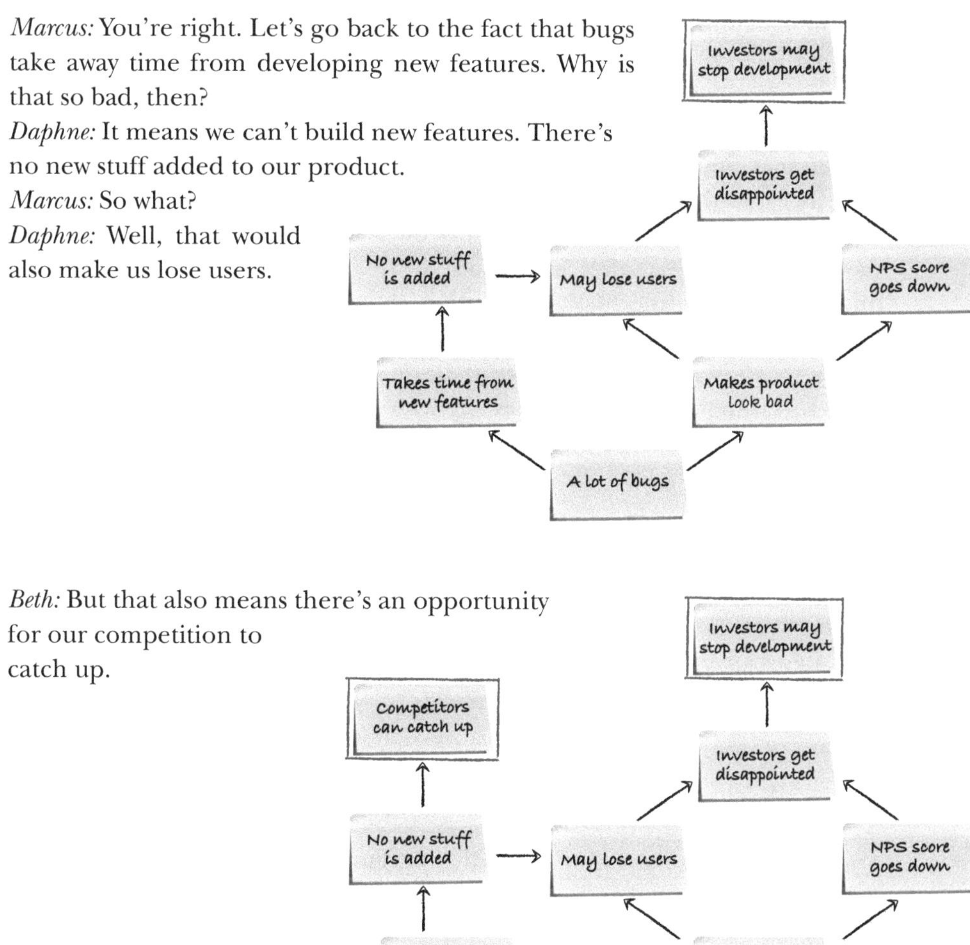

As you can see, the team quickly came up with reasons why this issue is important to look at and learned a lot about the problem in the process. Using the approach described here, they've now reached one or more top nodes of the tree. They now know the impact of not doing anything about this problem. Let's now work our way down to the root of the evil to find out what the real reason behind the problem is.

FINDING THE ROOT CAUSE OF THE PROBLEM

The second part is digging downward into the root cause by asking "Why?" questions. Just like with the "So what?" questions, you start from the problem statement and create stickies for each answer to the "Why?" questions.

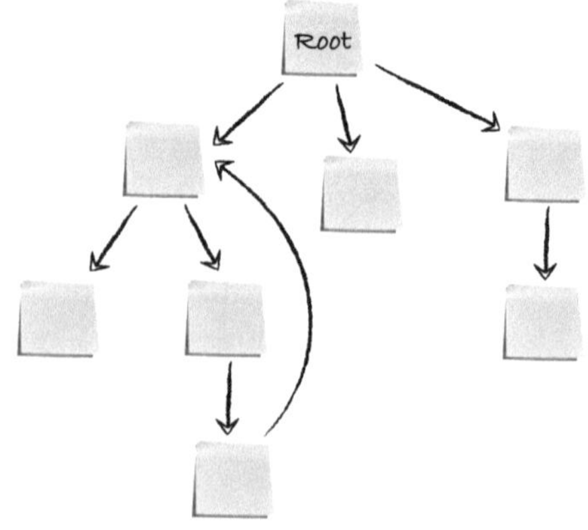

You'll end up with a lot of branches here too, but keep digging deep. Remember to draw arrows and lines that show how the stickies relate to each other.

You may find that you create a circle of references, so that a loop is created. These are special places that need your attention: they're called *self-enforcing loops.* These are things that pose the risk of creating a vicious circle of things that keep feeding each other.[8] Make a circle around those loops or make them stand out somehow, so that you remember to do something about those problems.

Here's an example of the team going for the root cause:

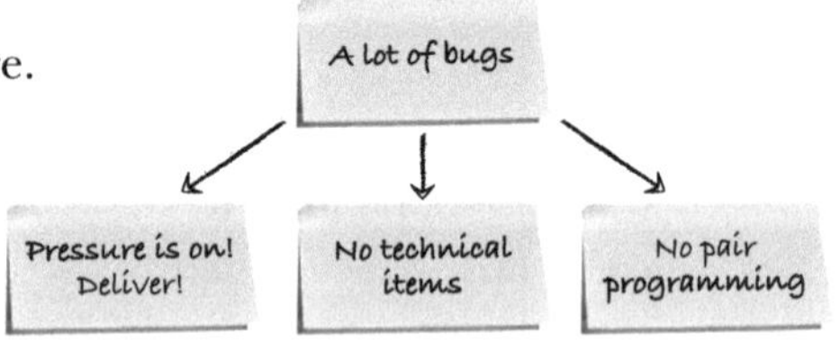

Joakim: We have many bugs; why?
Adam: We've been under a lot of time pressure. It's deliver, deliver, deliver.
Daphne: We don't do any technical work items anymore.
Eric: We have stopped pair programming.

Joakim: Ok, why don't we do any technical work items?
Adam: Because of the time pressure.
Eric: And the same goes for the pair programming. People think that it takes longer.
Joakim: That's what we call a self-enforcing loop. Let's indicate those with red arrows.

Joakim: So why has the time pressure been on?
Adam: Well, it's the May release coming up …
Joakim: Why do we have a time pressure to deliver that?

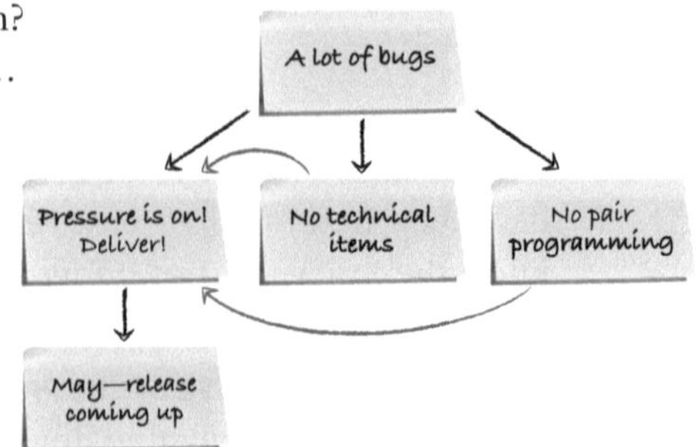

[8] For example, we're stressed, so we take shortcuts and hence start to cut back on quality, which makes us more stressed, forcing us to take more shortcuts, cutting back on quality. That in turn makes us stressed and forces us to … What? Ah—you got it. OK. I'll stop now. It's a circle—it's hard to know if you're there yet.

Adam: We didn't get to decide what went into the May-release backlog. That created a much bigger backlog than we could handle.

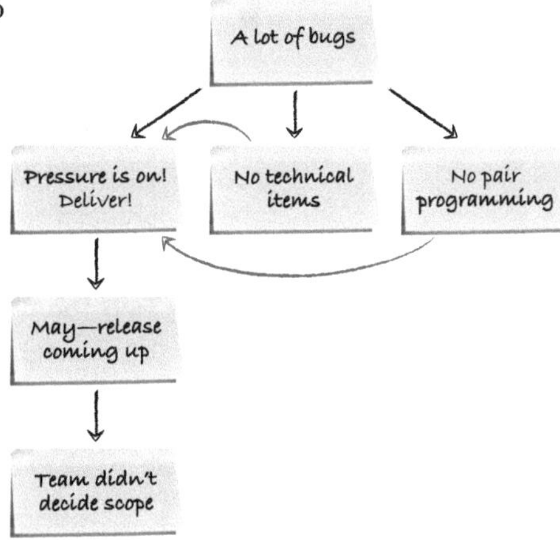

Joakim: Why didn't we have any say on that, then?"
Eric: Because Sales didn't care to ask us?
Daphne: Nope, that's not true. They asked us, but we weren't allowed to take time out of development on the February release, remember …
Joakim: OK, so that's another way that the pressure on delivering is hindering us. Another self-enforcing loop.

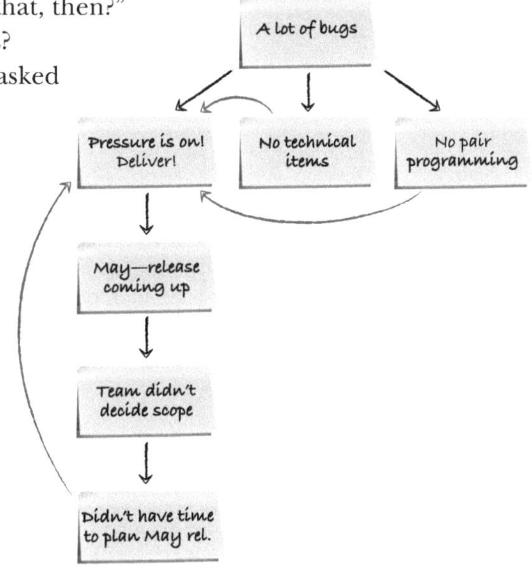

As you probably see from that dialogue, root-cause analysis is a razor-sharp tool that quickly cuts to the root of the problem and the business impact. This might raise some big questions, so make sure you have an atmosphere of problem solving rather than blaming in the room. Reminding people about the goal of the workshop before you start and that you want to find "unrealized improvement opportunities" in your process and not people who have failed could be one way.

Root-cause analysis

* The five whys
* Finding the real reason to solve the real problem
* Find the impact of a problem
* Find the real root cause of the problem
* Visual and cooperative exercises

10.3 Kanban Kata

Retrospectives are great because they allow time out of your normal flow to improve your process. In your normal work, you can also work on improvements, such as small things that you can fix right away (fixing that step in the build process that often fails) or steps toward a bigger goal (lowering the average lead time of your work items).

Kanban Kata is another way to implement process improvements. *Kanban Kata* is a series of questions and forms that help you to improve in small steps, in a continuous flow, so that improvement work and ordinary work are intermingled. It's a great way to get a process around the continuous improvements in your team, pioneered by our good friend Håkan Forss.[9] We like Kanban Kata because it's along the lines of

9 Visit him at @hakanforss on Twitter and at http://hakanforss.wordpress.com.

continuous improvement, inspired by the way Toyota does it—making process improvements an integral part of normal work. It also complements normal retrospectives in a nice way for kanban teams.

Kata? Toyota Kata?

The strange word *kata* is commonly used in martial arts. It refers to the practice of doing a set of predefined movements in order to create a muscle memory of the movements. You try to make the movements as exact and precise as possible, and practice them over and over again, striving for perfection. The idea is that when you finally find yourself in a real combat situation, these basic movements are in muscle memory so that you don't have to think about *how* to do them.

The step from martial arts to process improvements can feel big and steep, but it all has to do with a book called *Toyota Kata* by Mike Rother (McGraw-Hill, 2009, http://amzn.com/0071635238). In this book, the author describes how Toyota has implemented the ideas of continuous improvement in practice. Toyota Kata is nothing that Toyota itself talks about, but rather it's the way that the author describes the practices he has observed in his research and studies of Toyota.

Håkan Forss has applied the ideas from the *Toyota Kata* book to kanban for software development and called it Kanban Kata.

A kata—a number of precise questions that you follow to a point—might feel contrived at first, but remember that a kata is a series of predefined steps that you follow in order for them to become muscle memory. A kata is written a certain way so that ultimately it trains you to do the right thing without thinking. In this case, the kata trains you in process improvement.

10.3.1 What is Kanban Kata?

The easiest way to introduce Kanban Kata, now that you know the origin of it, is through an example. In this section, we'll introduce the three katas, or improvement dialogues, that make up Kanban Kata:

- *Daily Kata*—A way to start including improvement work in your daily meetings
- *Improvement Kata*—A formalized way to improve your process
- *Coaching Kata*—Focuses on improving the learners (the people in the team): a coaching technique

In the imaginary world where the Kanbaneros reside, we've sent Håkan to the team for a couple of days, and you'll see how their way of tackling improvements and daily work has changed. Håkan has introduced the whole team to Kanban Kata and given Frank (the team lead) some extra hours of introduction.

DAILY KATA

You join the team and Håkan[10] around the board for a morning meeting that Frank has started:

"Alright guys, what are we trying to achieve?" Frank asked, facing the team.

"We're aiming to have code ready for release every Wednesday; that's tomorrow," Daphne said.

Frank looked down at a little card he held in his hand. He looked up again and continued: "Where are we now?"

"There is a risk that we won't be able to release tomorrow," Adam said, a bit disappointed.

"What obstacles are in our way now?" Frank asked.

"We have work items 22 and 33 checked in with no problems," Eric said.

"There are a couple of problems jeopardizing the release," Adam stated.

"What are they?" Frank asked.

> **5 questions for daily meetings**
>
> 1. What are we trying to achieve?
> 2. Where are we now?
> 3. What obstacles are in our way now?
> 4. What's our next step, and what do we expect?
> 5. When can we see what we've learned from taking that step?

[10] We use a LEGO® avatar to represent Håkan. This feels very appropriate to us because Håkan not only is a big LEGO® fan but also has used LEGO® elements in his presentations in a very effective and entertaining way. And we can disassemble him if he starts to complain about how we describe Kanban Kata.

"Right now we can't build the master branch. There are some nasty merge problems that need resolving," Daphne said, clinching her fist in an I-will-wring-that-problem's-neck-in-a-second movement.

"What's our next step, and what do we expect?" Frank continued.

"I'm looking into the build errors for the master branch right now," Daphne said. "With the help of Eric, we expect to find the problem soon."

"When can we see what we've learned from taking that step?" Frank asked.

"We'll probably find a solution in an hour or two." Daphne looked at Eric, who nodded his agreement.

"Alright, let's meet back here before lunch." Frank checked his watch. He continued: "Anything preventing flow right now?"

"Yeah," Adam started, as he pointed to the red sticky for story 46, "we have some questions regarding the business rules. They block us from finishing up the specifications and test specs, and development will be waiting too."

"Alright, what's our next step, and what do we expect?" Frank asked.

"We have a meeting booked with Cesar and Beth for 2:00 PM today. We expect that meeting will clear it up," Adam said.

"When can we see what we've learned from taking that step?" Frank asked again.

"We can share what we learned at tomorrow's morning meeting," Adam answered.

"Great. Be sure to add the resolved date to the blocking sticky when it's resolved."

"Anything else preventing the flow right now?" Frank urged them on.

There was some murmuring in the group, but no one had anything else stopping them. Frank closed the meeting with a perky, "Alright people—stop starting, and start finishing." They all looked at Joakim, who stood in the back, and then burst out laughing at Frank using that statement in such a cheerful manner.

IMPROVEMENT AND COACHING KATA

When the group dissolved, Frank went up to Håkan and asked, "Did I do alright?"

"Yeah, that was great. What was the biggest difference from your normal standups?" Håkan asked.

"Well, probably the focus on learning and that I underlined taking small steps. Also I think the 'what do you expect' part made us think about what we did before we started, in a good way," Frank said.

"Yes, that was what I heard too. Great work!" Håkan said. "Should we move on to the next kata, then?"

"By all means, sensei," Frank said and winked. They went back to the board, and Håkan started by asking, "What is the target condition?"

"We're still working with our long-term goal of reducing lead times for all our work items, as we decided a month back. Our hypothesis is that it can be achieved with the same number of people that we have today on the team." Frank continued, "We are reducing the lead time on the board to five days, for items classified as medium."

"What is the condition now?" Håkan asked.

"We're getting there; at least, it feels a lot closer now," Frank said.

"What do you base that on? Can you show me some data?" Håkan asked.

"Sure thing, here's our work-item run chart for the lead times." Frank pointed to a chart next to the board.

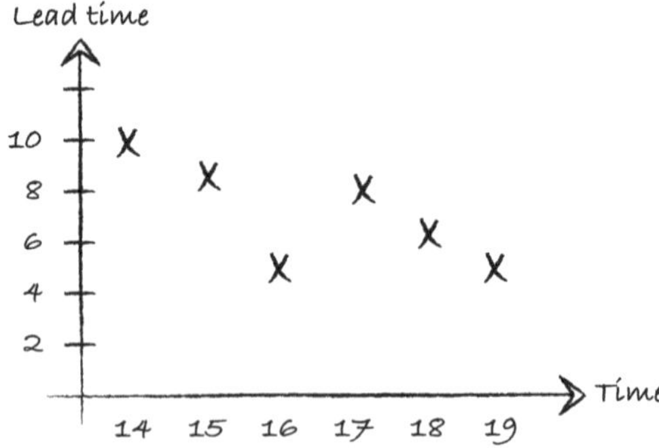

"Can you explain to me what you see?" Håkan asked.

"Yes: in this diagram we have tracked the lead times for medium-sized work items. We can see that for the last items we're close to five days, our target condition," Frank said.

"What was your last step?" Håkan asked, after turning over the five coaching questions card (shown later in this section).

Frank grabbed a Plan-Do-Check-Act (PDCA) cycles record form[11] and pointed to the row from the last coaching session.[12]

PDCA CYCLES RECORD *(Each row = one experiment)*

Date: 20130426	Process Metric: Lead time medium items
Process: Mobile banking	

Step	What do you expect?	Coaching Cycle	EXPERIMENT	Result Observe closely	What We Learned
Document the setup process	To better understand the process			Many steps are done manually—even ones that can be automated.	We could quite easily automate a lot of steps in the setup process.

---

[11] A PDCA cycles record form can be used to track your decisions and progress through the improvement work.

[12] The forms and cards in this section are taken from *The Improvement Kata Handbook*, Copyright © 2013 by Mike Rother, all rights reserved. Issued under the Creative Commons license. You can download yours here: http://mng.bz/Kweb.

"To document the test setup process."

"What happened?" Håkan prompted.

"Well … we went through a normal test setup and documented everything we did," Frank said, a bit unsure.

Håkan nodded acknowledgment before asking, "What did you learn?"

"It was quite easy to see a number of steps in the test setup process that could be automated, if not all of them," Frank said.

"What obstacles are now preventing you from reaching the target condition?" Håkan asked.

"There's a number of issues, and right now …" Frank said, and then listed the obstacles for Håkan.

"Which *one* are you addressing now?" Håkan asked.

"The test setup time," Frank said.

"What is your next step?"

"We're starting to automate the complete test setup today," Frank said proudly.

"Do you expect to be done with that by the next time we meet?" Håkan asked sneakily.

Frank smiled as he remembered. "Smaller steps that we can finish in a short time are preferred … right, sensei?"

"Yes." Håkan smiled.

"Well, we could probably start automating the loading of the test data. That's a pretty easy one."

"Sounds reasonable. What do you expect, when taking that step?"

"Well, at least 80% of the time spent to set up the database should be cut," Frank answered.

"And what would the time be?" Håkan asked.

Frank did some calculation in his head, and then said: "That would be about four to five minutes, at least."

"Good. We want to be as precise as possible," Håkan explained. "When we're more precise, it's clear whether we've reached the expected outcome or not. The important part isn't reaching the expected outcome, but that we can learn by comparing the outcome to what we expected to achieve. The kata is all about learning so we can improve in small steps over and over again. Getting back to the kata," Håkan said, "when can we go and see what we have learned from taking that step?"

"We expect to have it done at the end of the week."

"Great. Let's meet back here again on Friday at 10:00," Håkan said, as they ended the coaching session.

Håkan and Frank headed for the coffee machine and kept talking about the test setup. The improvement work was on a roll, and it felt like they had good control over the process. That calls for coffee!

10.3.2 What happened

In this example, you saw three katas being used: the Daily Kata, the Improvement Kata, and the Coaching Kata. You could see the rather strict form in which both Frank (in the Daily Kata) and Håkan (in the Coaching Kata) used a set of predefined questions, known as the Five Questions.[13]

If you feel that the way these katas (questions and forms) are formulated doesn't suit you and your team, then you could formulate your own. But the questions should then be followed to the letter, as you would have done with the ones suggested here. Repetition is the key to getting it perfect.

> *Repetition is the mother of all knowledge. Now do the assignment again.*
>
> —Lennart Wistedt, Marcus's fourth- to eighth-grade math teacher

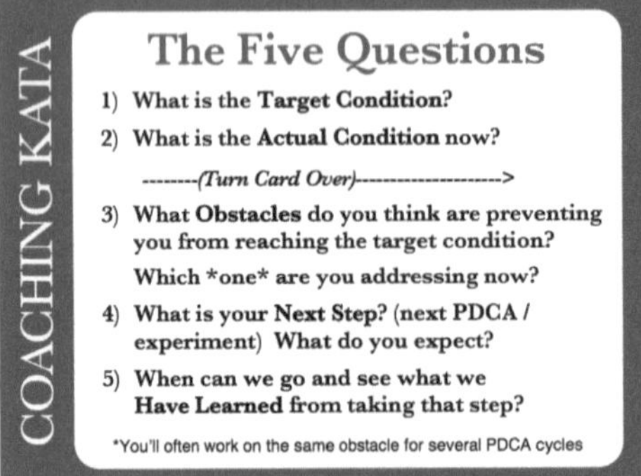

COACHING KATA

The Five Questions

1) What is the **Target Condition?**
2) What is the **Actual Condition** now?

--------*(Turn Card Over)*-------------------->

3) What **Obstacles** do you think are preventing you from reaching the target condition? Which *one* are you addressing now?
4) What is your **Next Step?** (next PDCA / experiment) What do you expect?
5) When can we go and see what we **Have Learned** from taking that step?

*You'll often work on the same obstacle for several PDCA cycles

Reflect on the Last Step Taken

Because you don't actually know what the result of a step will be!

1) What was your **Last Step?**
2) What did you **Expect?**
3) What **Actually Happened?**
4) What did you **Learn?**

------------------------------>
Return

Did you also notice the focus on learning and taking small steps? For every little step the team took, they first were asked for the expected outcome. Then they were asked what they learned from what happened. That's the scientific method at play: developing a hypothesis, making a prediction of what will happen, performing an experiment, observing the data, and reflecting on the difference between the prediction and what happened.

10.3.3 Why does this work?

Kanban Kata puts a strong focus on learning in a structured manner. It consists of three katas, or routines, if you like, that build on the scientific method. The nice part about using the scientific method is that no result is bad; it's only a result. You'll use the outcome to learn and to improve your next hypothesis.

> *There is no such thing as a failed experiment, only experiments with unexpected outcomes.*
>
> —R. Buckminster Fuller

[13] Used under Creative Commons; see http://mng.bz/Kweb.

The next secret to why Kanban Kata works is that it takes small steps. You're trying to improve from your current condition toward an improved target condition. The road toward the target is unknown, and the best way to navigate it is in small steps. These steps are the experiments that you're conducting based on your hypothesis.

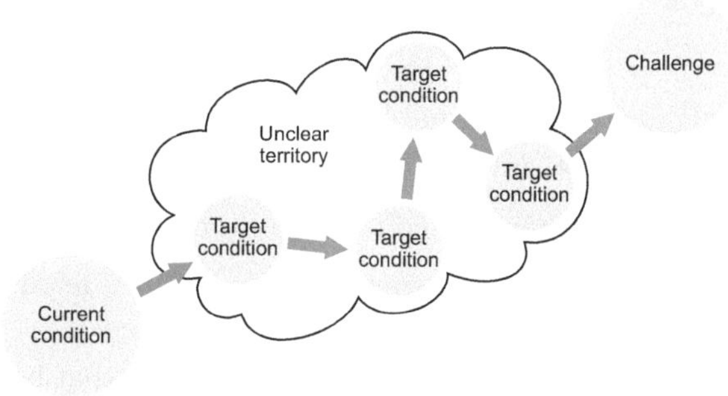

That brings us back to the results of the experiments and the fact that they're only that: results. Even making mistakes or taking wrong turns is OK, as long as you learn and improve from there. Getting from your current condition to the target you've set for yourself means going through unclear territory. You're bound to take some wrong turns—but that's OK, as long as they're small steps and you can correct your bearing toward your challenge on the way to fulfill your vision.

In the Kanban Kata, you're using routines (see the questions that Håkan was using earlier) that guide you through the different katas. They help you create new habits, a new mindset of continuous learning and improvement. That's where the real gain is in using Kanban Kata: creating habits, a mindset, throughout the organization, of making small, small improvements, every day.

Kanban Kata

* Continuous improvement through a set of predefined questions
* Based on the scientific method
* Take aim at your vision, and take small steps to get closer
* We talked about three katas:
  - Daily Kata—Focus on your day-to-day activities
  - Improvement Kata—Focus on improvements in your process
  - Coaching Kata—Improving the learners

10.4 Summary

This chapter talked about process improvement and common improvement practices:

- Continuous improvement and respect for people are core to kanban.
- Kanban helps you discover improvement opportunities.

We then turned our attention to a couple of common practices for improvements:

- A retrospective is a way for a team to look back on their process and see how they can improve it.
- Root-cause analysis is a tool that helps you find the root problem so you don't only fix the symptom.
- Root-cause analysis also guides you to see *why* the problem is worth solving.
- Kanban Kata is a continuous-improvement tool that is based on how Toyota makes improvements.
- There are three katas within Kanban Kata:
  - *Daily Kata*—Including improvement work in your daily work
  - *Improvement Kata*—A formalized way to improve your process
  - *Coaching Kata*—Improving the learners
- The "kata" in Kanban Kata indicates that you follow a set way of working toward a goal, until the routine becomes second nature and making improvements becomes the way that you normally work.

In the next chapter, we'll take a look at how metrics can help you know whether or not you're improving.

11 Using metrics to guide improvements

This chapter covers

- Metrics and how they can help you improve
- Some common metrics and visualizations used by kanban teams
- How to find good metrics for your team

Chapter 10 talked a lot about improvements and starting to make changes to your process in order to try to improve. We like to think about it as doing experiments that you've not yet validated, because you can't really know in advance whether you're improving or not. When conducting these experiments, you need some way of knowing whether they improve your process. To know that, you need to measure how your work works. There's a strong community around metrics for teams using kanban and Lean. In this chapter, we'll show you a couple of commonly used metrics and discuss what you could learn and improve by using them.

As with most things in kanban, you want to visualize the metrics in order to know what's happening. We'll introduce you to a couple of common visualizations and diagrams. And we'll show you how to create the diagrams from your workflow data and how to interpret them to see what's going on in your process.

Let's dive right in and talk about some common metrics that teams using kanban and Lean often find useful.

11.1 Common metrics

This section takes a look at some common metrics that you can easily capture by using a visualized workflow on a board, like the ones we've used so far in the book. This will give you a good indication of how your process is working for you, how fast you're moving stuff from idea to production, and more.

A WORD FROM THE COACH Remember to always include the team in the process of deciding on a metric so that they have their say about what's a good metric for them. These are merely suggestions to get your discussion going. Also remember to mix these "process"-related metrics with metrics showing that your efforts are making a business impact.

Let's start with one metric that's easy to capture: cycle (and lead) time.

11.1.1 Cycle and lead times

WHAT ARE THEY? Measure how fast work is moving through your process and where it slows down.

WHAT CAN YOU LEARN FROM THIS METRIC? By measuring lead time, you can see the actual improvement in time-to-deliver/market and predictability. You can also see the due-date performance—whether a certain item is on target against what you thought it should be. With the lead time captured, you can also analyze where the work item has spent its time and start tracking lead-time efficiency to see whether the work item is mostly waiting, blocked, being reworked, or actually being worked on.

Cycle time refers to the time a work item takes to go through *part of the process*—for example, doing development and testing. *Lead* time, on the other hand, refers to the time taken to finish the *complete process*, from idea to finished feature in production.

Lead time is generally more interesting to track because it shows you the *entire* process. Cycle time narrows down the focus to only part of it, which might miss another part of the process that could give you valuable information. If you're improving only for part of the process, you may miss some other bottleneck that slows the lead time.

The following example board shows the cycle times a team tracks for development and testing. The complete lead time is also indicated, as you can see from the complete workflow.

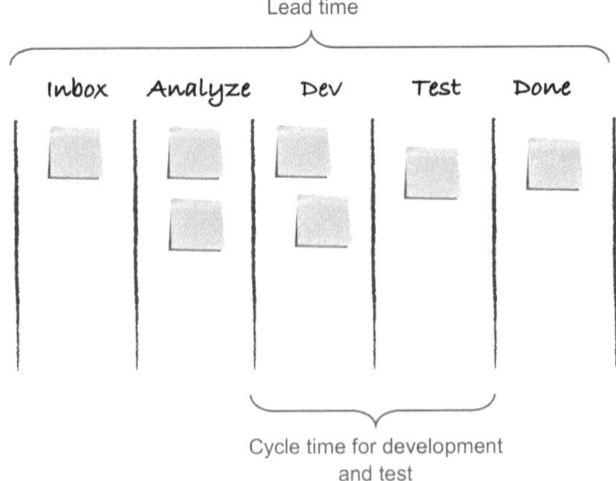

The lead time for the complete process is often a bit harder to get hold of, because you may not have it under your control or visualized on your board. Strive to track the time for work items for as much of the process as possible to get the complete picture.

Cycle time vs. lead time

To better understand the difference between lead and cycle times, consider the first Scrum project that Marcus took part in. The team consisted of six happy developers, and we created working software every third week. The cycle time of our development was therefore three weeks. But was that helpful to the business?

Not that much. When we were "done" after six sprints, we learned that a three-month testing phase was waiting for all the work we had done. And after that, we missed the quarterly release cycle by one week and had to wait another three months before releasing our software to the users.

Sadly, that didn't matter much for our total lead time, because we understood that the requirements for the application had been written a year and a half before we even started.

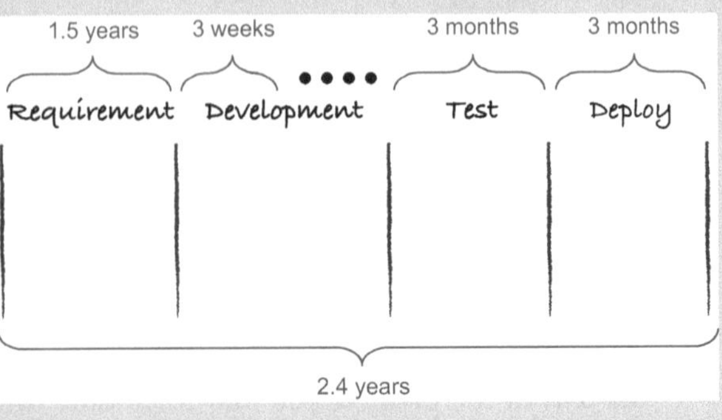

The cycle time (considering development only) for a single feature was three weeks, but the lead time for that same feature was two years and four months.

That's the difference between cycle and lead time. Although reducing the development cycle time may be useful, the big improvement opportunities can be found elsewhere.

The lead time should be as short as possible so that work flows quickly through the complete process. Note that focusing on shortening the cycle times can sometimes be bad for the overall lead time. This is known as *optimizing locally*. Say you've optimized development time, and it's now a couple of days. This has consequences for others around development; can requirements be written in small chunks to keep the developers busy? Can testers handle being given new items every other day? It may even be wise to slow down the developers in order to have the work flow more smoothly through the process. By measuring lead and cycle times, this is easy to spot. (Read more about that in chapter 7.)

CAPTURING THE METRIC

Cycle and lead times are metrics that are easy to capture and track. With a visualized workflow like a board, you can start today. Note the date on each work-item card as you put it on the board. When the work item reaches the last column on your board (Done or In Production, for example) note that date. The difference between these two dates is the cycle time for your process. It's the total lead time if you have the entire process on your board from idea to production.

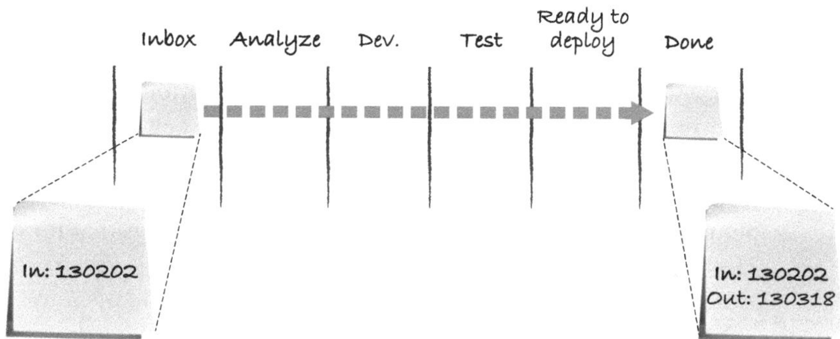

In this example, you see a work item that entered the board (in the Inbox column) on 2 February 2013. It reached the Done column on 18 March 2013. Subtracting those dates from each other gives a total lead time of 44 days (31 working days in Sweden that year).

Capturing the cycle time is equally simple. Do that by "stamping" the work item with the date it enters the column you're interested in: for example, when it enters the Dev. column and then again when it reaches the Ready to Deploy column.

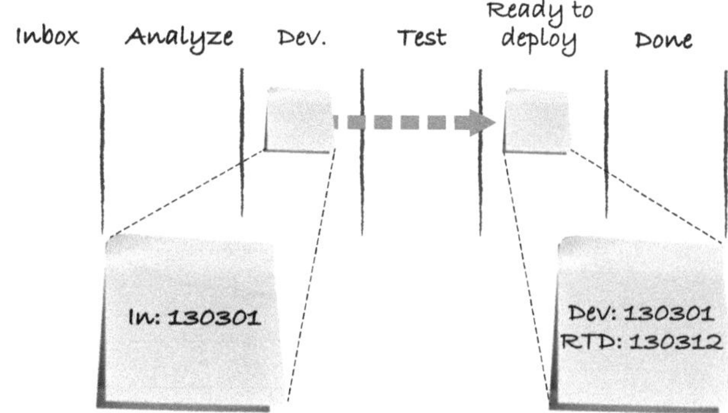

You can see that this work item entered the Dev. column on 1 March and reached the Ready to Deploy column on 12 March. That gives a cycle time of 11 days (8 working days).

ANALYZING THE METRIC

With these two metrics in hand (lead time of 44 days and a cycle time for development and test of 8 days), the team can now start to do some analysis and ask questions about how their work is behaving. Eight days is only about 20% of the total time. Has this number (eight days) gone up or down? What should it be? Where's the rest of the time spent? Should they start tracking cycle time for other parts of the process to know more?

When asking questions like that, you'll soon realize that the individual cycle and lead times aren't so interesting. The trends over time are much more interesting. It might be that the first item you tracked was exceptionally fast or slow. You need a bigger sample to see whether you're improving over time. You can do that with statistical analysis (see section 11.2.1 for an example of this) or by visualizing your trends.

When you've tracked the lead time, you can also start to analyze it:

- Is the time measured *normal* for a work item of this size and type? With a large enough sample, you can start to make predictions for work items as they enter the board (see section 9.1.4 on Disneyland wait times).
- You can use the lead time date to make prioritizations. Say, for example, that a medium work item usually takes five to eight days to complete, and you have one with a due date in six days. With that information in hand, you can start to prioritize it over other work if you notice that it begins to slip behind its predicted schedule.
- One interesting exercise is to break the lead time down and see where the actual time is spent. For a total time of 30 days, where is that time mostly spent? How much is spent waiting or blocked? How much is rework? Analyzing that can help you find bottlenecks and make big improvements.

VISUALIZING THE METRIC

The team tracks the trends of the lead and cycle times on two simple diagrams that they've drawn on the whiteboard next to their workflow. This can be done as a simple scatter diagram, like the one shown next. (You could use a tool like Microsoft Excel to

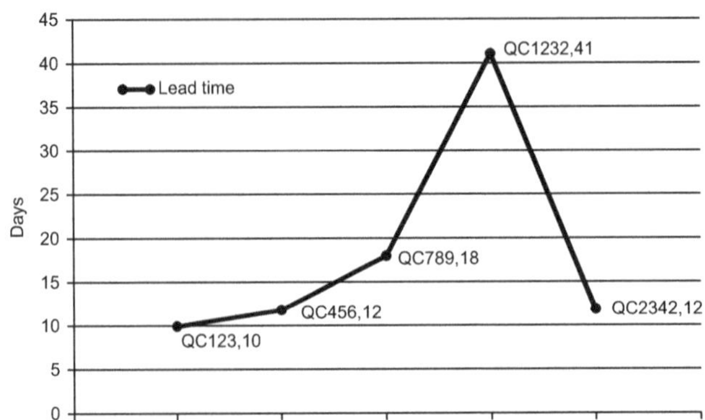

draw the diagram, but we've found it simpler to get started by plotting it out on the whiteboard.)

The diagram doesn't have to be correct to the decimal point. The important thing is to visualize the diagram and put it up on the wall for everyone to see. Make it big! You want everyone to see it and be able to reflect and ask questions.

You could track both the cycle time for the different parts of the process and the total lead time. You can display that in a stacked column chart showing the distribution of time in the different stages of the process, as shown in this diagram.

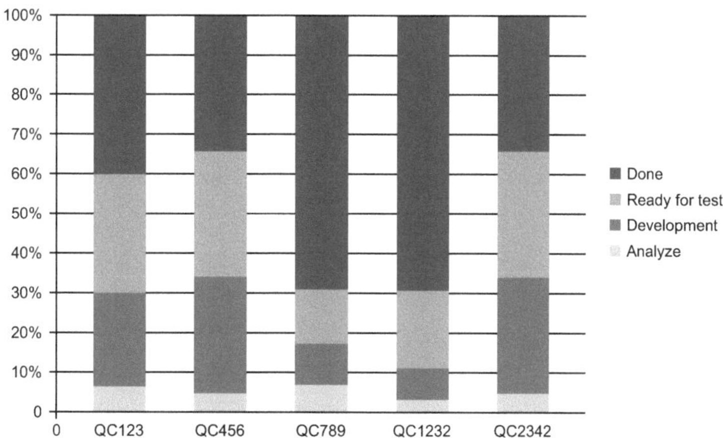

Section 11.2 looks at how to use this data in more advanced diagrams, like a control chart and a cumulative flow diagram. But don't underestimate simple diagrams like these as a good start.

Even though focusing on shortening lead times is a Good Thing because it leads to a better flow as we talked about in chapter 7, you might miss other information if you focus solely on that metric. For example, if you focus on lead time, you may not notice that it's been a week since you put something out in production. This is why you can complement your lead-time metric with a focus on the *throughput* of your process.

11.1.2 Throughput

WHAT IS IT? Measures the rate at which the process produces completed work items.

WHAT CAN YOU LEARN FROM THIS METRIC? You can learn whether your efforts to improve the flow by reducing WIP, slicing stories, and investing in automation such as continuous delivery and so on are paying off. Are you actually improving delivery frequency and thereby shortening feedback loops?

Throughput is defined as *the movement of inputs and outputs in a production process*[1] and roughly translates to "how much stuff we complete per time unit." Another way of putting it (that we like better) can be found in the Theory of Constraints community: *Throughput is the rate at which a system achieves its goal.*

Tracking throughput helps you focus on moving stuff through your process and ensuring that work gets done and not merely worked on. Higher throughput (more items completed per period) is better to strive for, but not at the cost of quality.

CAPTURING THE METRIC

As with lead time, throughput is pretty simple to capture: count the number of completed work items per week (or month, or whatever suits your granularity needs). On a visualized board, you could count the number of work items in the Done column each Friday and then clear the column.

---

1 See http://en.wikipedia.org/wiki/Throughput_(business).

VISUALIZING THE METRIC

Throughput is easy to visualize as a scatter diagram or stacked column chart that shows how many items you complete each week, for example. Here's one example of how that can be visualized:

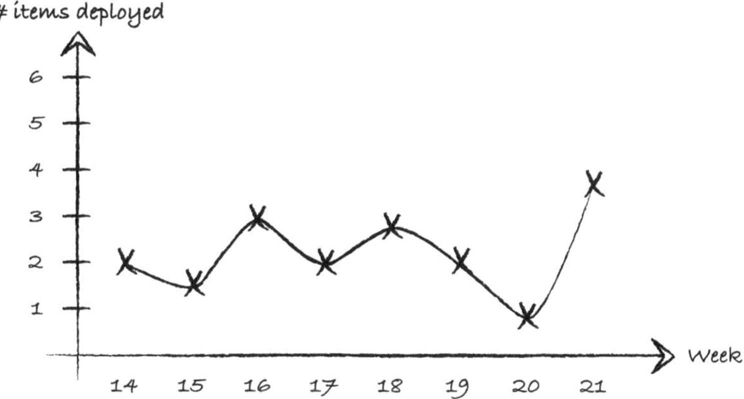

Again, you could use fancy tools to create this diagram if you wanted to, but you don't need to. The only thing that's important is that it's visualized for the team and others who are interested.

ANALYZING THE METRIC

Analyzing throughput can help you focus on getting stuff done. We've seen teams where "everything works just fine" but that didn't deliver anything for a month. By adding a small visualization that showed how much they were getting out the door each week, they started to focus on delivering again.

Throughput can also be a balancing metric for lead-time improvements. If you're reducing lead time and throughput goes down, it could be that you've reduced WIP too much. For example, say that you really try to optimize for great lead time and set your WIP limit to a single work item. That work item can't move any faster, because every person available on the team is working only with that item. The moment you need someone to help out or answer a question, they have time to do so. But that may be bad for throughput because nothing else except that single item is being worked on. Maybe (and probably) the WIP is too low.

11.1.3 Issues and blocked work items

WHAT ARE THEY? Measure items that are hindering the flow.

WHAT CAN YOU LEARN FROM THIS METRIC? How blocked work items are affecting your lead time/lead-time efficiency. How good/fast are you at unblocking/resolving issues? Are you improving?

Issues and blocked items are things that are hindering the work flow. Issues or defects tell you that you're not producing at the right quality, and they're definitely things that you want to be notified about. Blockers stop your work from flowing smoothly. You want to clear those and make sure you have as few of them as possible.

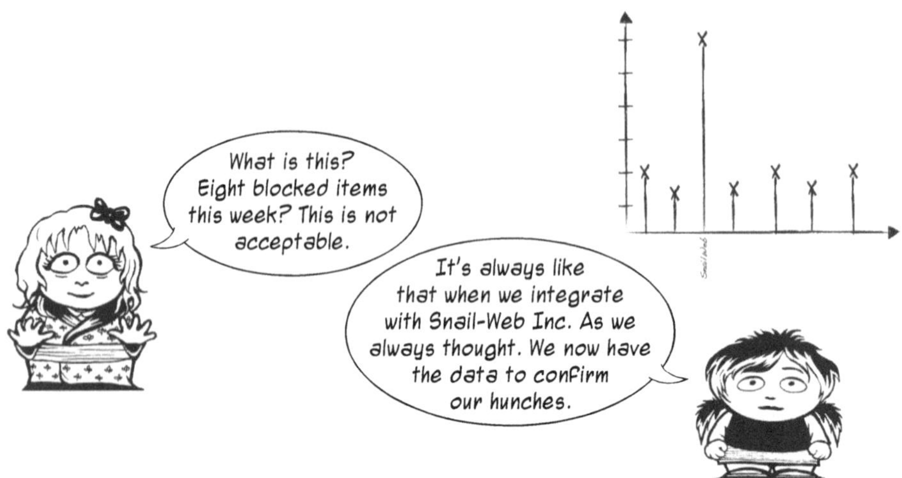

Tracking issues can be the balancing metric that makes sure you don't run your process too fast. Imagine that you only focused on reducing lead times, for example, and that someone wanted to improve that metric. One way to accomplish that is to be sloppy: that would surely make things go faster.[2] With a quality-focused metric—tracking the number of defects, for example—you make sure the lead-time metric isn't focused on *ad absurdum*. You can read more about quality metrics in section 11.1.5.

Blockers often happen when you're forced to wait for others to take over your work or give you input before you can keep working. Discussions about how to resolve problems like these are easier and more to the point if they're backed up with data.

For example: "We've tracked the number of items that we're waiting for from you, and it's increased by 30% in the last month, and here is the data that shows you that trend" is a much better argument than "I feel that we're waiting for a lot of your stuff." With concrete data in hand, you can discuss what to do about it. Or suppose you've done something about clearing blockages—how can you know whether that measure had any effect? You need some kind of metric, before and after.

CAPTURING THE METRIC

With a visualized workflow, these two metrics (defects and blockers) are easily captured by counting the number of items on the board:

---

[2] At least for a while. Sloppy code has a tendency to be hard to maintain and becomes slower and slower to move around in.

- Number of defects = Number of pink stickies at any given time, or per week, for example
- Number of blockers = Number of stickies with a blocked marker attached to them

VISUALIZING THE METRIC

This is easily drawn as a scatter or stacked column chart showing the trends. Are you having more blocked items now? Since you did that bug-fixing week, has the number of new bugs been kept at the new low or is it rising again? What was the reason for having that many bugs in the last week?

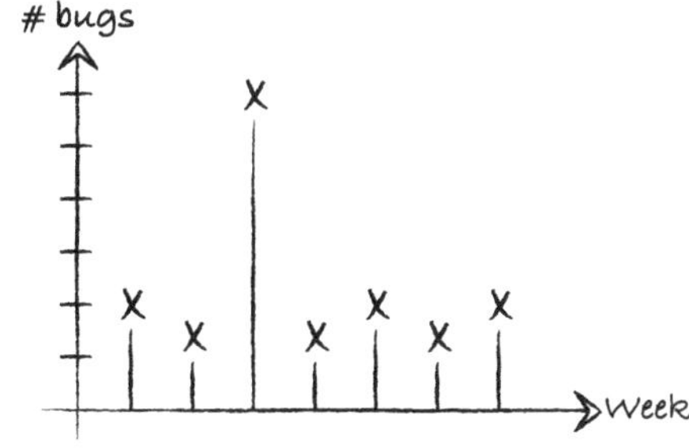

You could track other stuff that's important for your process (making sure you're always doing a certain number of new or technical maintenance features, for example). You can track and visualize these in the same way we've described here.

ANALYZING THE METRIC

The number of blockers is interesting to analyze because these are the things that slow you down and reduce your lead-time efficiency. For the blockers that do occur, make sure you're resolving them fast. Some teams track each day that a work item is blocked with a progress indicator on the blocker sticky (see section 4.4). That data can lead to interesting discussions and improvement opportunities around resolving blockers and how to prioritize that work—or around flow, because you really don't want to be blocked at all.

11.1.4 Due-date performance

WHAT IS IT? Measures how well promises and deadlines are kept.

WHAT CAN YOU LEARN FROM THIS METRIC? You can see if a due date is likely to be met in the predicted lead time and build a track record that makes you trustworthy and dependable. This in turn helps you build trust with your stakeholders.

If an item has a due date attached, you want to make sure to hit that due date. That date is often there because a business opportunity exists on the date or a fine is due if it's missed. Some people talk about due dates as part of their service-level agreement (SLA) with surrounding departments and stakeholders.

CAPTURING THE METRIC

When dates like these are important to your team, you need to track them. It's not hard to do from your board because you can note the date the work item was completed and compare it to the due date.

VISUALIZING THE METRIC

For metrics like these, a pie or circle chart probably is the most suitable. This gives you a quick overview of how many work-item due dates are met and missed.

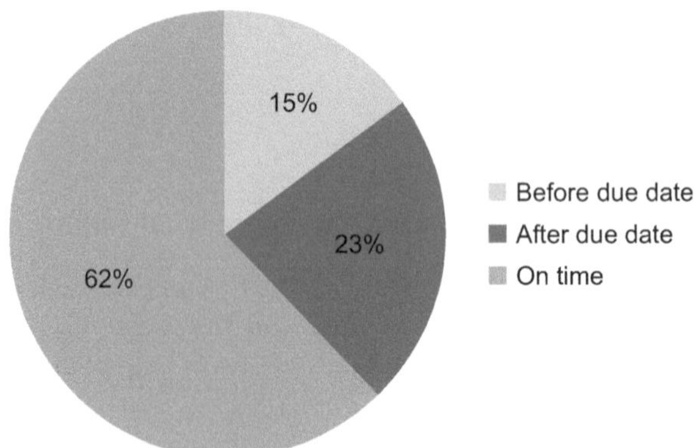

ANALYZING THE METRIC

Due-date performance can be something that you use to communicate with other teams and stakeholders, but it also helps you prioritize and motivate your own team. If an item is slipping behind, according to the predicted due date, you can prioritize it higher than other work: "We don't want to screw up our great track record!"

With a long and solid track record of being on time, you often build trust with teams around you and your stakeholders. But this can also lead to improvement discussions: "We hit 95% of our due dates except for items that have to do with Vendor B. What can we do about that?"

11.1.5 Quality

WHAT IS IT? Measures the quality of the work and whether features that give value to stakeholders and customers are being delivered.

WHAT CAN YOU LEARN FROM THIS METRIC? Quality is great to use as a balancing metric for other improvements, such as improving lead time. It can also be a metric to see whether your quality-improving efforts (automated testing, paying down technical debt, and so on) are paying off.

Quality is a tricky concept, and a thorough treatment is beyond the scope of this book. It can be interpreted in many different ways. We don't want to dwell on that big subject here. We'll adopt Gerald Weinberg's definition: "Quality is value to some person."[3]

This definition is, of course, vague and open to interpretation, but so is quality. A friend of ours was very disappointed to find a lot of spelling and grammatical errors in a book he had written. But it was voted the #1 agile book that year, with more than 20 five-star reviews on Amazon. What is quality for that book? A flawless product that no one uses isn't quality.

CAPTURING THE METRIC

There are a lot of alluring metrics around quality that you can capture quite easily:

- The number of defects/bugs per build or release of the product. This is probably best captured as a trend that shows how the number changes over time.
- The number of defect work items on the board per time unit. This shows how much of your resources are spent on fixing bugs.
- You could track most metrics that we've mentioned so far (lead time, throughput, and so on) separately for defect work items.

By now you should sense a big *but* coming up … and here it comes: *but* just because these things are easy to track doesn't mean there's value in tracking them.

> *Quality, I patiently explain, is not the absence of something in management's eyes, that is, defects, but the presence of something in the consumer's eyes, that is, value.*
>
> —Alan Weiss[4]

And yes, that idea of quality is much harder to capture and track, but it's also more valuable to track for the business impact you're trying to achieve. In the words of

[3] From *Quality Software Management: Systems Thinking* (Dorset House, 1991, http://amzn.com/0932633226).

[4] *Million Dollar Consulting* (McGraw-Hill, 2009, http://amzn.com/0071622101).

Gojko Adzic: "Don't cling to defect tracking tools as if they were a safety blanket; define what quality means in your context."[5]

How do you know if you've created value for some person? That's a harder metric to capture and can only be answered by asking those for whom you want to create value. There are a lot of different ways to go about that: polls and interviews, net promoter scores (NPS), and number of likes on Facebook are a few we've heard about.

You've now ventured outside your own process and need to tap the *product* you're creating for data in order to capture the metric. Maybe new functionality needs to be built into the product to see and know what users think and how they're using it.

Google Analytics, Optimizely, and Google Tag Manager are common website tools that monitor traffic and can follow the way users interact with your pages. They can give you a lot of information about the quality of the product and features you're building.

VISUALIZING THE METRIC

Quality metrics can take many shapes, so we can't give you a great tip on *one* way to visualize yours. We can say this: make it big, make it visual, and put it on the wall. A Google Analytics dashboard on a screen next to the team will gain a lot of attention and trigger praise, questions, and discussions—exactly what you want in order to improve even more.

ANALYZING THE METRIC

If you manage to capture the value you're creating for your users, you're in a great position for some really interesting analytics. Then you can make small changes to your product (some[6] call them experiments) and see how the metrics you're capturing are changing based on them. This can even lend itself to what's known as *A/B testing*—that is, releasing two versions of the same functionality and seeing which one performs better.

To take a real example that Marcus was involved in, let's say you want to have as many users as possible registered on your site. Right now you see a big drop-off in the registration module. You think it has to do with the CAPTCHA[7] module that has people reading hard-to-read symbols and entering them in another box. So you devise an experiment and release one version of the registration form with the CAPTCHA turned on and one version with it turned off. Now you can measure the difference in conversion (from unregistered users to registered users) and see whether you should use the CAPTCHA algorithm or not.[8]

This is valuable data that can help you improve the business impact you create with your product. This is also a subject that is way bigger than we have room for in this

---

5 See his blog entry "Bug statistics are a waste of time" at http://mng.bz/kKIT.

6 See http://theleanstartup.com/.

7 See http://en.wikipedia.org/wiki/CAPTCHA.

8 Can you guess the "winner" of the alternatives? CAPTCHA turned on beat CAPTCHA turned off by 5% over a week's worth of experimenting. No one in the entire company guessed that. Neither did you, we presume. The result of the experiment contradicted our hypothesis. Now—how would you act on that information?

book. To learn more, try the awesome book *Impact Mapping* by Gojko Adzic (Provoking Thoughts, 2012, http://mng.bz/12J0) as a starting point.[9]

11.1.6 Value demand and failure demand

WHAT ARE THEY? Measure how much work is caused by systemic failures—work that must be redone, for example.

WHAT CAN YOU LEARN FROM THE METRICS? How to increase capacity for value delivery through systematically reducing failure demand.

Failure demand is a concept invented by Professor John Seddon (*I Want You to Cheat!* Vanguard Consulting Ltd, 1992, http://amzn.com/095197310X). It can be understood as "demand on a system caused by failure to do something or do something right for the customer." The opposite of failure demand is *value demand*, which is the real reason that the system exists. Value demand means things you want the system to do. It goes without saying that you want to minimize *failure* demand where possible.

Examples of failure demand are plentiful, sadly, but can range from having to redo work because of bad specifications, to not understanding each other and hence producing the wrong things, to bugs and defects, to overloading support functions due to poor quality or instructions. Failure demand includes anything that takes your focus away from doing the things you want to do: delivering features that make a business impact.

Measuring failure demand versus value demand can be hard because it sometimes comes down to what *you* think an item is. Implementing a new aspect of a search feature, for example—is that value demand (new feature please) or is it failure demand (you should have included the feature the first time around)?

---

9 See also http://impactmapping.org/.

CAPTURING THE METRIC

It follows naturally that because it's sometimes hard to classify work items, it can also be hard to capture the metric. Our suggestion is to not overdo it but rather find an easy way to classify the work item. For example, vote at the end of a work item's life: was this mostly failure demand or value demand? Some work items (like defects) fall naturally into one category that's hard to classify as anything other than failure demand.

VISUALIZING THE METRIC

Once you have a way to classify value demand versus failure demand, you can visualize the trends as two graphs and see how they're doing against each other. Or you can write a big percentage on the board: "Last week we had 25% failure demand—10% less than the week before."

ANALYZING THE METRIC

This metric can be an eye-opener for many teams—and the stakeholders around them—regarding where the team's time is really spent. When you have those numbers in front of you, you can start to see what you can do about the situation. Why did the failure demand occur, and what was the root cause of it (see section 10.2)?

11.1.7 Abandoned and discarded ideas

WHAT ARE THEY? Measure how many items in a particular backlog (or inbox column) are discarded instead of going into the development workflow and how many items in the development workflow are discarded.

WHAT CAN YOU LEARN FROM THE METRICS? Too few discarded ideas means you don't have a lot of options, so maybe you're not innovating or taking enough risk. Too many items in the development column being discarded means you're starting work you shouldn't.

This is a metric that's easy to overlook because we, in agile methods, encourage changes. It's even in the word *agile*—to be able to change quickly. But how many teams have you seen count the ideas or work items taken off the board? Often they're discarded and not thought about until they resurface.

CAPTURING THE METRIC

An easy way to track the items you take off the board is to have a trashcan or basket where you move work items that you discard. You can then make note of those items and maybe even count the number of discarded ideas per time unit (per week or month, for example). This data can be the context for a fruitful discussion later.

ANALYZING THE METRIC

You can read some interesting facts from those discarded items. Although the first, natural reaction is to think that it's a bad thing to keep moving items off the board, you still want to discard some items. If you don't discard anything that's moved up on the board, you could argue that you're not innovating enough. The lust for discovery is killed by your steadfast backlog that shouldn't be changed.

On the other hand, if you discard too many items, it might be hard to keep the goal clear. This is even worse if you start working on items and then discard them. That can be measured by the number of items in development that you then discard. If that number is high, it means you start a lot of work that you shouldn't have started. That in turn can beg the question whether you should invest more time investigating or discovering in the earlier phases, upstream from your team.

This section took a look at some common metrics that we've seen kanban teams use and get value from. The visualization of metrics is an important part of making the metric known and important to everyone on the team and people around the team. Although the simple diagrams in this section are a great start, the next section dives deep into two well-known and powerful diagrams: process-control charts and cumulative flow diagrams.

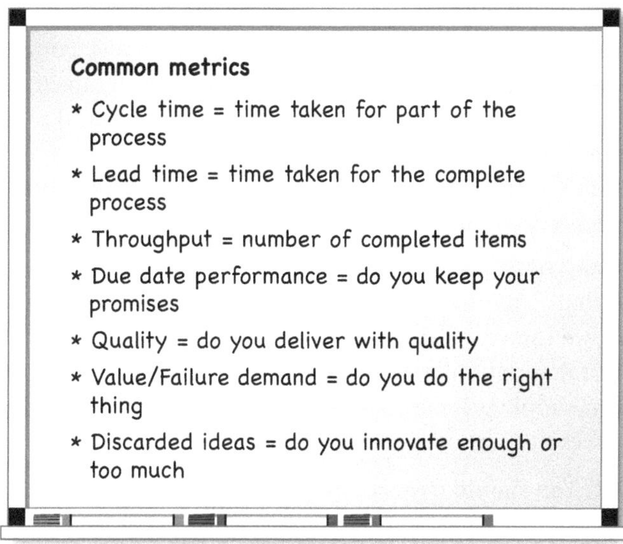

You already have all the data you need to produce these new, powerful diagrams with a visualized workflow. It's a matter of drawing them. Let's see how it's done.

A WORD FROM THE COACH Probably no team should capture and track all the metrics that we've suggested in this section. But for the ones you're tracking, make sure you have explicit, visual policies in place to help you remember what to track when an item is completed. It can be a simple as a checklist, so-called *exit criteria*, in the Done column: "This is what needs to be done before the item can be moved off the board."

11.2 Two powerful visualizations

The previous sections introduced you to a couple of common metrics and gave you hints on how to visualize them. Most of the diagrams suggested are simple to both draw and understand, but they're also limited in their use. They often show one aspect of your process, and you need to cross-reference several diagrams to get a more holistic view of how things are going.

In this section, we take a look at two commonly used diagrams. They're a bit more advanced to produce than the simple scatter, pie, and stacked column charts you've seen so far, but they also give you more information as a reward for your efforts at drawing them. We show you what kind of data you need to track and how to draw the diagrams, and finally what kind of information you can get out of them.

This section isn't about how to use Excel (or any other tool, for that matter). We only show you the kind of calculations you need in order to draw a simple version of the diagram.

11.2.1 Statistical process control (SPC)

Statistical process control (SPC) is an approach to quality control that involves much more than just drawing a diagram. Covering SPC is well outside the scope of this book, but we want to introduce you to a diagram that we've found useful called the *statistical process control chart.* There's an underlying theory that we think you also should know about in order to be able to interpret and understand the SPC chart correctly. It's called the *theory of variation.*

THEORY OF VARIATION

One thing that's easy to overlook is the natural variation found in every system. We assume that we can reach around the average result every time. But that's not the case, due to natural variation. John Seddon has formulated a theory of variation[10] that, through four simple principles, says you can't expect work and workers to perform on the average result that you track and measure.

Principle #1: You should expect things to vary—they always do.

There's natural variation in every system, so you shouldn't be surprised that you get different results from different people, or from the same people on different days.

With a small sample, you can't really tell if it's good or bad, and whether it's within or outside the normal variation for that kind of work. Using an SPC chart, you can see whether the variation is predictable (within the control limits) or unpredictable (outside the control limits).

For example, the performance of a worker may look excellent. When you get a bigger sample, though, you see that it was just what to expect given natural variation.

---

[10] See "There Is a Better Way" at www.systemsthinking.co.uk/variation.asp.

Principle #2: Understanding variation will tell you what to expect.

Let's say you have a team that has tracked the lead time for their work over the last couple of weeks, as visualized in this chart:

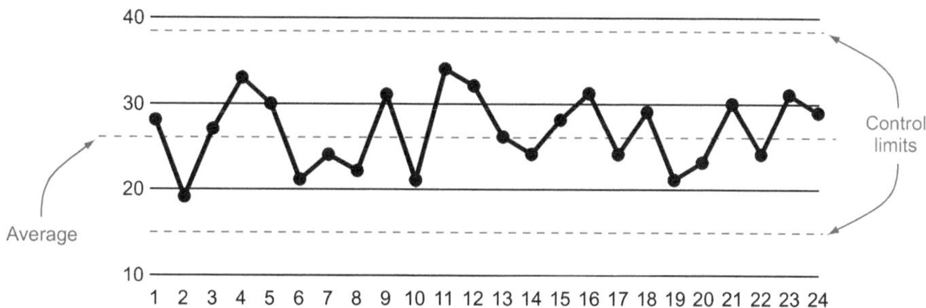

Having upper and lower control limits in place tells you that the team's result will sometimes be as low as the lower limit (in this case, 15) and sometimes as high as the upper limit (in this case, 38), but more often around the average (in this case, 26.5).

Strangely enough, teams often expect to be average (or better) every time. But that's not going to happen, because we are human beings working on knowledge work in a context that naturally has variations.

Consider the example of setting targets for the lead time in the team just mentioned. If you set it to the average, the team will sometimes be over it (and go home sad) and sometimes be under it (and go home happy). You know this will happen because there's natural variation in the process. If you set the target toward the upper control limit, the team will often go home sad, because they will miss it a lot. In reality, many teams will begin doing better, because they're trying to reach that target. But at what cost? It's not uncommon for teams to start cheating[11] or gaming the system to reach the target.

Targets in processes with variations don't motivate people, but they *can* demotivate people. If you read the work of Dan Pink (*Drive*, Riverhead Books, 2001, http://mng.bz/yM3h), you know that what really motivates people isn't targets but autonomy, mastery, and purpose.

> *If you give a manager a numerical target, he'll make it, even if he has to destroy the company in the process.*
>
> —W. Edwards Deming

Principle #3: Work on the causes of variations, which are always found in the system.

> *A bad system will defeat a good person anytime.*
>
> —Attributed to W. Edwards Deming

[11] For example, start doing sloppy work that is faster but will come back and slow them down later.

The majority of performance variation is found in the system itself, outside the control of the individuals who work in it. Consider all the things that affect your current situations: policies, roles, organizational structure, procedures, requirements, funding, and information, to mention a few. All of these are examples of things that (normally) lie outside the control of the team. Things like these also cause the natural variation in the system. Again: the things that cause the natural variation lie outside the control of the team.

Managers should be to try to minimize the variation by working on the things in the system that cause variation.

Principle #4: Understanding variation tells you when something has happened.

In an SPC chart, you can see if a single value is a *special cause* (lies outside the control limits—see the circled point on the graph) or if it's a *common cause* (within the control limits and hence an effect of natural variation). You need to be aware of the difference so you don't act as if every variation is a special-cause variation.

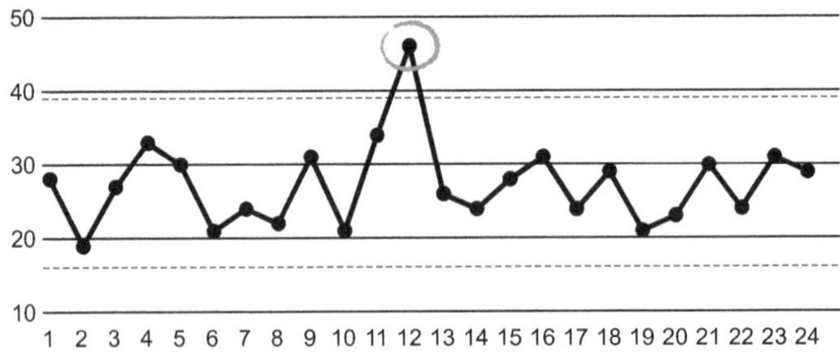

For example, it normally takes Joakim 20–40 minutes to drive to work. But one day he had a flat tire, and the journey took him 1 hour and 25 minutes. Should that single incident change the way he drives? Or should he buy a new car? If it's super important that he is never, ever late, maybe he should invest in a Vespa and keep it in his trunk in case of future flat tires. But more likely, he should treat that incident as a one-off that won't impact his driving that much. If he starts to have flat tires often, he might check into his driving habits or the quality of the tires he buys.

THE SPC CHART

A *statistical process control chart* (or control chart, or running chart, or SPC chart for short[12]) shows trends on how the process is doing over time. Usually you track lead or cycle times (see section 11.1.1), but you can use a running chart to track other metrics as well.

The *statistical* part of the name implies that you're applying statistical analysis with the chart, and that's completely correct. With statistical analysis, you get a better view

[12] "Beloved child has many names" is a Swedish saying, so it's safe to say that SPCs are loved, we suppose.

of the real trend by excluding the occasional highs and lows (also known as *outliers*) and keep your focus tight on the trend in the data.

WHAT DATA DO YOU NEED TO DRAW ONE?

You don't need much data to be able to draw a control chart—in fact, you only need the lead time for each work item. That said, you can make the chart more interesting if you have a few more values, all of which you get from your visualized workflow:

- Identifier or title of the work item, so you know which work item a certain point in the diagram refers to.
- Start and stop dates, used to calculate the lead (or cycle) time for the work item. You could just track the lead time as a single number,[13] but having the Start and Done dates can prove useful for narrowing the scope of the diagram, for example.
- Work item type, which allows for interesting filtering and scoping (for example: what was the lead time for defects in May?).

As you can see, all that data is sitting on your board, waiting for you. It's easy to capture.

HOW DO YOU DRAW ONE?

The simplest version is drawn by calculating the lead time (Done date minus Start date) in days and creating a scatter diagram showing this data. You've already seen simple diagrams like this in this chapter. Adding a trend line makes it easier to analyze the data.

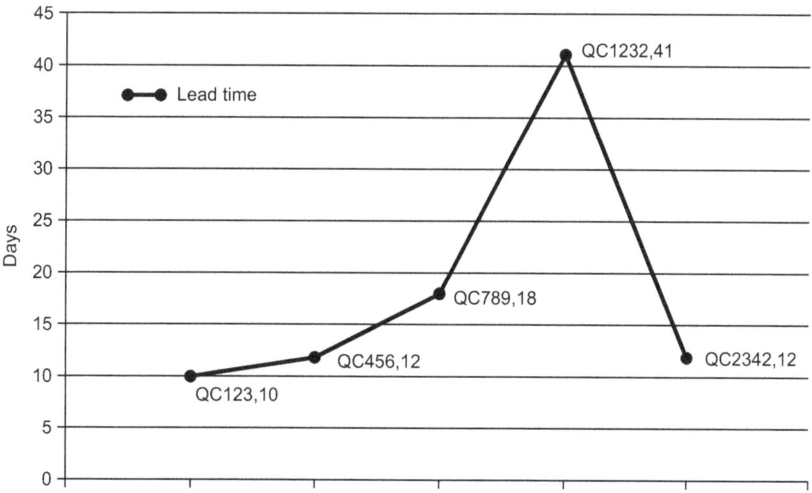

[13] For example, by noting the date you put the sticky on your board and then counting the days until you moved it into the Done column.

You can include the identifier or title of the work item if you want a way to refer to it, but the chart can easily get cluttered, and you may take away the focus from the trend.

A slightly more advanced method would be to plot different lines or even different diagrams based on the work-item type. You can easily do that by using filters for your data before you create the diagram.

Finally, you want to put the *statistical* into *statistical process control charts*, and in order to do that you need some formulas for average lead time, the one sigma, and the upper and lower control limits. Consider the following data:

Id	Title	Start	Done	Lead time in days
123	Work item #1	2013-01-01	2013-02-01	31
124	Work item #2	2013-01-10	2013-02-02	23
125	Work item #3	2013-01-13	2013-02-03	19
126	Work item #4	2013-01-15	2013-02-08	24
127	Work item #5	2013-01-18	2013-02-09	22
128	Work item #6	2013-01-20	2013-02-10	21

- *Average lead time* is an easy one: take all the lead times and divide them by the number of items you've tracked. For this example, that would be (31 + 23 + 19 + 24 + 22 + 21) / 6 = 24 days.
- *One sigma* is a bit tricky to understand and calculate. A *sigma* is a value that helps even out the effects of outliers. A statistical rule called the 68-95-99.7 rule[14] states that 68% of all values lie one standard deviation (called *one sigma*) from the mean. With two sigmas from the mean, you cover 95% of all values. Finally, with three sigmas, you cover 99.7%. Calculating one sigma[15] from a sample is pretty advanced mathematics, but thankfully almost all spreadsheet programs have formulas for that in their arsenal.[16] With this sample, you get STDEVP(31, 23, 19, 24, 22, 21) ≈ 3.7.
- The *upper control limit* is now (after doing the mind-bending sigma stuff) easy to calculate. You use an upper control limit of one sigma above the average, therefore, according to the 68-95-99.7 rule, taking 68% of the population into consideration. In this example, this adds one sigma to the average: 24 (average lead time) + 3.7 (one sigma) ≈ 28 days.
- The *lower control limit* is equally easy to calculate. Subtract a sigma from the average. In this case, that would be: 24 (average) – 3.4 (one sigma) ≈ 20 days.

[14] See http://en.wikipedia.org/wiki/68-95-99.7_rule.

[15] See http://en.wikipedia.org/wiki/Standard_deviation.

[16] In Excel it's called DSTDEVP, and for Google spreadsheets it's called STDEVP.

HOW DO YOU READ IT?

This calculation will produce a diagram that looks something like this:

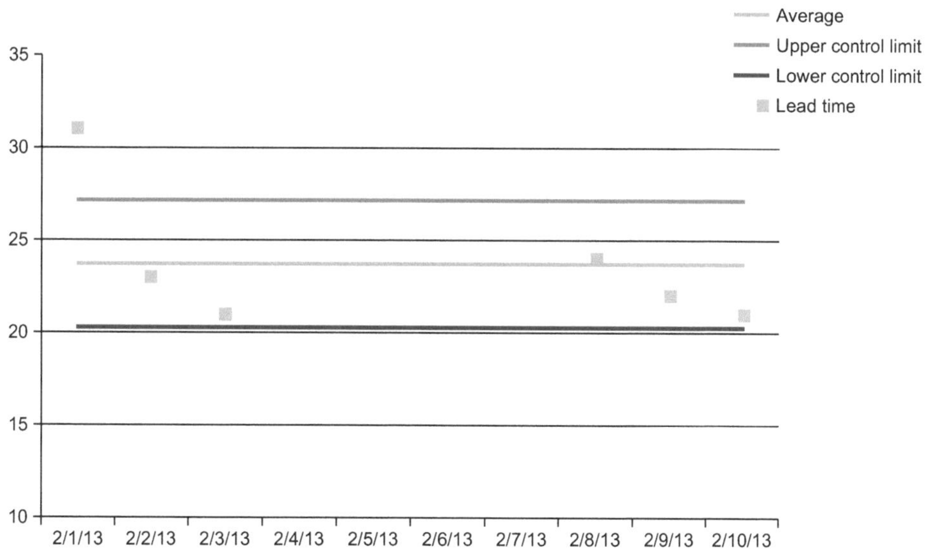

With this diagram in place, you can get a lot of information:[17]

- You don't have to care too much about the first work item because it's an outlier (based on the data you have right now). You can easily see that because it lies outside the *upper control limit.*
- The difference within the control limits isn't too big, meaning you have a pretty high accuracy for the lead time of your items. But wait a minute. This sample is minimal (and made up), so you can't say how you're doing with a bigger sample. What you want to watch out for is whether the *spread* (the distance between the upper and lower control limits) is big, meaning items are different in size, and predictions are harder to make. Could that be something that you can improve on? How would you do that?
- There's a nice trend on display here because the lead times go down. Why is that? Are these special work items, or have you changed your ways of working? How can you reinforce this trend? If the trend is going the other way, what do you have to do to stop it?

Remember the theory of variation (covered earlier) and that every system (and process) has natural variation. Take that knowledge into consideration when reading an SPC chart.

---

[17] Yes, this is an example, with just a couple of data points. The analyzing you're doing may be overthrown as new data points—new work items—are completed.

A statistical process control chart is a nice tool and not hard to read. It's also easy to capture the data needed to draw one. Let's now turn our attention to a diagram that's a bit more advanced at first glance. After getting used to it, you'll soon see that it's not hard to read and that you can get a lot of information out of it: the cumulative flow diagram.

11.2.2 Cumulative flow diagram (CFD)

A *cumulative flow diagram* (CFD) is full of information that can be useful as background material for a discussion on process improvement. After an initial introduction, it's easy to read, and the metrics are also easy to capture from your visualized workflow. Drawing the diagram is simple after the discipline involved in gathering the data.

The CFD is growing in popularity in the agile community and has been called the successor to the Scrum burn-down chart.[18] Let's dive in and see how you can draw one yourself.

WHAT DATA DO YOU NEED TO DRAW ONE?

In order to draw a CFD, you need to know *the number of work items* you have in each step of your board per day.[19] You can easily track that by counting them. The only trick is that you can't capture this data *after* you've taken the stickies down off the board.[20]

Here's an example board, as it looked on a certain date (2013-01-10, to be exact):

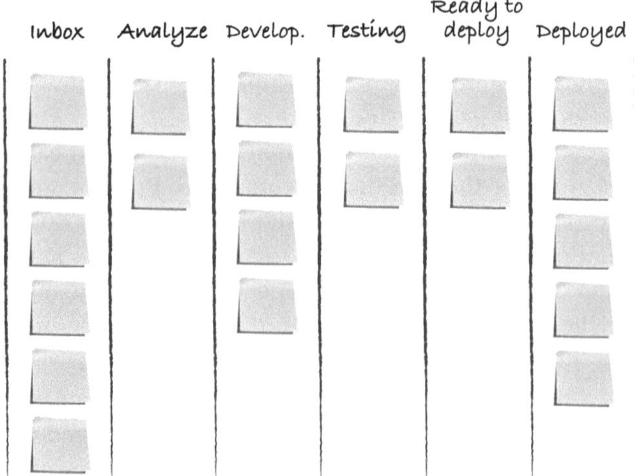

[18] A burn-down chart is often used by Scrum teams to track their process during a sprint, by showing how much work (often in story points) is left to do.

[19] Theoretically it could be any regular interval, but a daily interval not only is the most commonly used but also seems appropriate for most teams.

[20] If you're not Sheldon Cooper or have eidetic memory—or have taken a photo of the board each day.

Over time, the team has counted the number of items in each step and gathered the data in a table like this:

Date	Inbox	Analysis	Development	Testing	Ready for Deploy	Deployed
2013-01-05	4	1	2	2	2	1
2013-01-06	5	2	4	2	2	1
2013-01-07	4	2	5	2	2	2
2013-01-08	5	2	5	3	3	2
2013-01-09	6	2	5	3	2	4
2013-01-10	6	2	4	2	2	5

In the table you can see the number of items in each stage of the process at a certain date. The last column is accumulated (hence *cumulative* flow diagram) as we keep deploying more and more items into production. For example, on 2013-01-09 we had three work items in Testing, and the accumulated number of Deployed items was up to four.

A lot of numbers are displayed here, but don't feel discouraged. It's simple to track the data in a spreadsheet. Remember to do it daily, after every daily standup or at another recurring event that happens at regular intervals.

HOW DO YOU DRAW ONE?

Drawing a cumulative flow diagram is easy. If you're using spreadsheet software, the diagram type you're looking for is called something like Stacked Area Diagram. You create that diagram by selecting the data and having the software create the diagram for you.

Remember that you need to lay out the areas in the order of the columns in your process. In this example, that gives you the following: the Inbox area needs be on the top in the diagram, followed by Analysis, Development, Testing, and so forth. Some spreadsheet software[21] orders them alphabetically by default and hence messes up the diagram. Make sure the data is in board-chronological order.

If you draw this diagram manually, it's a matter of plotting items from each column for each day. Start from the bottom, and note how many Done items there are. For the next position, add the number of items in the next column to the Done column.

For example, in the Ready for Deploy column on 2013-01-10, we had two items. In the Done column, we had an accumulated value of five. Adding those together (2 + 5) means the Y value should be added at 7 for Ready for Deploy.

---

[21] *cough* Excel *cough*

Here's an example of how the data looks in a stacked area diagram, when it's drawn by Microsoft Excel:

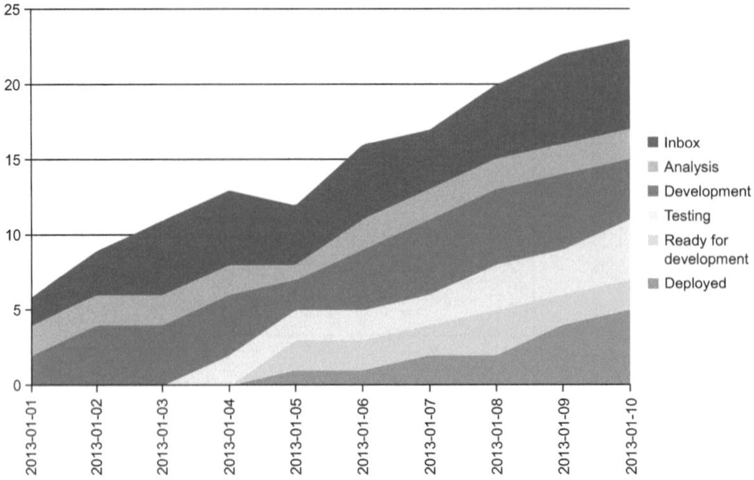

HOW DO YOU READ IT?

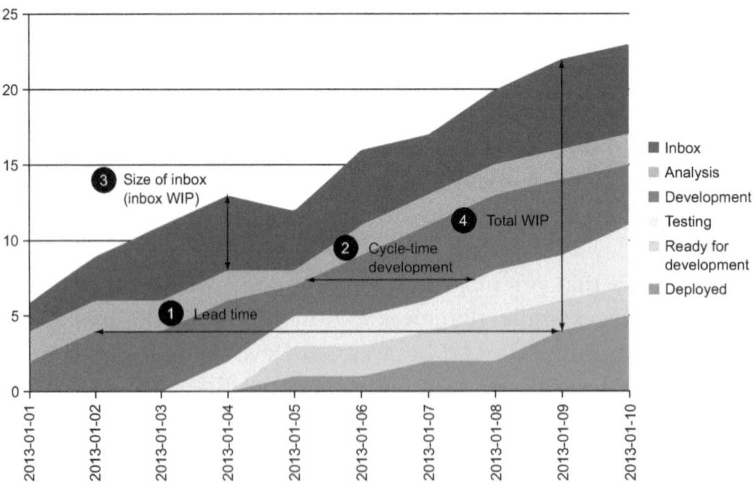

One of the main reasons for the CFD's popularity is that it shows you a lot of information. Here are a few things that you can pick out from the diagram (indicated with the same numbers on the previous diagram):

1. The lead time can be seen in the diagram as the total horizontal length of the colored area in the diagram, on any given date.
2. Cycle times for parts of the process can also be seen as the start of the area of interest. We've measured development time here.

3 The size of the backlog is shown as the height of the top-level area. That's the number of items in the Inbox. The same measurement can be done to any area at a given time to see the WIP for that column.

4 You can also measure your total WIP at any given date by measuring the height of all the areas down to Deployed (the Done step).

Other things of interest are shown in a CFD:

- You can also see the relation between WIP and lead time. The more work you have in process (number 4 in the previous diagram, the total height of all the areas), the longer your lead time will become (number 1 in the diagram). This can be an eye-opener and a great discussion point for the team to see how lower WIP makes work items flow faster through your process.
- From the areas, you can get a lot of information. For example, the growing Deployed area (the bottom area) shows the number of features delivered over time. And the Development area shows how many items are being developed at any given time.
- The Inbox area (the top area) shows how many items aren't being worked on yet. In the example diagram, the Inbox is moving with the other areas, which means new stuff is added to the Inbox from time to time. If a project had a fixed backlog, and nothing was added to it over time, the Inbox area would shrink over time.

As you can see, there's quite a lot of data that you can get out of this diagram and look back on for analysis. For example, what happened when you started to pair program? Did the WIP go up or down? At the same time, what kind of effect did that have on the cycle time for Development? Did that also effect the lead time?

All these questions and more can be answered using the CFD, which is a great tool for kanban teams to help them analyze their progress. You need to be diligent when it comes to capturing the data, but it's also rewarding because the CFD shows a lot of information in a nice way.

Common diagrams

* Statistical process control chart (SPC) or running chart shows lead and/or cycle times
  - Can be hand drawn in a simple manner
  - The "statistical" part adds data that shows outliers clearly
  - Start and stop dates needed to draw one
* Cumulative flow diagram shows amount of work per step in your process
  - Day-by-day status needed to draw one
  - Contains a lot of information, work in process per step, lead/cycle time

11.3 Metrics as improvement guides

We've now talked a lot about different metrics and diagrams and other visualizations, and you may think it will be hard to pick the right one for you and your team. Remember that a metric is (often) not important in itself but is rather a guide for your improvement work. Metrics help you know whether you're improving or not. With metrics in place, you can take a more experimental approach to learning and improving, because you can't really know before you start whether you're going to improve.

This section covers some things to think about for your metrics and how you use them. Kanban is based on three simple principles, one of which is *visualize work*. You visualize work in order to see and know information that you otherwise would have missed. This information helps you make informed decisions about your process, the status of your work, and how you can improve.

Metrics are like visualization for improvements. Metrics are there to help you determine whether the changes you make, in order to improve, lead to an improvement or whether you should try something else. With a good visualized metric, you can start to have discussions based on data instead of based on hunches or beliefs (anecdotal evidence).

When you measure how your work is behaving, you can also begin to see how changes you make in order to improve affect those metrics. You can do small experiments and see how they affect the metric you're trying to improve.

MAKE IT VISUAL

One way to visualize metrics is through diagrams like the one below. Visualizing your metrics doesn't improve your process, but it does start discussions based on the data rather than on a gut feeling. Questions are raised, experiments can be tried, and the effect of those can be tracked in a more controlled way because you can see how the experiment has changed your trend.

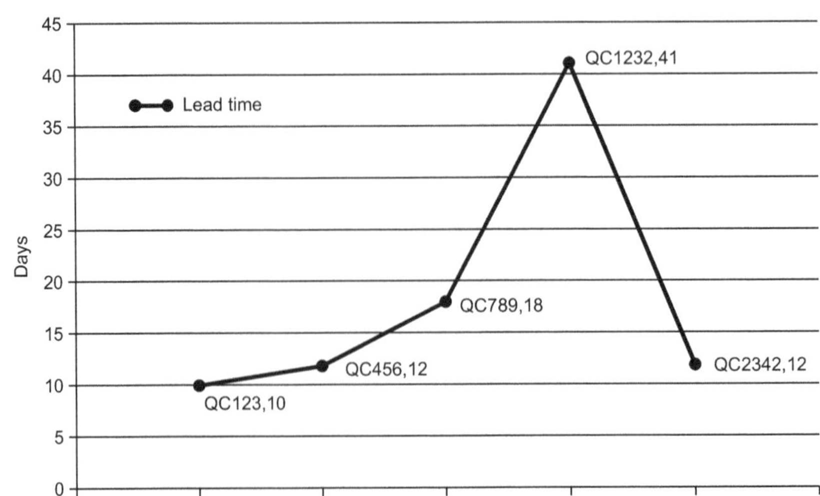

If you're still not convinced, try the simplest possible thing you can come up with from this chapter—tracking lead times, for example. Make the metric visual and big, and put the data on the board. Involve the metric in your discussions; refer to it as you talk about your work. Pretty soon people will begin talking, questioning, and discussing. In these discussions, the team will talk about improvements to the process.

ARE YOU MAKING A BUSINESS IMPACT OR NOT?

When you're looking for metrics, you should start out with what's important for you and your business. What goals are you trying to reach? How do you know if you're heading in that direction? These are sometimes not easy questions to answer and track metrics around, but you should still strive to find data that shows whether you're making a business impact.

Let's say your business is trying to get more users on your site. If you track and visualize that close to your board, you can glance at that number and see if your efforts are impacting that number, reason about the work that you're doing next, think about the effect it will have on the business goal, and so on. In short, you make the business goal apparent and try to connect it closer to the work you're doing.

YOU GET WHAT YOU MEASURE

You get what you measure. Measure the wrong thing and you get the wrong behaviors.

—John H. Lingle

Set up a goal or metric, and you'll soon start seeing people change their behavior to reach that goal. That, at first, might seem obvious and to be something you'd want; but when you think about it, it's a bit dangerous, too. If you start to measure how long each support call takes in a call center, you'll find that people begin closing calls early rather than focusing on helping the customer. Workers in the call center will prefer short calls over longer ones, even if that means their customers won't get the help they need. Metrics may drive the call-center employees toward the wrong behavior.

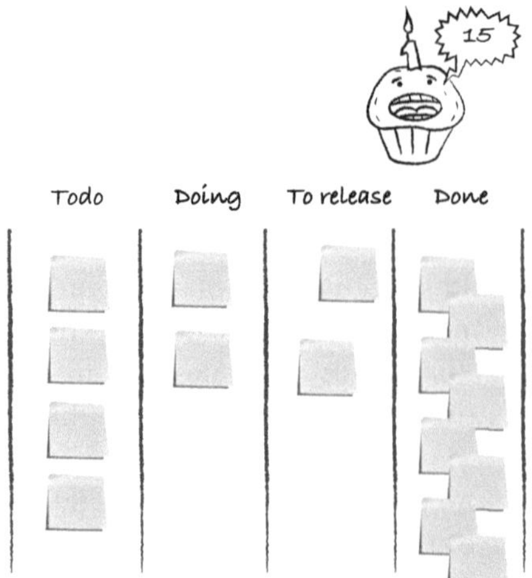

The knowledge that "you get what you measure" could also be used to your advantage. One such technique is to put a limit on the amount of work in the Done column, sometimes referred to as the *cake limit* (see chapter 12). When the limit is reached, the product owner comes in with cake and distributes it to the team. What kind of behavior could this drive? The team could start making smaller stories that are done more quickly and hence fill up the Done column with work items more quickly. And that's a good thing: smaller stories that move faster across the board—yes, please.

BALANCE YOUR METRICS

In your search for a good metric, you should also make sure you don't focus all your energy on one metric. This could make you forget about other important aspects of your process. Imagine that you have a metric on throughput (number of items completed per week, for example). With a strong focus on only this metric, your team could easily get burned out, making people hate work and even eventually leave. Or they may cut corners with code quality that will only result in more technical debt and finally slow down your process.[22]

To handle this problem, we suggest that you try to find *several* metrics that balance against each other. An example could be to focus both on lead time (time it takes for work through the entire process) and quality (number of bugs in production, for example). With these two values, you try to make sure you don't fall into the trap of starting to take shortcuts to get a lower lead time.

MAKE THEM EASY TO CAPTURE

Tracking a metric requires that you gather it in some way and then visualize it or show it to the people who care about it. Make sure the gathering doesn't take a lot of effort. If the metric is hard to gather, you'll end up in a situation where you have to prioritize gathering process data against "doing the work," risking that it won't be tracked at all. Also, you want the metric to be able to change as your process changes. If you use metrics for which you've invested a lot in gathering the data, you risk not wanting to change, or you may even stop caring about them. That could make introducing new metrics harder because now you're tracking several metrics, which could give you contradicting results.

[22] We've actually heard a couple of stories of developers being fired because they cared "too much" about code quality. They were adding tests around a non-tested code base when they "should have put new features into production"—a behavior that might stem from focusing too much on one thing, one metric.

PREFER REAL DATA OVER ESTIMATED DATA

Try to use real data rather than estimated values. Real data is data you can get from measuring the way your work works, the quality of your work, how the product is being used, and so on.

Unlike estimated data, real data can't be argued with. You can always question the way an estimate has been done and how the numbers came about, but with real data you're facing the facts directly. You can still have discussions around the number, why it's like it is, and what to do about it, which we think is a Good Thing. You want to continuously improve the quality of the data and the ways you gather the data.

Note that real data doesn't automatically mean precision. Real data can, for example, be asking people to vote with a fist of five[23] to the question "Are we having fun right now?" This is also data.

Tracking where we spent our time

There's a firefighting squad at Spotify. Their main responsibility is to handle emergencies that occur in the backend systems and keep them running. Naturally, the team experienced a lot of *reactive* work. But they soon realized that they had to start doing some *proactive* work to keep the system in shape and handle problems before they became emergencies.

We decided to try to track where they spent their time: on proactive or reactive work. This is a metric that could prove hard to track: should we use time sheets, track hours on paper, or estimate?

The team came up with a simple yet telling approach. After each day, they posted a sticky on a board that indicated where they had spent their time that day (mostly).

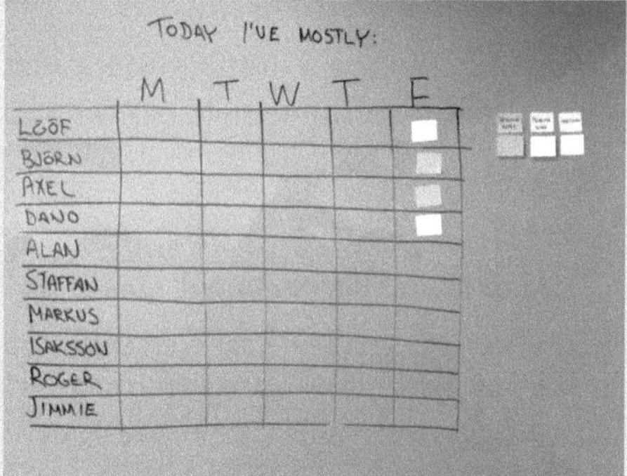

We collected the data during a week and then summarized it to get a bigger picture. Pretty soon we saw trends and could start doing something about it.

That data wasn't perfect, but it was good enough for our needs.

[23] Raising one to five fingers in response to a question.

USE METRICS TO IMPROVE, NOT TO PUNISH

Metrics are powerful motivators that can help you to see and follow your progress toward a better result. But, as with all powerful tools, they can be misused. One common misuse we've seen is to set goals for teams and then hold them accountable for the outcome of those goals. Rather than motivate the team, the metric is used to punish the team for bad results.

Don't get us wrong here; you want the team to strive to reach the goal and be accountable for the result, but there's a subtle difference in intent. That difference can be found in who sets the goal. Is it a goal that the team has set up and committed to? Or is it a metric that's been assigned to the team by some outside person, such as a manager or stakeholder?

Make sure you include the team in the development of the metric. Doing so builds commitment and the feeling of the metric being "ours" rather than "theirs."

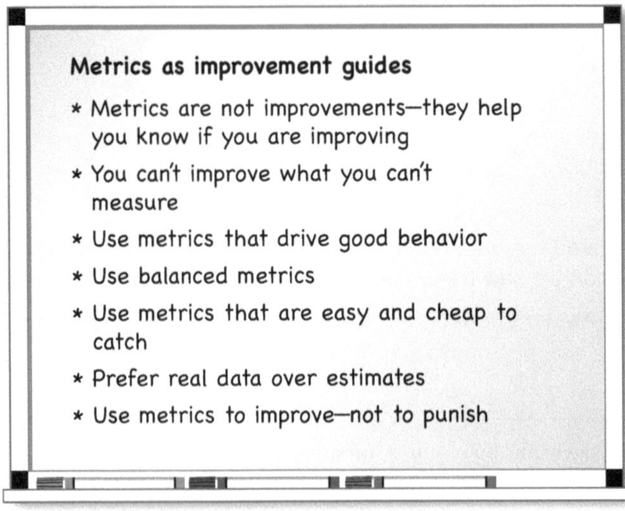

11.4 Exercise: measure up!

You now have another opportunity to try this for real in your team. Sit down and discuss the metrics that would help you know the status of your process:

- Do you have any metrics in place already? Are they good? Do they help *you* to know what's going on?
- Can any of the suggested metrics be tried and experimented with? How would that help you?
- Are there any other metrics that you want to introduce?
- What kind of behavior do you want to encourage? Will the metric help that?

Start simple and easy. Remember that metrics are often hard to stop measuring once you begin. Make sure everyone knows the purpose of the metric and that you don't push metrics on the team. They should rather come from the team. "No metrics right now" is a valid outcome of the discussion. Ask again later if you or anyone else sees the need.

11.5 Summary

In this chapter, you learned about metrics and how they can help you track your process:

- In order to know if you're improving or not, you measure your process behavior and analyze these metrics.
- Metrics are like a visualization of your process's health.
- The following are common metrics that kanban teams use:
  - *Cycle time*—Time taken to complete part of the process
  - *Lead time*—Time taken to complete the whole process
  - *Throughput*—How many items get done per week (or month or whatever)
  - *Number of issues and blockers on the board*
  - *Due-date performance*
  - *Value demand versus failure demand*—Demand on a system caused by failure to do something or do something right for the customer
- These are common diagrams that kanban teams use:
  - *Statistical process control (SPC) chart*—A visualization of lead and cycle times
  - *Cumulative flow diagram (CFD)*—Shows a lot of information about your process based on the number of items per stage in your process per day
- Finding a good metric can be hard. Remember the following:
  - You get what you measure.
  - Don't focus on a single metric—use balanced metrics.
  - Use metrics that are easy to capture, or make them so.
  - Prefer real data over estimates.
  - Use metrics to improve—not to punish.

12 Kanban pitfalls

This chapter covers

- How to avoid common kanban pitfalls and criticism
- The number-one mistake when starting to use kanban
- The fact that kanban isn't a process at all, at least not as you might think

By now you should have plenty of reasons to use kanban in your process. You can show interested people that kanban has improved and continues to improve your process. Because of the approach that kanban takes to change management ("Start where you are and improve from there"), most teams and organizations don't object too loudly to kanban and the principles it's built on.

That said, some criticism comes up from time to time. It wouldn't be fair if we didn't at least touch on the most common issues and how to deal with them. For the most part, the criticism focuses on pitfalls that are easy to fall into if you don't look out. We wrote this chapter so you know what to avoid.

The aim of this chapter is twofold: to introduce you to some commonly raised objections and then to help you avoid the pitfalls identified by this criticism. Learning about the ways people criticize is a great way to improve—it helps make sure you steer clear of bad things.

Let's take the bull by the horns and start with criticism that came up in the early years of kanban, leveled by one of the founders of Scrum.

12.1 All work and no play makes Jack a dull boy

PITFALL Kanban can end up becoming boring, with just work item after work item lined up, and no natural interruptions, celebrations, or cadences.

SOLUTION Compared to Scrum, kanban gives you the freedom to detach the different ceremonies, such as planning, review, and retrospective, from each other, depending on how the work actually flows through your process.

(Everyone who checked the door to see if Jack Nicholson was ready to break in with an axe, raise your hand.) The heading of this section is a quote from the famous horror movie *The Shining*, in which an overworked author[1] just keeps typing the phrase "All work and no play makes Jack a dull boy" on his typewriter. It's also what we thought we heard[2] Ken Schwaber say when he criticized the early kanban community. The real quote is this:

> *God help us. People found ways to have slack in waterfall, to rest and be creative. With Lean and Kanban, those hiding places are removed. We now have a progressive death march without pause.*
>
> —Ken Schwaber[3]

Ken Schwaber is, together with Jeff Sutherland, the father of Scrum. He was commenting on the lack of iterations in kanban. To him, kanban was just a long list of work lined up, with no end in sight: just work, work, work.

That doesn't sound too nice, does it? Sadly, he had a point, especially considering many of the kanban implementations we've seen at our different clients and workplaces.

---

1 Neither Marcus nor Joakim had reached that point at the time of writing. Our families are safe. But Marcus has not dared to give tricycles to his twins.

2 It's a bit of a stretch but it made a great heading, don't you agree?

3 "Waterfall, Lean/Kanban, and Scrum," http://mng.bz/OrXd.

Kanban is very lightweight and is easy to get up and running. As we've mentioned a lot already, it's just a few simple principles. If you're already doing Scrum or some other iteration-based method, you can even *remove* stuff like iterations, if you want. Before long, you end up with just a continuous flow of work and "no slack … to rest and be creative."

But that's not how it needs to be, and it's not how kanban was intended to be. Quite the opposite! Kanban never said to remove iterations. But it does give you the freedom to *detach* the ceremonies of other methods—such as planning, reviews, and retrospectives—from each other.

Kanban doesn't say anything about having the same cadence for different ceremonies or not. If you find that useful, by all means go ahead and do that, but don't be unnecessarily constrained by it. Take the opportunity to defer decisions until the "last responsible moment,"[4] when you have the most information in your hands. Using kanban, you can also greatly benefit from showing your stakeholders what you've done and how you're progressing, with demonstrations and reviews.

Back to the criticism of Ken Schwaber that we started this section with. He could be right, but it doesn't have to be that way. Make sure you take time for reviews, retrospectives, and other good practices. But do them when it's the right moment, not because a certain amount of time has passed or when the iteration is over. Do it when needed—just in time rather than just in case. We talk about this in the chapter on planning (chapter 9), where we describe cadences.

Finally, using WIP limits will drive you to collaboration, and you might also end up with "slack … to rest and be creative" from time to time.

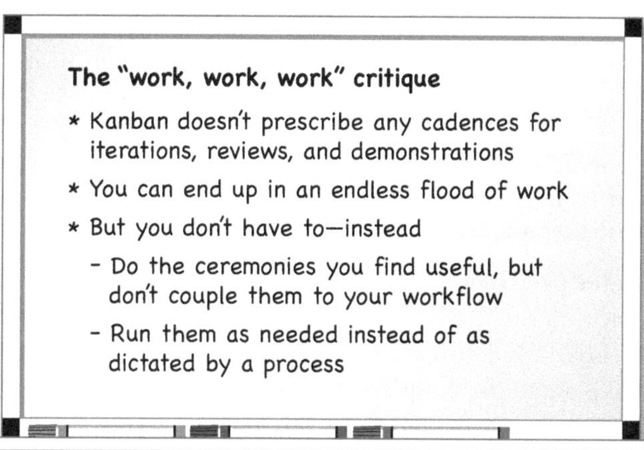

[4] Mary and Tom Poppendieck, *Lean Software Development*, Addison-Wesley Professional, 2003, http://amzn.com/0321150783.

12.1.1 Creating cadences for celebration

To fight the risk that your process is just "work, work, work," you could and should have a cadence for celebration. It's as important as other events that we've talked about, and it's a great way to boost morale and team enjoyment. Cadences for celebration can take many forms, and there's often no shortage of creativity when it comes to inventing new ways to celebrate. In this section, we'll introduce you to two ways of having celebration cadences as part of your process.

FREQUENT FLYER MILES

With frequent flyer miles, the team can collect points for the work they're doing. They can then use points to do something fun together. The points work much like an airline's frequent flyer miles—after you travel a certain number of miles, the airline gives you some points to spend on free trips, upgraded hotel rooms, or other perks.

The team and the stakeholder come up with some way to track the points earned by the team and decide what to do when the team reaches a certain point threshold. For example, when you've completed 50 story points or 20 work items, you have a pizza and gaming evening at the office.

We've also seen teams working this in layers, which allows the team to save points for even greater rewards. For example, you can have the pizza and gaming night at the office at 50 points, or you can save up points for the next level, 100 points. That's when the stakeholder takes the team out on the town for laser tag, dinner at a nice restaurant, and so on.

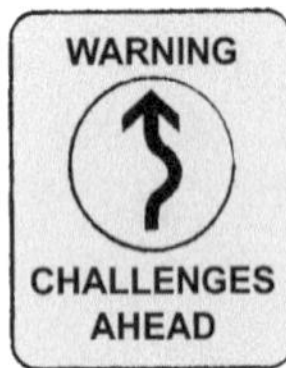

WARNING We should probably mention here that it's possible to go overboard with the rewards. Dan Pink talks about this in his book *Drive: The Surprising Truth about What Motivates Us* (Riverhead Books, 2011, www.danpink.com/books/drive). Pink cites several studies indicating that for knowledge work, the result has a tendency to get worse if you pay more, give higher bonuses, and so on.

Use the perks and celebrations we suggest here as a way to have a good time with your team. Don't let them be the only reason that people are doing work for you. Read more about that in *Drive*.[5]

WORKING TO THE CAKE LIMIT

Another way to create a cadence for celebration is to have a WIP limit on the final column of the board. It confused us at first when we saw that on a board at Spotify, but as the team[6] explained the concept, it made great sense. It's also a nice way to extend the use of the mechanisms in kanban to this area.

---

5 Spoiler alert: autonomy, mastery, and purpose drive us—not more money, nor pizza and beers for that matter.

6 The team at Spotify quickly understood the mechanics of kanban and used it to introduce a pull mechanism for celebration. Creative and fun!

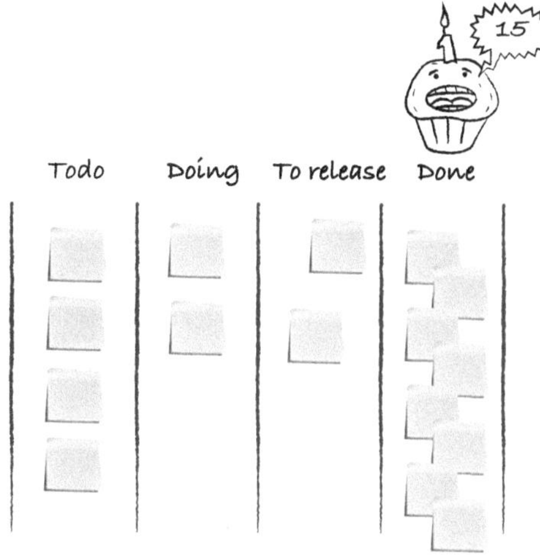

The WIP limit on Done limits the number of items you can put in that column. Let's say you set the limit at 15 items. That means after you've filled the Done column with 15 items, you can't finish any more items. You're up to your WIP limit for Done. Not only that, but work also starts to back up in the workflow (because nothing can move forward), creating an increasing urgency to clear the Done column.

The only way to clear the Done column is for the stakeholder to bring cake[7] and thank the team for work well done. It's both brilliant and fun, and it shows the principles of queues and bottlenecks in a nice way.

Let's continue on to another criticism about the flow that's the heart of kanban. In short: there are no timeboxes in kanban, but you can add them if you see the need.

12.2 Timeboxing is good for you

PITFALL Kanban has no built-in timeboxing. You want timeboxes because they help you prioritize and make necessary trade-offs in scope, time, and cost.

SOLUTION You can have timeboxes where they're beneficial. In flow-based processes, without iterations, timeboxing can be implemented with SLAs and deadlines per work item, for example.

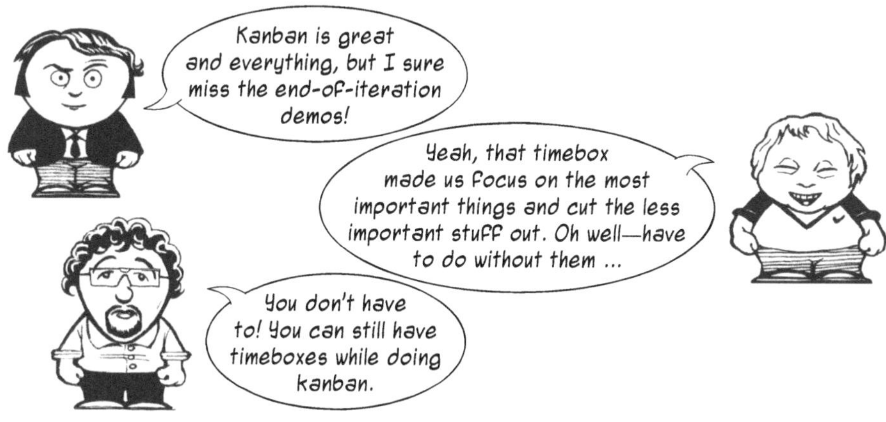

[7] Or something else that the team enjoys and is allowed to eat and drink during working hours.

Timeboxing is a powerful technique that helps you maintain focus and make the necessary decisions to deliver the *right* things on time. The following triangle is one way to show what timeboxing is all about. It illustrates the trade-offs you have to make in any project, but in particular for software projects (sometimes called the *iron triangle* or *triple constraints*).

This triangle balances scope, time, and cost against each other. *Scope* refers to the scope of the features someone wants. *Cost* is how much money it will cost—for example, how many people are on the team and which hardware/software is needed to build it, and other costs. *Time* represents how long the endeavor will take, or the due date when the project needs to be done.

In the middle of the triangle is a fourth[8] aspect: *quality*. You can take quality into consideration and make trade-offs with it. More often than not, that creates problems afterward in the form of technical debt that needs to be paid off. We don't often recommend trading with quality but rather suggest trying to make the quality as good as possible, considering the other aspects.

> **Technical debt**
>
> *Technical debt* is a metaphor that Ward Cunningham coined. It helps you think about the things that you should have done to your code, were too rushed to do, or were too sloppy to introduce. As with financial debt, technical debt involves interest. If you don't do anything about the technical debt, the interest grows over time (in the form of extra effort needed to keep the code in working condition), and soon you find yourself just paying off the interest. This creates a situation where you can't develop new features because all of your resources are spent keeping the system running.

[8] Yes, fourth. In a triangle. Stay with us.

Back to the triangle. The crux of it is, you can't fix all three of these aspects. Actually, you could, but you'll see later why that would be considered bad. For the sake of argument, let's say that you agree that you can't fix time, scope, and cost.

What are your options, then?

- You can *fix time and scope and let the cost vary*. "We'll be done with this exact feature at 0900 on 14 May, but it's going to cost us." Most companies and stakeholders don't like that setup. And for the most part, it's very hard to make software development projects go faster by throwing more people[9] on the team. Typing code isn't the biggest constraint in software development; learning and understanding are.[10]
- Let's *fix scope and cost instead and let time vary*. "We'll have this exact list of features ready, and it will cost $47,343, but we don't know when we'll be done." This is also something that most companies shy away from—it's often worse than letting the cost vary. Companies want some sort of predictability, and saying, "We don't know when we'll be done" is more uncertainty than most organizations can cope with. Another (possibly bigger) problem with this approach is that it assumes that you can know the scope before starting something and that there will be no new discoveries. For these reasons, "fixed scope" is rarely really fixed anyway.
- That leaves *fixing cost and time and letting scope vary*. "We'll be done at 0900 on May 12, and that will cost you the salary for these six guys during that time. But we don't know what will be done by then." Although that sounds scary at first, this is actually a business opportunity. It gives you the chance to order the list of items you want the team to do in business-value order, doing the most valuable ones first. Or if the business values are hard to see or know, you can sort the list of items to do in order of how much you can learn or how much risk you can reduce. With a quick estimate, the team could probably guess how far they would get.

The last approach is known as *timeboxing*—fixing the time (and cost) for when things are to be done and adjusting the scope accordingly.

---

9 "Nine women don't give birth to a child in a month" is something that a witty colleague has often said to Marcus to get the message across.

10 If you need more evidence for that, just ask anyone involved in a project if it would proceed more quickly if they got the opportunity to do it all over again. They will most likely say, "Yes, of course." Then ask them why. What made you go slower the first time around?

Fix all the aspects! Do it! Do it now!

We said that you can't fix all three variables—scope, cost, and time—in the triangle. That's not quite true. You could, but that approach creates other problems.

If all aspects are fixed, something has to give when you're running late or need to make trade-offs. Because all three aspects are fixed, the only thing left to trade off is quality. That means you're starting to get sloppy or doing things faster than you can handle. That will eventually come back and bite you in the form of technical debt. When forced to fix scope, time, and cost, we often increase our estimates to take risk into consideration.

Never has that been more bluntly apparent than in a certain review meeting Marcus was once in. The project had gone under (!) budget, and the business was very pleased but wanted to know why. The IT project manager was a bit uneasy with that question but finally said, "Well, we always add 30% to our estimates before we send them to you. Just to handle the risk of our being wrong."

That made the business people burst out laughing. When they calmed down, they managed to say, "When we get your estimates, we always add 30%. Just to handle the risk of your estimates being wrong."

Fixing all three aspects is bad in more ways than first meet the eye, because it means you're delaying feedback and putting off decisions until it's too late to do something about them. For example, if you give the estimate (for example, 10 weeks), and you realize halfway through that it's not going to take 10 weeks, you'll probably need to increase your estimate. If you've "buffered" the estimate by 30%, you'll probably wait a little longer before raising the issue, and more time and money are wasted.

Let's get back to the critique about kanban and timeboxes. By now you can see the good things that timeboxes bring with them. The main thing is that they provide a constraint that you take on that makes sure you prioritize and do the most important stuff first.

In iteration-based processes like Scrum and XP, natural timeboxes are built into the process. In Scrum, they're called *sprints*: timeboxed iterations for which the team takes on the top features in the product backlog. The time and cost are set beforehand, and the scope the team takes on is ordered in business value. If the team fails, the least valuable features are the ones that don't get done during the sprint.

A flow-based process like kanban doesn't have timeboxes built into it. It's just a flow, right? It's a long, never-ending river of work coming toward you. Well, it doesn't have to be like that. You can create timeboxes of your own, for single work items, sets of work items, or columns in your process, for example.

Using deadline dates on your work-item cards, SLAs, and different classes of service (see chapter 8) is a way of making sure you get some constraints into your system. That, in turn, helps you focus on getting the right things done first.

Iterations and timeboxes encourage you to trim the tail of how much work you can squeeze into the iteration. This can be helpful and beneficial because it may nudge you into splitting big work items in two and pushing the second part to the next iteration. When you're done with the first part of the work item, you may find that the second part wasn't really needed.

When you, in a flow-based process, focus on individual items, you're instead trimming off the tail of each story in the same way. You might move an advanced feature (like a nice drop-down box for selection, for example) into a work item of its own and use a text box with the numerical value instead. And lo and behold—perhaps your users are advanced enough that they like entering the numerical value better, and it turns out to be even quicker for them.

The "timeboxing is good" critique

* Timeboxing is a great technique that helps you focus on what's important
* Kanban doesn't say anything about using timeboxes
* But you can have timeboxes in kanban:
  - Due dates for work items based on size
  - SLAs for different types of work or classes of service
* Trimming of work for iterations or for individual work items

We've now tackled two criticisms that often come up around the way flow-based processes behave. Another one relates to the subtle and non-intrusive way that kanban can be introduced. Can that really be criticized? Yes, as you'll find out in the next section.

12.3 The necessary revolution

PITFALL Kanban takes an evolutionary approach to change management and urges you to start where you are, agree to pursue incremental change, and respect current process and roles. But what if you need a revolution? What if the organization or the team needs to be shaken and stirred a bit?

> **SOLUTION** You're in control of the tempo at which you want to improve. Use a lower WIP limit to provoke more improvement opportunities, for example. Or start using new practices such as test-driven development (TDD) and pair programing at a tempo that's suitable for your organization.

Kanban is great because it starts where you are. You can begin using kanban without changing a thing. Merely visualize the way you work and limit the number of items going on at the same time. From that, you can improve and evolve your process as you learn more.

This is good news because it means you easily can introduce kanban into almost any environment, regardless of the process you're working with today. There's no big bang, no changing of titles and roles—you can keep working as you used to. The visualization part is something that even the most avid opponents of new ways of working can often live with, as long as you keep it aligned with the ways you work now.

In short, kanban can be introduced as an *evolution*, avoiding painful revolutionary changes. By now, you may wonder how on Earth this can be a criticism of kanban. It's easy to see, in fact: it turns out that sometimes you need a revolution. Sometimes you need to shake things up and get your organization to wake up. In order to survive or take advantage of new business opportunities, you might have to change a lot, and change fast. If that's the case, then you should probably go with a tried-and-tested method (like Scrum or XP) and then add the kanban principles on top of that to drive improvement. You can think of it in terms of risk assessment: a small, malleable team, with a willingness to try something new and a great coach nearby, can probably take a lot of change without risking too much. On the other hand, if you're a Cobol team in a big, conservative bank organization, the risk of changing is greater.

The great news here is that you're in control of the tempo at which you improve with kanban. With more aggressive, lower WIP limits, for example, more improvement opportunities will present themselves. Putting stuff out in production earlier and more often will provide feedback faster and thereby give you even more reasons to change and improve. If you end up with too many problems to improve on at the same time, you can always push back from your WIP limits again and handle the biggest issue first, as normal. (Read more about how to control the WIP limits in chapter 6.)

You can add practices from other methods for your needs, as you see fit. For example, pick up some practices from XP, like pair programming or test-driven development, to get a handle on your code quality. Or you might start looking into impact mapping and specification by example to get a grip on the early stages of your feature's life and a make sure you're building the *right thing*. In recent years, continuous delivery and the ideas behind Lean startup have become popular. These methods focus on shortening the feedback loops in your process so you can get feedback on your new features more quickly. The principles of kanban can be of great use here to help you visualize and track the quick flow of your features.

In short, you're in control of your process improvement's speed and reach. Make sure you improve at the speed that you and your organization can handle. But don't go too slowly: sometimes you need a revolution.

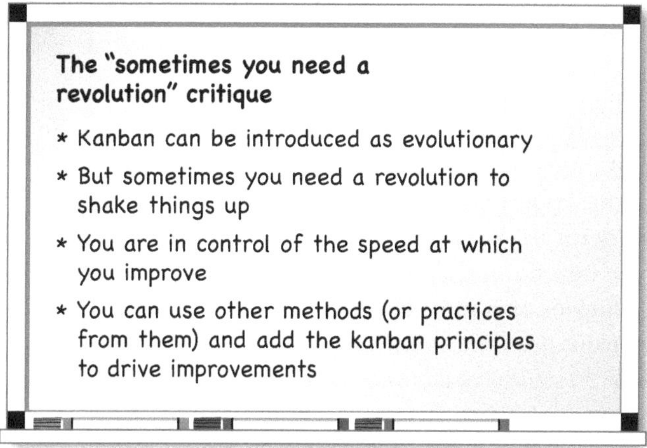

Speaking of too slowly: for some teams, kanban can become an excuse to stop doing the good practices that were already in place. That's the topic of the next section.

12.4 Don't allow kanban to become an excuse to be lazy

PITFALL Because it's just three simple principles, kanban doesn't dictate much at all. This can sometimes become an excuse to stop doing things that are helping you today. You may become lazy.

SOLUTION Keep doing the practices you have found useful until you see a good reason to stop using them. When they hinder your flow, then you can start questioning how or whether you should do planning, estimating, iterations, and so on.

Some teams that start "doing" kanban stop doing the good practices that some other method has given them, such as standups, retrospectives, and reviews. We often hear stuff like "We used to plan our work, but now, with kanban, we've stopped that." Other teams are the opposite and don't begin with agile practices in the first place. "Scrum doesn't work for us! We tried a planning meeting yesterday, and it was boring. Instead we'll do the new thing called *kanban*. It's simply a standup (we might remove it later) and some stickies on a wall. That's enough for us."

These teams miss out on one important aspect. We'll let you in on a secret, this late in the book.[11] Lean in real close to the page. There. Here we go: you can't do kanban. Once again, a bit louder: *you can't do kanban.*

Yes, you read that right. You can't "run kanban" at your company. You can't even "switch from Scrum to kanban." What you can do, and get a lot out of, is apply the kanban principles to your process. Kanban can be said to be a *meta-process*—an improvement process for processes.

[11] Well, we already said this, actually. In chapter 2, we said that kanban isn't a process like others, but rather a meta-process that you can apply to other processes you're already running.

If your head spins because of that sentence, don't feel bad. It's like that for all of us,[12] at least in the beginning. But this is actually great news, because it means you can apply kanban to whatever method you're working with today and improve from there.

Back to the teams that stop doing other stuff because they have "started doing kanban instead": kanban says nothing about stopping practices that help move work through your workflow or that improve the quality of the process you're working on. After doing kanban for a while, you may end up questioning your current practices and begin wondering whether they really provide value. But until then, keep doing them as if nothing has changed. Because it hasn't. You've just started your improvement journey with kanban.

Until you find good reason to stop, keep doing the following: retrospectives, reviews, and sprints (with a planning session at the beginning and a review at the end). Keep writing lengthy specifications documents and handing them over in the next phase in your process.

Kanban will soon show you what's slowing down your flow. On your visualized workflow (on the board, for example), you can see when work items are stacking up. Your metrics and diagrams may help you see where the process is slowed down. These things may eventually lead you to start questioning the way you write specifications, handoffs, sprints, and so on.

One of the things that we've seen many kanban teams run into is not using WIP limits. You'd think that most teams would think about that (because it's one of only three principles), but it happens a lot. Here's a very common scenario that many teams end up with when introducing kanban into their process:

[12] Except for Torbjörn Gyllebring (@drunkcod), who has made a name for himself by going around explaining that "kanban isn't your process" to the kanban community.

A lot of teams start using kanban principles without any WIP limits. This is a mistake, in our opinion. With no WIP limits, there's no tension to drive you to improve your process. You can just keep adding work in process when problems arise. Often this manifests as a lot of blocked or waiting work items on the board.

You can liken this to an iteration that can be extended indefinitely. There's no incentive to complete the scope for the iteration on time—you can always extend the scope.

Remember the true nature of a WIP limit: it's not a rule, but a guideline and a discussion trigger. Without it, there's no reason to have the discussion. You just keep adding work to your process, and there's no mechanism to ask whether you should do this or not.

One common reason that WIP limits are never introduced is that it may seem daunting to come up with the "correct" number for the WIP limit. Chapter 6 contains a number of suggestions for this. One that's really easy to get started with is called "Drop down and give me 20" (see section 6.3.3). You basically pick a large number and then drop the WIP limit (allowed number of work items) gradually until you start running into problems. Then ease back a bit on the WIP limit and start doing something about your problems.

Finally, remember that there isn't a correct WIP limit. The WIP limit is just a tool you control that helps you drive improvements. Without it—no reason to improve.

First retrospective ever

For one client, Marcus facilitated the first-ever retrospective for a team that had been working together for about 15 years. Only recently had they started visualizing their work and been introduced to the principles of kanban.

Like many teams in their situation, they hadn't added any WIP limits yet. Sure enough, during the retrospective, the top thing to improve was how to handle and manage tasks that were unexpectedly added to their workload. The team had realized that these items were disruptive for their flow, slowing down the work they did.

They realized that a simple WIP limit would make a discussion take place when a new item was about to be introduced. The product owner was happy with three escalation levels:

- Put it at the end of the backlog: "We'll take it when we get there."
- Put it at the top of the backlog: "We'll take that next, after finishing the things we're doing right now."
- Push it into the Doing column at the cost of other work: "We'll drop whatever we're doing now and do this instead."

The interesting thing is that before the WIP limit was in place, there was no real reason to even have such a conversation. Items were just shoved onto the current workload, and everyone tried to cope under the new load.

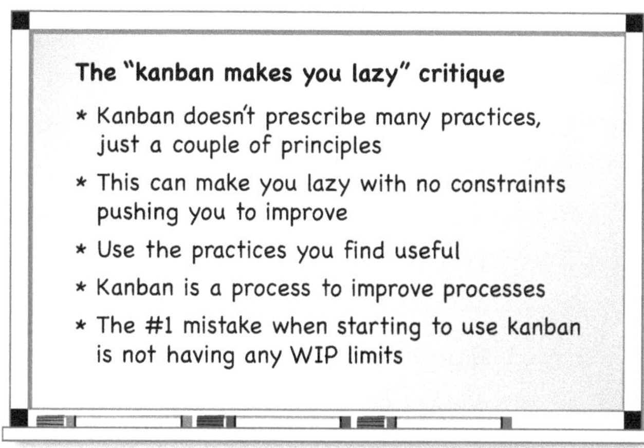

Don't let kanban become an excuse to stop your good practices. Kanban should help you improve your process, not make it worse.

12.5 Summary

In this chapter, we took a look at some pitfalls and at the criticism that's been raised about kanban. We also showed how you can avoid falling into those traps:

- Kanban can end up just being a long flow of work that seems never-ending—it's just work, work, work. Make sure that doesn't happen to you by adding cadences for reviews, retrospectives, and planning as needed.
- No timeboxing is suggested when using kanban, which can remove the constraint you need to finish stuff and make trade-offs to do so. To tackle this, add timeboxes to individual items; use deadlines/due dates or SLAs.
- Kanban is great because it starts where you are: you don't have to change a thing about how you work to get started with kanban. But sometimes you need a revolution:
  - Nothing is hindering you from taking on new roles or ways of working.
  - You can also control the tempo at which you improve by limiting WIP, more or less. Less WIP means more opportunities to improve.
- Kanban is a meta-process—an improvement process for an already-existing process. Don't remove things that work today merely because kanban doesn't say anything about them.
- The number-one mistake when starting with kanban is to begin without any WIP limits. This means there's no constraint pushing you to improve.

13 Teaching kanban through games

This chapter covers

- Using games and simulations to teach the principles of kanban
- Leading discussions that help teams apply these principles in their daily work
- Using the getKanban simulation as a standalone introduction to kanban

This chapter presents some games we've played and used to introduce teams to kanban. We didn't invent them, so we'll try to attribute them correctly. Some of the games in the agile community are almost mythical and seem like they've been around forever. The true source or creator can be hidden in all the variants and changes made to the game over the years. We've gone through our network of colleagues to try to find the sources for the games we introduce—hopefully we've tracked down the correct ones. If we've failed to do so, we're sorry; please help us correct this by sending us a message via the Author Online link at www.manning.com/kanbaninaction.

As you start to use kanban with your team and at your workplace, you'll soon find others around you who are interested in what you're doing. It might even be the case that you've begun to introduce others to the concepts. If you're anything like us, you'll soon be teaching kanban concepts and practices.

You could give your colleagues this book and say, "Talk to me again when you've read this!"[1] But we've found that running a concrete, practical exercise makes the concepts stick much better. This idea is loosely founded in the thinking behind experience-based learning defined by David Kolb (*Experiential Learning*, Prentice Hall, 1984, http://amzn.com/0132952610).[2] We often start our presentation with a game or exercise that shows a principle in action and then refer back to what was learned as we present the theoretical concepts in kanban. In the introduction, we play Pass the Pennies with the team to show them why they'd want to limit WIP.

For each game covered here, we add some tips, comments, and questions to get a discussion going and help the learning process. The following table shows a short summary of the games and the concepts we'll talk about.

Section	Game	Concepts taught
13.1	Pass the Pennies	Limiting WIP leads to shorter lead times.
13.2	The Number Multitasking Game	Limiting WIP leads to shorter lead times. Multitasking leads to lost time and poor focus and quality.
13.3	The Dot Game	Limiting WIP, tweaking the process toward even faster flow, collaboration. Little's law and pushing more items into the system increases WIP, which in turn slows the flow down.
13.4	The Bottleneck Game	Improve flow in a system using the Theory of Constraints.
13.5	getKanban	Improve your process by using the kanban principles in practice.
13.6	The Kanban Pizza Game	Improve your process by applying the kanban principles, limiting WIP, and doing retrospectives in short increments.

That's quite a few games, so let's get going right away with a quick, practical game that shows why limiting WIP is a great idea.

1 And by all means do!

2 See also "What is experience-based learning?" at http://mng.bz/9Ik1.

13.1 Pass the Pennies

Pass the Pennies (sometimes called Flip the Chip) was mentioned in chapter 1, when Marcus and Joakim played this game with the Kanbaneros. The game is a fast and engaging way to introduce the concept of WIP and show why limiting WIP is a good idea. As you may remember from chapter 5, limiting WIP will make your work flow faster through your process. After playing the game, you can have a discussion about limiting the WIP. What are the "pennies" that you're passing around in your process? How do you go about limiting the amount of work? What would happen if you did?

We've seen a lot of eye-opening "Aha!" moments when playing this game with teams, and we've heard people bring up the game years after it was played. Pass the Pennies takes about 15 minutes to play, and you should allow at least 15 minutes more to discuss what you learned.

13.1.1 What you need to play the game

You need the following to play the game (including nine players, preferably):

- 4 workers who flip the coins
- 4 managers who time their worker
- 1 customer or project manager (can be played by you, the facilitator, if needed)
- 20 coins of equal size
- A table to play on
- 5 stopwatches (or phones with stopwatch applications)
- A whiteboard or flipchart to write results on

Make sure you've read about and understand the game and preferably have played it yourself, before you try to facilitate it. This goes for every game and exercise you run and teach to others.

13.1.2 How to play

The objective for each role is as follows:

- *Workers*—Flip all the coins and pass them to the next worker in line.
- *Managers*—Measure the *effective* time that each worker is flipping coins.
- *A customer*—Determines the total time in two aspects: the time it takes for the first coin to be delivered, and the total time (until the last coin is delivered).

The game is played in three iterations: 20-, 5-, and 1-coin batches. In each iteration, the game is played exactly the same, except that the WIP (batch size) is lowered. The goal, process, and order of the exercises stay the same.

Seat the workers around the table with a manager standing behind each worker. Instruct the managers to use the stopwatch to track the effective time the worker is working. Ask the customer to measure the time for the first coin delivery and the total time for all coins to be delivered.

When the first 20-coin iteration is underway, you'll have plenty of time to draw a table for the result on the whiteboard, like the one at right. Wait to note down the results until the iteration is over. When all the results are added, pause for a moment for the players to reflect on them.

	20		
Worker 1	0:20:6		
Worker 2	0:10:5		
Worker 3	0:13.4		
Worker 4	0:25.0		
First	1:18:0		
TOTAL	1:18:0		

Each manager-worker pair can be allowed a short "motivational talk," for fun.

Now tell the team that you're not happy with the result and that you want run the next iteration with five coins. Be sure to remind everybody that the only thing changing is the WIP. Measure the whole time that each worker is working.

	20	5
Worker 1	0:20:6	0:25:5
Worker 2	0:10:5	0:23:5
Worker 3	0:13.4	0:26:4
Worker 4	0:25.0	0:24:7
First	1:18:0	0:18:9
TOTAL	1:18:0	0:40:0

When the five-coins iteration is over, note the results. You can see the results we had with a team in the table to the left. The results will probably raise a few eyebrows, because the time to first delivery went down a lot: from 1:18 to 18 seconds in our example! The overall time was also greatly improved, dropping from 1:18 to just 40 seconds. Give the team a couple of minutes to talk and reflect on what happened.

	20	5	1
Worker 1	0:20:6	0:25:5	0:21:2
Worker 2	0:10:5	0:23:5	0:21:7
Worker 3	0:13.4	0:26:4	0:24:6
Worker 4	0:25.0	0:24:7	0:32:6
First	1:18:0	0:18:9	0:04:8
TOTAL	1:18:0	0:40:0	0:37:0

Before long, though, you should start the final, one-coin iteration. Use the same goal and rules as before. When the last iteration is over (it goes by quickly), note down the result. You should end up with a table like this (with columns for 20, 5, and 1).

Make sure to thank everybody for playing, and then start a discussion to analyze the results.

13.1.3 Questions for discussion

We often ask questions like these to trigger a discussion:

- What happened to the total time? Why?
- What happened to the time for each individual worker? Why?
- How did it feel to play the game? When was it stressful? When was it calmer?
- Can this game be translated into your work?
  - What are the coins in your work?
  - What isn't applicable in your context?
  - What would happen if you lowered the number of "coins" in your context?
  - What's hindering you from doing that?
- What can't be translated into your work situation?

Feel free to add other questions as you see fit or as the discussion wanders.

13.1.4 Main take-aways

From the previous result tables, you can easily see that the time for the first coin goes down a lot. This is typically what happens with small batch sizes that are moved through the value chain in a continuous flow.

For each individual worker, the times usually (but not always) trend upward. This can trigger a discussion about how, when you optimize for flow, resources may not be used 100%. You can talk about what the team is optimizing for or if it's important that everyone is fully utilized at all times.

This is also a good time to discuss lead time (from start to finish) versus cycle time (times for each individual worker). What are their customers interested in—finished stuff or great resource utilization?

13.1.5 Tips and variants

Someone will almost certainly object that this is a simplification, and it sure is. But the simulation is done to illustrate a principle: that less WIP (number of coins) makes your work flow faster through the process. How can that principle be translated into your work context? In the simplest form, the coins represent work items, although work items are often of different sizes and complexity. The principle of limiting WIP still applies, though. You can read more about that in chapters 5 and 6.

Pass the Pennies takes nine people to play. But you can slim it down in several ways and still make great use of it:

- Play with only three stations.
- Let the workers time themselves.
- You, the facilitator, can play the customer.

NOTE To the best of our knowledge, this game seems to have been created by a man called Joe Little, under the name Scrum Penny Game.[3] There are a lot of variants (Flip the Chip, for example), and we've heard others mentioned as probable creators of the game: George Dinwiddie, Jeff Sutherland, and Henrik Kniberg.

13.2 The Number Multitasking Game

This game is a simple simulation that can be played with a single person. It shows that less WIP improves lead times and helps alleviate stress and pressure. Although a single player can play this game, we have scaled it to include up to 65 people.

This simulation is another way to illustrate the value of limiting WIP, but it has additional properties that we think make it a little more interesting. Pass the Pennies shows only one concept, but shows it well. The Number Multitasking Game is a bit more realistic and takes other aspects of your work into consideration. The discussion after the game will be about multitasking and the bad effects of having work pushed to

---

[3] See "Comfortably Scrum: Scrum Penny Game" by Tommy Norman at http://mng.bz/4R01.

you. That's more realistic than Pass the Pennies, in our opinion. The game takes about 10 minutes to run.

13.2.1 *What you need to play the game*

You need the following to play the game:

- 3 different-colored pens per player
- 2 sheets of paper per player
- A manager who times each player (this role can be played by the facilitator, if needed)
- A stopwatch (or a phone with a stopwatch application)

13.2.2 *How to play*

Ask the people playing to help you with three *important* tasks that your company has coming up. Here are the tasks:

1. Write the roman numerals I through X in a column from top to bottom. Use a black pen for this task.
2. Write the letters A through J in another column from top to bottom. Use a red pen for this task.
3. Write the numbers 1 through 10 in a final column from top to bottom. Use a blue pen for this task.

Introduce all the tasks as top priorities and vital to the company's survival. In the first iteration,[4] you want to utilize the "resources" (the players) to the fullest and therefore want them to spend equal amounts of time on each project, because they're all important. Instruct the players to write row by row. Here is an example of someone going through the first three rows:[5]

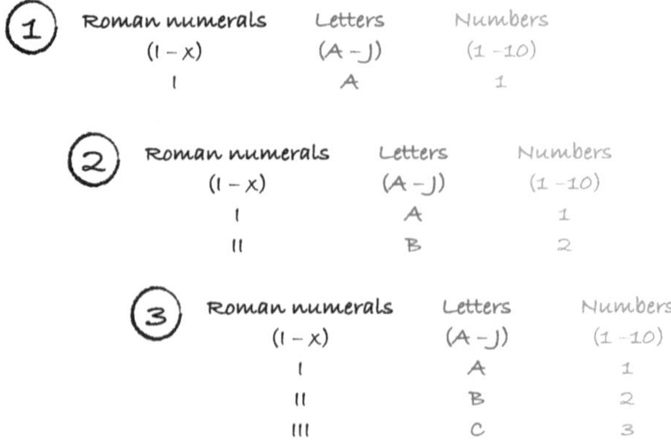

[4] *Iteration* here means finishing all the tasks: the roman numerals, the letters, and the number columns.

[5] This instruction seems hard for some people to grasp, so be sure they understand that you want them to write the numbers row by row.

The manager will time the players for each task as well as record the total time (when all the tasks are done). When the iteration is over, note the time for each task under it on the paper (or on the whiteboard). You'll find that each task takes quite a long time to complete (usually over a minute) and that all of them are finished with just a couple of seconds in between. An example result is shown in the table to the right.

	Row by row	
Roman	1:20:0	
Letters	1:22:0	
Numbers	1:24:0	
TOTAL	1:24:0	

Leave a few seconds for reflection, but then move on to the next iteration. Explain that you've now thought it over, and it turns out the first task (roman numerals) is the most important one. The letters task is the second most important, and the numbers turn out to not be that important at all.

Ask the players to do it again, but this time focus on what's most important first and finish it before continuing on to the next task. In other words, work column by column, like this:[6]

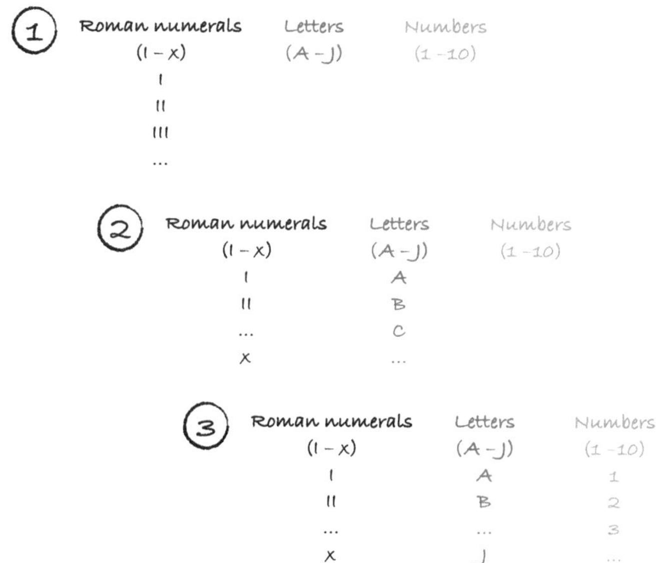

[6] You might have to be very specific here and say something like, "First all the roman numerals, then all the letters, and finally all the numbers. Column by column."

As before, note the time for completing each project and the total time for all the projects to be completed. As you'll notice, the times typically play out something like this table:

	Row by row	Column by column
Roman	1:20:0	0:12:0
Letters	1:22:0	0:12:0
Numbers	1:24:0	0:08:0
TOTAL	1:24:0	0:32:0

Here you can see that the completion time for each individual task has dropped dramatically—from 1 minute 20 seconds to just 12 seconds for the roman numerals, for example. Also notice that the total time has been reduced from 1 minute 24 seconds to merely 32 seconds. Ask the players to point out these differences before you do for a better "Aha!" effect.

Be sure to thank the players for playing the game, and then start the discussion.

13.2.3 Questions for discussion

These are a few of the questions we use to start a fruitful discussion after playing this game:

- What happened to the total time? Why?
- What happened to the times for each individual project? Why?
- Was the first round harder? Why?
- Does the simulation resemble your work situation?
  - What are your individual projects?
  - What does "switching pens" represent in your context?
- How are projects prioritized at your company? Do you know what's most important to work on right now?
- How many projects/different things are you working on right now?
- What happened to the quality of the produced result?
- How did the first approach feel? Did the second approach feel better?

13.2.4 Main take-aways

The results should show an improvement in lead time (total for all three projects). The time for the first project is dramatically improved, often by 70–80%.

Not only that, but quality is often improved as well. This has to do with the fact that you don't have to switch tools (pens) in the second iteration. Most people also find it quite hard to write the roman numbers from I–X, and the second iteration allows for more concentrated focus on each project. Writing the numbers 1–10 is easy for most.[7]

Most people find the first approach much more stressful, due to the fact that they're switching tasks all the time. By reducing the amount of stuff going on at the same time, you not only increase the focus and quality of your work but also improve the lead time for each project.

NOTE This origin of this game was also hard to track down. It seems to have evolved from a lot of different agile simulations. The exercise resembles the Multitasking Name Game that Henrik Kniberg[8] uses. Kniberg hints that he, in turn, has adopted his from other simulations he's seen done by others—for example, Mary Poppendieck.

13.3 The Dot Game

The Dot Game is a simulation of a software-development project that shows the benefits of limiting your WIP. It also has some additional features regarding software development that make it a bit more interesting than the two games we've looked at so far.

The Dot Game shows interesting developments for a software team that starts to limit WIP. First you see what happens with the flow, but it also shows how you can start to think about changing the way you work to help the work to flow (another of the kanban principles). The game takes about 45 minutes to run.

A WORD FROM THE COACH This game is hard work at certain positions and can be stressful at times. Make sure everyone involved volunteers and that you keep it fun. We've had people grow angry during this game, and that's not what you want. Make sure everyone understands the fun of it.

13.3.1 What you need to play the game

You need the following to play the game:

- 8 players (although you can play one role yourself)
- A table with 6 chairs for the 6 seated players
- A whiteboard or flipchart
- Loads of rectangular stickies—at least 300
- Little stick-on dots (colored labels) in 4 different colors (see section 13.3.7 for cheaper alternatives)
- A premade template that acts as the specification for what is to be made
- A project manager with a stopwatch to measure time
- A customer (this role can be played by the facilitator)

---

7 The record time for that is 2.8 seconds, done by an Avega Group employee.

8 See "The Multitasking Name Game – or How Long Does It Take to Write a Name?" at http://mng.bz/YR06.

13.3.2 How to play

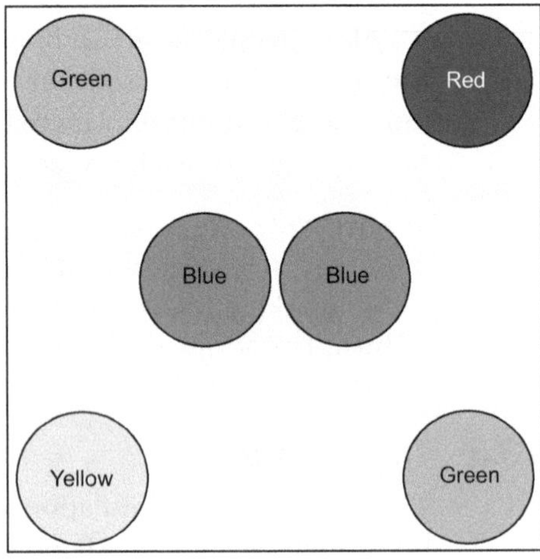

You can have a little role-playing fun and introduce yourself as the owner of a factory that creates stickies with colored dots on them, like the one to the right (hold it up for the group to see).[9]

The goal of the exercise is to create as many of those dot-covered stickies as possible within five minutes. You have a well-thought-out and established process, and you're now considering starting a factory in this room. The process calls for six willing workers. You ask people if they're willing to help you. Introduce each role and describe its task. Invite volunteers to take a seat at the table. Here are the roles,[10] in order of the process:

1. *Business Analyst*—Removes a sticky from the pack and hands it to the next worker.
2. *Technical Analyst*—Puts a yellow dot in the lower-left corner and hands the sticky to the next station.
3. *Designer*—Puts a red dot in the upper-right corner and hands the sticky to the next player.
4. *UI Developer*—Adds green dots in the other two corners and passes the sticky on.
5. *Developer*—Adds the two blue dots in the middle and passes it to the Tester.
6. *Tester*—Makes sure the produced items are up to quality standards. If so, the items are delivered to the customer.
7. *Project Manager*—Times the procedure. Place the Project Manager at a whiteboard or flipchart to note down the times. The Project Manager times how long it takes for the first delivery (the first thing that reaches the customer). The Project Manager also warns the team when only one minute is left and announces when time is up (after five minutes).
8. *Customer*—Accepts the finished items. We often play this role ourselves and put "pressure" on the team as needed to keep the exercise interesting and fun.

Seat people as shown in the diagram.

---

[9] This means you'll have to create a template sticky before the game starts.

[10] Feel free to use job titles from your current workplace if you like.

13.3.3 First iteration

When everyone is seated, once again show them the template sticky and put it in the middle of the table. Tell them that your process has been optimized for working in batches of five items: the Business Analyst takes five stickies from the pack and hands them to the Technical Analyst, who adds yellow dots to all five of them and hands them on to the Designer, and so on. Let them know you're going to evaluate them individually. Each station should produce as much as possible and not care whether the following stations are keeping up or not. We want everyone to be effective, right?

Don't answer too many questions (there often aren't that many at this stage), but strive to get the first iteration going as soon as possible. The Project Manager kicks off the game by starting the timer. As soon as the game is started, take the Customer[11] aside and tell them that only two things should be evaluated for acceptance of items:

- The dots at the edges should be as close to the edges as possible, but not over them.
- The blue dots in the middle should be as close together as possible but not overlap.

[11] The Customer can be instructed in advance if you have the time. Or play that role yourself.

Instruct the Customer to only answer direct questions and not give away the acceptance criteria unless asked specifically.

When the team is in the middle of playing through the first iteration, you can head over to them and motivate them to produce as much as possible. When the first batch of stickies arrives to the Customer, the Customer accepts or rejects the stickies based on the criteria described earlier. Don't say anything as to why.

Make sure the Project Manager notes the time for the first delivery (which usually takes about two and a half to three minutes) on the whiteboard and warns the team when there's one minute left.

When the iteration is over, ask the Project Manager to count the following:

- Number of completed items
- Number of accepted items
- Number of items in process (items "on the table" that weren't delivered)

Note all of these results on the whiteboard in a table like this:

	5	
First delivery	2 mins 22 secs	
# Done	13 items	
# Accepted	4 items	
WIP	66 items	

Explain to the team that you're disappointed with their performance. The Customer wants these items. Badly! Can they please get their act together and go faster, already?

Stop here and ask the people how it felt and how it went:

- You should see a bottleneck piling up after the Business Analyst (who has an easy job). Why did that happen? Were there any other bottlenecks or uneven flows?
- What if the Tester found flaws? What could the Tester do about them? What should they have done?
- Ask the team about the acceptance criteria: are they known? Who knows about them? What can be done to find out the criteria? Have the Customer briefly answer any questions the team may ask, and then move on to the next iteration.
- What's the value of all the items on the table that aren't delivered? None, in the eyes of the Customer. They're wasted.

Little's law in the Dot Game

In the original game instructions, Little's law is introduced (see chapter 5). We usually don't do that, for two reasons:

- We often mess up the calculation in the heat of the moment.
- We think that the point comes across with the data presented on the white-board anyway.

But if you feel up to the counting challenge, you could tell the team that the time for the first delivery is quite misleading. Let's see Little's law in action using our numbers, as noted in the table we created during the first iteration.

	5	
First delivery	2 mins 22 secs	
# Done	13 items	
# Accepted	4 items	
WIP	66 items	

Little's law teaches that cycle time is calculated as follows:

Cycle time = work in process / throughput

Throughput, in turn, is calculated as follows:

Number of items finished / time

With the numbers from the example, that gives us the following:

WIP: 66 items that were *in* the process
Throughput: 13 completed items / 5 minutes = 2.6 stickies per minute
Cycle time: 66 / 2.6 stickies per minute = 25.4 minutes per sticky!

That's a big difference from the already-bad 2:22 minutes for the first delivery.

This can also be explained on the table by having people realize that a sticky removed from the pack needs to "travel through" all the stickies on the table. The first batch had no items in front of it and hence moved faster through the system.

13.3.4 Second iteration

Explain to the team that in a desperate attempt to improve the output and quality of this workforce, you're going to try something really crazy: for the second iteration, you'll change absolutely nothing about the process except the number of items worked on at the same time. They'll work in batches of one, not five.

The Business Analyst takes one sticky from the pack and hands it down to the Technical Analyst, who adds a yellow dot and hands it down to the Designer, and so on. Work as before, but with one item at a time.

Start the next five-minute iteration when the team is ready. This time you can go around and make sure people are working as they should. Be sure to check the delivered items for quality (or help the Customer). See that the Project Manager warns the team when one minute is left and lets them knows when the time is up.

Note the results for the second iteration, which probably looks something like this:

	5	1
First delivery	2 mins 22 secs	36 secs
# Done	13 items	28 items
# Accepted	4 items	17 items
WIP	66 items	29 items

Stop here and discuss the result:

- What happened with the time for the first delivery?
- What about the number of delivered items?
- Why did the quality (accepted items versus number of done items) improve? Somebody may say that this was easier during the second iteration because they now know what to do. That's correct—and it's also exactly the point that you want to make. They now know what to do because they asked the Customer during the discussions after the first iteration and adjusted to the new information, right?
- Where's the bottleneck now? Who has a lot of items in front of them? Often the bottleneck appears in different positions than it did in the first iteration.

13.3.5 Third (and final) iteration

Announce your resignation to the team. It's hopeless. You have no clue how to improve the process to produce any good results from this team. The team can now, all by themselves, come up with ways of improving the process in order to produce as much as possible and waste as few items as possible.

In our experience, many teams need some input here to get going.[12] You could ask them who's responsible for quality and what they should do about that. Or how they can make sure to waste as few items as possible. Team members may ask whether they can trade places, and you can allow that, but there is a penalty: people who trade jobs have to slow down on the new work to make it more realistic. A tester doing development probably won't do it as fast as a developer.

[12] We've also seen some super-creative variants here, including walking around the table and having the Customer walk with the team, correcting mistakes and giving input as they walked. You'd be surprised at what people come up with. Allow them to think for a while before giving them hints.

Give the team a few hints, and then allow for three minutes of self-organization to get ready for the last iteration. If you have people in the room who aren't seated around the table, make sure to ask them for input on improvements as well.

When the team is ready, run the third iteration as before: five minutes, warn when one minute is left, and time the first delivery. When the five minutes are up, you'll end up with a table like this:

	5	1	?
First delivery	2 mins 22 secs	36 secs	36 secs
# Done	13 items	28 items	23 items
# Accepted	4 items	17 items	20 items
WIP	66 items	29 items	10 items

As the result is noted, start a discussion:

- How did that last iteration feel? Common answers are "chaos" or "unstructured." Is that bad?
- What happened with the time for the first delivery? Usually it goes up a little bit. Why is that?
- What happened with the quality? It's often improved greatly. Why?
- How much was wasted? Why?

Make sure to thank everyone for playing this quite stressful game, and end the session.

13.3.6 Main take-aways

This game shows a lot of things worth noting:

- With smaller batches, the lead time goes down and quality goes up.
- By doing a retrospective and adjusting the way you work after each iteration, you improve the result. Ask the team, after the last iteration, whether they think they would improve further if they got another try. Most teams say yes.
- You need to ask questions of and collaborate with the Customer to know what they want. A perfect specification isn't enough.
- There's no use pushing work into a system that's overloaded. The first position in the first iteration is usually a great illustration of that. We've seen Business Analysts with more than 200 stickies ready to be picked up by the next station. This is what Mary Poppendieck calls "wishful thinking," meaning those items will not happen (faster) just because you stack them there. In fact, they will slow the system down by increasing your WIP (read more in chapter 5).

13.3.7 Tips and variants

This game takes time. Allow one complete hour for the game, although you may run through it in 45 minutes. Take a break after the game. Here are a few additional thoughts:

- Don't forget to create the template before you start.
- The green and blue dots run out first. If necessary, buy more—you'll probably need those.
- To save money, you can run this game with the players drawing dots with colored markers instead of placing dots. Doing so adds some features to the game because errors can't be fixed easily, and it's harder to have the quality be consistent when it comes to size and form.
- If you have somebody else playing the Customer, make sure they aren't too picky. That puts the focus on the wrong place. Take time to instruct the Customer before the session and make sure that only the set acceptance criteria are taken into consideration.
- Take notes of any comments during the iterations. The comments can then be revisited during the discussions.
- Invite any people who weren't playing the game to join the conversion, but only *after* each round. You don't want them to interrupt the players in miditeration.
- In the retrospectives between rounds, give everybody plenty of time to talk. This is where learning takes place. Let the players talk first; the people looking on (if any) can talk after that.

NOTE Al Shalloway of Net Objectives created this game.[13] He based it on the Lean Manufacturing Cup Game.[14] He also kindly reviewed this section for us, for which we're grateful.

13.4 The Bottleneck Game

The Bottleneck Game effectively teaches the five focusing steps from the Theory of Constraints (see chapter 7). The Theory of Constraints views a process as a system with at least one bottleneck (constraint) that slows production down. The five focusing steps are techniques that help identify, elevate, and manage the bottleneck(s) to get a better flow.

This Bottleneck Game resembles the Dot Game in some ways but is a bit more elaborate. It focuses more on bottlenecks[15] and the Theory of Constraints' way of approaching problem solving.

---

[13] "The Dot Game," http://mng.bz/lONY.

[14] Martin Boersema, "The Lean Cups Game – What's summer without a few cold ones?" at http://mng.bz/0Von.

[15] Duh! With a name like that, we kind of knew …

The game is well documented. You can download it for free from www.agile-coach.net/coach-tools/bottleneck-game/.

13.4.1 What you need to play the game

This is a team exercise, and each team consists of from four to seven people:

- You need plenty of space for each team in a long production-line format.
- Print the instruction sheets from the website to distribute to each player according to their role.

13.4.2 How to play

The game is played in three rounds, with concepts being introduced as part of the game. The complete game takes about two to three hours to play and can be extended with a workshop that applies the things you've learned to real-world situations.

The goal of the Bottleneck Game is for each team to create as many pairs of paper hats and boats (like the pair to the right) as possible and at the same time make sure not to waste paper. The suggested game process is set up to reveal some bottlenecks. The presentations and tutorials help the attendees to use the five focusing steps (from the Theory of Constraints) to resolve these bottlenecks.

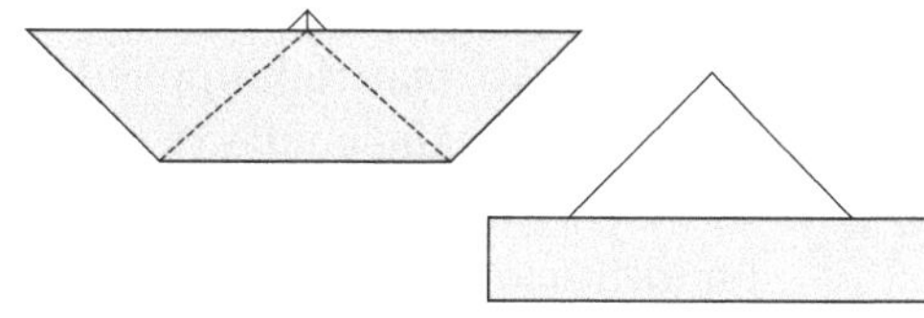

The five focusing steps

The five focusing steps are based on the simple premise that there's at least one bottleneck in your system. If there weren't, the flow through the system would be totally unrestricted, and the throughput would be instant and unlimited. Any improvement made to the biggest bottleneck is an improvement of the throughput for the entire system.

Here are the focusing steps to follow to manage a bottleneck:

1. Identify the constraint that slows down the throughput. For example, testers are always overloaded with work.
2. Exploit the constraint so that it's used to its full capacity. For example, make sure the testers only do testing and nothing else.
3. Subordinate other activities to the exploitation of the bottleneck. For example, make some other function do the non-testing work to help the testers out. This is OK because the other function isn't the bottleneck.
4. Elevate the constraint. For example, have other functions do testing too, or hire new testers. This is often slow and expensive, so don't try this until you have tried the first three steps.

(continued)

5 Rinse and repeat. Make sure that, at every point in the process, here if not earlier, you check to see that no other function has become the bottleneck. For example, making sure testers only do testing and nothing else may very well have resolved the situation, but now deployment is the constraint of the system. In that case, move your efforts to manage deployment as your bottleneck.

You can find more details and background in the excellent book *The Goal* (North River Press, 2012, http://mng.bz/bRak) by Eliyahu Goldratt, which formulates the Theory of Constraints.

The process that is simulated is optimized further and further into the game to manage the bottleneck to achieve a quicker and smoother flow.

13.4.3 Questions for discussion

The extensive material supplied on the game's website gives you a lot of suggested discussion topics and guidance on running the subsequent workshop with which you can extend the session. The material contains a complete and extensive session handbook for instructors, job instructions for workshop attendees, and ready-made handouts for attendees to keep.

13.4.4 Main take-aways

The main things the Bottleneck Games reveals are as follows:

- How a bottleneck can be managed by using of the five focusing steps from the Theory of Constraints.
- How the Theory of Constraints, and what you've learned in the exercise, can be applied to a real situation.

NOTE This game is released under the Creative Commons Attribution-Share Alike by Pascal Van Cauwenberghe and Portia Tung. The game and all needed material can be downloaded at www.agilecoach.net/coach-tools/bottleneck-game/.

13.5 getKanban

getKanban is a full-fledged kanban simulation that in itself is an introduction to kanban and its principles. The game is a fairly complex board game with excellent documentation. You should probably play it at least once with someone else before trying to facilitate it yourself.

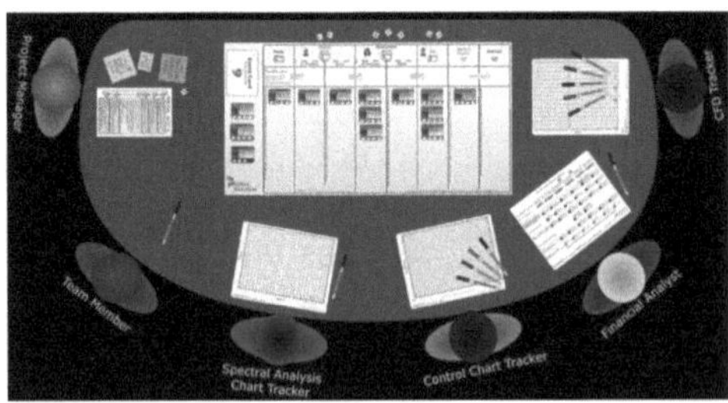

The game comes in three modes: quick play, standard, and advanced mode. Each mode is increasingly more detailed and hence takes more time to play. You should allow at least two and a half to three hours for the advanced mode and should include a short introduction to kanban before starting the game.

getKanban costs money[16] and can be ordered from www.getkanban.com. It's well worth the investment. You can also print the game materials from earlier versions of the game yourself, for free.

The getKanban game is ever-evolving, and you can expect updates to the game continuously. The version we briefly describe here is version 4.

13.5.1 What you need to play the game

You need the following to play the game:

- The getKanban board game. All necessary materials are included in the box.
- About 6 players per board (minimum of 4 players to make the game interesting).
- A big clear table space.
- A whiteboard or flipchart to track results and explain concepts is useful.

13.5.2 How the game is played

Giving complete instructions on how to play getKanban is well beyond the scope of this book. That's described in the getKanban game itself. Consider this section a short introduction to the game.

In the game, you play a software-development team that creates a product that customers are subscribing to—for example, an online service. The official objective of the game is to gain as much money as possible, but other objectives can be used too, such as finishing as many items as possible, for example.

You play through a number of days with the software-development team, starting a couple of days into an ongoing project, so you're thrown directly into the action. Progress is determined by the throw of a pair of dice—the higher the rolls, the more work (analytics, development, or testing) is done by the team. The work effort can be rerouted, so that development work values can be used in testing, for example, as part of team strategy.

Throughout the game, event cards are introduced with features the team needs to take into consideration. There will be bad bosses making "stupid" policies that throw the plans overboard, conferences that can give you additional subscribers, and some work with value that's not determined until later in the game.

Each round follows a strict schedule that helps you play through the round, update your earnings, and see some metrics and draw diagrams to help keep track of your progress. It's all very detailed and easy to follow and can in itself be a great introduction to the diagrams and metrics used in kanban.

---

[16] $450 per game at the time of writing.

The team strategy in picking which items to focus work on and how to distribute the work (values from the dice) determines whether they're successful or not.

13.5.3 Questions for discussion

There are ample opportunities for discussion during the game, but in the end a wrap-up discussion should focus on the following:

- What did you learn?
- How can you apply this in your current context?
- What surprised you about how the game played out?

13.5.4 Tips and variants

You can change things when you run this game if needed. Here are a few of the tweaks that we have used or seen:

- As a facilitator, you should be ready to walk around the group and help them, answering questions and giving them tips. The game has quite a few rules, and following them all during the first run-through has proven a daunting task for most groups with whom we've tried the game.
- Set aside plenty of time for playing this game. An introduction to kanban is probably needed before you play. The game takes at least 90 minutes to play. You should probably set aside at least 30 minutes to discuss the game with the attendees afterward. All in all, the session may last two and a half to three hours, if you include breaks.
- Although the game is controlled in part by the event cards, you can play it more than once. Different focus and strategies and how they affect the outcome are interesting variants you can introduce.
- You can play an online version of the game by yourself at https://getkanban.corporatekanban.com. It's both cool and a bit awkward and sad, we know, but it can be a good way to run the exercise to prepare yourself, or to point people to for follow-up.

13.5.5 Main take-aways

The main take-aways from the getKanban games, for us, are these:

- See kanban in action for real. The game touches on a lot of areas of using kanban and the principles kanban builds on. The concept of limiting WIP and the *pull principle* (pulling work into action just in time rather than keeping a stock of work, just in case) are shown in practical use.
- How a kanban board works and can be laid out.
- How to build and use metrics and diagrams such as cumulative flow diagrams and control charts.

- How to use the metrics and information created by the process to optimize business outcome.

READ MORE At www.getkanban.com, you can read much more about this game. Although the game is for sale, it's also open-sourced, and you can contribute to its progress.

13.6 The Kanban Pizza Game

This is another kanban simulation game that can be obtained (for free) from the Agile42 website (http://mng.bz/kYN7). The game takes about an hour to play, making it quicker than the getKanban game, and can be played with less preparation. It does require a lot of props, and you probably need someone to help coach the team during the game to reach its full potential.

The game is quite fun and easygoing. It's a perfect team-building exercise[17] that also teaches something useful. The overarching objective is for the team to "feel" how kanban works in practice.

13.6.1 What you need to play the game

The Kanban Pizza Game website has lots of information on what you need to get started. Quite a few things are listed, but nothing that you wouldn't find in most offices or office-supply stores.

Besides the props, you'll also need the following:

- 5 players per team (4 players could also work).
- A game leader (who has experience playing the game).
- A table to play on: one table per team that can accommodate all team players easily. A lot of pizza is going to be shuffled around on the table.
- A whiteboard or flipchart for reporting.

13.6.2 How to play

The objective of the game is to create pizza slices (which add points) but avoid wasting pizza slices that don't get done (which deduct points). The Customer orders complete pizzas, and the team only gets points for fully completed orders. The team with the most points wins.

[17] Because it quite naturally builds up an appetite for pizza, the session can be rounded off with pizza for everyone. Not the paper version, though.

The simulation leader takes the role of someone who opens a new pizza restaurant and hires the players to work for them. All the materials and tools for creating pizza slices are supplied to the team.

The game is then played in four iterations, as follows:

1. Bake/create pizza slices any way the team feels like, in an arbitrary process.
2. Introduce the concept of "orders" (batches of slices) and workstations that physically limit WIP.
3. Introduce a product variation in the form of a pizza with a different recipe and workflow.
4. With all the parts of the game in place and the experience the team has acquired from the previous three iterations, let them self-organize and come up with process improvements.

After the formal game, continue to a debriefing session to lock in learning points from the game.

13.6.3 Questions for discussion

You can use questions like the following to open up a discussion after running this game:

- What happened to lead time as you introduced WIP limits? Why?
- Did you feel stressed? How can you improve on that?
- What happened when a new product was introduced?
- What similarities or connections can you make to how you work?
  - What are the pizza slices?
  - What about the board?
  - Who's ordering pizzas?

The creators of the game also suggest that you keep going from here and start to create your own visualized workflow with the principles learned in the game. It sounds like a great idea but will probably require some coaching or help to handle questions that might arise. In this way, the game can be used as a lead-in for the team to start using kanban for their work.

13.6.4 Main take-aways

These are the goals of the game:

- Experience kanban and the kanban principles in action.
- Understand and experience the effect of limiting your WIP.
- Inspect your process, and self-organize to improve the process.
- Create a kanban board to reflect your workflow.

To be able to get a feel for how a pull system works in practice is a great thing that's pretty hard to do. That's what this game accomplishes.

There's quite a lot of documentation on the website, but to get the full potential out of the game, you need to have hands-on experience. You're probably best off playing the game for yourself with some friends before trying to run it with others. Better yet, find someone who has experience running the game, and have them run it with you.

NOTE The game was created by Agile 42 (www.agile42.com) and is licensed under the Creative Commons Attribution-Share Alike 3.0.

13.7 Summary

This chapter showed you some games and simulations that can help you introduce the main concepts of kanban to people who haven't heard about it before. In our experience, games like these are great ways to learn kanban and the principles it's built on. We've overheard people talking about the Dot Game they played a year ago when discussing a problem with the flow on their board. And we've heard people remind each other to not make "more pizzas than the system can currently handle."

Although the games are important, what's most valuable is the discussion that follows. Make sure you've prepared a lot of questions to pose to your team. You want them to reason about what happened and transfer that to their work lives.

appendix A *Recommended reading and other resources*

We both are avid readers and have read many texts over the years that influenced us and taught us a lot about kanban, Lean, agile, and more. In this appendix we share our top list of works to learn from.

We've grouped them by topic and given a sentence or two to tell you a little about each item, why we chose it, and what we find about it that's particularly good.

A.1 Books on Lean and kanban

- *Kanban: Successful Evolutionary Change for Your Technology Business* (David J. Anderson, Blue Hole Press, 2010, http://amzn.com/0984521402)—This is the book in which David J. Anderson defines and explains the Kanban Method. It's basically a must-read if you're interested in kanban. This book will teach you everything about how David and others came up with kanban and why and how it works.
- *This Is Lean: Resolving the Efficiency Paradox* (Per Åhlström and Niklas Modig, Rheologica Publishing, 2012, http://amzn.com/919803930X)—This great little book clearly explains the foundational thinking behind Lean and delivers a good definition of what Lean means. It's written by Professor Per Åhlström and researcher Niklas Modig from the Stockholm School of Economics and is an easy read of about 160 pages.
- *The Toyota Way to Continuous Improvement: Linking Strategy and Operational Excellence to Achieve Superior Performance* (Jeffrey K. Liker and James K. Franz, McGraw-Hill, 2011, http://amzn.com/0071477462)—This book is the result of 20 years of studying Toyota and other Lean companies. It describes the

philosophy and principles behind the Toyota Way and how Toyota implements the Toyota Production System in its daily business. The authors also share their advice on how you can change your company into a learning organization.

- *Toyota Kata: Managing People for Improvement, Adaptiveness, and Superior Results* (Mike Rother, McGraw-Hill, 2009, http://amzn.com/0071635238)—Rother looks beyond what Toyota does and tries to understand how and why. He then formalizes this into a method called the Toyota Kata. It's a real eye-opener. The Kanban Kata that we talk about in chapter 10 is based on this book.
- *The Principles of Product Development Flow: Second Generation Lean Product Development* (Don Reinertsen, Celeritas Publishing, 2009, http://amzn.com/1935401009)—This dense book on product development contains 175 principles synthesizing knowledge from a vast array of fields, from telecommunications networking to military doctrine, into a second-generation Lean theory that goes beyond the faith-based approach and advocates applying an economic view to decisions.
- *Lean from the Trenches: Managing Large-Scale Projects with Kanban* (Henrik Kniberg, Pragmatic Bookshelf, 2011, http://amzn.com/1934356859)—This book presents a short case study on implementing Lean and kanban in the Swedish Police. The author is one of the prominent agile figures in Sweden.

A.2 Books on agile

- *Scrum and XP from the Trenches* (Henrik Kniberg, Lulu.com, 2007, http://amzn.com/1430322640 or free as a downloadable PDF at www.infoq.com/minibooks/scrum-xp-from-the-trenches)—This book is an excellent, pragmatic introduction to Scrum and some agile practices. It has been the start of the agile journey for many people, including Marcus. Thanks, Henrik!
- *Extreme Programming Explained: Embrace Change* (Kent Beck, Addison-Wesley Professional, 1999, http://amzn.com/0201616416)—This book is an introduction to extreme programming (XP), one of the first agile methods. It describes several of the most important agile practices used by many kanban teams.
- *The Agile Samurai: How Agile Masters Deliver Great Software* (Jonathan Rasmusson, Pragmatic Bookshelf, 2010, http://amzn.com/1934356581)—This book is short, pragmatic, fun, and a good introduction to agile and a lot of practices around it. It includes many practical tips and can be used as an introduction. We've left this book with clients we've visited as reference literature.
- *The Art of Agile Development* (James Shore and Shane Warden, O'Reilly Media, 2007, http://amzn.com/0596527675)—This detailed introduction to many agile practices (particularly XP) is great for the novice and advanced beginner, but it also presents some new perspectives and good exercises for more experienced practitioners.

A.3 Books on software development

Even though this isn't a book on software development as in writing code, we have found the following books interesting and have learned a lot from them that we can use in practice to assist our kanban teams:

- *Specification by Example: How Successful Teams Deliver the Right Software* (Gojko Adzic, Manning, 2011, www.manning.com/adzic/)—Specification by example is a practice to ensure that you're building the right thing: what's needed, not only what the customer wanted. This book does an excellent job of describing all the aspects and consequences of specification by example (a.k.a. behavior-driven development or acceptance-driven development).
- *Test-Driven Development: By Example* (Kent Beck, Addison-Wesley Professional, 2002, http://amzn.com/0321146530)—This book provides a great introduction to test-driven development (TDD) through a thorough case study that shows you the how-tos in small, fine-grained steps.
- *Growing Object-Oriented Systems Guided by Tests* (Steve Freeman and Nat Pryce, Addison-Wesley Professional, 2009, http://amzn.com/0321503627)—In this book (known in inner circles as the GOOS book), the authors show how TDD can be applied in the larger world. It includes a lot of practical examples and tips throughout.
- *Clean Code: A Handbook of Agile Software Craftsmanship* (Robert C. Martin, Prentice Hall, 2008, http://amzn.com/0132350882)—This is a must-read for any agile developer. It shows you how to write clean and maintainable code. It will probably also make you ashamed of your own code (as it did for Uncle Bob himself).
- *The Clean Coder: A Code of Conduct for Professional Programmers* (Robert C. Martin, Prentice Hall, 2011, http://amzn.com/0137081073)—Uncle Bob turns his attention to the professional developer and scrutinizes what it means to be a great developer. This is done through many anecdotes and funny stories that make you think about your profession in a new way.

A.4 Books on business and change management

- *The Goal: A Process of Ongoing Improvement* (Eliyahu M. Goldratt, North River Press, 2012, http://amzn.com/0884271951)—Imagine writing a book on the Theory of Constraints. Imagine how boring that book could be. This is the opposite. It's a gripping and entertaining novel that teaches you about the Theory of Constraints while following the destiny of Alex Rogo. This is done in such a subtle way that you almost don't notice it until you're done.

  It's one of the best books we've read!
- *Switch: How to Change Things When Change Is Hard* (Chip Heath and Dan Heath, Crown Business, 2010, http://amzn.com/0385528752)—This book teaches you about making changes: personal changes, helping others change, and changes

to organizations. It gives you a practical framework for making changes and contains loads of examples and studies to back it all up.

This book made us feel almost as though we were cheating by knowing all these techniques when we'd finished reading it. You can get that feeling, too!

- *Made to Stick: Why Some Ideas Survive and Others Die* (Chip Heath and Dan Heath, Random House, 2007, http://amzn.com/1400064287)—Here's another great title by the Heath brothers that talks about making your ideas sticky, which in turn is a way to improve the change process. It provides lots of cases (the opening case will stick with you forever, as an example) and practical tips.
- *Fearless Change: Patterns for Introducing New Ideas* (Mary Lynn Manns and Linda Rising, Addison-Wesley, 2004, http://amzn.com/0201741571)—This book contains a lot of small patterns: ways, thoughts, and practices that can help you bring about change. After a short narrative about the ideas behind the patterns, the book presents a long list of patterns that you can start tomorrow. It's a must-have for any change agent.
- *The Lean Startup: How Today's Entrepreneurs Use Continuous Innovation to Create Radically Successful Businesses* (Eric Ries, Crown Business, 2011, http://theleanstartup.com/book, http://amzn.com/0307887898)—This book talks about applying Lean concepts to ideas: more specifically, business ideas; and even more specifically, startup ideas. These ideas range from using the scientific method for exploration to A/B testing to validate your hypothesis. Soon after reading it, you'll start to realize what many others have seen: Lean Startup can be applied to your business regardless of whether you're a startup.

A.5 Other resources

Although we both read a lot, the kanban community is moving fast. In order to keep up with the latest news and happenings, we follow a lot of online resources such as mailing lists, blogs, and Twitter accounts. Here are a couple of our favorites:

- *Kanban dev Yahoo mailing list*—This is an extremely active mailing list for all things kanban. All the big names in the Lean software development movement are active on the list, and you'll be sure to get great answers fast. http://finance.groups.yahoo.com/group/kanbandev/.
- *Personal Kanban 101*—This site introduces the ideas of Personal Kanban. http://mng.bz/61Zn.

A.5.1 Noteworthy blogs

Here are some of the blogs and sites that we often visit:

- http://joakimsunden.com (Joakim Sundén)
- http://www.marcusoft.net (Marcus Hammarberg)
- http://positiveincline.com (Mike Burrows)
- http://www.agilemanagement.net (David J. Anderson)

- http://hakanforss.wordpress.com (Håkan Forss)
- http://dannorth.net (Dan North)
- http://flowchainsensei.wordpress.com (Bob Marshall)
- http://availagility.co.uk (Karl Scotland)
- http://brodzinski.com (Pawel Brodzinski)
- http://www.dennisstevens.com (Dennis Stevens)
- http://blog.crisp.se/author/mattiasskarin (Mattias Skarin)
- http://leanandkanban.wordpress.com (David Joyce)
- http://blog.jabebloom.com (Jabe Bloom)
- http://www.klausleopold.com (Klaus Leopold)
- http://www.software-kanban.de (Arne Roock)
- http://lizkeogh.com (Liz Keogh)
- http://zuill.us/WoodyZuill (Woody Zuill)

A.5.2 Noteworthy Twitter accounts

Here are some of the Twitter accounts that we follow on Lean, kanban, and agile, in alphabetical order:

Chris Achouiantz *@ChrisAch*
Gojko Adzic *@gojkoadzic*
Agile Borat *@AgileBorat*
David J. Anderson *@djaa_dja*
Jurgen Appelo *@jurgenappelo*
Kent Beck *@KentBeck*
Jim Benson *@ourfounder*
Jabe Bloom *@cyetain*
Pawel Brodzinski *@pawelbrodzinski*
Martin Burns *@martinburnsuk*
Mike Burrows *@asplake*
George Dinwiddie *@gdinwiddie*
Håkan Forss *@hakanforss*
Torbjörn Gyllebring *@drunkcod*
Kurt Häusler *@Kurt_Haeusler*
Ron Jeffries *@RonJeffries*
Liz Keogh *@lunivore*
Henrik Kniberg *@henrikkniberg*
LeanKanbanConference *@LeanKanban*
LeanKit *@LeanKit*
Klaus Leopold *@klausleopold*
Janice Linden-Reed *@jlindenreed*
Bob Marshall *@flowchainsensei*
Henrik Mårtensson *@Kallokain*
Uncle Bob Martin *@unclebobmartin*
Benjamin Mitchell *@benjaminm*
Niklas Modig *@LeanOnMyself*
Dan North *@tastapod*
Michael (Doc) Norton *@DocOnDev*
Staffan Nöteberg *@staffannoteberg*
Jeff Patton *@jeffpatton*
Mary Poppendieck *@mpoppendieck*
Jonathan Rasmusson *@jrasmusson*
Donald Reinertsen *@DReinertsen*
Karl Scotland *@kjscotland*
Al Shalloway *@alshalloway*
James Sutton *@LeanSE*
Jean Tabaka *@jeantabaka*
Adam Yuret *@AdamYuret*
Woody Zuill *@WoodyZuill*

appendix B
Kanban tools

Some of the more common questions and suggestions we get when presenting kanban are about tooling: "Surely there must be an electronic tool to track stickies," "But what if we're distributed geographically? Would an online board be better?" and so on.

There are loads of tools out there, and many of them are useful and great. We haven't talked too much about online, electronic tools in this book for a simple reason: this is a book about the principles and thinking of kanban and not about the tooling. When you understand the principles, you can bend the tools to your will.

We often suggest to new teams that they start on a physical board and then move to an electronic tool when they've got the hang of it. Not that you can't start electronically, but there's often a tendency to not change much in electronic tools if, for example, it's something that's hard to do and that takes time.[1] When you start using kanban, you want it to be super simple to change your process as you see the need: like wiping a whiteboard and starting over.

Make sure the tool isn't dictating what you can do with your process. A tool is something that should serve you, not the other way around.

Here's a list of tools that we have used or heard good things about. This list was probably old the moment we wrote it down, so keep your eyes and ears open for newer, better, and cooler tools.

The lists ahead are in no particular order. We didn't get paid by any of these vendors, nor do we lean toward any of the tools (because we prefer physical boards when we can have those). We did a quick shout-out on Twitter and got few suggestions.

[1] For example, we've both worked at a company that had "Greenhopper guys," who were the only ones who knew how to and had the authorization to change the board.

B.1 Standalone tools

These tools can run standalone; you don't need another product underneath them. In some cases, you can import work items from other tools such as JIRA, Team Foundation Server, and so on, but in most cases these tools are separate systems.

B.1.1 LeanKit Kanban

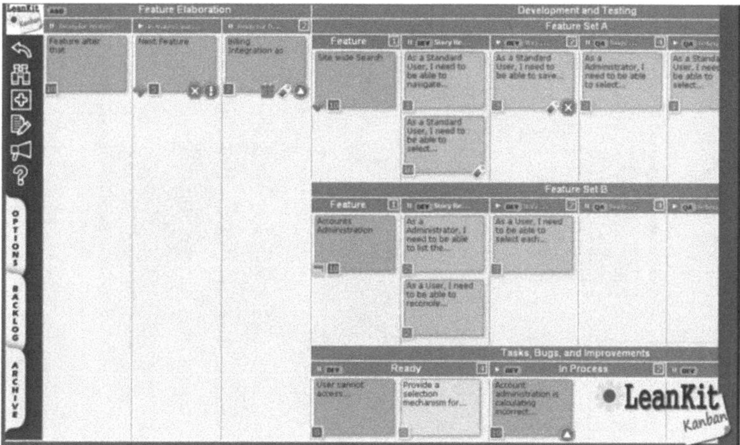

LeanKit Kanban (http://leankit.com) is a lightweight kanban tool that supports many of the advanced practices discussed in this book. In fact, we've used it during the planning and writing of the book. Despite the tool's lightweight nature, it's powerful and supports many ways of working. Everything from simple personal boards to advanced organization-wide processes can be modeled in the tool. The free version allows for up to 25 users and 10 boards.

B.1.2 AgileZen

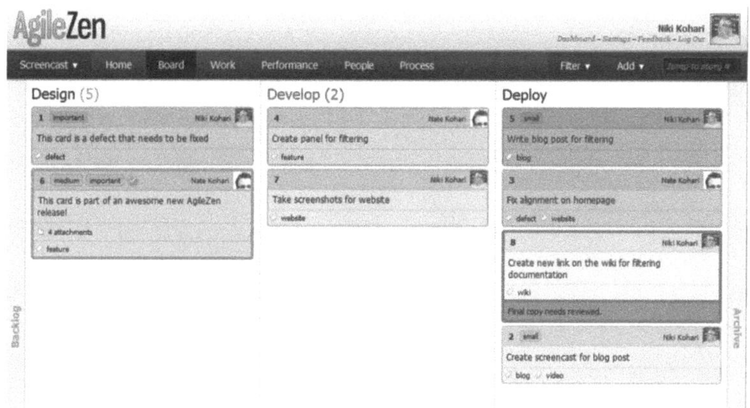

AgileZen (www.agilezen.com) is a simple kanban tool that can be used from the personal level all the way up to the level of large organizations. It has a free introductory-level plan for one user and one sample project that helps you get to know the product.

B.1.3 Trello

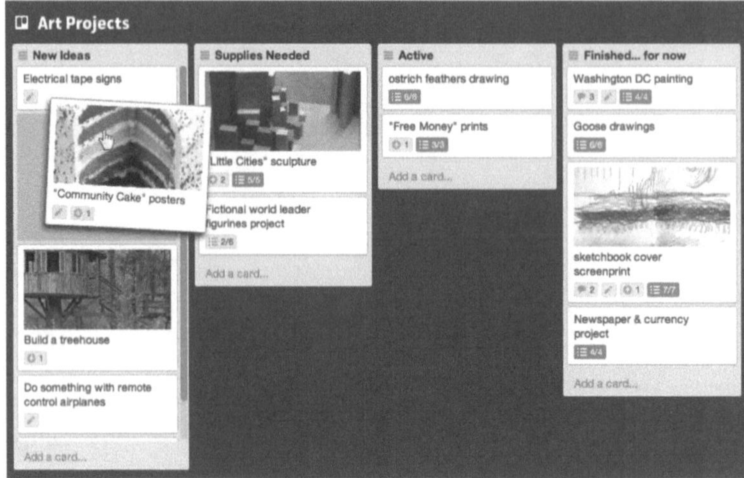

Trello (https://trello.com) is a simple organizational tool. It can be used to visualize your kanban process, but it's not only geared toward kanban. Therefore, some features that you might expect (WIP limits, for example) are missing. It's still useful, though: it's easy to get started with, and it's completely free.

B.1.4 KanbanFlow

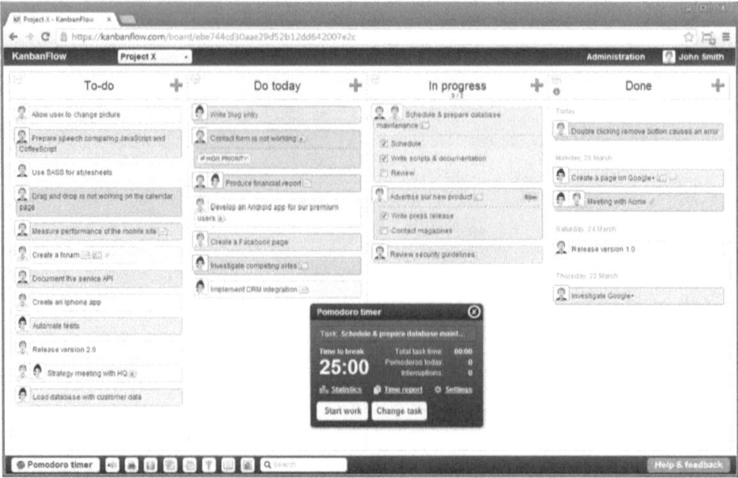

KanbanFlow (https://kanbanflow.com) is another tool we've heard great things about. It focuses on simplicity and supports most of the common use cases, including some that you might not have thought of before (built-in Pomodoro timers,[2] for example). It's free with an unlimited number of users, and it offers some extra features in the paid version.

B.1.5 Kanbanize

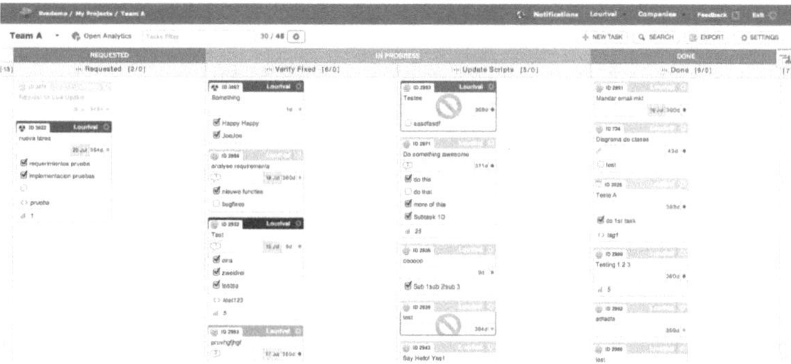

Kanbanize (http://kanbanize.com) looks promising, although we haven't used it. The feature list is extensive, and it offers a live demo of the tool. There's also a free Community version.

B.1.6 Kanbanery

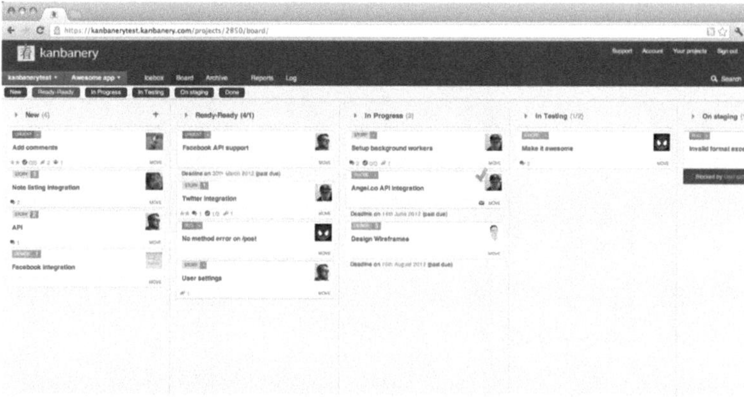

Kanbanery (https://kanbanery.com) is another tool with an extensive feature list, and it supports importing work items from other tools (via CSV files). There's a free 30-day trial plan.

---

2 The Pomodoro technique is a personal time-management technique that helps you focus your work into short timeboxes.

B.2 Tools on tools

These tools are installed as add-ins to existing systems.

B.2.1 JIRA Agile

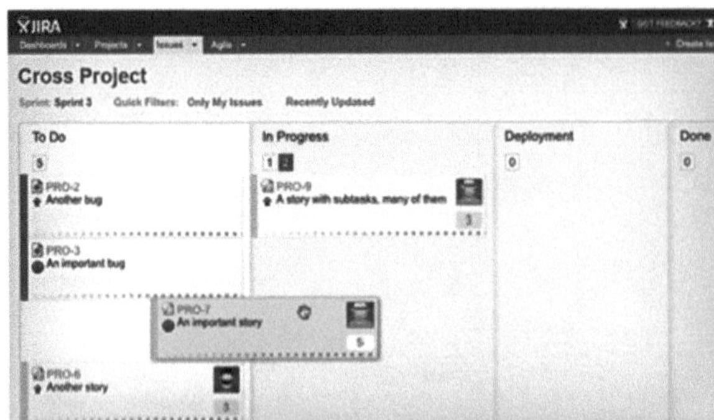

JIRA Agile (www.atlassian.com/software/jira/agile) is Atlassian's kanban tool for use in combination with its popular issue-tracking system, JIRA.

B.2.2 Kanban in Team Foundation Service

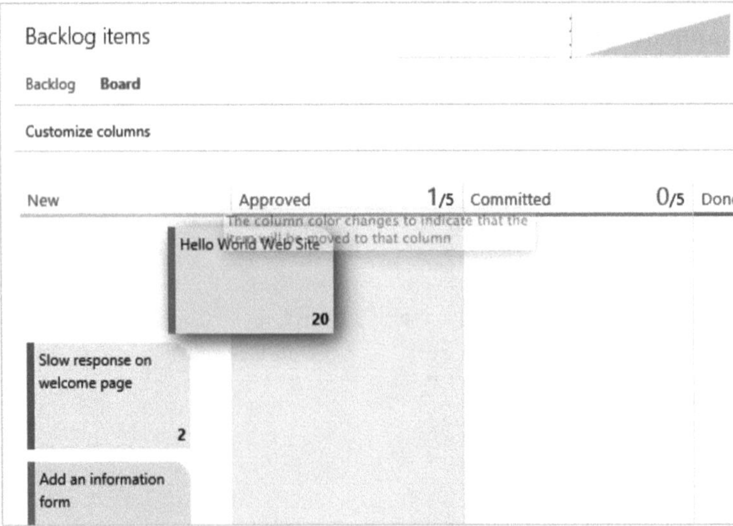

Microsoft provides built-in support for kanban boards in its project-management tool, Team Foundation Service (TFS). For users of TFS, this is a very useful addition to the suite (http://mng.bz/4vd0).

B.2.3 HuBoard

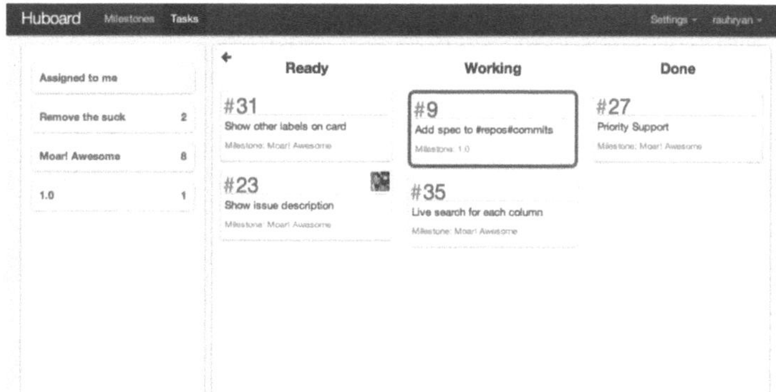

HuBoard (http://huboard.com) is a GitHub kanban system that is built on top of its issue-tracking system.

index

A

B

C

D

H

I

J

K

T

U

V

W

X

Z

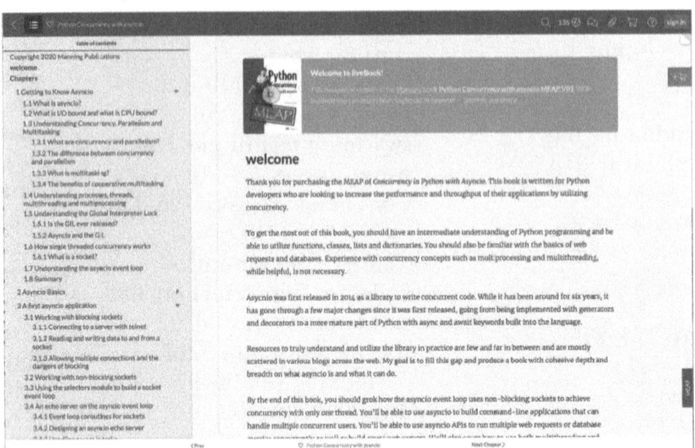

A new online reading experience

liveBook, our online reading platform, adds a new dimension to your Manning books, with features that make reading, learning, and sharing easier than ever. A liveBook version of your book is included FREE with every Manning book.

This next generation book platform is more than an online reader. It's packed with unique features to upgrade and enhance your learning experience.

- Add your own notes and bookmarks
- One-click code copy
- Learn from other readers in the discussion forum
- Audio recordings and interactive exercises
- Read all your purchased Manning content in any browser, anytime, anywhere

As an added bonus, you can search every Manning book and video in liveBook—even ones you don't yet own. Open any liveBook, and you'll be able to browse the content and read anything you like.*

Find out more at www.manning.com/livebook-program.

**Open reading is limited to 10 minutes per book daily*